DOSTOEVSKY

DOSTOEVSKY IN 1872

Painting by Perov

DOSTOEVSKY

His Life and Art

by

AVRAHM YARMOLINSKY

CRITERION BOOKS   NEW YORK

Copyright © 1957 by Criterion Books, Inc.
Library of Congress Catalog Card Number 56-6213

Second Edition, completely Revised and Enlarged

MANUFACTURED IN THE UNITED STATES OF AMERICA

FOREWORD

TO THE SECOND EDITION

A REVISED edition of a book published in 1934 on a subject as compelling to-day as the phenomenon of Dostoevsky scarcely requires an apology. In the last twenty years a limited amount of hitherto unknown material relating to the novelist's biography has come to light. The new data, a re-examination of some of the old sources, but chiefly second thoughts, have led me to recast many passages. One such is the account of his father's murder. Parts of Chapters IV to VII have been altered and expanded with a view to emphasizing young Dostoevsky's responsiveness to radical ideas. His trial as a political prisoner is here presented more amply. Some details have been added to the story of his involvement with Polina Suslova. Somewhat fuller treatment is accorded his journalistic writings, and the comment on practically all his major works has been thoroughly revised. The last chapter, part of which deals with his posthumous reputation, has been almost entirely rewritten. To what is said there it should be added that during the liberal era which dawned soon after Stalin died, in 1953, there was a return to greater appreciation of Dostoevsky's work. The seventy-fifth anniversary of his death was observed with a spate of notices which included qualified eulogies of an official nature. While invoking Lenin's authority in calling for a critical attitude towards the novelist's performance, the government newspaper hailed him as "one of the greatest word artists of all countries and peoples." The Communist Party daily claimed for his novels "a progressive significance in the development of Russian culture." A new and mammoth edition of his collected fiction was started, and there were indications that the Dostoevsky studies, broken off two decades previously, were to be resumed.

What figured as Appendix I in the first edition is now a section of Chapter XXI; the substance of Appendix II has been incorpor-

v

ated into Chapter I. A new feature is a table of important dates in Dostoevsky's life, which should prove useful for ready reference. The Bibliography has been brought up-to-date. Naturally I have made every effort to correct the few factual errors that crept into the earlier text.

I am deeply indebted to my wife, Babette Deutsch, for her help in preparing both the original and the present revised work.

A.Y.

CONTENTS

CONTENTS

LIST OF ILLUSTRATIONS

CHRONOLOGY

EXCEPT for those relating to Dostoevsky's sojourn in Western Europe, the dates in this table, as throughout the book, are Old Style, and so, being of the nineteenth century, are twelve days earlier than if they were reckoned by the calendar now in general use. Practically all his writings first appeared in periodicals.

The spelling of his name is a concession to Anglo-American usage. "Dostoyevsky" would be phonetically a closer rendering. The stress falls on the third syllable, though the novelist himself is said to have accented the second.

Fyodor Mikhailovich Dostoevsky born in Moscow.	October 30, 1821
Mother dies.	February 27, 1837
Admitted to Military Engineering School in Petersburg.	January, 1838
Father murdered.	June, 1839
Graduates from Engineering School and is enrolled in the Petersburg Corps of Engineers as a draughtsman.	August, 1843
Retires from Government service.	October, 1844
Poor Folk, published.	January, 1846
The Double, published.	February, 1846
First epileptic attacks?	1846-47
Imprisoned as political offender.	April 23, 1849
Netochka Nezvanova, published.	1849
After all preliminaries to public execution last minute reprieve and announcement of actual sentence.	December 22, 1849
Deported to Siberia in irons.	December 24, 1849
A convict at Omsk.	Jan., 1850—Feb., 1854
Periodic epileptic attacks begin.	1853
Starts military service as a private in Semipalatinsk.	March, 1854
Obtains officer's commission.	October 1, 1856
Married to Marya Dmitrievna Isayeva.	February 6, 1857
Permitted to retire from service and leave Siberia.	March, 1859
Settles in the capital.	December, 1859
"The Friend of the Family," published.	1859
Edits *Vremya* and *Epokha,* monthlies.	1861-1865

The Insulted and Injured, published.	1861
The House of the Dead, published.	1861-62
First trip abroad.	Summer, 1862
Intimacy with Polina Suslova.	Winter, 1862-63
"Winter Notes on Summer Impressions," published.	1863
Foreign travel, part of the time in the company of Polina Suslova.	August-October, 1863
"Notes from the Underground," published.	1864
Wife dies in Moscow.	April 15, 1864
Death of his brother, Mikhail.	July 10, 1864
Trip to Germany.	Summer, 1865
The Gambler, published.	1866
Crime and Punishment, published.	1866
Married to Anna Grigoryevna Snitkina.	February 15, 1867
Goes abroad with his wife.	April, 1867
Daughter, Sonia, born in Geneva.	March 5, 1868
Infant dies.	May 24, 1868
The Idiot, published.	1868
Daughter, Lubov, born in Dresden.	September 26, 1869
The Eternal Husband, published.	1870
Returns to Petersburg with family.	July, 1871
Son, Fyodor, born.	July 16, 1871
The Possessed, published.	1871-72
Edits *Grazhdanin,* a weekly.	1873-74
The Raw Youth, published.	1875
Son, Alexey, born.	August 10, 1875
A Writer's Diary, published.	1876-77, 1880-81
Death of Alexey.	May 16, 1878
The Brothers Karamazov, published.	1879-80
Delivers address at Pushkin Festival in Moscow.	June 8, 1880
Dies in Petersburg.	January 28, 1881
His widow dies at the age of 72.	June 9, 1918

DOSTOEVSKY

CHAPTER ONE

A CHILD

HE is held in the arms of his mother before the altar of the village church. She has lifted him up to receive the sacrament and to kiss the chalice. Suddenly a dove flies in through an open window, flutters a moment in the warm air fragrant with incense, and darts out through the window on the other side. He starts away from the chalice, crying: "A dove! A dove!"

He is bigger now: he has turned three. Nurse has just brought him into the parlour to show her charge off to the company. He kneels, facing the icon in the corner, and before them all he says his bedtime prayer: "All my hope I place in thee, Mother of God; shelter me under thy mantle." "What a clever little boy!" the guests exclaim.

These were Fyodor Dostoevsky's earliest memories. They were of a kind natural to a child born into an Orthodox household established in the hallowed city of Moscow. Religious observances were a matter of course both to that unhappy army doctor, his father, and that good woman, his mother. Church attendance belonged to the daily routine. The family had but a step to go, for a chapel, named for Saints Peter and Paul, was attached to the hospital, on the staff of which the father served and where they had their living quarters. Indeed, it was in this chapel, accustomed to the hasty funerals of the poor, that little Fyodor was baptized, on a November day, under the sponsorship of four godparents, one of them his mother's wealthy sister, Aunt Kumanina, who stood godmother to all his brothers and sisters. The children were also taken—and these were memorable occasions—to the great cathedrals of the city and to the sanctuaries behind the red swallowtail ramparts which wall in the Kremlin heights. The aged little churches with their glowing domes, their chimes filling the quiet

1

lanes in which they nestled—the peace of these was to be shadow-less in remembrance. Each summer, up to the time Fedya was ten years old, his mother bore off her little flock on a long, leisurely pilgrimage to the shrines of the Troitzkaya Lavra. Besides pious memories, they brought back from the trip, which lasted nearly a week, toys of peasant make. It may well have been at the monastery that he saw "possessed" women exorcised at mass—a fearful and touching scene. Always at church the poor crowded at the entrance. The boy felt curiously drawn to these ragged men and women who bowed so low and prayed so earnestly.

Perhaps it was in these early years that some event deeply coloured by emotion came to be associated for him with the enchant-ment of the sunset hour. It may have been his mother holding him up before the icon while she prayed for the Virgin's protection, one still summer day as the sun was sinking. Or was it his having been touched, for the first time, as a child of eight, in a peculiarly inti-mate way by religious feeling? It was the Monday of Passion Week and he was at mass with his mother. The sun slanted in through the window and illumined the incense that was eddying upward toward the cupola. A young acolyte placed an enormous book on the lectern in the middle of the church, opened it, and read: "There was a man in the land of Uz, whose name was Job; and that man was perfect and upright and one that feared God and eschewed evil. . . ." The little boy was shaken with a strange ecstasy in which awe was mixed with happiness. The three thousand camels, Job praying for his sons because they might have sinned in their feast-ing, Satan talking boldly to God, the righteous man rending his mantle and falling down upon the ground and crying in his bereave-ment: "Blessed be the name of the Lord!"—all these details of the story took hold of his imagination and stirred him strongly. He was a deep child. If Job's faith touched him, Job's rebellion must also have had an echo in his heart. At all events, the boy grew into a man who was never able to read those pages without what he called "morbid elation." Nor was the curtain ever wholly to close for him upon this drama of God and man.

The children came in two sets: Mikhail was the eldest; one year later, on October 30, 1821, Fyodor was born; the next year Varvara came, and in 1825, the last of the elder group, Andrey. Four years later twin girls were born, one of whom lived only a few days—the children were not spared the sight of the little coffin. In due time there were two more additions to the family.

Fyodor was inseparable from Mikhail, and "Little Tail," as they nicknamed Andrey, was generally allowed to tag after them. The band was captained by Fedya. Though not a well child, he was full of high spirits. "I am not surprised, my dear, at Fedya's mischief," his mother wrote to his father, apparently in reply to a report about the boy's behaviour, "for that is what we have to expect from him." He was the inventor, the explorer, the mime. Whenever the family went on a trip he was in a fever. He would perch aloft on the coachman's box until they came to a station and then he would be poking his snub nose everywhere at once. After seeing a trapeze artist at a public entertainment play the part of a Brazilian ape, Fedya came home and was an ape for weeks. Once at a festival, he saw a runner racing with a handkerchief between his teeth, and for days afterwards he raced through the hospital park, a handkerchief fluttering from his mouth. Little encouragement as there was for it, he liked to imagine himself an athlete. In his eagerness, he would cheat at cards when, on the great holidays, especially at Christmas time, the family indulged in a game. The little gambler persisted in it, although he was invariably caught red-handed. "A perfect flame!" —that was how his parents spoke of this sensitive, fidgety, boisterous son.

The flame burned in a close atmosphere. The sizeable household, which included seven servants, was confined to an apartment of three rooms and a large kitchen. The nursery, a windowless alcove of the dark pearl grey foyer, was presided over by Alyona Frolovna, a mountain of a woman, who was forgiven her bulk, her prodigious appetite, her habit of taking snuff, because of her limitless devotion to the family. The living quarters were no brighter for being situated in a wing of a charity hospital. What also clouded the air of home was the father's morose and irascible disposition.

The elder Dostoevsky had made his own way and had had a rough road to travel, which had not sweetened his temper. His family had come down in the world. Its pedigree has been traced to a boyar who in 1506 received a land grant which included part of the village of Dostoevo, in the region of Pinsk. He was probably descended from a Tartar chieftain who emigrated from the Golden Horde, so that in Dostoevsky's case, as in Turgenev's, the old adage about scratching a Russian holds good. In view of the novelist's intense animus against Poles and Catholics, it is noteworthy that some of the branches of the family were Polonized and embraced Catholicism. Others, like the one from which he stemmed, held to their Russian nationality and the Orthodox or Uniate faith.

The son of a priest with a parish in a town of the province of Podolia, the boy had been sent to divinity school as a matter of course. He had not remained there, and it is said that he ran away from home and never spoke of his early years. It is certain that in 1809, at the age of twenty-one, he entered the Imperial Military-Surgical Academy in Moscow. He was in his senior year when Napoleon's army invaded the country, and he was forthwith put to work taking care of the wounded and fighting an epidemic. He remained an army doctor until 1820, when he retired from the service, having married the daughter of a Moscow merchant, of pure Russian stock, the previous year, and settled down to civil practice, as physician in the dispensary of the Mariinsky Hospital for the Poor. In the parlour hung a gilt-framed pastel portrait, showing him in his gold-braided uniform. Fedya usually saw his father, however, in the black frock coat, the white vest and stock, which was the professional attire of a doctor, and wearing a decoration. He had the orders of Saint Anne and Saint Vladimir, which enabled him to regain the rank of hereditary noble *(dvoryanin)* that his forebears had lost when they became members of the clergy.

Mikhail Andreyevich, as his associates and few friends called him, was a sickly, moody man, given to fretting and complaining. His sullenness and self-righteousness would give way to self-pity and self-abasement. At once sentimental and mean, he was a prey to jealously and groundless suspicions. When his wife was carrying her last child, he chided her because she was suffering from heartburn—a condition she had not known in any former pregnancy. She gathered that the symptom had roused his mad suspicion of her infidelity, and for the sake of his peace of mind she solemnly swore that she had been faithful to the vow she had made at the altar sixteen years previously. It took all her tenderness to cheer him during his attacks of hypochondria and depression. She argued that they were happy in each other and in the love of their children, and that they had nothing more to desire, certainly not wealth. The children's love of their father must have been tinged with fear and, perhaps, resentment. Not seldom their mother or the nurse had to shield them from his uncontrollable rages. And, although he spared the rod, he was a stickler for discipline and a believer in hard-and-fast rules, which did not lighten the oppressive, puritanical atmosphere that he created in the home.

The mother appears to have been a kindly, devout, not uncultivated woman, with a good deal of practical sense, which she may have inherited from her father, the merchant, and with so delicate a constitution that she was able to nurse only the eldest of her children.

Fyodor was deeply attached to his mother. "When you left us, beloved Maminka," he wrote, at the age of thirteen, in his earliest known letter, with real feeling and the scantiest punctuation, "I became exceedingly sad and now whenever I think of you I am overcome with such sadness that I can't chase it away at all if you knew how much I want to see you I can't wait for that joyful moment. Every time I think of you I pray God for your health. Let us know, beloved Maminka, if you have made a safe journey kiss Andrushenka and Verochka for me I kiss your little hands and remain your obedient son F. Dostoevsky."

As long as he lived, he kept a miniature which had belonged to his mother. It represented a flying angel and bore the inscription:

J'ai le cœur tout plein d'amour,
Quand l'aurez-vous à votre tour?

O heart! When will you be filled with the love which alone is man's salvation? This was the question that Dostoevsky, overflowing

with bitter hatred and equally bitter compassion, would never cease
to ask.

III

The day, which began early, was filled with set labours and staid
pleasures. As soon as breakfast was over. Fedya and his brothers
were at their lessons in the canary-coloured living-room, where the
family also took their meals. At twelve the doctor returned from
visiting his patients, and dinner was placed on the table at one.
The father took his after-dinner nap of two hours in the parlour,
with Andrey by him to chase away the flies with a freshly cut linden
branch, and woe to the boy if he was inattentive! At four o'clock
in the afternoon tea was served, after which the doctor went out
again, and the family breathed somewhat more easily. The long
winter evenings were spent by the light of tallow candles (wax
tapers were reserved for company, lamps the doctor disliked) in
the cobalt-blue parlour, over a volume of Karamzin's patriotic history or a novel. If it was a romance by Ann Radcliffe, at least one
of the listeners, thrilled with delicious horror, would dream feverishly of it afterwards. Promptly at nine o'clock the family went in to
supper, and then the children said their prayers before the icon, bade
their parents good-night, and so to bed.

Rarely did Fedya's parents, by going out of an evening, release
the spirit of boisterous fun which thrives in a large family but
which here the father's presence tended to subdue. Visitors were
infrequent. Among those who came to the house, mostly during
the day, were the doctor's colleagues and, chiefly, the relatives.
There was grandfather, who came to dinner once a week. There
was great-uncle, a genial and cultivated old gentleman who taught
at the University of Moscow. There was Uncle Mikhail who, like
his sister, played the guitar, and who left one of his instruments
at the house, so that there were duets on his regular Sunday visits.
But his appearances ceased abruptly, for a reason that was not di-
vulged to the children. He had tried to seduce one of the servants
and, on being reprimanded for it in his sister's presence by the
doctor, had spoken to her disrespectfully, whereupon the doctor
gave him a slap which ended their relations. There were the cousins
and the aunts, especially Aunt Kumanina, who would drive up in

style, with a postilion in front and a footman behind to help her
with all the packages of fruit and goodies that she would bring.
Having no children of her own, she was all the more devoted to
her poor sister's family, and until Fyodor was in his late teens
played an important part in his life. All these relatives were on
the mother's side, a fact that Fyodor must have noticed.

The monotony of the daily pattern was relieved by the holy
days, and then there was the eighth of November to prepare for:
the solemn occasion of the father's name-day. That day the doctor
put aside his cares, devoting it, as he claimed, first to God, his "sole
consoler in this grievous life," and second to himself. The two
older boys would recite their felicitations in French, after having
handed their father the scrolls on which these were written in their
best penmanship. The hero of the day, pleased by the performance,
would melt, and embrace his sons with warmth.

Another outstanding event, impatiently awaited, was the visit of
one of the peasant women who had acted as wet-nurses to the children. She would come on a winter morning and be shown into the
parlour. After a short prayer before the icon, she would greet the
mistress of the house and kiss the young ones, among whom she
would distribute whey-cakes she had baked for them in her village
home. Then, since lessons must not be interfered with, she would
retire to the kitchen.

She reappeared in the unlighted dining-room when dusk shrouded
the birchwood chairs upholstered in green morocco, on each of which
a small and eager occupant perched waiting for her stories. A
spell lay over the hour. The silence was so complete that one
could hear plainly the scratch of the doctor's pen as he sat in the
next room entering prescriptions on his patients' charts. Not to disturb the parents, the nurse would talk in a whisper, spinning out,
with a gusto no less naïve than her listeners', the old stories in
which the Fire-Bird and Bluebeard and that cunning son of a
priest, Alyosha Popovich, played their wonderful or fearful parts.
The more terrifying of these tales, muttered in the shadow-filled
room, must have heightened Fedya's fear of the dark. There was,
too, one old woman who told them stories from the Arabian Nights,
and of course there were tales about holy men and holy places.
Cheap editions of fairy tales, printed on coarse grey paper and

illustrated with crude coloured pictures, lay about the nursery, so the children did not have to depend solely on the nurses' lore.

One especially memorable occasion was a performance of Schiller's *Robbers*, which Fyodor witnessed at the age of ten. On certain holidays and regularly during Carnival Week, the children made long visits to their great-uncle, who had no offspring of his own. He and his wife lived on Novinsky Boulevard, near the park where street fairs were held, with their bands and dancing bears, clowns and strong men, puppet-shows and Indian knife-jugglers, "Russian mountains" and swings. It was nominated in the bond that he would be allowed to take them there, although the doctor must surely have considered the entertainment vulgar.

Summer brought the young people a measure of freedom. The garden attached to the hospital was their natural playground. They were not, however, allowed to go there without a nurse or some other guardian—indeed, until Fyodor was sixteen he was not permitted to leave the house unaccompanied. The doctor had definite ideas about the proprieties. He would not let the children indulge in any game except "horses," handball and the use of bats being proscribed as dangerous and unseemly. Here and there, strolling along the paths or seated on the benches, were figures clad in loose gowns of camel-coloured wool or ticking, according to the weather, with white bonnets and slippers without heels. These were the convalescent patients, and among the many prohibitions that hedged in the children, none was more rigid than that which forbade them to address these people. Fedya could not keep himself from violating this rule. The seamy side of life fascinated him from the beginning.

On a fine summer evening the family would march in full force to a neighbouring park, which was known as Mary's Grove. As they passed the gates of the Alexandrovsky Institute for Girls, a copeck or a groat would be tossed at the feet of the sentinel who was standing there, gun in hand. The way led through crazy streets and alleys, and the doctor improved the occasion by discoursing to his sons on acute and obtuse angles, curves, and broken lines. Even when they were beyond the city limits the children had to walk sedately, and a scamper or a romp among the birches was out of the question.

Dostoevsky's second wife remembered his having spoken of his "happy and placid childhood." Looking backward late in life, he said that, in spite of "all deviations," his parents had earnestly striven to be among the "best" people in the highest sense of the adjective. Again, he mentioned, with a flash of pride, his having come of "a Russian and pious family." One fancies that the actuality was not as decorous as it appears both from his remarks and from his brother Andrey's smug reminiscences. The fact that neither hide nor hair of the father's relatives was to be seen, and that no mention was made of them, must have given Fyodor the feeling of living in a lopsided family. Certainly the personality of the father was not conducive to an atmosphere of serene gentility. One suspects that as a child Fyodor looked upon things that do not belong to the life of "a Russian and pious family."

I V

The doctor's income was small, as his salary was but six hundred roubles a year and his private practice modest. Nevertheless, he was intent upon becoming the owner of a piece of land in the country as behooved a *dvoryanin*. Real estate agents began to haunt the flat, and one fine summer afternoon when Fyodor was nine, the doctor, having taken leave of his wife and kissed the children, seated himself in a covered *troika* and drove out of town, to look over a bit of land with a view to purchase. Within an hour or two the family was dismayed to see him back again; he had forgotten his passport, without which it was not permissible to travel. He got his papers and set off again. The incident was considered an evil omen, a notion that seems justified in the light of later events. The immediate result of the journey was that he became the owner of Darovoye, a village in the province of Tula, a distance of a hundred miles from Moscow. The acquisition was solemnized by a mass in the Iberian Chapel.

The following year after Easter, the mother, accompanied by the older children, made the momentous journey to Darovoye, and took the management of the estate into her capable hands. Forthwith a fire razed the village to the ground; moreover, the new landowners found themselves involved in litigation. To safeguard their interests they rounded out the property by acquiring a tiny neigh-bouring hamlet, which went by the name of Cheremoshna or Chermashnya. The entire holding cost 12,000 roubles. In the 1930's Darovoye became a collective farm named for Dostoevsky.

It must have relieved the elder Dostoevsky to think that now he could pass on to his heirs not merely his name and his noble rank, but also a sizable estate and nearly one hundred "souls," i.e. male serfs. But the purchase put a great strain on the family resources. To swing it, the doctor must have spent his wife's *dot* and gone heavily into debt. After the fire at Darovoye money had to be advanced to the peasants to enable them to put up new huts, and some of the loans were never repaid. The property proved a liability rather than an asset. Henceforth the doctor often found himself in dire straits. At one time, having taken five roubles in advance on his salary, he had not a copeck to look for when they were spent—an experience with which his son Fyodor was to be painfully familiar. This was all the harder for the doctor to bear, as there was a streak of the miser in him. Like many a thwarted man, he would quibble over small expenses, so that his wife had to plead with him to buy a pencil-box for Mikhail, who seems to have been reduced to beg-ging from his schoolmates. In her absence, the doctor would write to his wife for an exact accounting of the silver left in the town apartment, and she would list everything meticulously, from the tray, the milk pitcher, and the slop basin, down to the broken silver tablespoon and the two battered saltcellars in the chiffonier. He is perturbed. He can find only five of the six spoons she men-tions, and the broken one is nowhere to be discovered. Perhaps she is mistaken; he believes he has had no more than five spoons since she left. As for the broken spoon, she should try to remember whether she hadn't locked it up elsewhere. For he keeps the keys by him constantly. He also wants an inventory of everything in the storeroom, with mention of any of his wife's dresses, blouses, and caps that she may have left at home. One can't be too careful with thievish servants about.

When he complained of being short, as he frequently did, his wife replied soothingly: "Don't worry about sending me money. As it is, I have left you with nothing. Get along as well as you can, my dear. For the time being I am not in need, and should I be so, I hope to have some oats left to sell." She was an excellent manager, knew how to deal with her serfs, a rough lot who had the reputation of horse thieves, and so meticulous in her accountings to her husband that he described her letters as "business records." She would report to him that God had given them increase in the shape of a peasant lad and a girl as well, since a son had been born to their Nikita and a daughter to their Fedot; that the sow had presented them with five young; that the ducklings were thriving, but that the goslings were being depleted by the uncertain weather, and that only one hen was setting.

From now on the summer was a season of release for the children, who spent it in the country with their mother. The doctor came out rarely and for short periods. The summer residence was the Darovoye "manor house," a four-room cottage, made of plaited boughs stuccoed over. The children used it chiefly as a dormitory. The house was surrounded by venerable lime trees under which they took tea, and beyond it was an orchard and a thick birch wood which climbed up and down ravines. Fyodor was so much attached to this place, with its green darkness, its steep gullies, and its silence broken only by the rustle of leaves underfoot and the abrupt soft crash of a squirrel leaping overhead, that they called it "Fedya's Grove." Not that Maminka liked them to play there: she was constantly warning them about snakes and rumoured wolves. To keep the children occupied, she had a pond dug, where they bathed, fished, and boated.

Each of the brothers had a *troika,* a three-horse team, of his own, consisting of peasant boys and girls. They would save up part of their dinners and, when the meal was over, take it to the stables, which were located under some bush. Imitating the horse-dealers whom they watched at the fairs, they would look into the creatures' mouths, lift up their legs to examine the hoofs, and so on. Sometimes savages, armed with bows and arrows, and fiercely feathered, prowled in the shadows of the lindens, and tents were pitched in the darkest part of the copse. Actually, there was only one tent, the feathers had once been worn by tame geese, and under the war paint the pale features of Fyodor and Little Tail were plainly visible. It was Mikhail who daubed the faces and even the bodies of the tribe, and it was Andrey who was destined to record its adventures in sentimental retrospect, but it was Fyodor who led them when they raided the enemy's stronghold in the birch wood, and indeed on most other occasions. When Fyodor was not chieftain, he was Crusoe, in a game of his own invention, with Little Tail for Man Friday.

There was an ancient wooden chapel near the cemetery beyond the lime copse. Entering it one day through the door which was never locked, they took the icons from the shelves and formed a procession. Carrying the images and chanting canticles and prayers, they marched along as they had seen the priests do, "blessing the fields."

Fyodor would hang about the peasants at work and would run errands for them, while they would let the little master put his hand to the plow or hold the reins. The raw clods crumbling under the harrow, the uncouth figure of a peasant merging into his field, the tangled thatch roofing a grey hut—such elements of the rural scene must have found lodgment in the boy's mind. But the impressions that remained with him for life were rather of the folk than of the landscape. He was always to remember a moment of sharp panic and the comfort he received from one of his father's plowmen. It was a clear, windy August day, and he was going to the birch grove to gather mushrooms, when the cry of "Wolf!" tore through the midsummer hush. Screaming with terror, he ran straight to a peasant who was walking behind his plow. It was their serf, Marey.

"Hearing my outcry," Dostoevsky tells the story, "he stopped his mare in surprise, and when I caught, on the run, the plow with one hand and his sleeve with the other, he noticed my fright. 'A wolf!' I cried out, panting. He threw up his head and looked around. 'Where is the wolf?' 'Shouted . . . someone just shouted: "A wolf!"' I stammered. 'What are you talking about? What wolf? You imagined it, my boy. There aren't any wolves here,' he mumbled, trying to reassure me. But shivering with my whole body, I tightened my hold of his *zipoon* [coat]. I must have been very pale. He looked at me with an alarmed smile, apparently anxious for me. 'See how frightened he is—oh, oh!' he shook his head. 'Enough, sonny. A child, eh?' He stretched out his hand and suddenly stroked my cheek. 'Well, enough, sonny. Christ be with you, cross yourself.' But I did not cross myself; the corners of my lips trembled, and this seems to have struck him particularly. He gently stretched out his large soil-stained finger with its black nail and gently touched my quivering lips. 'A child!' he smiled at me with a long, motherly smile." The boy was at last reassured and, after Marey had made the sign of the cross over him, went away.

In a sense, Dostoevsky clung to Marey's *zipoon* all his life. The People, whom he identified with the peasantry, were to him the vessel of grace and the source of salvation, although he may have had flashes of recognition that, in the words of one of his characters, he was placing laurel on lousy heads.

CHAPTER TWO

SCHOOL DAYS

THE DOCTOR believed that instruction could not begin too early, and when Fyodor was four years old he was set to learning his letters, literally at his mother's knee. He was not as quick as Mikhail, a fact of which he was made painfully conscious by the family's mockery. His primer was a book illustrated with quaint lithographs and entitled: *One Hundred and Four Histories Chosen for the Benefit of the Youth from the Old and New Testaments, by Johann Hübner, accompanied by pious reflections.* The first lesson concludes with these reflections: the power of God is immense; the wisdom of God is infinite; the loving-kindness of God is ineffable. It was with these religious axioms that the pupil was always to be deeply concerned.

Later on two tutors were called in. The deacon taught the older children "God's law." The card table would be opened in the living-room, and the four of them, together with the ecclesiastic, would sit at this worldly piece of furniture to recite their lessons from Metropolitan Filaret's *Principles*, which opened thus: "The one God worshipped in the Holy Trinity is eternal, that is, He hath neither beginning nor end to His Being, but always was, is, and shall be." Having reviewed the assigned portion of this edyfying text, the deacon would give the better part of his time to telling Bible stories. Of the flood, of Joseph and his brethren, of the Nativity, he spoke with so much gusto that even Maminka, who sat near by, dropped her knitting to listen. Did the good man ever give Fyodor the thrill of religious awe awakened in him by the reading from the Book of Job? Did he unwittingly raise in the boy the first stirrings of the doubt that was to torture him to the end of his days?

Monsieur Souchard taught the children French. This *émigré*, after changing his name in an excess of patriotism to the Russian form of Drashusov, eventually opened a small preparatory school, which was attended by Fyodor and Mikhail. In one respect this

14

establishment resembled Dotheboys Hall: the staff consisted of the members of the master's family. Since none of them had any Latin, that language was not in the curriculum. Dr. Dostoevsky took it upon himself to supply the deficiency. The lessons, which were given in the evening, were an ordeal. The pupils did not dare to sit down or even to lean against the table, but stood for the whole period, as Andrey remembered, "like little idols," spouting their declensions and conjugations. At the slightest mistake the doctor would fly into a rage and call them "lazybones" and "dolts." He never struck them. His worst punishment was to stop the lesson.

The doctor liked to repeat that he was a poor man, and that after his death his boys would have to shift for themselves. He was, however, prepared to make heavy sacrifices to provide his sons with the education of gentlemen. At the age of thirteen Fyodor, together with his inseparable companion Mikhail, was entered at Chermak's, one of the better boarding schools in Moscow. Instruction here was offered by teachers from the university, and if the curriculum was rather stiff, the atmosphere was homelike. The pupils took their meals with the headmaster and his sons, and if a boy had a sore throat he was dosed and coddled by Mme. Chermak. Fyodor made himself somewhat conspicuous by protecting the newcomers against the tyranny of the older boys. The presence of his brother must have contributed to his comfort. It is doubtful if he had any chums at school, in spite of the fact that secretly his heart hungered for friendship; his touchiness and sensitiveness stood between him and his companions. He seems to have been, in words that he used of another boy, "doomed to solitude," a nature flung back upon its "own resources and dreams."

Every Saturday morning the doctor's carriage, driven by one of his serfs, went to fetch Fyodor and Mikhail home for the weekend. The two free days were crowded. The father, a practical-minded man, had the older boys give lessons to Andrey, Fyodor's subjects being history and the Russian language. Then there was church attendance. And there were always books and magazines about that Fyodor wanted to read. Books had been his refuge from the beginning. On one occasion the boys appealed to their parents for arbitrament as to who was the greater poet, Zhukovsky or

Pushkin. Family readings in the evening had long been an institution, the father and mother taking turns at the book. Mikhail,
who was himself given to verse writing, cared more for poetry,
and Fyodor for prose, but both had an unlimited admiration for
Pushkin. Fyodor had a special liking for literature that took him
away from his surroundings—the novels of Walter Scott, the plays
of Shakespeare, or books of travel. In his daydreams—the boy indulged his fantasy—he journeyed to Italy or the East, and thought
seriously of running away to Switzerland.

At home he had practically no visitors. The father, besides
being a disciplinarian, was something of a snob. One of the reasons that his sons lacked friends was that he rigidly censored their
contacts with their contemporaries. Once or twice, it is true, the
Dostoevskys gave an evening party for the young people, but this
was not much of a diversion. Decidedly, the brothers lacked the
social graces, and they had to be all but driven to the dancing
floor. Fyodor especially had a shy and reserved manner. Only
when he felt completely at home would he express his uncompromising opinions. Then he would speak hotly and sharply.
Often the doctor would be moved by his son's fiery outbursts to
a warning which was more prophetic than either guessed: "Eh,
Fedya, enough! You will not get off with a whole skin! Mark
my words: you will yet wear a red cap!" He meant the cap worn by
privates in the Siberian regiments, which were recruited partly
from convicts who had done their term.

II

And now the two elder boys were in their middle teens, and
it was high time to begin thinking about what to make of them.
There was no question of consulting their inclinations. It was only
natural that the army doctor should decide upon a calling having
to do with the army. He resolved to place them at the military
engineering school in Petersburg, an exacting and exclusive institution. When the decision to send them there was taken, their
mother was far gone in consumption. The disease had developed
rapidly. Toward the end she looked almost a stranger, not only
because of the ravages of illness: too weak to comb her own hair

and considering it indecent to let others do it, she had it cut. Mikhail and Fyodor had to part from her even earlier than they had feared. She died before they left.

About the same time, in the northern capital, another death occurred which was a fresh blow to the two brothers. On January 29, 1837, Pushkin died of a wound received in a duel. The news only reached the Dostoevsky household a month later, at the time of the mother's funeral. Fyodor kept repeating that if he had not been wearing mourning for his mother, he would have asked his father's permission to put on black for Pushkin. An elegy on the poet's death was so often on the brothers' lips that Andrey was to remember every word of it forty-five years later. Was it that Fyodor concentrated his attention on the less personal bereavement in order to take his mind off the deeper pain? The loss of his mother grieved him all the more because his relations with his father were not intimate and probably not happy. Now there was no one to stand between him and this morose and irascible parent who loved but was apt to antagonize his children.

It was only meet that the orphaned boys should not leave home for the strange, rather terrifying and fascinating place which the school must have meant to them, without again visiting the shrines that had hallowed their childhood. Escorted by their Aunt Kumanina—for who was closer to them than she?—they made a pilgrimage to Troitzkaya Lavra. There was now a sacred place for them nearer home: their mother's grave. The brothers had been allowed to select the inscription for the stone, and had chosen an epitaph from Karamzin: "Rest, dear dust, until the joyous morn."

At last came the day of departure for Petersburg. It was then May, for they had been delayed by a stubborn affection of the throat that attacked Fyodor. A solemn mass was served, and the boys occupied their places in the *kibitka,* beside their father, who was going with them to the capital.

It took them nearly a week, travelling, as they had to do, by coach, to cover the four hundred miles which separate Moscow from Petersburg. On their recent trip to the monastery, the boys had relieved the more tedious stretches by reciting verses to their aunt. The widower was probably not in the mood to respond gratefully to this sort of thing, but Mikhail pleased himself and his brother, on this more momentous journey, by maintaining his habit of writing three poems a day, while Fyodor kept composing mentally a novel of Venetian life. The *kibitka* jolted along the dust-padded road across a bare, monotonous landscape, but he was drifting in a gondola that ruffled the coloured shadow of palaces, under a proud sky. En route, the boys decided that on arriving in Petersburg they would make it their business to visit the site of Pushkin's duel, and also find their way to the dead poet's old quarters, to behold the room in which he had breathed his last. Dr. Dostoevsky had seen to it that his sons' heads were packed with theorems and dates as their luggage with necessaries, but there were things tucked away in Fyodor's mind of which he had little inkling. Peculiarly sensitive to all the mean and sordid aspects of his surroundings, the adolescent boy fled to an ideal world, which may have seemed nearer now that he was at the entrance to a new life, in a new city, among new people.

Before he reached his destination, an ugly incident took him out of his dreams. One evening when they were all at an inn where they were waiting for their horses to be watered, fed, and rested, Fyodor, looking out of the window, saw a *troika* halt at the steps of the posting station across the street. A tall, corpulent man with a purple face, wearing the gaily-plumed tricorn of a military courier, leapt out of the vehicle and dived into the building. A moment later a fresh *troika* pulled up, and the driver, a peasant lad in a red shirt, carrying his coat on his arm, jumped onto the box. The courier came out at once and took his seat, but without giving the driver time to start, he rose and began striking him with his great fist. The lad hunched forward and lashed the middle horse with all his might. The team leapt ahead, but the courier was not satisfied. As long as Fyodor, watching greedily, could see them, he kept on beating the coachman, who never stopped flaying the horses. The picture, which with time took on a symbolic character, remained with him always.

III

Once in Petersburg, the doctor placed his sons with a coach who was preparing a group of boys for entrance to the engineering school, and after six weeks of paternal supervision interlarded with sight-seeing, went back the way he had come. They never saw him again.

Months of hard work were in store for the two brothers. In addition to cramming mathematics, fortfication, artillery, they had to study mechanical drawing and take an intensive course in military drill, a subject of major importance at the school. It was only on Saturdays and Sundays that they could snatch time to write home. On his return from Petersburg the doctor had retired from the service, given up his practice, and settled at Darovoye, taking with him the younger children. In one letter the drudges speak wistfully of the occupations that engage their brothers and sisters in the country. They take occasion to remind Varenka of her promise to study and read Karamzin, and Fyodor hopes that his quondam pupil, Andrusha, is not as careless of his history as he used to be. In the autumn it will be his turn to enter Chermak's. "So for a long time yet you will have to look out for your children's education: you have so many of us," they tell their parent, adding with chilling reasonableness, "Judge for yourself, then, how earnestly we pray to God that He should preserve your health, which is so precious to us." Their joint letters home, apparently written by Mikhail, but signed by both, indicate interest in affairs at the farm: the crops, the new wing which is at last under way, and they abound in expressions of piety and filial regard.

When September came, and examinations with it, they wrote home: "Time itself can't keep pace with us. We're always poring over a book." With the Lord's help, however, they hoped to come through. They worked harder than ever, and when they visited the Kazan Cathedral they did not neglect to say a prayer. Their industry was calculated to please their father, but he must have frowned over the news that in order to be presentable at the examinations, the boys had been compelled to buy new hats, at the shocking price of seven roubles apiece. He seems, however, to have been as generous as his limited means allowed, and for the time being the boys were in funds.

But soon real troubles commenced. Mikhail, who had always been considered the stronger of the two, was turned down by the school doctors on the grounds of poor health. His own explanation was that this was a pretext, so that both brothers should not be an expense to the Government. And then Fyodor, who had come through the examinations brilliantly—indeed, practically at the head of the list, was assigned twelfth place because, for one thing, some of the boys had bribed the authorities. Fyodor had nothing with which to grease their palms and would have been ashamed to buy priority in any case. He was serving his monarch, not these grafters. The injustice of it galled him. To make matters worse, he was refused the scholarship on which his father had counted. Preference had been shown to boys whose fathers could better afford to pay tuition. What would become of them? "But," they wrote home, "the Lord will not forsake poor orphans." When Aunt Kumanina, on hearing the news, volunteered to pay the tuition, should her brother-in-law swallow his pride and permit it, Fyodor felt that his prayers had been answered.

It was not until January, 1838, that he found himself a member of the company of *conductors,* as the students in the lower grades were called. Among other formalities he had to take an oath of allegiance to Emperor Nicholas I, for he was now in military uniform. After some delay Mikhail entered a military school at Reval (now Tallin). And so Fyodor lost the companion from whom he had been inseparable since the beginning, just when he needed him most. In commenting on this misfortune, he wrote to his father that blind Fate played with man as with a toy, but that perhaps God ordered everything for the best. His circumstances at the time were not calculated to strengthen the latter sentiment. He was making his way alone in an unfamiliar, hostile world.

I V

There was something oppressive about the very look of the place: the Cyclopean walls, the huge portals flanked by obelisks, the vast chambers massive with bronze and marble, the chilly statues and sombre historical canvases, the granite stairways leading to long draughty corridors. The school was housed in that cross between a palace and a fortress which the mad Paul had built for himself, and in which he had met his violent death. It was said that one of the oval rooms had been the scene of weird rites, performed in secret by an outlawed mystic sect, which in the early part of the century was fashionable in high places. The boys doubtless pointed out to newcomers the hidden passages, the secret staircases, the chambers where the throne had once stood, where the emperor had dined, and the one where, it was whispered, he had been strangled one night by one of his own courtiers.

A harsh spirit governed the school. The boys could expect no leniency here. In addition to the academic work, there were lessons in singing, dancing, and fencing, as well as sentry duty and the eternal drill. It was only during the summer, when the students went camping as part of the training-course, that there was some relief from the routine. The boys lived in tents pitched just outside Peterhof (now Petrodvoretz), the old imperial residence. The constant drill was hateful to Fyodor, and the out-of-door life bored him then as it always would, but at least the absence of classes allowed more leisure for reading. It was natural that there should be martinets among the instructors. When the bayonets quivered because the class faced the sun and was dazzled, one drill sergeant would shout in a rage: "Attention! Never mind the sun! There is no sun on parade!" During his first term Fyodor had to take part in five parades within three months, all of them reviewed by the Grand Duke Michael and the Tsar. May was marked by the agony of the gala parade reviewed by the entire Imperial family. Since the Polish insurrection of 1831, which had revealed Russia's need for fortifications, the emperor had taken particular interest in military engineering, and he had kept a fond eye upon the school, which responded to his frequent visits with every mark of fervent devotion.

The strict discipline and the strenuous work were perhaps less hard for a sensitive boy to bear than the conscienceless cruelty and the rigid conventions of his schoolfellows. In the first letter Fyodor wrote home after he entered school he said that he was beginning to get used to the routine, but that he could say nothing good about his companions. A newcomer, who was contemptuously referred to as a "hazel hen," was victimized as a matter of course. He was subject to a protracted hazing process. The unfortunate would undergo severe beatings and when he was ready to creep into his bed, might find it flooded. He would be required to lick up ink, and if he gave signs of squeamishness would be forced to repeat obscenities. A hazel hen would suffer in silence, for complaint rendered him a pariah. An immemorial feud raged between the upper and the lower classmen. On one historic occasion, a member of the senior class considering himself slighted by a younger boy, there was a fight, in the course of which some youths ran for their rifles. The commander of the company checked hostilities before the guns were brought into action, and assembling the whole contingent and lining them up, commanded reconciliation by shouting the order: "Kiss to the right! Kiss to the left!" It was only in such extraordinary cases as this that the authorities intervened. During Fyodor's second year at school there occurred a mysterious scandal, so grave that several of his companions were demoted, and for a time all out-going letters were censored.

The hazel hen who answered to the name of Dostoevsky, a pale boy with freckles on his snub nose and an inward look in his small deep-set grey eyes, wore the military uniform of a *conductor* as though it were a misfit. And indeed, in this training-school for builders of fortresses, he was a misfit. Not that the raw-skinned daydreamer was a softy. There was a strength in him that his fellows respected in spite of themselves. But he did not join in the fun, and for the most part kept his own company. He formed the habit—which was to last his lifetime—of working late into the night, long after everyone else in the house was asleep. A proctor making his rounds would notice a lonely blanketed figure hunched over a desk beside a draughty window in the light of a single tallow candle. The quiet, the half-darkness, he would explain, disposed him toward work. He impressed his schoolmates as a solitary, who never laughed and seldom spoke, who would be customarily seen carrying his equipment as though it were a martyr's irons, and striding along in his jerky fashion, with a concentrated stare. They nicknamed him "Photius" after the fanatical archimandrite who ruled Alexander I, or perhaps after the Byzantine patriarch who championed the Eastern Church, and twitted the pale, retiring boy with being "a mystic or idealist."

He was good in all the academic subjects, except mechanical drawing, of which there were four kinds, but he did not get on with his teachers as well as he might have, at least in the beginning. When the first year was over, he found that he had not been promoted, in spite of the fact that by his own account he had passed the examinations with flying colours. He blamed this misfortune on

certain teachers who, he believed, had held his rudeness against
him. He took the blow so hard that he was ill in bed for several
days. Another whole year to be spent in this beastly class! That
he should be left behind, while, through favouritism, nonentities
were advanced! O meanness of man! O harshness of Heaven! Such
was the tone of his reflections on the event. "Oh, God," he wrote
in a letter to his father on October 30, 1838, "what have I done to
bring down Your wrath upon me? Why do You not send me Your
grace, that I might rejoice the tenderest of parents? Oh, how many
tears this has cost me! I felt sick when I heard the news." He goes
on to beg his father not to take it to heart. This by no means implies
that he will be expelled. Surely, he is not altogether lacking in
ability! In writing to Mikhail he confesses that in his mortfication
he wanted to crush the world with one blow. Never before had he
known what it meant to have his *amour-propre* injured. When he
said this, he was forgetting the previous occasions on which his
self-esteem had been wounded. His relations with his teachers improved with time, but the taste of humiliation remained.

Mikhail, too, wrote home in an effort to comfort his father and
perhaps to shield Fyodor from paternal wrath. The doctor indeed
needed solace: on getting the bad news he had collapsed and only
a copious bleeding had saved him, he believed, from a fatal stroke.
By way of balm Mikhail offered such reflections as that whom the
Lord loveth He chasteneth, that, conversely, "all these physical
joys and all this filthy happiness in which the heart and the mind lie
swaddled in a pitiful stupor are merely the mockery of Fate . . ."
and that "in misfortune man becomes more man and thereby nearer
to the Divine Ideal." In thus exalting the virtues of suffering Mikhail sounded a note which was to become a major motif in his
brother's thinking.

CHAPTER THREE

A RAW YOUTH

At school Fyodor lived in a turmoil of thought and emotion, dominated less by the adolescent's ecstacy than by the adolescent's despair. "I don't know if my sad thoughts will ever cease," he writes to his brother the first summer. "It seems to me that the world has taken on a negative meaning." The idea of suicide is not far from his mind: "To see nothing but the hard shell under which the universe languishes, to know that one explosion of the will is enough to break it and allow one to merge with eternity, to know this and yet live on like the lowest of creatures—how terrible! How faint-hearted man is! Hamlet! Hamlet! When I think of his wild, tempestuous speeches in which resounds the groaning of a numbed world, then . . . my soul is so oppressed by sorrow that she fears to fathom it lest she turns and rend herself." A postscript to the letter suggests a singular way of escaping from responsibilities and harassments: "I have a project: to go mad. Let people rage, let them doctor me, let them try to restore me to sanity."

As time goes on, he does not cease to indulge himself in this melancholy mood. "Brother," he writes in the autumn, "it is sad to live without hope." The present depresses him, the future horrifies. He is breathing a chill, sunless air. Often his state is that of the Prisoner of Chillon after the death of his brother:

> *I had no thoughts, no feeling—none—*
> *Among the stones I stood, a stone. . . .*

It is a long time since he has known "an explosion of inspiration." He is not visited any more by "poetry, the bird of paradise." His dreams have abandoned him, and "the marvellous arabesques" that his fancy used to trace "have shed their gilt." The thoughts that used to kindle his soul have lost their heat.

Again he breaks off his complaints to plunge into muddled philo-

24

sophizing. Mikhail's remark to the effect that to know more, one must feel less, is dismissed by his brother as "delirium of the heart." Love, the soul, Nature, God, can only be known, he insists, through the heart, not through the intellect, which is a "material faculty," a machine set into motion by "the spirit's fire." Thought generates in the spirit. Thoughts are whispered to the spirit by the heart. Philosophy is not merely an equation in which Nature is the unknown quantity. It is poetry that apprehends the ultimate, which is the proper object of philosophy. Fyodor would have his brother know that poetic and philosophic ecstasy are the same, and philosophy is but the highest degree of poetry. Some of these anti-rationalist notions, fragments of a romantic system of ideas, will be the anchorage of his mature thinking.

He had few companions to whom he could open his heart as he did to Mikhail. Only three or four of his schoolmates fell under his influence. Yet if he was backward at forming personal relationships, he attached himself with violence to those friends whom he made. He knew the transports of friendship as celebrated by the romantics. One object of his amical passion was a striking young man five years his senior, whom he had first met at the inn where they stopped on arriving in Petersburg. During the weeks of tutoring, after their father had left them, this Ivan Shidlovsky had been in the habit of visiting the brothers every Sunday, looking after them like a fond relative, and accompanying them to church. When he was alone, Fyodor clung the more closely to the companionable youth. Of a winter evening he would make his way through the snowy streets to the humble lodging of his friend, and they would spend exquisitely melancholy hours together. The spirituality of Shidlovsky, his sensuousness, his literary talent—he wrote poems expressing the desire to govern the universe and gossip with God—his golden tongue, his ready tears, his easy ecstasies, his sufferings as a victim of unrequited love—everything about this tall, ascetic-looking youth enchanted the lonely boy. Here was "the proper image of a man," such as Shakespeare and Schiller had painted.

Shidlovsky was also friendly toward Mikhail, with whom he exchanged fervent letters. In one of them he explained that he loved his correspondent, firstly, as a confidant, and secondly, as a poet with a serene view of the world. His own view, at least at the moment of writing, was that "God is good, or He would not be God, that the universe is the visible, palpable beauty of this goodness, and that their essential identity is truth." On another occasion he told Mikhail that he envisioned the laurels awaiting him, in the same breath invoking Werther and Chatterton, and declaring that the bottom of the Fontanka Canal beckoned to him as the nuptial bed beckons the bridegroom. "*Ach*, why weren't you with us?" Fyodor wrote to his brother on New Year's Day, 1840, as he counted over the precious memories of the past year, in which Shidlovsky loomed so large. "I remember how tears flowed from his eyes as he read your poems. He knows them by heart." During the summer Fyodor saw little of this comrade, who was making ready to leave the capital. They spent their last evening together walking the streets of a Petersburg suburb, recalling the past winter, which had been peopled by the shades of Homer and Schiller, and discoursing of Mikhail, of themselves, of the future.

Then Shidlovsky stepped out of Dostoevsky's life, but not out of his memory. He had strengthened his young friend's notion that writing was the only worthy occupation, since it furnished an avenue of escape from sordid reality. Years later this odd fellow entered a monastery, but soon retired to his estate without taking off his cassock, and divided his time between drunken orgies and fits of piety. He would be seen preaching the Gospel to a crowd of awestruck peasants near a tavern, and he made pilgrimages to various shrines, but in the end the bishop forbade him entrance to the monastries on the ground that he corrupted the monks.

Shortly after he became intimate with Shidlovsky, Fyodor found himself involved in another violent friendship, which he surrounded with mystery, perhaps because he considered it too precious to expose to vulgar comment. It seems to have consumed itself briefly and intensely upon a plane where life merged into literature. In his letter of New Year's Day he was telling Mikhail: "I had a comrade with me, a creature whom I loved so much! You wrote me, brother, that I hadn't read Schiller. You are mistaken! I learned Schiller by heart, I talked him, I dreamed him, and I think that Fate has done nothing more fitting for me than to let me know the great poet at just this period of my life: at no other time could I have responded to him so fully. Reading Schiller with him, I verified by him the noble, ardent Don Carlos, the Marquis Posa, and Mortimer. This friendship brought me so much sorrow and joy! Now I shall be silent about it eternally. But Schiller's name became for me a cherished, magic sound, calling up many reveries; they are bitter, brother; that is why I said nothing to you about Schiller! . . . I am pained when I hear his name."

This friend, he confessed, had been closer to him than Mikhail, for whom, he went on, he had never had any real brotherly feeling, although he loved him for his verse, the poetry of his life, and his misfortunes. But in the same breath he laid balm to Mikhail's soul by enlarging on the joy that a letter from him brought with it. When one arrived, he looked at it, turned it over in his hand for a minute or two, fingered it to find out how ample it was, and then, having thoroughly examined the envelope, he put it in his pocket unopened, and spent a "voluptuous" quarter of an hour before he eagerly picked the treasure's lock, a way he was to have with precious letters.

The mysterious friend vanished, to be heard of no more. Mikhail remained. Whatever he may have felt about Fyodor's temporary disaffection, he must have warmed to the praise of Schiller. He had himself once written to their father: "Let them take everything from me, let them leave me naked, but give me Schiller, and I shall forget the whole world." Dostoevsky was ultimately to revolt against Schilleresque idealism, and yet something of it always remained with him.

There were other authors whom he was reading with enthusiasm, and both brothers took their literary opinions sufficiently to heart to quarrel over them seriously. The first season at camp Fyodor read prodigiously. He devoured, among other things, the whole of that weird fantast, Amadeus Hoffmann, almost all of Balzac, Goethe's *Faust*, as well as his lyrical poems, and a great deal of Hugo. He dipped with equal relish into the older writers and into current books, nor did he neglect native authors. His enthusiasm is as violent as his taste is eclectic. He prizes highly *The Confessions of an English Opium Eater*. Of Balzac he exclaims: "His characters were created by the intelligence of the universe. Not the spirit of an age, but the struggle of millenniums has prepared for such a dénouement in the soul of man." Both Hugo and Racine command his admiration. *Phèdre* is the quintessence of truth and poetry: it matters little that this Shakespearian theme is executed "in plaster-of-Paris rather than in marble." As for Corneille, he is "almost a Shakespeare." Only offended angels speak as Auguste does in *Cinna*. "Have you read *Le Cid?*" he asks his brother, who had dared to disparage the French classics. "Read him, you wretch, and lie in the dust before Corneille!"

He was studying life at secondhand, through literature. Yet already it was clear to him that his true pursuit was not the building of fortresses, but "the meaning of man and of life." He was, he wrote Mikhail, making sufficient headway with this study, since he was spending his best hours with the greatest writers "freely and happily." For all his moodiness, he had moments of serenity and full self-confidence. In one of these moments he wrote to his brother: "Man is a mystery. It must be unravelled, and if you give your life to the task, do not say that you have wasted it; I devote myself to this mystery because I wish to be a man."

II

In addition to his metaphysical ache, and the difficulty of adjustment to the uncongenial environment, there was another hardship that beset the raw youth. From the beginning of his stay at school he felt the pinch of penury, which was to fret him practically to the end of his days. At home he had done without pocket money because, in his father's opinion, a gentleman's son required none. Living as he now did in a boarding school, his needs were nominally provided for. Yet there were all kinds of demands on his purse. When a review was in prospect the boys, most of whom came from well-to-do families, bought new apparel, and he had to do likewise or risk being remarked by the emperor. And then there were paints and brushes to be got, and the French circulating library—he simply must join it. On October 30, 1838, he was writing home: "Send me something without delay. You will pull me out of hell. Oh, how terrible it is to be in this extremity!" Such modest sums as he received, he found hard to keep. Money burnt a hole in his pocket, and being frequently without a groat, he fell into the habit of borrowing. The unseemly situation was calculated to wound his pride deeply. He borrowed to pay the priest's fee when he took communion. He borrowed the price of a stamp, to send a letter to his father, and sometimes he had to enclose a missive to Mikhail with that of a friend. Soon he was in debt to the tune of fifty roubles. "Save me," he wrote to his father. "Send me sixty roubles. . . . My God, I know that we are poor. But Heaven is my witness, I do not demand anything excessive."

Two months later he repeated the same cry, which was to sound in his letters to relatives and friends so often throughout the years to come. "I have a head, I have hands," he tells his father. "If I were free and thrown upon my own resources, I would not ask a copeck from you. I would put up with iron poverty." He recognizes that the parents' want "must be fully shared by their children." But he is in the service, and, as he says plainly, must either conform to the standards of his fellows or be outlawed. Camp opens early in June, and that means extraordinary expenses. He is willing to forego tea and sugar, although if one has to spend hours in a canvas tent in the rain, or when one comes in from practice tired and cold, these are no luxuries. Indeed, the previous year at camp he had been taken ill for want of them. But what he must have is two pairs of plain boots, since the Government does not supply enough, and a chest in which to keep his belongings, particularly books. "For how," he adds, "how can I pass the time without books?" Moreover, the tent holds only cots: bundles of straw, covered with sheeting, and so the orderly must be paid to find a place for the chest. Nor can he be expected to do without boot-blacking, and such things as writing paper and stamps, and all that costs something. He requires at least twenty-five roubles, besides the fifteen he has on hand. "And so send me this sum by the first of June," he writes, "if you wish to help your son in his terrible need. I dare not demand; I am not asking too much, but my gratitude will be boundless." Fyodor was perhaps moved less by actual need than by a fear of being looked down upon by his more prosperous companions. At least one of his schoolmates managed without any tea of his own, since the school provided tea morning and evening, without extra boots, being content with what the Government supplied, and without a chest, although he claimed to be as great a reader as Dostoevsky.

The doctor, who had no way of checking his son's statements, in reply to his pitiful plea pointed out that he had had a succession of ruinous seasons on the farm: after a long and bitter winter, during which they had had to sacrifice the very thatch on the roofs to keep the cattle from starving, there had been a spring drought which spelled famine; further, he hadn't ordered a new suit of clothes in four years, and was without a groat. Nevertheless, he enclosed a remittance for ten roubles more than his son had requested.

This was the last letter that Fyodor received from his father. Wrapped up in his own troubles, he probably knew little of what was going on at home, or of how wretched an existence the widower had been leading since his retirement. Living alone on the farm, without his customary occupations and contacts, he rapidly went to pieces. Like thousands of isolated provincial gentlefolk, he tried to drown his loneliness in his cups, and, for want of better company took one of the servants for his mistress. His old fits of rage came upon him more frequently and with greater violence. It is vaguely reported that he suffered from peculiar seizures. He would be heard talking aloud to his dead wife. As time went on he was practically never sober, and behaved like one half mad.

One June day, a fortnight after having written to Fyodor, he was killed by his Chermashnya serfs. The identity of the murderers was known to the local peasantry and even to the priest. Nevertheless, there was no trial. It is said that the Moscow relatives, arriving on the scene, easily learned the true story, but succeeded in persuading the police to see the death as the result of apoplexy. Since a number of men were involved, bringing the culprits to justice would have meant sending them all to Siberia. The family argued that this would only result, on the one hand, in the loss of so many workers to the heirs, and, on the other, in a blot on the family scutcheon. In any event, the scandal was hushed up so carefully that no breath of it reached the general ear until over eighty years after the tragedy.

Under these circumstances gossip, embroidering upon rumour, gave rise to several versions of the way in which the doctor had met his death. According to one, his anger had been roused as he was inspecting the work that some of his Chermashnya serfs were doing in an outlying field, and he let loose on them. One of the peasants answered him impudently and then, in fear of a flogging, rushed upon the master and with the help of his fellows did him in. It was said that for two days the body lay at the mercy of the weather and the crows. Another version has it that the murder was a premeditated one, in which over a dozen men, practically the entire male population of Chermashnya, took part. Dostoevsky's daughter reported that her grandfather had been suffocated by his coachman with his own carriage cushions. But though the tale varies, the fact is left in no doubt that it was one of those acts of vengeance against a brutal master which were ominously on the increase at the time. Long years afterwards, his ugly disposition was still remembered by the old inhabitants and contrasted with his wife's kindness. One aged peasant, upon being told that Fyodor Dostoevsky had become famous, observed that it could not be true that he was a great man: from such a one as his father nothing good could come.

Fyodor seems to have been the first to learn the dreadful news. He passed it on to Mikhail. Afterwards Mikhail recalled that on the night of June 8, apparently the fatal date, he had seen his father in a dream sitting at his desk, his hair all white, and that looking at him thus, he became so sad that he began to cry, and then went over and kissed his father without being noticed. He had waked with fear in his heart. Fyodor wrote to Mikhail "that he had shed many tears over their father's death. Oddly enough he went on to speak of his hopes, his faith in the future and in himself, his growing sense of being at peace with the world, his freedom from the tumult that had agitated his soul: now everything in it is calm, as in the heart of a man who hides a deep secret." One gets the curious impression that the tragedy was in the nature of a release for the boy.

As a grown man Dostoevsky is said to have disliked speaking of his father. One can only speculate upon what was his feeling for him, or rather upon what was his attitude toward the father image in the early years. Perhaps it is here that one must look for the matrix of that emotional ambivalence, the love-hate motif, which he eventually erected into the law of the heart. His letters home were few and far between—he was always pleading the pressure of work. At least once he expressed his attachment in emphatic terms, but with an emphasis that rings false: "My God, how long it is since I last wrote, how long it is since I tasted those moments of true, cordial bliss, true, pure, exalted . . . bliss which is experienced only by those who have someone with whom to share the hours of rapture and sorrow, who have someone in whom to confide all that goes on in their hearts! Oh, how greedily I now drink in this bliss!" There is no doubt, however, that occasionally Fyodor had been filled with pitying tenderness for the unhappy, hysterical, narrow-minded, spasmodically generous man who was his father. "I am sorry for our poor father!" he had once written to Mikhail. "A strange character! How many misfortunes he has sustained! It is bitter, even to tears, that there is nothing to console him with. And do you know, Papasha completely lacks knowledge of the world. . . . But he is deeply disappointed in it—this seems to be our common lot." A son who thus compassionated the living surely felt a greater pity for the dead. In any event, the eighteen-year-old Hamlet must have brooded long over the murder, a murder hedged about with secrecy and unavenged. One suspects that he carried the scar of the crime to the end of his days.

And now what was to become of the family? Of the seven children, at least five still needed parental care. Mikhail conceived the idea of settling in the country and bringing up his brothers and sisters, and Fyodor applauded this generous impulse. It remained however, a pious wish. Mikhail stayed on at Reval where, as he had written his brother, he was "plucking the flowers of love," the reference being doubtless to his infatuation with Emilia Ditmar, who was, before long, to become his wife. Meanwhile, there was the matter of guardianship to be decided immediately. Mikhail begged the Kumanins to undertake this responsibility, but although they were ready to do a good deal for the children, particularly the younger ones, they declined, and eventually the office was entrusted to Varvara's newly acquired husband. This Piotr Karepin, to whom the Kumanins had been at pains to marry off the eldest of the Dostoevsky girls, was a substantial citizen in the Government service in Moscow. He was a widower, already past forty, while his bride was a girl of seventeen. Although Fyodor, being away at school, was not present at the wedding, the marriage, with the grave discrepancy in the ages of the couple, seems to have made a shocking impression upon him.

III

Fyodor spent, or, as he would have said, wasted, more than five years at the Engineering School. He never really managed to make an adjustment, and at the end of his stay there he was much the same retiring, self-absorbed daydreamer that he had been at the beginning. His mind was of the sort that could draw but small sustenance from the scientific subjects which prevailed in the curriculum. Mathematics he could not bear. It was a subject so useless, he had once written to his father, that it was positively foolish to study it. It was a mere soap bubble. His school record was good on the whole. He cursed and crammed—and passed. But in the end all this laboriously acquired information dropped away from him as water rolls off a duck's back. The chief effect of his training seems to have been to cultivate in him a distaste for the sciences. His abilities as a military engineer may be gauged by the fact that at the final examination he is said to have submitted a plan for a fortress without providing for gates. The friend who tells the story says that the emperor's scrawled comment: "What fool did this?" so rankled in Dostoevsky that he finally decided to leave the service.

As time went on he chafed more and more under the yoke of his uncongenial duties. He had been at school less than two years when he wrote to Mikhail that his sole aim was to be free. He was depressed by the thought that he was engaged in work unworthy of him. "How sad life is, and how burdensome its moments," he reflected, "when . . . you feel that the soul's flame is being beaten down and extinguished by God knows what; when the heart is being torn to shreds—and why? Because of a life worthy of a pygmy rather than of a giant, of a child, not of a man." In his isolation, he told his brother, he had grown brutish. Left alone after a brief visit from Mikhail (he came in January, 1841, to take examinations for promotion to officer's rank), Fyodor was plunged into deeper despondency. He had nothing to hope for except that he might win a million roubles. The gambler's demon was already at his elbow.

Now and then, however, he was filled with the prescience of limitless power. The future was his. There was a kind of fire in his soul, in which he firmly believed. Freedom—that was the thing!—

freedom and one's calling! The mere thought of such happiness
made his soul expand, allowing it to grasp the greatness of life.
He approached this longed-for freedom when, in August, 1841,
he was promoted to the upper section of the school, known as the
Engineering Academy, and therewith received the rank of ensign.

As a commissioned officer he could have his lodgings outside
the school and taste something of independence. There were now
many afternoon hours to devote to reading and—what was perhaps
more necessary to him—writing. It is certain that he had obeyed
the literary impulse even while he was still an inmate of the school.
At least some of those nocturnal hours that he spent wrapped up
in his blanket beside his candle must have been given to setting
his fancies down on paper. Although he shared Mikhail's passion
for poetry, he did not try his hand at verse, lacking, according to
one friend, the requisite patience. When Mikhail, having taken
his examinations, was leaving Petersburg, Fyodor gave a farewell
party at which he read passages from his plays: *Maria Stuart* and
Boris Godunov. He was still at work on the first-named play in
1842, attracted to the subject both by his passion for Schiller and
because he had seen Lily Loewe in the title-rôle of the German
drama. Nothing of these early efforts has been preserved.

In the autumn of the first year that Fyodor was living in his
own quarters, Andrey came from Moscow to stay with him and be
tutored by him for entrance examinations to the school. He found
Fyodor sharing a gloomy apartment of two rooms with a schoolmate, Adolf Todleben. Eventually the two brothers set up house-
keeping together in a roomier flat. Here some of Fyodor's friends
would drop in after dinner, and the evening would often end with
a card game, played for such stakes as they could afford, and much
relished by Fyodor. There were other amusements, too, in the form
of the theatre, the ballet, and concerts by such artists as Liszt and
Rubini. The small allowance he received from the family guardian
was of course inadequate, and as usual he was frequently reduced
to borrowing. His creditors included Andrey, who was getting an
occasional remittance from the Kumanins. Nevertheless, he managed to send a respectable sum to Mikhail when, early in 1842,
at the age of twenty-one, that impecunious if enterprising young
man married his Emilia. That year Fyodor passed his examinations

successfully, and was promoted to the rank of sub-lieutenant, next above that of ensign. The school rated him as very zealous in the service, good as regards his mental capacities, his morals, and the care of his equipment, and proficient in "God's law" and the art of laying mines, among a score of other subjects.

Now there was only one more year of this drudgery. There was little but the hope of speedy release to distinguish it from the preceding years. One change was the absence of Andrey, who, having been admitted to the School of Architecture, was living at the dormitories. The petty, matter-of-fact person that his younger brother had turned out to be was no companion for Fyodor, and he was rather relieved to be free of him. As for the rest, there were the same dull classes, the same worries over making both ends meet. He had a remarkable faculty for getting rid of money. It almost seemed as though he were striving for the penury that he found so distressing. His health was rather poor and, whether out of carelessness or despondency, he refused to take care of it. Books were as ever his meat and drink. The year brought him at least one new book that was to prove a source of endless interest and delight. It was Gogol's *Dead Souls*. Here was the Human Comedy in Russian terms and, moreover, a work that to the discerning eye held promise of being the preface to a Divine Comedy.

Dostoevsky marked the great occasion of the passing of his finals in June with a dinner in the private room of a fashionable restaurant. In spite of the wine and a piano, the night was probably less festive than he could have wished, for he had dragged the friend who was his sole guest out of a sick-bed to help him celebrate the end of his servitude. The following day he set off for Reval to visit Mikhail. His month's leave over, he returned to Petersburg, carrying with him a complete wardrobe, including linen, such things being cheap in the prosperous Baltic city. He may also have taken back with him the distaste for everything German which was one of his many pet prejudices. He was within two months of his twenty-second birthday when, in August, 1843, he graduated, and forthwith entered the Government service as a draughtsman in the Petersburg Engineering Corps.

CHAPTER FOUR

THIS IS FAME!

H E did not intend to follow the profession for which he was trained. Literature, not military engineering, was to be his life-work. And yet there he was, stuck in the service. His circumstances were as uncertain as ever, in spite of the fact that now, being a draughtsman in government employ, he had a small salary in addition to the income from the estate. Part of the winter he shared living quarters with a friend, a physician by the name of Riesenkampf. Mikhail had made the arrangement in the hope that the orderly German would have a steadying influence on his brother. The association did not last and failed of the desired effect.

As before, Dostoevsky lived from hand to mouth. The arrival of money from home—Moscow was still that to him in a vague way—was a great event. His voice gained assurance, his step became jaunty. He paid his creditors, he feasted, he tried his luck at billiards and cards. But a brief day or two of riotous living saw him back again on a diet of bread and milk got on credit or paid for with money borrowed from friends and usurers. He was plagued not so much by lack of money as by inability to spend it sensibly.

It may have been at this time that he became so intimately acquainted with the shabby taverns of the city and noted, as he never noted the details of the natural scene, such smells and sounds as the reek of burnt fat and greasy napkins, the stuttering air from *Lucia*, the shouts for the waiters, the clicking of billiard balls, the songless nightingale pecking at the bottom of its cage.

Dostoevsky had long ago conceived the notion of giving up his share of the inheritance in exchange for a lump sum, but the guardian would not hear of it. Sometimes a few of his roubles found their way into the pockets of the doctor's patients who were mostly poor folk. Dostoevsky was attracted to them much as he had been to the inmates of the charity hospital where he had lived as a child

He hung around the waiting-room. He drew them out over a cup of tea. He studied them. He sank himself in the pinched, warped lives of the penniless and ailing. Here was the stuff for his pen.

For himself, he was not content to remain poor. He was full of grand money-making schemes, half commercial, half literary. In collaboration with Mikhail and a friend he would translate a thriller by Eugène Sue, publish it on his own, and reap a profit of four thousand roubles. Or they would get rich by issuing a complete Russian Schiller. There must be a public for these sublime writings! Then there were George Sand and Balzac to translate. He hoped to get at least one hundred roubles for his version of *Eugénie Grandet*, but he had no cash with which to pay for the copying of the manuscript. If only Mikhail would lend him ten roubles for the purpose: he swore by Olympus, by his just finished play, by his future moustache, that his brother would get half of the proceeds. One could so easily fail to hook a fortune for want of a few roubles' bait. Eventually this translation found a place in a magazine, the others all coming to nothing. Still, translation seemed a road to ease. Mikhail must go on with Schiller. *Don Carlos,* issued on their own with an introduction by him and a poem to the dramatist by Mikhail, was bound to be a hit. And then there was money in writing plays. Why not toss off a popular melodrama? But no, potboilers be damned! He would write only what was worth writing, and that as well as he could.

The service was as distasteful to him as school had been. It was, indeed, intolerable. He compared it to a diet of potatoes. He had endured only eight months of it when he spoke of retirement as a foregone conclusion, and indeed before long tendered his resignation. Why, he argued, waste one's best years? Besides, he was being assigned to a post in the provinces. And what on earth would he do without Petersburg? How he was to make a living did not worry him. He would find a crust of bread somehow.

The step he had taken deprived him at once of a dignified position with a chance of advancement, and of a salary which, though small, was steady. He knew that he would have to justify himself in the eyes of the Moscow relatives, particularly his brother-in-law who, as guardian, held the purse strings. In the letter that he addressed to Karepin ten days after he had sent in his resignation, he said that he had been forced to resign because of his debts. He had been assigned to a distant post and, to save his honour as an officer, would have had to settle with his creditors before leaving Petersburg. He named fifteen hundred paper roubles as the amount of his indebtedness, although he confined to Mikhail that it was no more than eight hundred, a large part of which he owed to his landlord: he had rented a rather expensive four-room flat because he liked the looks of the owner, and, to save firewood, was occupying only one room. His situation, he told Karepin, was desperate: he had no clothes, no food, and would soon be reduced to sleeping under the colonnade of the Kazan Cathedral. What other course was open to him when he had no one to count on, and his own brothers were ready to cheat him out of his rightful due? His demand for a lump sum, in lieu of his share of the inheritance, must finally be granted. He would be content with a payment of five hundred roubles down and another five hundred in monthly instalments. Then he would clear off his debts and start life anew. He wound up with the threat that if his plea remained unanswered he would sell his share in the estate to a stranger.

The guardian unmoved, advised him to withdraw his resignation. Whereupon Dostoevsky admitted that he may have acted rashly in resigning, but declared that he would rot in debtors' prison— he would have to go there without trousers, he told Mikhail— rather than re-enter the service before his affairs were in order. As to compounding his share of the inheritance, that was positively his duty now, since it would be said that as a free lance he might become a charge on the family. At any rate, he was writing for the last time.

Again Karepin sent advice instead of money. He also had a few hard words to say about his ward's greed, and, animadverting on his literary ambitions, warned him against being carried away by Shakespeare, who was really only "a soap bubble." Dostoevsky replied with a letter that he described to Mikhail as "a gem of epistolary polemics." He told Karepin to mind his own business, blamed his debts on the loansharks with whom Petersburg was overrun, and abruptly opened his heart to this man, of whom he had an unprintable opinion, by announcing that the exploration of life was at once his study and his diversion. In conclusion he set a definite date by which he must have the money. It passed, and there was not so much as a word from Karepin.

In the meantime his resignation had been accepted—on October 19, 1844. He was at the end of his rope. "I am left alone," he wrote to Karepin, "without hope, without help, abandoned to all calamities: nakedness, beggary, shame, infamy. . . ." In addition to everything else, he was sick. Wouldn't Karepin agree to the arrangement, after all? It would be his salvation. It might even enable him to re-enter the service. If there was no ready money, why not borrow? Let Karepin at least, for Heaven's sake, send on a statement that he could show his creditors, as to his financial expectations. If he didn't get the money, he would simply turn over his share of the estate to the sharks to whom he was in debt. These dealings with his brother-in-law strengthened any disagreeable impressions of him Dostoevsky may have had. "Karepin drinks, f——s, s——s, swills vodka, has a rank in the service, and believes in God." Such is the thumbnail sketch of the man that he drew for Mikhail.

Although it was months before he finally received the five hundred roubles, he did not have to go to prison. He was given to exageration and was as readily depressed about the sad state of his purse as about that of his body. Nevertheless, it is certain that when his resignation made him, at the age of twenty-three, a free man, his circumstances were dismal. He was making his start in life under the most inauspicious auguries.

I I

What kept up his courage through all his troubles was one great hope. While he was parading his wretchedness before Karepin, he was writing to Mikhail that he was finishing a novel. Here was something definite to build on. He would sell it to a magazine or, better yet, he would publish it himself, with part of the money he expected from the guardian. But when, at long last, he did get the coveted five hundred, it was not enough to pay his debts, so that publishing his book was out of the question. Besides, much as it had pleased him while he was working on it, he had no sooner finished it than he decided to rewrite it completely. He cut, he added, he polished. It was only in March of the following year that he considered the job done.

By then it was too late in the season to issue the novel in book form. Should he hand it over to a magazine for a song? No. He was writing, as he told Mikhail, not for glory, but for bread. Not that he would, for the sake of the money, do less than his best. He would follow in the footsteps of Pushkin, of Gogol. Those supreme craftsmen were sure of their monuments, and of their money, too. No, he would tighten his belt, arm himself with patience, lay aside three hundred roubles, even if he would have to go into debt again, and in the early autumn when people returned to town hungry for something new, he would stake his last chance on printing the thing himself, and either be ruined or make a pile of money. Should the novel fail, he would probably hang himself. He concludes the letter by telling his brother of an article he had been reading about German artists who had died in penury, committed suicide, or gone mad: "I am still terrified. One must be a charlatan."

Five weeks of tormenting worry go by, and he is forced to a fresh decision. He is now apparently sharing two rooms and a kitchen with his old schoolmate, Grigorovich. They stoke their own samovar and get their own meals themselves. These are often extremely frugal, sometimes consisting of rolls and barley coffee. At least he has clothes enough to last him for two years. The money that was to have been saved up for the publication of the book has vanished. Besides, well-informed people have assured him that it would be bad business for him to issue the novel on his own. And so he will submit it to *Otechestvennye zapiski* ("Fatherland Notes"), a monthly which has the enormous circulation of twenty-five hundred copies. If the thing is accepted, his future is assured. He has new ideas that before long will increase his fame threefold. He has put away childish things. When he does not write, he reads. He can fairly feel his mind expanding, his powers growing. He has revised his novel again, greatly to its advantage. This, he assures Mikhail, is absolutely the final revision. He won't touch it again. If the book is accepted, he will have the heart and the time to undertake the translations of Sue and Schiller. If it is rejected, he will probably throw himself into the Neva.

Dostoevsky's entrance upon the literary stage was a piece of crude melodrama, of the sort in which both his art and his life abound. The manuscript of *Poor Folk* did not, after all, land upon the desk of the editor of *Fatherland Notes*. Instead, it found its way, just how is not quite clear, perhaps through Grigorovich, into the hands of a pushing, prodigiously active young man, who was then little more than a hack, but with a sound business head on his shoulders: Alexey Nekrasov. Dostoevsky had read his first collection of verse, a thin little book in pink covers, while still at school. The man was now a publisher in a small way, and was on the lookout for manuscripts for a miscellany that he was planning to issue. In this enterprise he was to have the help of Belinsky, the arbiter of the intellectuals of the period. This critic had gathered about him a group of young men who formed the nucleus of the so-called Westerners. For the most part sons of the gentry, they were liberals in an age of reaction, chafing against the autocratic régime of Nicholas I and dreaming of a Russia rebuilt on the European model.

Was there anything in *Poor Folk*, after all, to recommend it to a critic of Belinsky's calibre? So much depended on the fate of this story! All Dostoevsky's faith in his performance could not quiet his fears as to what was to become of it and him. The late spring was ushering in the short, luminous "white nights" of the North. Restless with the knowledge that Nekrasov had his tale, Dostoevsky left his rooms to spend an evening with a former schoolmate. They passed the time together rereading Gogol's *Dead Souls*. It was almost dawn when Dostoevsky returned home.

The night was too rare for sleep. He opened the window and sat beside it, breathing the mild, disturbing air. Suddenly the bell rang. It was just four o'clock. The door opened and in burst Nekrasov arm in arm with Grigorovich. They rushed up to the dumbfounded watcher of the dawn and put their arms about him. They seemed near tears. From their incoherent words Dostoevsky made out that they had started to read *Poor Folk* in the evening, that they had spent the night over it, and that it had stirred them so deeply that they had to come to the author at once. Suppose they found him asleep! They would wake him up. They had to tell him.

Here was an hour to savour and remember. They talked, not only of his story, but of truth and poetry, they quoted Gogol, and every second word was of Belinsky. . . . Vissarion Belinsky: he would see the story that very day, Nekrasov promised the young author, shaking him by the shoulders. And then they left him, with the absurd injunction to sleep. For a long time Grigorovich, lying on the divan in the adjacent room, heard him pacing back and forth.

At first Belinsky proved sceptical about "the new Gogol" that his fellow editor was pressing upon his attention, and two or three days passed before he touched the manuscript. But he, too, stayed up all night to finish it. In the morning he clamoured for the author. And so Dostoevsky was brought before the great critic. There was something solemn about the tone and bearing of the slight, frail man. Dostoevsky, awed as he was, could yet discern the nature of this solemnity. It was not that of a pompous, self-important person, but that adopted by a man of stern integrity about to say grave and weighty words. What Dostoevsky heard, in substance, was that he had written a great book, a book that reached depths beyond the grasp of the author himself. As Belinsky proceeded, his excitement mounted, and as usual on such occasions, his voice grew shrill, while his assumed dignity melted into enthusiasm.

Dostoevsky came away from the interview intoxicated. He stood still on the street corner overlooking Anichkov Bridge, near which Belinsky lived, and stared at the bright day, at the sky, at the unaware pedestrians. In all his dreaming he had never figured to himself anything like this. He was on the threshold of a new world. His whole being was buoyed up by "timid elation." He was not worthy of this glory. Well, then, he would make himself worthy. He, too, would become part of the sacred circle of which Belinsky was the master. He would be faithful. This was the greatest moment that he had known or, indeed, was ever to know.

III

The exaltation could not last. A man of his unstable temper was bound to suffer more than most from the dejection that follows intense excitement. Besides, there were enough worries to cancel those high moments. The summer brought a breathing spell in the form of a trip to Reval to visit Mikhail and his wife, whom he had not seen for two years. He returned to Petersburg by sea, and as the boat was crossing the stretch of water between Kronstadt and the capital, he was assailed by a weariness of the spirit not a little complicated by a weakness of the flesh. He was seasick. He was thinking miserably of having left behind him, for an indefinite period, his brother and his new sister-in-law who, however badly situated, had each other to comfort them. The flat, lifeless landscape, as the dirty little steamer churned up the Neva, repressed him hideously. He was overwhelmed by a sudden dread of the future and a reluctance to go on living.

He came back to his empty, expensive, unpaid-for flat, had a brief interview with his creditors; bought paper and pens, and was in such bad humour that he could not make up his mind either to sit down at his desk or to visit the one friend who was in town. He would have been undone by melancholia if he had not been distracted by money troubles. And yet these very difficulties interfered with his work, which was of the sort that must mature slowly. "What a pity," he wrote, "that one must work to live!" Still, there was something to be said even for his spleen: it had given him two new ideas and a fresh situation for the new story, "The Double," with which he was busy. The spleen persisted. It was not merely that he was penniless and had to live on credit. He was, as was frequent with him, a victim of the mood that begins with depression, passes into apathy and self-neglect, and goes on to a self-contempt that is an equal mixture of fury and despair.

Early in October money matters took on a fairer complexion. Nekrasov paid down part of the sum agreed on and promised to settle the account shortly. He had bought the novel for 150 roubles, but now in a fit of compunction, he voluntarily added another hundred. Here, in advance of publication, before it had even come back from the censor, half the town was talking about *Poor Folk*. Grigorovich was his self-appointed *claqueur*. It was also a matter of general knowledge and satisfaction that he had begun work upon another piece. He had become the darling of the Belinsky circle. In his paternal tenderness, the little man, forgetting that he was shorter than Dostoevsky, would tell everyone: "He's a little bird," adding as he held out his hand three feet from the floor, "but he has sharp claws." Belinsky's affection for him, as Dostoevsky told his brother, was due to the fact that the critic saw in his writings the justification of his own views. But Dostoevsky's understanding of the matter could scarcely lessen his pleasure. And there was something else in the offing. He was to be one of the editors of a satirical paper which would poke good-natured fun at everything offensive to the group. Dostoevsky projected for the paper a serial to be called *A Valet's Memoirs of His Master*. It was a good scheme, and would mean a fair monthly income.

As the season progresses, he is lifted to the pinnacle of glory. He is an *habitué* of the favourite haunt of the Belinsky coterie: the drawing-room of Nekrasov's friend, Panayeva. The great critic loves him to distraction. Arriving fresh from Paris, Turgenev, a poet, an aristocrat, handsome, rich, keen, has become enamoured of him. But his fame is by no means limited to literary circles. Wherever he goes, he says, he is treated as a wonder. Whenever he opens his mouth, people repeat to each other: Dostoevsky has said this, Dostoevsky thinks of doing that. He would run short of paper, he tells Mikhail, were he to enumerate all his successes. He has met a lot of very fine people—in fact, he is in high society. Prince Odoevsky has begged for the pleasure of a visit from him. Count Sollogub is tearing his hair because he cannot get hold of this genius everybody is talking about. As a matter of fact, the Count went so far as to call on the author, in an effort to lure this prodigy into what he called his "menagerie." The young writer seems to have been thrown into confusion by the appearance of his titled and loquacious visitor. The latter carried away with him the impression of a sickly-looking, abashed, yet withal attractive young man, possessed of a great deal of reserve and *amour-propre*.

Success did not seduce Dostoevsky into resting on his laurels. He had no end of ideas. In a single night he wrote a complete story and sold it in the morning for thirty roubles. Read aloud in Turgenev's rooms before the whole company, it caused a furore. Now Belinsky felt sure of him: he could handle such a variety of subjects. The story in question is entitled "A Novel in Nine Letters." It is a humorous piece in the manner of Gogol, deriving comedy more from the style than from the situations. The plot, in which shady business dealings and cuckoldry play a part, is a rather farcical one.

There were still days when he was without a copeck, and, of course, the debts had not been wiped out. But that no longer worried him. Money was sure to come. An editor, hearing of his straits, begged him please to accept the loan of five hundred roubles. He needed the money. The Minnas, Claras, Mariannas were prettier than ever, but frightfully expensive. Perhaps he liked to boast a bit about these exploits, as about his infatuation with the clever and beautiful Mme. Panayeva. Turgenev, he declared, joined Belinsky in scolding him for the irregular life he was leading. Belinsky kept watch over him in the most fatherly fashion. " These people," Dostoevsky writes, "don't know what to do to show their affection for me, they are in love with me, one and all."

The miscellany, with *Poor Folk* in it, is out. It appeared on January 15, 1846. It is the literary topic of the day. He has, he tells Mikhail, thrown a bone to the public. Let the pack fight over it. The fools are making him famous. They are taken aback by a work from which the author has completely effaced himself. And then too there is the novelty of his analytical approach, of his probing. As for his own set, they are agreed, and Belinsky along with them, that he has outstripped Gogol himself. "My future, brother," he sums up the matter, "is a most brilliant one."

"The Double," too, is out. It took longer to write the story than he had thought, but it was a matter of three or four days between the setting down of the final period and the printing of the piece in *Fatherland Notes* a fortnight after the appearance of *Poor Folk*. It is, the author informs Mikhail, ten times better than *Poor Folk*. The clique declare it a work of genius and say that there has been nothing like it in Russia since *Dead Souls*. Further, the story brought in more than twice as much as its predecessor. And he was in receipt of other moneys as well. In fact, in the course of some six months he has spent a small fortune.

IV

The winter months flash by. There are so many impressions crowding upon him, so many new contacts, that he has no time to collect himself. Ideas swarm about him. His pen never stops. In two months he counted thirty-five mentions of him in various articles. This is fame! Yet there are flies in the ointment. His friends, after praising "The Double" extravagantly, have, on second reading, found it wanting. The larger part of the public, too, has dismissed it as prolix and, what hurts the author more, dull. The thought that he has deceived the expectations of his audience and ruined what could have been a masterpiece is a thorn in the flesh. The distress makes him literally sick. What is more, the shift in public opinion has altered his own view of his work. Now the thing disgusts him. Much of it was written hastily and in moments of fatigue. Alongside of brilliant pages, he has come to see, there are vile nauseating passages. And then there are money difficulties. He has been rash enough to accept 250 roubles for "goods" that he has not yet produced. And now the cash is spent, and he is again without a groat.

He is busy with several new projects. There are two stories, very terse and with thrilling tragic plots, for a miscellany planned by Belinsky, also a trifle for *Fatherland Notes,* and a novel for Nekrasov. Although a number of new writers have appeared, supremacy is still his and he hopes it will remain so indefinitely. Never before has his mind been so furiously active.

His elation was short-lived. By May he was sunk in a mood that mixed apathy, anxiety, and the feverish expectation of some change for the better. Again he spent part of the summer with Mikhail and his family in Reval and returned armed with the resolution to live modestly and write slowly. He manages to get along, but works badly, and has no prospects. To escape from the impasse in which he finds himself he conceives the idea of running away to Italy. On what? Well, he will publish on his own a collection of his writings and make a thousand roubles on it by the first of the yea.. In order to tide him over, he could, of course, get an advance on an unwritten story, but that is just what he is trying to avoid. He has been doing that sort of thing too long; to keep it up would only be to continue slavery. He is resolved to achieve his emancipation. The thousand roubles will permit him to pay off his debts and keep him in Italy for eight months. To find himself in that land of romance had been his dream since childhood. There he will start a novel, at which he expects to work two years. The plan is ripe in his head. At last he will be able to write something to please himself, without being hurried or hounded. Also he will be in a position to dictate his price. On his return, he will find himself in clover, what with the second part of the novel ready for publication and another volume of collected short pieces, both old and new, to be put on the market.

The grandiose plan fell through. He postponed the trip until the autumn. The delay fretted him. He was not prepared to resign himself to half portions either of fame or of wealth. He busied himself meanwhile with his story, "The Shaved Whiskers." He would dangle it before the hungry eyes of the magazine editors, watch them scramble for it, and fling it to the highest bidder. Of course, if he could publish it separately, that would be even better. Alas, he had followed the bad example of Aesop's milkmaid. A few weeks pass, and all his projects are so much spilled milk. The edition of his collected stories is a vain dream and so is the Italian journey. Furthermore, when he had reached almost the end of "The Shaved Whiskers," he was suddenly overcome by the feeling that he was merely repeating himself and jeopardizing his reputation. He must bring forward something fresh, new, startling, or he was lost. The manuscript of "The Shaved Whiskers" has not been preserved. He must have destroyed it in disgust. What did appear in the October issue of *Otechestvennye zapiski* was the short story, "Mr. Prokharchin," at which he "had slaved the whole summer," as he put it.

By January, 1847, he expected to finish yet another story, which was going brilliantly. Then he would take off a whole year to write the novel that was tearing at his vitals. But one must live. So he would publish *Poor Folk* and *The Double* as separate volumes, and only issue his collected writings two years later: "This will be extremely advantageous, for I will take in money twice and make myself famous." If only he had the capital with which to be his own publisher! The book-publishing industry, be it said in passing, then in its infancy in Russia, was suffering from the business depression the country was feeling at this time. He offered Mikhail one-fourth of the profits of the undertaking for the loan of two hundred roubles, which would make him independent of printers and booksellers. Booksellers were scoundrels. But this time, Mikhail, who was often in straits himself and who had a growing household to support, failed to respond as usual, and the publishing venture was indefinitely postponed.

V

To make matters worse, in the second winter of his fame, Dostoevsky had a falling out with Nekrasov and, indeed with the entire circle. When he had first appeared in Mme. Panayeva's drawing-room, where the group met so often, the fair-haired youth with the restless grey eyes and the nervously twitching lips struck his hostess as pitifully ill at ease. Turgenev described him as a mole who had crawled out into the light of day. He had moments of abysmal shyness. His eyes would hide behind their lids; his head would seem to withdraw like a turtle's; his words would come in gasps. But as his visits became more frequent, his bashful manner gave place to a tactlessly forward one, which these clever literary people failed to interpret as another sign of shyness. They saw merely that he was obstinate and cocky and that his fame had gone to his head. Indifferent to the fact that they had to do with a thin-skinned youth who had been too abruptly pulled out of his dark self-communings into the public eye, they behaved like a crowd of schoolboys baiting an offensive newcomer. Led by Turgenev, who was generally the life of the party, they would encourage Dostoevsky in his contrariness and amuse themselves with the spectacle. Instead of laughing off these attacks, he took them seriously, seeing himself as the victim of envy, and fairly choked with gall.

One evening Turgenev was making sport of a man he claimed to have met in the provinces who imagined himself a genius. Dostoevsky, trembling in all his limbs and white as chalk, ran out before the story was finished. He never came back. The one member of the circle whom he continued to see, reported that he spoke of them as envious, heartless nonentities. Their own tongues were not quiet. The very hands that had set him on a pedestal now none too gently took him down. His erstwhile admirers were now his detractors. They circulated a rumour that the young author had demanded a special decoration, some said a gold border, on the pages of the miscellany containing *Poor Folk*. An epigram, tossed off by Turgenev and Nekrasov and dedicated to Belinsky, described Dostoevsky as a new pimple glowing on the nose of literature, assured him that the Sultan was about to send his Grand Vizier for him, and referred to his having fainted when introduced to a society belle at a fashionable soirée—an actual occurrence. The gold border figured here too.

Nekrasov was just then starting a new magazine, *Sovremennik*, (The Contemporary), or rather reviving an old periodical by that name which had been launched by Pushkin, and the quarrel lost Dostoevsky this market. According to Nekrasov, Dostoevsky had come to him to demand that a certain critical article about him be withheld from publication; he had mentioned the epigram, fumed, and threatened, until the editor had concluded that the man had gone out of his mind. One unpleasant aspect of the break was that Dostoevsky was obliged to refund the sum he had accepted as an advance. The result was that he agreed to work the entire winter for *Fatherland Notes*, and in return, Krayevsky, the editor of that periodical, was to pay all his debts. So here he was again, enslaved as before, with no prospect of escape.

He continued to see Belinsky for several months after his break with the rest of the coterie. And then that link, too, snapped. Not long afterwards Dostoevsky was to blame the estrangement on their failure to agree on the proper function of literature. He may indeed have objected to the critic's emphasis on the writer's moral and didactic mission, seeing it as a brake on the freedom and spontaneity of art. But the fact that Belinsky had grown cool to his work is more likely to have proved fatal to a friendship which, to begin with, was pitched in too high a key, particularly for one as touchy as Dostoevsky. The previous year Belinsky had been praising him unreservedly. Here, he had said, was a genius who must make his way slowly and whose fame would be at its zenith when talents that might temporarily eclipse him were forgotten. But in his survey of the literature produced in 1846, he found "monstrous defects" in "The Double" and deplored the fantastic element in it. "In our time," he opined, "what is fantastic occurs only in insane asylums and comes under the jurisdiction of physicians, not fiction writers." He rejected "Mr. Prokharchin" because of an obscurity scarcely illuminated by sparks of talent. In his review of the literary output of the following year, he dismissed "The Landlady," which had appeared in the autumn, as utterly false and, moreover, unintelligible. In a letter to a friend, dated February 14, 1848, he was even more outspoken. " 'The Landlady' is awful rubbish," he said. "He (Dostoevsky) has composed other pieces since, but every new work of his is another failure. In the provinces people can't stand him, and in the capital they speak with hostility even of *Poor Folk*. How we've fooled ourselves about this genius! . . . I, the foremost critic, acted like an ass raised to the second power."

He had hailed the author of *Poor Folk* as the hope of what he called the Natural School, a novelist who dealt with the realities of Russian life in a spirit of protest, however indirect, against social injustice, and it pained him to notice that the young man's performance was taking on a totally different complexion. Disappointed in the writer, he was also cured of his infatuation with the man. He discovered that, like Jean Jacques Rousseau, whom he abominated, Dostoevsky believed that the whole world envied and persecuted him.

He died shortly after dictating—he had been too weak to write—the letter just mentioned. Dostoevsky's relationship with the critic lasted less than two years, but it left an indelible mark on his thinking. At school he had been an enthusiastic reader of George Sand and thus may have caught a whiff of socialist ideas. In the early forties they were beginning to seep into Russia, in spite of the rigid censorship set up by Nicholas I. By 1843, in Petersburg, the works of the French exponents of socialism were, in the words of a contemporary, "the object of study, ardent discussion, questions, and all manner of hopes." The doctrine had gone to the head of Belinsky, among others. Several years before Dostoevsky came to know him he had announced in a letter that for him socialism was "the alpha and omega of faith and knowledge." His socialism was a humanitarian credo, at once ethical and emotional, involving summary rejection of the existing order, emphasis on the importance of the external conditions of man's life, and concern for the welfare here and now of every human being. But people are so foolish he said to himself, that you have to get them into Eden by force. This did not daunt him. "Fierce Vissarion" was not one to consider doing things by halves. "To make even a small fraction of mankind happy," he wrote to a friend, "I am perhaps ready to destroy the rest by fire and sword." He adopted the motto: "Sociality or death!" and applauded the eighteenth century for guillotining "aristocrats, priests, and other enemies of God, reason and humanity." His devotion to reason and humanity never flagged, but, under the influence of Ludwig Feuerbach's ideas, he turned against the Deity. Shortly before he discovered Dostoevsky he was writing to a like-minded friend: "In the words 'God' and 'religion' I see darkness, chains, and the knout. . . ." While for some of his contemporaries socialism conjured up the vision of a new Christianity destined to regenerate mankind, Belinsky saw it as a scheme of secular meliorism based on a purely materialistic outlook.

In later years Dostoevsky asserted that he had "passionately" embraced the critic's "whole teaching." Of this he gave a none too coherent account. In 1846, he wrote, Belinsky had initiated him into the world of the "new ideas" which were to become "the future law" of all mankind. He must then have shared the master's dream of a Golden Age in which all men would live as brothers on a new earth under the rule of Reason. And, like Belinsky, he must have believed that socialism, far from destroying freedom, placed it upon "a new and adamant foundation"—a conviction that he would in time indignantly repudiate. The critic's arguments against religion must also have shaken his disciple, even if the uninhibited invective to which Belinsky was given in the heat of polemics and which was directed even against the personality of Christ rubbed him the wrong way. In any event, it must have been during his long talks with the critic that the nodus between socialism and atheism was established in Dostoevsky's mind.

CHAPTER FIVE

A SICK SOUL

DOSTOEVSKY'S quarrel with the *Sovremennik* circle coincided for him with a brief period of well-being. "Never," he wrote Mikhail, in the same letter in which he announced his break with Nekrasov, "has there been such abundance and serenity in my life, so much evenness in my character. Never have I known such physical health." New images were crowding into his mind as never before. He believed that he was actually undergoing both a moral and a physical regeneration. This amazing change he attributed to the influence of a group of new-found friends centring around three young men—the Beketov brothers.

With these, the eldest of whom had been a schoolmate of his, Dostoevsky set up a kind of communal *ménage* on Vasilyevsky Ostrov, in an outlying section of the city. "They cured me," he wrote, "with their company." He was as eager for comradeship as only a solitary who found sociability difficult could be. Even when he was in the midst of pressing work, he wanted someone near him. Here with the Beketovs there was no lack of companionship. There were Dutch-treat dinner parties and an occasional picnic Of an evening there would be ten or fifteen people at the house, gathered, one fancies, around the samovar, and bubbling over with talk. It was not unlike that in which the Belinsky coterie indulged. Here was the same animus against oppression, the concern for social justice, the Westernist orientation, the tendency to think of human condition in naturalistic terms.

The communal household was not only of spiritual benefit to the young man: it had as well the advantage of economy, the expenses not exceeding three hundred roubles a year per person. "So great," he exclaims, "are the benefits of association." The term meant co-operative living and was prominent in the socialist vocabulary of the day. The arrangement did not interfere with his privacy.

He had a room of his own, where he spent much time at his desk. He was at work on a novel: *Netochka Nezvanova*. Occasionally he broke off at seven o'clock to divert himself with the Italian opera, choosing, for cheapness, a gallery seat. He needed distraction, for writing was a strain, although, strangely enough, he wrote best and fastest when his nerves were at their worst. He felt as though he were being tried by the editors, the critics, the public, and he hoped to win the case with his novel, to the undoing of his enemies. His main problem was to deliver enough copy to Krayevsky to work off his debt by the time summer came. Other periodicals offered better rates, but since he had taken an advance from Krayevsky, he was under the man's thumb.

He would not publish what he was writing until the whole thing was finished. He would keep at his job even if the sky came crashing around his ears. He knew the measure of his ability and would not go astray. Meanwhile, being pinched in pocket, he had to depend on the help of "kindly people." He would "perish" if it weren't for them. Besides the novel, he was writing a story: *The Landlady*. It was in the manner of *Poor Folk*, only better. "My pen," he blusters, mixing his metaphors, "is guided by a spring of inspiration that leaps straight from my soul." The novel will appear at the end of the year, and will wipe the floor with his former friends of the *Sovremennik* set who are now trying to bury him. Once he has published this novel, he will issue it separately at his own expense, and *Poor Folk* and *The Double* as well, and then perhaps Fate will smile upon him. Meanwhile, life, what with poverty, the constant sense of being driven, the unbearable fatigue, is the same hell that it has been ever since he first achieved his "doubtful fame."

When he was thus complaining of his circumstances, he was no longer sharing quarters with the Beketovs, who had moved away from the capital. There was no trace of the euphoria that had resulted from his association with the brothers, and he was again in the thick of his anxieties and distresses. In his loneliness he began pleading with Mikhail more earnestly than ever to retire from the service and come to settle in Petersburg. He would be sure to find work. Perhaps he would make a literary career for himself as a translator. Everybody was doing it. Dostoevsky hinted that he might even make peace with Nekrasov for Mikhail's sake. At least they would be together, and so they would gain courage and their strength would be doubled. In ten years they would have three hundred and fifty thousand roubles. The benefits of association—the word is never far from his pen-point—would be theirs.

Mikhail succumbed to his brother's enthusiasm. Yes, he agreed, association was a great and sacred thing. He would tender his resignation and move to the capital, with the expectation that his Emilia and their three children would join him there later. What with selling the furniture and borrowing, he might bring with him as much as two hundred roubles, and this would be the foundation of their future fortune. They would want accommodation for a servant—one of their serfs—and they must have a lodging with firewood supplied. In the autumn of 1847 Mikhail arrived in Petersburg, to the great joy of his brother and the regret of all those wishing to inquire closely into what Dostoevsky was doing and thinking during the two or three years that followed, for with Mikhail in the same city he had no need to pour himself out in letters to this, his sole confidant.

I I

To add to the difficulties that beset the young author, his health was wretched. A sedentary life and long periods of overwork must have aggravated a condition due to more fundamental, if obscure, causes. When he resigned from the service he had talked vaguely of being ill. He had been in the habit of neglecting himself and avoiding doctors. Now just the contrary was true. The months that had followed his initial success had been filled with more definite complaints. He suffered from nervous spasms of the throat. He feared "nervous fever." If he failed to have sea bathing in the summer, he didn't know what would become of him. At the end of April, 1846, he explained his silence to Mikhail on the grounds of having been at death's door. "I was terribly sick, suffering from an irritation of the entire nervous system, and the ailment attacked the heart, causing it to become congested and inflamed—a condition which was barely checked by leeches and two bloodlettings." He was by then out of danger, but far from recovered. In his doctor's opinion the illness had been developing for three or four years, and recuperation would be a correspondingly long process. He was to diet and lead an orderly, quiet, and utterly lean existence, and perhaps have a change of scene. This grave illness is never mentioned again.

That summer an advance received from Krayevsky enabled him to have a visit with Mikhail at Reval. But before he left town he had to undergo more doctoring. On a May morning in 1846 he went to a certain young medico named Yanovsky, recommended to him by a recently acquired friend, to be treated for a minor complaint. The doctor, being a man of literary interests, must have been somewhat flattered to be consulted by the celebrated author of *Poor Folk*. Looking at this patient with a more attentive eye than usual, he noted that his visitor was below medium height (actually, he measured five foot six), but broad-boned, especially in the shoulders, and with remarkably large hands and feet, that his fine soft hair was blond to the point of whiteness, that his forehead was unusually well developed, his pale grey eyes small and restless, and his lips thin and compressed, giving a look of concentration to the face. The doctor was surprised to see that the patient held himself not like the graduate of a military school that he was, but rather in the slouching fashion of a divinity student. His black jacket was of excellent cloth, his vest of black cashmere, his linen fine and immaculate, and he carried a topper—indeed, he looked almost fashionable, except for his shoes, which were shabby.

The examination showed that there was no trouble with the vital organs, except that the heartbeats were irregular and the pulse uneven and "remarkably compressed, as with women and people of nervous temperament." To a very marked degree the patient exhibited the traces of having suffered from such diseases of childhood as rickets and scrofula.

While he was treating Dostoevsky for the local disorder, which he did not choose to name—was it an unmentionable ailment?—the physician came to suspect that, in addition, his patient was probably afflicted with an obscure affection of the nerves. He was led to this notion partly by Dostoevsky's account of a nervous condition to which he had been subject in childhood, partly by what he

saw of the man's disposition and consititution. As the doctor may
have known, Dostoevsky's heredity, too, was bad: he was the son
of a consumptive and a dipsomaniac who had strange seizures, and
one of his uncles drank himself to death. That the family tree bore
bad fruit may be seen from the fact that one of his brothers became
a hopeless drunkard and one sister a psychopath. A few weeks'
treatment was sufficient to cure the patient of the local ailment,
but the nervous trouble persisted. The doctor was soon to recognize its true nature.

Dostoevsky's character was in itself indicative of his affliction.
He was irritable and suspicious, given to magnifying trifles and
distorting ordinary facts. There were times when he behaved
paradoxically: he adored his little godson, Mikhail's first-born
and his own namesake—he was cross with him about nothing; he
admired and respected his brother's wife—he was rude to her; he
looked up to his brother—he treated him as an inferior. "Sometimes when my heart is swimming in love," he wrote to Mikhail,
"you can't pull a kind word out of me." Extraordinary circumstances, he claimed, could sometimes bring him to show his true
feelings, but too often his ill temper and sullenness caused him to
be misjudged by those around him. He gave as a reason for his
behaviour that his nerves refused to obey him, and rightly connected the discrepancy between the way he felt and the way he acted with
his illness.

Another symptom was his hypochondria. He complained of pal-
pitations of the heart. His condition threw him into a panic. The
projected trip to Italy was planned, he told Mikhail, not for his
pleasure, but for his health. Should he try Priessnitz's cold water
cure? He must do something. He also spoke vaguely of inflammation of the brain. He came to believe that the climax of his illness
was something like temporary insanity. It was of this period that
he said: "For two years on end I suffered from a strange moral
ailment. I fell into a hypochondriac state. There was even a time
when I lost my reason." He was past middle life when he wrote
reminiscently to Dr. Yanovsky: "You loved me and looked after
me, mentally deranged as I was (now I know that that was what
was wrong with me). . . ." Toward the end of his life he elaborated
a curious theory as to the cause of the derangement. It had been due,

he asserted, to abdominal plethora, which produced haemorrhoids, hypochondria, and consequent nervous and mental disorders. His brother Nikolay, he said, was a sufferer from the same ailment.

Sometimes Dostoevsky was afraid to go to bed. Suppose he were to fall into a sleep resembling death? Spending the night with a friend, he begged that they would not be too quick to bury him, should they think him dead, and he pictured the horror of waking in the grave. He would leave a note on his table to the effect that he should not be buried too soon. Now and again he felt as though death were paying him a call—a loathsome and terrifying experience. He may well have been remembering his own sensations when, in *The Insulted and Injured,* he described the mystic terror of his hero: the dread of an inconceivable and impossible something turning into a horrible, ruthless reality, a dread no less harrowing because the mind is divided between an understanding of its folly and an inability to reject it.

He fell into the habit of dropping in at Dr. Yanovsky's bachelor apartment every day and sometimes spending the night. If he came early, he would not breakfast before glancing at himself in the mirror and having the doctor look at his tongue and feel his pulse.

He turned to Yanovsky for more than relief from his hypochondriac obsessions. Here was a man who knew the secret workings of the body, the diseases of the flesh and the mind. There was so much to be learned about the nervous system, about the brain, about insanity. For one who felt himself always trembling on the verge of a nervous breakdown, there was something of both fascination and terror in the subject. He would pump the doctor. He would borrow medical tomes. What especially caught his attention, as it did that of so many of his contemporaries, was phrenology. Assiduously Dostoevsky felt his own bumps and discovered, not without satisfaction, that his skull was shaped like that of Socrates. He had the same development of the frontal bone, over the perceptive and reflective organs, the same jutting superciliary ridges, the same absence of projections in the supraoccipital bones where the lower instincts and sentiments were located, amativeness among others. This he found truly remarkable. Yanovsky must have seen for himself that he was "no petticoat chaser." What he was fond of was not the petticoat at all, but the cap: the kind worn by his friend Maikov's mother, Yevgeniya Petrovna. Indeed, according to his friend and physician, Dostoevsky had never shown signs of a passionate interest in women. Riesenkampf, who had known him earlier, also found him indifferent and even hostile toward them. Barring his brief infatuation with Mme. Panayeva, one finds no sentimental involvement of the slightest consequence. On the other hand, there is some indirect evidence that the young man did not lack sexual experience and that it was of a kind that he looked back upon with shame. It remains true, however, that his early writings are curiously sexless. Only in his mature work does passion find its voice.

III

In addition to his physical distresses, his irritability, his hypochondria, his "moral ailment," Dostoevsky came to show symptoms of a more specific and far more alarming character. About the time when *Poor Folk* was on the stocks he was subject, if Grigorovich's testimony is to be credited, to seizures, which were usually followed by two or three days of mental misery. On one occasion the two friends were walking together and met a funeral procession. Dostoevsky wanted to beat a retreat, but before he could go any distance he had a "fit" so violent that he had to be carried to the nearest grocery, where with great difficulty he was restored to consciousness.

Another friend saw him in a mild attack in the summer of 1846 or '47. It was late at night, a small party was drawing to an end, when Dostoevsky's face changed queerly and a frightened look came into his eyes. A few moments passed and then in a hollow voice he asked: "Where am I?" and ran to the window for air. When his host came into the room, after seeing the other guests off, he found him sitting on the window sill, his face twisted, his head bent to one side, his body shaking convulsively. He doused him with cold water, but Dostoevsky, without coming to himself, ran out into the street. The alarmed host dashed after him, but could not keep pace with him, and jumped into a cab. When he caught up with him at the gates of a hospital, a couple of blocks away, Dostoevsky was in a calmer state and allowed himself to be taken home. He explained that he had run to the hospital with the vague notion of finding help there.

Dr. Yanovsky saw him in the throes of a serious attack three times. The first of these occurred in July, 1847. One day the doctor was drawn like one hypnotized to Saint Isaac's Square, although he had no business there, a fact that Dostoevsky afterwards adduced as proof of the significance of forebodings. As he was crossing the square he ran into his patient, clutching the arm of a military clerk. Hatless, his coat and vest unbuttoned, his cravat untied, Dostoevsky was shouting that he was dying and calling for Yanovsky. His pulse was pounding away at the rate of more than 100, his head thrown back and held rigid, and his body beginning to shake with convulsions. The doctor took him home, opened a vein, drawing coal-black blood, and kept him at his apartment for several nights.

In the case of the second attack witnessed by Yanovsky, just as in the instance reported by Grigorovitch, it was something that had to do with death which appears to have touched off the paroxysm. It was caused by the death of Belinsky. When Dostoevsky brought the news to Yanovsky one May morning in 1848, he was in such a state that the doctor insisted that he remain with him. All went smoothly during the day, but at three o'clock in the morning the doctor heard heavy stertorous breathing in the room where Dostoevsky was sleeping. He went in to him and found him lying on his back in convulsions, with open eyes, foaming lips, and protruding tongue. The third attack occurred in the early spring of 1849, also late at night, after an unpleasant incident at a meeting of a discussion group of which Dostoevsky was a member. Again he ran to Yanovsky for help when he felt the seizure coming on. The doctor describes in as "violent and characteristic," adding that his patient also had many light attacks.

Not that Dostoevsky understood the nature of his trouble. He called it humorously "kondrashka with a little breeze"—the "breeze" was apparently his way of describing the premonitory sensation as of a current of air experienced before an epileptic attack, and kondrashka is the popular term for a stroke.

At the time Yanovsky recognized that Dostoevsky was suffering from epilepsy, which in his opinion first showed itself in 1846, if not earlier. Grigorovich would have it that the malady was already apparent in his school days. Another friend said that Dostoevsky had suffered from the disease "since his childhood," and accounted for it thus: "Something terrifying, unforgettable, tormenting, happened to him in his childhood, the result of which was his falling sickness,"—an opinion in which Dr. Yanovsky concurred when he was in possession of most of the facts. "It was precisely in his childhood," the physician then wrote, "that Dostoevsky had a dark, gloomy experience such as never passes without leaving a scar, even if it occurs in maturity, and which so affects the temperament as to lead to nervous diseases and consequently to epilepsy." It is clear from the context, however, that the doctor was referring not to a specific trauma but to the oppressive atmosphere which the father's tyrannical behaviour created in the home.

That Dostoevsky's illness was caused by a shock and that this occurred early in his life is the story related by Orest Miller, co-author of the first biography of the novelist. He was told by a person "very close" to Dostoevsky that his malady dated from his "earliest youth" and was connected with "a tragic event in their family life." Unable to corroborate this statement, the biographer discreetly withheld all details. If this "tragic event" was the assassination of the father, his reticence is intelligible, since mention of the matter was forbidden by the relatives. It may be noted that Dostoevsky's daughter, in her life of his, mentions a family tradition to the effect that the news of the murder brought on the first epileptic seizure. That Dostoevsky had Smeryakov, in *The Brothers Karamazov*, contract epilepsy at the age of twelve is perhaps of some significance.

These suggestive, if meagre and uncertain clues, together with scraps of evidence derived from Dostoevsky's writings, have led to the formulation of a psychoanalytic theory of the origin of his trouble. Unlike lesser lights, Freud himself, realizing how scant and dubious the information is, was not dogmatic on the subject. He was inclined to see in the novelist's ailment not an organic affection, but rather the symptoms of a neurosis. "The most probable assumption," he wrote, "is that the attacks go back to his childhood, that the symptoms were mild to start with, and did not assume epileptic form until after the terrible experience of his eighteenth year, the murder of his father." The key with which he tried to unlock the mechanism of Dostoevsky's neurosis was the familiar one of the Oedipus complex.

The Freudian theory sees the boy as a creature torn between love and hatred of his father, the hatred being all the more savage since it was kept under and hidden from his pious and filial self. On the one hand, in the inmost depths of his heart he longed for the satisfactions of a tender union with his father; on the other, he feared him, broke out in revolt against him, and unconsciously wished his death. The news of the slaying comes as the tidings of fulfillment, both joyful and terrible. Are not his hands stained with his father's blood? Did he not commit the murder, in will, if not in deed? Henceforth his sense of guilt will be heavier than ever and find a dozen subtle ways of shaping his life. His epileptic attack, with its premonitory moment of bliss, due to the granting of the death wish, its period of unconsciousness and subsequent distress, is then a punishment meted out to him by his own conscience and at the same time a fond identification of himself with his dead father. The psychoanalyst sees a special meaning in the fact that the attacks were released by such experiences as the sight of a funeral procession, the news of the death of Belinsky, the man who had stood to him *in loco parentis*. It is perhaps of significance that the theme of a child believing itself responsible for the death of its parents is touched upon in two of Dostoevsky's early tales, and that the father-son relationship and the crime of parricide play an important part in his major fictions.

His epilepsy has also been diagnosed as genuine, one physician opining that it was based on "an endocrine abnormality." When doctors disagree, the layman must remain in doubt. One thing is certain: Dostoevsky's attacks manifested themselves at least as early as 1846, when he was twenty-five, and plagued him for the rest of his life, while his super-sensitive, misanthropic, unstable disposition, marked by hypochondria, a strong religiosity, and a tendency to take refuge from reality in a dream world, answers to the description of the epileptic personality as presented in medical literature. An eminent authority on the disease has stated that it develops in most cases when the patient is in his teens, and another physician maintains that the epileptic make-up is discernible from earliest childhood. Exactly when Dostoevsky's initial seizure occurred, what caused the malady, and what its true nature was, will probably always remain open questions.

CHAPTER SIX

REBELLION?

O F a Friday evening Dostoevsky would occasionally make his way—sometimes taking Mikhail along with him—to a small frame house on Pokrov Square, walk up a stairway lit by an ill-smelling lamp in which hempseed oil burned smokily, and emerge into Petrashevsky's rather dingy drawing-room. He had become acquainted with the man in 1846. It was the following year, around Lent, that he made his first appearance at Petrashevsky's Fridays—they had started some two years earlier. Like the opera, the circus, and Nilsen's sermons, the gatherings at the house of this small official in the Foreign Office were then one of the institutions in Petersburg about which visitors to the capital would write home. Dostoevsky found there, wrapped in a fog of tobacco smoke, about a score of people: officers, government clerks, teachers, literary men, university students. There were some *habitués* and many transients, and the host, a short, thick-set, hirsute young man, with lively black eyes and nervous gestures, darted from one group to the next, too intent on having the minds of his guests meet to bother about their being properly introduced to each other. The names of some Dostoevsky never learned.

The samovar would be purring, the piano might be opened, and before the company broke up in the small hours the table would be spread with a modest supper. Cards were banned. The place was a cross between a social club and a debating society. What chiefly drew the men together was the talk. It was of the kind that could not but attract a disciple of Belinsky. Ideas were touched upon, sentiments were voiced that scarcely befitted faithful communicants of the Orthodox Church and loyal subjects of the Emperor. Domestic and foreign news was discussed, official measures freely criticized, the antics of the censors and other abuses denounced; serfdom was attacked, the family and religion questioned. Quite a few of Petrashevsky's guests were free-thinkers or, indeed, atheists, and he himself once described Christ as "a well-known demagogue who ended his career rather unsuccessfully."

Dostoevsky contributed little to the casual conversation. Reserved and taciturn, he gave the impression, when he did speak, of possessing the earnestness and ardour that make a good propagandist. On one occasion he moved the company deeply by describing from hearsay the flogging of a corporal who had avenged himself on a brutal officer—a punishment which he was to witness more than once. An acquaintance had it that at the spur of the moment he was "capable of appearing on a square with a red flag." After the revolutionary events which marked the year 1848 in the West, the tone of the gatherings became somewhat more formal. Occasionally there would even be a chairman who wielded a bell in the form of a hemisphere with a handle representing Liberty. Sometimes a speech would be delivered on a definite topic, such as social reform or the principles of political economy. Dostoevsky gave a talk in which he dealt with a psychological theme that is the subject of several of his stories: the dwarfing of personality. Again, a man might read a manuscript, perhaps a story with a purpose. The host, who was a born proselytizer, had no stomach for pure art. He insisted that literature was merely one of the means to the great end of regenerating society.

In addition to holding his at-homes, Petrashevsky had organized a small co-operative lending library which included forbidden foreign publications. The Dostoevskys, both Fyodor and Mikhail, belonged to it. Such bootleg literature was smuggled over the border in quantities.

The works of the French socialists figured prominently among the books circulated by Petrashevsky. The doctrines of the Utopians, particularly those of Fourier, commanded the allegiance of many of his visitors. Just at the time when the Fourierist colonies that had sprung up in New York, New Jersey, Pennsylvania, Wisconsin, and on the shores of Lake Ontario, were falling into decay, seeds of the faith were sprouting on the cold banks of the Neva. A few Russian heads were giddy with the dream of a world of harmonious, strictly patterned living, of a true society in which men would be at one with nature and their own kind, and know neither fear, nor hate, nor envy, nor cruelty—in short, a cross between a planned Paradise and the land of Cockaigne. Unlike the Americans, who had an opportunity to test out their theories, the Russian Fourierists, under the stern paternalism of Nicholas I, had to confine themselves to idle discussion. Since there were no means of carrying them out, there was no limit to the extravagance of the schemes hatched by these dreamers. On a certain Friday Dostoevsky listened to a proposition that the world be divided into two halves, one to be given to the Fourierists, the other to the communists, for social experiments. "Let them live as good neighbours," the speaker is reported to have added, "and borrow from each other the good things each has." To this the host took exception. There was nothing, he argued, that the Fourierists could borrow from the communists, except perhaps atheism. A fanatical follower of the French reformer, he looked forward to living in a phalanstery himself and it is said that he attempted to induce his own serfs to form one but that they had burned down their Eden.

On April 7, 1849, eleven men met at dinner to celebrate Fourier's birthday. The occasion they were marking, the first speaker declared, was bound to accomplish "the transformation of the planet and of the human beings that inhabit it." After setting forth the master's doctrines at some length, he touched on matters of immediate concern to his hearers, saying: "My fatherland is in chains, my fatherland is enslaved." He ended, however, on a note of hope, exclaiming: "Transfiguration is at hand!" There was general applause, and two men embraced him. Petrashevsky, who rose next, extolled Fourier's system as the only one that was capable of harmonizing society with human nature, but did not underestimate the difficulties of planting the seed of socialism in "the savage soil" of Russia.

The third speaker was most eloquent. He painted the life around him in the blackest tones, but ended on a note of proud rhapsody. "We have come here not to lament and tell pitiful tales; on the contrary, we are full of hope, triumph, and joy. . . . We must remember the greatness of the cause for which we are struggling. To restore the laws of Nature, trampled upon by the doctrines of ignorance; to restore God's image in man in all its grandeur and beauty, to set free and organize the lofty, harmonious passions hitherto restrained and crushed; to destroy the capitals and cities and to use all their materials for other buildings, and to turn this life of torture, disasters, poverty, shame, and disgrace into a life harmonious and abundant with joy, wealth, happiness, and to cover all this poverty-ridden earth with palaces and flowers—that is our great task, than which there is no greater on earth. . . . We here in our land will begin the transformation, and the whole earth will accomplish it."

Dostoevsky was not present at the dinner. He could not work up much enthusiasm for Fourierism, which, as a matter of fact, he knew at second or third hand. The regimentation involved in the Utopian schemes disturbed him. He felt an urge toward comradeship, communal living, togetherness. But he also had a jealous sense of his own free and unpredictable self, his own inviolable will. Moreover, that feeling for reality which was coming to restrain his daydreams made him look quizzically at the prospect of recruiting radiant phlanges from brutalized serfs. Yet he had not lost his interest in the tender-minded socialism into which Belinsky had initiated him. It was based on the attractive premise that evil had no roots in human nature, and it held the promise of a Golden Age to come. Also it was comforting to find that so many of these French reformers kept invoking the name of Christ. A volume on one of Petrashevsky's shelves contained a supplement wherein a certain Victor Meunier argued that the teachings of Christ were akin to the most revolutionary doctrines of the times and that were He to walk the earth again, He would be court-martialed. Belinsky had once spoken in the same vein. Pierre Leroux went so far as to identify the society that was to be with the universal Church. The idea would eventually become central to Dostoevsky's thinking.

Petrashevsky was an internationalist and he favoured the transformation of the Russian empire into a federated republic, like the United States of America. But however radical his views, he was no revolutionary. A firm believer in progress under the tutelage of reason, he held that the Fourierist variety of socialism offered his compatriots a way to achieve the good life peacefully. This conviction was not shared by all those whom he drew into his orbit. Harsh facts broke in on Utopian reveries. Among the frequenters of the Fridays there were a few individuals with a less feeble grasp on Russian realities. Further, they were by temperament less given to follow the counsels of gradualism and moderation. Violence was already exerting its attraction upon some. It would seem that Dostoevsky belonged to this handful of potential militants, capable of acting in defiance of the law.

II

As has been said, the coterie that centred around Petrashevsky had none of the earmarks of an organized body. There were those in the company who came to feel the need of setting up something in the nature of a formal association. One of them, an army officer, Nikolay Mombelli, was the author of an essay in which he suggested that the Tsar be put on a diet of the Vitebsk peasants for a few days—their bread looked like dried horse dung mixed with straw. He and another man conceived the idea of establishing what they vaguely called "a brotherhood of mutual aid." The matter was discussed privately by half a dozen people, including one Nikolay Speshnev.

Among Petrashevsky's guests he stood out as a strikingly handsome figure and a magnetic personality. A substantial land-owner, he had lived abroad a good deal. There was a touch of the Byronic about him, something at once splendid and sinister. It was rumoured that during his stay in Dresden he had had at least two desperately romantic affairs with Polish ladies. Bakunin called him a gentleman from head to heel; Petrashevsky called him a man of masks. While abroad, he may have come under the influence of the early communists. At one of the Fridays he made a speech to disprove the existence of God. He seems to have begun by declaring his intention to spread by word of mouth "socialism, atheism, terrorism, everything, everything good in the world," and advising his hearers to do likewise.

There was general agreement that "the brotherhood" should be a secret society run by people of republican views. One man suggested that its rules include the threat of death to any informer. The purpose of the projected organization was a moot point. Speshnev cut in on the hemming and hawing by indicating that he favoured "a purely political society," engaged in propaganda and preparing for "insurrection." It was seldom that this bold word was heard at the Fridays, and then only when talk turned to the condition of the serfs. On one occasion Dostoevsky himself is said to have welcomed a revolt of the peasants if that was the only way in which they could obtain freedom.

Speshnev was to insist later that he had mentioned insurrection in order to bring the discussions of "the brotherhood" to an end by frightening the participants. The matter was, in fact, dropped. Nevertheless, Speshnev, for one, apparently did not abandon the idea of a secret society working for a violent upheaval. He believed that a revolution might occur in Russia within a few years. There was nothing fuzzy about his socialism. He favoured nationalization of the land and government control of both agriculture and industry.

It was this man who for a while seems to have exerted a strong influence on Dostoevsky's thinking. There is something enigmatic about their relationship. "Now I am with *him,* and I am *his* . . . Do you understand, I have Mephistopheles of my own?" Dostoevsky told Yanovsky, if one is to credit the doctor's reminiscences set down many years later. Yanovsky has it that his friend was referring to having borrowed no less than five hundred roubles from Speshnev. "I'll never be able to pay back this sum," Yanovsky quotes Dostoevsky as saying; "and, besides, he won't take just money—that's the kind of man he is." Was there another element in the situation? Among Speshnev's papers the police found a pledge to the effect that "the undersigned" had joined "the Russian Society" and had obligated himself "to take part openly and fully in the uprising and fight, when the Committee had decided that the time for rebellion had arrived," as also to enlist other members, and have each sign a like pledge. Speshnev assured the authorities that the paper was nothing but a draft, without significance, and that it had not been signed by anyone nor, indeed, been shown to anyone. To account for Dostoevsky's feeling that he had sold his soul, it has recently been suggested that he actually took this pledge, but there is nothing to support this conjecture.

By the winter of 1848-49 some of those who had been attending the Fridays were also meeting elsewhere. A number of men, Dostoevsky among them, drawn together by a plan to issue a literary miscellany, had decided to start "a salon" of their own. The explanation that they had grown tired of the serious talk and wanted to have intimate "literary-musical evenings" may have been camouflage. According to Speshnev, the chief reason for secession was the suspicion—a well-founded one—that secret service agents had been planted at Petrashevsky's. The group met at the lodging of the poet Pleshcheyev and later at the apartment of another minor writer, one Durov, each member paying three roubles for his share of the refreshments and the rent of a piano.

At a gathering in Pleshcheyev's room Speshnev urged the authors present to send him manuscripts that were sure to be barred by the censor, saying that he would have them printed abroad and smuggled into the country. During the very first meeting at Durov's, Mombelli again harped on the necessity for "people of advanced views" to form a close association. A student by the name of Filippov proposed that the group make a systematic study of conditions in Russia, each member dealing with some phase of the subject, and that the results be circulated among "discreet people." Dostoevsky's essay, which, like the rest, never materialized, was to be on socialism. Filippov urged further that they secretly reproduce their manuscripts by lithography. This was a daring proposal. But everyone knew Filippov. Hadn't Dostoevsky seen the daredevil munch a cluster of green rowanberries the previous summer in the midst of a cholera epidemic, just to prove that he was afraid of nothing? Half of those present, not wishing to be taken for cowards, held their peace. When people finally broke into speech, it was to raise objections, cite difficulties. Two of the musical members of the company changed the subject by taking up their instruments.

Nothing further was done about the matter except to inquire into the cost of a lithographic stone. But Filippov did purchase the parts of a printing-press and took them to Speshnev's apartment. The enterprise seems to have been carried out with Dostoevsky's help. One winter day he called on his friend, Appollon Maikov, and asked leave to spend the night. In the course of the evening he announced that he had been delegated to invite Maikov to join a group of seven or eight men, including Speshnev and Filippov, who were setting up a secret press. They had left Petrashevsky out of it —he was "a fool, an actor," and couldn't hold his tongue. That

Maikov should have been approached with this request is rather surprising. Though an occasional guest of his old acquaintance, Petrashevsky, he was not politically-minded, and just then he was absorbed by a love affair and by a novel that he was writing.

Naturally, he balked at the idea. It meant certain ruin; further, he argued, the two of them were writers, impractical men, while politics was an eminently practical matter. "And I remember," he wrote thirty-seven years after the event, "how Dostoevsky, in a night-shirt open at the neck, sat like dying Socrates before his friends, and enlarged, at the height of his eloquence, on the sacredness of this undertaking, on our duty to save our fatherland, and so forth. . . ." The next morning Dostoevsky went off, having charged Maikov not to breathe a syllable about the matter. The setting up of a secret press in the Russia of Nicholas I was an undertaking tantamount to planting a bomb. All Dostoevsky's other acts against the constituted authorities were trifling by comparison.

If the press was actually set up, it certainly remained idle, though not for dearth of suitable copy. A number of subversive pieces were passed from hand to hand. One of them, written by Filippov himself, was a commentary on the ten commandments, in which the Tsar who does not side with the people against the masters and officials is described as "a ruler whose authority is not from the Lord but from Satan." It was read at a dinner given by Speshnev and attended by Dostoevsky along with other members of the Durov group. A story, entitled "Soldiers' Talk," from the pen of an army officer who was occasionally seen at the Fridays, was to be officially described as "revolting" and "intended to undermine the private soldiers' devotion to the throne and obedience to their superiors." There was great demand for copies of another piece: the lengthy letter addressed in July, 1847, by the outraged Belinsky to Gogol, on the publication of the latter's obscurantist book, *Selected Passages from Correspondence with Friends*. The missive was a vehement philippic against the bureaucracy, the Church, the institution of serfdom. For a government, Belinsky wrote, Russia had "a huge corporation of thieves and robbers." As for the Church, it had always been "a prop of the knout and a toady to despotism," and had nothing in common with Christ, who "was the first to instruct mankind in liberty, equality, fraternity." The Russians were fundamentally a level-headed and "a deeply atheistic people." They needed civilization, enlightenment. The first necessity was the freeing of the serfs, abolition of corporal punishment, respect for the existing laws. Dostoevsky received a handwritten copy of the epistle from Moscow and read it at Durov's, as well as at Petrashevsky's and elsewhere. The letter aroused "universal rapture," and it was decided to make several copies of it. This document, the last testament of his former mentor and the manifesto of Russian liberalism, was to become for Dostoevsky one of the chief instruments of a hostile fate.

But before doom fell, he was to know the stimulus of ideas, fantasies, beliefs, tapped from many minds. For a writer, there was even more pabulum in the faces, the voices, the gestures, the minutiae of personality, that these various contacts offered. Not that everything was seized upon and used at once. There was a laying-up of treasure, a perhaps only half-realized hoarding.

Young Dostoevsky's associations were by no means confined to radical coteries. The group that centred around Dr. Yanovsky was of a conservative temper, and so were the Maikovs. On Sunday evenings he would often repair to the spacious apartment near the Blue Bridge occupied by that family. Headed by a veteran of the Napoleonic wars who was a painter with academic laurels, it included four brothers. One of them, Valerian, a critic who crossed swords in the press with Belinsky himself, was drowned in the summer of 1847 at the age of twenty-four. Another, Appollon, was to be Dostoevsky's lifelong friend. At these gatherings he was bound to be exposed to the nationalist ideology which was just then taking shape. But it was not only here that he ran into it. By this time the discussion of these theories had gone beyond the Moscow salons and penetrated into the public prints of both capitals. Most young men in touch with their times were familiar with the Slavophil point of view: Russia was totally different from and superior to the West; Europe was mortally sick, Russia was bursting with health; while in the West the state, being based upon conquest, must live by violence and remain merely a formal, legalistic institution, the Russian body politic, having been founded by amicable compact between the people and their sovereign, could develop organically and peacefully; the Tsar's rule rested firmly on the

loving submission of his subjects; while Rome had imposed upon
Western Christianity a limiting rationalism, the Orthodox Church
had preserved a comprehensive spirituality which made it the sole
vessel of true Christianity. Some of these ideas were the unacknow-
ledged foundations on which the world of Dostoevsky's childhood
had rested. There was something reassuring and protecting about
a philosophy that exalted the ancestral order and the familiar faith,
that saw in the Tsar the image of the Father who by the mere fact
of his existence established and preserved the social framework.
But at this time Dostoevsky was not ready to accept these views.
He was to endure much travail of body and mind before they would
become his rod and staff. Now he was responsive to ideas of a
different order.

I I I

Dostoevsky's discontent with the state of public affairs may well
have been aggravated by his private harassments. Mikhail's arrival
in Petersburg did not bring all the blessings expected of it. Certainly
it brought no money. The sum of Dostoevsky's published work
for the year 1847 was the short story called "The Landlady," aside
from that bagatelle, "A Novel in Nine Letters," and several feuilletons. True, *Poor Folk* appeared separately, but *Netochka Nezvanova*, the novel upon which so much had been staked, failed to materialize, and indeed nothing is heard of it until two years later. The
situation was desperately discouraging. The brothers shared quarters
until Mikhail's family—his wife and three young children—came to
join him the following Easter. On Good Friday, when Dostoevsky
had to prepare some sort of reception for the newcomers, his creditors were all at his throat.

In 1848 he was more prolific, perhaps because of the sustaining
influence of his brother's presence. Mikhail, too, in addition to a
good deal of translating, did some original work. Dostoevsky came
out with four long stories and two lesser pieces. One of the latter,
"Polzunkov," appeared in the miscellany edited by Nekrasov, who
went out of his way to secure it—he could more easily give up a
friend than a contributor.

The winter of 1948-49 was one of penury and general wretchedness. Yanovsky offered him fifteen or twenty roubles of his own

and told him to borrow some cash from the alms-box into which he and his friends dropped their spare five-copeck pieces for beggars too proud to accept the free meal-tickets then in use. The friends had also, at Dostoevsky's suggestion, started a small co-operative loan fund. A drawer in the doctor's desk was the bank, the same drawer containing the rules of the institution written in Dostoevsky's hand. But he rejected Yanovsky's offer. It was not twenty or fifty roubles that he needed, but hundreds.

By New Year's Day his distress was acute. There was no getting along with him at all. He was more irritable than ever, more easily offended, and ready to make much of trifles. He complained more frequently of attacks of vertigo. He felt that he was going to pieces. And he owed money to everybody. As usual he borrowed from Peter to pay Paul.

The enormous sum Speshnev had lent him was no more a solution of his present difficulties than the sum he had received from the guardian had been. His original debt of four hundred roubles to Krayevsky had almost doubled. He felt as though he were in peonage to the man. The worst of it was that he was forced to botch his work. In order to pay off the debt, he told the editor, he was endangering his health, poor at best, and what was worse, injuring his name, his "sole capital." He began to look upon his work as drudgery that did not even yield bread. A mood of what he called "self-belittlement" took possession of him—a mood that gave way to self-assertiveness when he addressed Krayevsky. He wrote that the advance made him had been in the nature of a business risk, rather than a personal favour, that his vogue had been steadily increasing throughout the previous year, and he must be genuinely gifted if he could overcome "beggary, slavery, the fury of the critics who were solemnly burying [him], and the prejudice of the public." It was criminal to make a man so talented do less than his best.

He had previously agreed to turn over to Krayevsky practically everything he wrote, in return for fifty roubles a month, the minimum of subsistence. He was now faced with an unforeseen expense. One way of taking care of it would be to write a story for another review, but this would interfere with his work on *Netochka Nezvanova*, the first two parts of which had recently appeared in the magazine. It was essential to keep at it, so that at least the first six

parts could appear in successive issues. Besides, he wasn't writing
for money only. "I love the novel. . . . It's more precious to me than
the whole of *Fatherland Notes*. I wouldn't spoil it for one thousand
roubles a signature," he declared roundly.

The point of this outburst was that he wanted one hundred
roubles at once. Let it be considered an advance on the third and
fourth parts of *Netochka*—still unwritten—the remainder of the
sum that will be coming to him for those two parts to go toward
the amortization of his debt. He promises to deliver the third part
of the novel by the fifteenth of February. He must have the money,
though he knows that to accept it is against his own interest, since
it prolongs his slavery, and furthermore, after all that has passed
between him and Krayevsky, is indecent.

Dostoevsky received the hundred roubles that he had begged for.
Not that he delivered the third part of the novel by the middle of
February, as promised. He was only just finishing it by the end of
March. He was then in fearful straits, and wrote again to
Krayevsky, begging abjectly for ten roubles so as to throw a sop to
his landlady, whom he had not paid for two months. On the last
day of March he was telling the editor without a trace of compunction that he hadn't turned in the third part of the novel earlier because he had spent a month trying to write a story that would bring
him an additional fifty roubles. He hadn't succeeded: in fact, he had
only acquired a headache and ruined nerves, in addition to three
magnificent subjects for big novels. Krayevsky must have felt that
he had hold of an author who, whatever else was lacking, had all
the reputed irresponsibility of genius.

Without taking a moment's rest, Dostoevsky insists, he is now
plugging away at part four. It can't be delivered before April 8.
But how can he go on writing at all? When he accepted the money
in February, he swore to himself that he would never take another
advance. But he can't help himself. Easter is only three days off.
The remittance that should have reached him from relatives in
Moscow will only arrive after the holiday. This is one of the two
periods in the year when creditors refuse to be put off. "I will come
to you on Saturday," he announces. "For God's sake don't send
me away without a hundred roubles. I'll never ask another copeck
of you. My brother is my witness. Ask him." It he doesn't get the

money, Krayevsky will have no further instalments of the novel to offer his readers, for Dostoevsky will have to turn his hand to something that will bring an immediate return. After seven years of living on credit he is at the end of his tether. He must put a stop to this system of working off debts. He still remembers Good Friday of the previous year when, in addition to everything else, he had to prepare against the arrival of his brother's family. He can't face it again: he'll have cholera. And what of literature then?

Krayevsky did not send him away without the hundred roubles, but before the date set for the delivery of the fourth and fifth parts, he was writing to the editor again. This time he needs only fifteen roubles. He is fighting his small creditors as Laocoön fought the serpents. The fourth part of the novel, which he has not yet delivered, he promises, a second time, for the middle of April. But he must have fifteen roubles. Only fifteen roubles. "What are fifteen roubles to you? But for me they're a great deal. For a week I've been without a groat. Literally nothing. If you only knew to what I've been reduced. It's shameful to write about it. And what's the use? Isn't it disgraceful," he adds, with something between humour and pathos, "that the contributors to *Fatherland Notes* should be so poor?" Whether or not he got the fifteen roubles is not known, but Krayevsky never received the fourth part of the novel.

IV

On the twenty-second of April, Dostoevsky was on his way to the usual gathering at Petrashevsky's. It was an unseasonably warm evening. Drenched to the skin by a sudden shower, he stopped off at Yanovsky's to change his clothes and borrow fare for a cab. The doctors' pockets were as bare as the proverbial cupboard, and the drawer with the loan fund held only large bills. Yanovsky, rather than see his friend go out into the rain on foot, persuaded him to draw on the alms-box. Dostoevsky took six five-copeck pieces and left. He never paid back the money. The following morning he was roused out of his first sleep—he had come home in the small hours after stopping off at another friend's—arrested, and committed to prison in the Fortress of Peter and Paul.

CHAPTER SEVEN

THE CONDEMNED

SUDDENLY the hand of that sternest of fathers—the Tsar—was heavily upon him. He had sinned against him, and here was retribution. He was roughly pulled out of his familiar, if harassing, existence and thrust into a vacuum. He was stripped of his clothes, his books, his manuscripts, his very name. This number Seven, this thing in the filthy grey prison gown and felt slippers, locked up alone in an ill-lighted cell, treated by the silent guards and the examining magistrates as a creature set apart from men by the unnatural ways of the criminal—was he not a terrifying stranger tenanting the body of Fyodor Dostoevsky? But what nonsense! Come, he must get a grip on himself. If only he were writing, this nightmare would lift.

But writing was not to be thought of—he was not allowed paper and pen. The first days were particularly hard. Except for the few visits of the guards—they would bring him his meal of watery soup and boiled meat heavily seasoned to disguise its age—there was nothing to divert him. No human voice reached him, indeed no sound, save the grating creak of keys in locks and perhaps the muffled chime of the cathedral clock measuring off his hours.

What, after all, were the charges against him? What penalty might he expect? He did not know. He could perhaps reason himself into something like courage in the daytime, particularly if the upper part of the high window—the lower panes were chalked to opacity—showed a blue patch of sky. Yes, he had listened to wild talk against the constituted authorities, the established order, the Tsar himself, against property, the laws, the family, against God and the Saviour—he had contributed to it himself. But he was a writer, not a conspirator, and at heart a Christian and a patriot. Yet there were other times when everything looked black. At nine o'clock lights were put out, and as he lay on his straw pallet in an agony of sleeplessness for what seemed interminable hours, he must have touched panic. He had been reading forbidden books. He had been associating with hotheads. He had read Belinsky's letter at gatherings more than once and had it passed on to be copied. Of course, they were bound to find out about his part in setting up the secret press. He was without question a criminal.

The present was empty. The future did not bear thinking of. His mind naturally turned to the past, though that too was dangerous ground for a man in his situation. Only a few days ago he had been running about, trying to get a few roubles from Krayevsky—trying to squeeze blood out of a stone—trying to keep on his legs in spite of wretched health, trying to get on with *Netochka Nezvanova*, and all the while feeling at the end of his rope. And then came the night that had changed everything and made all that preceded it seem almost a lost paradise.

It was four o'clock in the morning when he had been awakened by the clank of a sabre and a soft, friendly: "Get up, sir!" The weapon belonged to an awkward gendarme stationed at the door, the gentle voice was that of a major of the gendarmerie. In the uncertain light Dostoevsky also made out the figure of a police captain with superb side whiskers. While he dressed himself with unsteady fingers, the two men searched his room, looking over all his books and papers. The police captain went so far as to rake over the cold ashes in the grate with Dostoevsky's pipe, and had the gendarme climb to the top of the stove to see if anything forbidden was concealed there. Noticing a bent silver coin on the table, he eyed it suspiciously and ended by placing it with the books and papers that they were confiscating. The last things that struck Dostoevsky as he left his disordered room were the scared face of his landlady and the stupid solemn look in the eye of his servant, frightened, but also impressed with the importance of the proceedings. Then there was the trip through the morning streets, and the headquarters of the political police near the Summer Garden. The doors of the detention room kept opening to admit more sleepy-eyed prisoners, under the escort of men in blue uniforms. Before the morning was over nearly two score people had been rounded up. Among them Dostoevsky was astonished to encounter his irreproachable brother Andrey, who had been arrested

by mistake. One literal-minded gendarme brought along with his
captive the woman found in that gentleman's bed. Most of the men
knew each other, and the day dragged on not too disagreeably, what
with the companionship and the fine dinner capped by good cigars.

It was late in the evening when Dostoevsky made the long trip
across the Neva to the fortress. In the guardroom he changed to convict's clothes, and then crossed the little drawbridge connecting the
main fortification with the Alexis Ravelin. Excitement had delayed
the fatigue of a sleepless night, and anxiety waited until he had
entered the squat old prison, walked through a dark vaulted passage and down a half-lighted corridor to find himself in this
shadowy, bare, ill-smelling cell. Rumour had it that men left this
northern Bastille either for the grave or the insane asylum.

At the end of a fortnight he was summoned to appear before
the investigating commission that was at work examining papers
and grilling the prisoners. He was interrogated about his education,
income, personal contacts. Four weeks passed before he had another
hearing. In addition to being examined orally he was given pen and
paper and requested to make a general deposition and to answer
specific questions in writing.

In his affidavits he admits having gone to Petrashevsky's on an
occasional Friday. But he asks: "Who has seen my soul? Who has
measured the degree of perfidy, wickedness and rebelliousness of
which I am accused?" If he made a speech once or twice, it was not
on a political subject. Perhaps he did sometimes express himself
with excessive heat, but that was momentary. Not that free and
frank discussion, within limits, can displease the authorities. His
own reputation is that of an uncommunicative person. He has few
friends and little leisure for them.

Like everyone else, he writes, he talked about such things as
censorship at home, the course of events in Western Europe. A
breath-taking drama is unfolding there, an age-old order is breaking
up. Was it a criminal offence to have felt concern about what is
happening in the land that gave Russia its culture? The crisis in
France is perhaps an historic necessity and may lead to happier
times. That makes him no enemy of autocracy. "There never was
anything more absurd to me," he declares, "than the idea of a
republican régime in Russia. . . . All the good things in Russia

since Peter the Great have come from the throne . . ." As for censorship, no one who loves literature can avoid discussing it. The differences between the writer and the censor are the result of misunderstanding, and all he ever said on the subject was in an effort to bring the two together. What was the use of having given him an education, if he is denied the right to have opinions of his own?

Yes, he read aloud Belinsky's letter, but he also read Gogol's reply. And not by so much as intonation or gesture did he indicate his own bias. Indeed, he is definitely out of sympathy with Belinsky's ideas. That letter is too bizarre, too soaked in gall, too full of wild assertions to lead anyone astray. It is obviously the product of a mind embittered and distorted by illness. He read it partly because it is something of a literary document, partly to clear himself of the suspicion that he still bore a grudge against this late friend with whom he had quarrelled. Besides, he owed respect to a man who had admirable qualities and was remarkable for his time. He admits, however, that he had made a mistake in reading the letter. As regards the mad suggestion for lithographing subversive pamphlets, made by Filippov—a lovable youth, but so hot-tempered and impetuous—it was because of his, Dostoevsky's, dissuading voice that the proposal had been rejected.

He was not, he points out, intimate with Petrashevsky and knew nothing of any plans he may have had. The Fridays were informal gatherings. If the chatter sometimes exceeded the bounds of propriety, it was because the guests felt that they were among friends, *en famille* as it were. At all events, he thought Petrashevsky was a ridiculous rather than dangerous character. Consider: he was an ardent Fourierist, and where? In Petersburg! Now Fourierism is a peaceful "system" that bewitches the soul and fills the heart with love of mankind. It does not encroach upon government, property, religion, the family. In France it may prove harmful, for there the starving proletarians in their desperation grasp at any means and are ready to use it as a banner. But "one need walk no more than twenty paces in a Petersburg street to realize that on Russian soil Fourierism can exist only in the pages of an uncut book or in a soft, gentle, dreamy soul." For his own part, he is devoted to the study of history and economics, and so he has investigated socialism in all its ramifications, but he has never been a socialist. Not that he can wholly condemn it. It is a false science like alchemy, but just as out of alchemy issued chemistry, so out of socialism there may arise for the common good "something harmonious, rational and beneficient."

It is clear that Dostoevsky did not recant and abjectly plead for mercy, as did so many of his fellow prisoners. Nor did he try to shift the blame for what he had said or done to other shoulders. That he was not quite candid and that he concealed certain facts is equally plain. He was obviously at pains to represent the whole affair as a matter of venial indiscretions and, by the same token, to minimize his own guilt and that of his comrades. Years later, long after he had repudiated his radicalism as a youthful aberration, he pictured the "Petrashevists," including himself, as far from impetuous but well-meaning innocents.

The investigating commission sat through the summer months, the official wheels grinding out in leisurely fashion what the Government was pleased to call justice. Meanwhile, Dostoevsky lay in prison. There were moments when he felt that he had never known any other life, and did not look forward to any other. Time, here as elsewhere, flowed unevenly. He marked off each day as it passed on an improvised calendar, but the end of the trial seemed as unimportant as it was remote. His appetite was poor, he was living on castor oil, sleeping about five hours a night, waking repeatedly, and suffering from abominable dreams. He had spells of dizziness when the floor swayed under his feet and his cell was like the cabin of a boat in dirty weather. He complained to Mikhail of his nerves, of a return of his throat spasms, of the opening up of old sores on his face and in his mouth, of a pain in his chest, of haemorrhoids. And yet, with it all, he felt that he had great reserves of strength to fall back upon.

On the whole, the horrors of the first weeks had abated. In some ways life here was not so different from what it was outside. He even managed to borrow ten roubles. He had distractions and occupations. He had learned how to communicate with the man in the cell next his by a system of knocks. A few letters from Mikhail reached him. In July he was permitted paper and pen, and so he could relieve himself of the stories that he had invented and had had to keep locked up in his head all these weeks. He had never written

with such a sense of satisfaction, and yet it was a severe strain
because there was nothing to divert him. If only he had books!
The prison library had a few edifying works, but he could scarcely
find much intellectual substance in travels to the Holy Land and the
works of Saint Dmitry of Rostov. And never had he so longed for
a glimpse of green leaves!

It was August before this desire was finally gratified. He was
permitted a short daily promenade in the prison courtyard. There
were trees there, and he counted them, as a prisoner will, and found
that with the big linden they numbered seventeen—unhealthy looking things, shaded as they were by the walls of the prison. But they
were green after all, and they reminded him of the hospital garden
in Moscow, where he and Mikhail used to play in the spring, of the
park at the engineering school where he had strolled as an unhappy
"hazel hen," of visits to Mikhail in Reval when early summer was
crowding the squares with green. The same month he was also
allowed a candle at night, another luxury. Occasionally Mikhail
managed to smuggle money and imported cigarettes in to him. And
then books drifted in—Schiller, Shakespeare, the Bible, and even
magazines. In the May issue of *Otechestvennye zapiski* he found the
last instalment of *Netochka* that he had sent to Krayevsky in those
almost unimaginable days before his arrest. It was unsigned: the
authorities could not allow the name of a political prisoner to
appear in print, but at least his story was there. Could he ever
again take up the thread of the unfinished tale?

II

The investigating commission discovered nothing aside from the
fact that there had been meetings at Petrashevsky's and elsewhere,
at which "pernicious" opinions and doctrines, especially Fourier's system, were freely aired and subversive manuscripts read. Both
Speshnev and Filippov confessed that they had tried to set up an
illegal printing-press, but the authorities failed to find any trace
of the press. The parts had been spirited away from Speshnev's
quarters after his arrest and presumably destroyed. No evidence was
discovered of the existence of any organized secret society or of any
attempts at revolutionary propaganda or action. Nevertheless the

high commission recommended that twenty-eight of the prisoners be court-martialled. Dostoevsky was among them, as one of "the most important" culprits. Accordingly the emperor appointed a special tribunal presided over by a general. It was then the end of September.

Dostoevsky was hauled before the judges and asked if he had any statement to make. This is what he wrote: "I have never acted against the Government with malice prepense. What I did was done without premeditation and much, so to say, inadvertently, as, for example, the reading of Belinsky's letter. If I ever spoke freely, it was only in the circle of my close intimates, who were in a position to understand me and knew in what sense my words were intended. But I always avoided disseminating my doubts."

Followed more weeks and months of solitary confinement. He anticipated the cold season with dread. A slit of bright sky seemed a guarantee of cheerfulness and health. The coming of winter aggravated his aches and pains. For two and a half months he was forbidden either to send or receive a letter. His purely cerebral existence, without impressions from the outside to feed his mind, was beginning to tell on him. He had the sensations of a man sitting in a chamber from which the air was being pumped. He was living entirely in his head, and his writing was squeezing the last juices out of him. And yet, strangely enough, he knew that at bottom all was well with him. Beneath the surface worries which fretted him, there ran a strong undercurrent of contentment. He was conscious of an inexhaustible store of vitality. He was at peace with himself and the world. Eventually he came to believe that his arrest had saved him from insanity. His curious serenity fits in with the theory that he unconsciously accepted this punishment as an atonement he had long craved. Here was assuagement for any sense of guilt that may have been lurking in some subterranean corner of his mind, disturbing gravely both his bodily well-being and his mental poise.

He did not know that the court, after six weeks of deliberation, had condemned him, along with fourteen others, to capital punishment by shooting. In due time the verdicts were reviewed by the highest judicial body known as the Auditoriat General. These jurists opined that since, in political crimes, no distinction was made between ringleader and follower, fully twenty-one of the twenty-three prisoners were legally liable to the supreme punishment. In view, however, of the prisoners' youth, their repentance, and the fact that they had not translated their designs into action, the high judiciary recommended to the monarch that terms of hard labour, of varying length, be substituted for the death sentence. In the hierarchy of guilt Dostoevsky occupied the tenth place, the list being topped by Petrashevsky, who received a life term.

Dostoevsky's sentence was to be eight years of hard labour in a Siberian fortress and the loss of all civil rights. The verdict listed two counts against him: the reading aloud of Belinsky's "criminal" letter, and presence at the reading of the "revolting" story, entitled "Soldier's Talk." The part he played in setting up the secret press remained unknown to the authorities.

A summary of the report drawn up by the Auditoriat General was submitted to the emperor on December 19. The fate of the prisoners was now in the hands of Nicholas. He decided not to treat them as harshly as he had the Decembrists, whose abortive rebellion he had so ruthlessly crushed on his ascension to the throne. He confirmed the commutation of the death sentences, and in some cases reduced the term of hard labour. Opposite the paragraph relating to Dostoevsky he wrote: "Four years [of penal servitude] and then into the ranks with him." The astounding severity of the sentences could only be accounted for by the hysteria which seized the Russian Government as it watched the thrones of Europe rock the revolution of 1848.

The emperor had a weakness for theatrical effects, in addition to immense self-righteousness. He gave orders that the death sentence should be announced to the prisoners in a public place in the presence of the populace and the troops, and that only after the men had gone through all the preparations for their execution, were they to be informed at the last moment that the Tsar in his ineffable charity had made them a present of their lives.

III

On the morning of December 22, Dostoevsky was aroused before daybreak. Something unusual was going on in the prison. He was given the clothes he had worn when he was arrested eight months earlier, and thus scantily protected against Christmas weather he was placed with a guard in a closed coach. There were more coaches containing other prisoners, and when they started on their way each vehicle was escorted by mounted gendarmes with sabres drawn. From the window he could see crowds of people walking in the same direction. He did not know where he was being taken. Though they went at a trot, the trip of three or four miles seemed endless. When he alighted, it was into freshly fallen snow. Just above the horizon a huge red ball was glowing dimly through the morning mists. The biting air seemed to pierce through his light clothing to his bones. Yet it was intoxicating. Glancing eagerly about, he found himself in a familiar place—Semyonov Square, with its orange barracks, and the cupolas of the cathedral veiled in haze. But the parade ground had an unusual look. It wasn't merely the crowds, nor yet the troops, lined up in square formation. It was that structure right in front of him, its three sides framed by soldiers, a railed platform, draped in black. Dostoevsky did not know that the height of the platform, like the speed of the horses that had brought him there, and every other detail of the drama that was to follow, had been determined by the authorities with the approval of the emperor.

More coaches kept arriving, bringing more men, some of them total strangers to him. Dostoevsky shook hands with the fellow prisoners whom he knew, exchanged a few words with them, stared at their changed, bearded faces. The general who seemed to be master of ceremonies put an abrupt end to their interchanges, and had them line up. Then a priest, in the vestments appropriate to a funeral, and carrying the cross and the Gospels, approached the prisoners and bade them follow him. They tramped after him in the deep snow, past the long line of troops, which had been chosen from regiments in which some of the prisoners had served as officers. Dostoevsky walked briskly. The men ascended the scaffold. Here they were rearranged and stood in two unequal rows. In a whisper—they were forbidden to speak—Dostoevsky told his neighbour the plot of a story he had written in prison. He was now in that state of calm that extreme nervous tension sometimes produces.

Answering the short command: "Present arms!" came the reverberant clanking of rifles. A court clerk stepped forward and stood between the rows of prisoners. They were ordered to bare their heads. Calling on each of the men by name, the clerk read off the verdicts. As he mumbled in the fashion peculiar to his kind, much of what he said was lost on his hearers, but not the identical phrase which recurred at the end of each verdict. Dostoevsky heard it like a refrain: "Petrashevsky . . . condemned to capital punishment by shooting." Other names were called, and finally, like the name of some stranger, his own: Fyodor Mikhailovich Dostoevsky. The mumbling went on as before and ended as before, with the incredible words: "condemned to capital punishment by shooting."

The reading lasted an unconscionable time. In his light clothes, his head uncovered, he shuddered with cold. Suddenly the sun, which had been hovering behind the mists, broke through, and somehow it came over him that they were not going to be executed. He said so to Durov, who was standing beside him. But Durov pointed out a cart covered with a mat which hid, he thought, their coffins.

The clerk finished his reading. With a kind of vacant intensity Dostoevsky watched his gestures as he carefully folded up his paper and shoved it into his side pocket. The clerk's place was taken by the priest. Choosing as his text St. Paul's judgment: "The wages of sin is death," he preached briefly to the condemned. In a voice that shook he told them that with bodily death all was not over, and that through faith and repentance they would inherit life eternal. He urged them to confess their sins and make their peace with God. Only one man was shriven. Dostoevsky, with the others, knelt to kiss the cross. One guesses that he did so like the condemned criminal in *The Idiot,* who pressed his lips to the cross greedily, as though in a hurry to possess himself of something he might need badly. With that act he knew himself abandoned by all men, beyond help, alone.

The gold-laced master of ceremonies dismissed the priest, who was lingering with the condemned, saying abruptly: "There is nothing further for you to do here, Father." Therewith two men in bright kaftans came forward and broke a sword over the head of each of the prisoners who was of the nobility, in token of the loss of the rights and privileges pertaining to their rank. Dostoevsky knelt with the other to suffer this disgrace. This over, the guards helped the condemned perform their last toilette: to remove their outer clothing and get into hooded white linen shirts with long sleeves—their shrouds. One of the men who could still joke asked: "How do we look in this attire?" And then, in silence, Petrashevsky and two of the others were led away from the scaffold to three grey posts and bound to them. They faced a firing squad of fifteen soldiers standing fifteen paces off.

For ten, for twenty, perhaps for forty minutes—how could he tell?—Dostoevsky had been living with the thought, the excruciating certainty, that he was about to die. It seemed impossible that these staring thousands, their faces red blurs in the frost, their eyes fixed upon the condemned, would go on living, while he must cease to exist, and now. He was the sixth. He must go with the next lot. So soon?

"Someone condemned to death," reflects Raskolnikov in *Crime and Punishment,* "says or thinks, an hour before his death, that if he had to live somewhere on a height, on a rock, and on a ledge so narrow that he had only room to stand, and around him, abysses, the ocean, everlasting darkness, everlasting solitude, everlasting tempest—if he had to remain standing on a square yard of space all his life, a thousand years, eternity, it were better to live so than to die at once! Only to live, to live, and to live! To live, no matter how!" In *The Idiot* the emotions of a condemned man just before his execution are described in detail. With five minutes left, he feels that there is an infinity ahead of him, that with so much intervening time there is no need yet to think of the final moment. He sets aside time for a last farewell to his comrades: two minutes; he allots a period to his last thoughts: two minutes; the remaining minute is for looking about him the last time. As he says good-bye to one of his comrades he asks him a trivial question and is deeply concerned over the answer. The two minutes come that he set apart for thinking to himself. "He knew beforehand what he would think about. He wanted to realize as quickly and clearly as possible how it could be that now he existed and was living and in three minutes he would be *something*—someone, or something. But who? Where?

He meant to decide all that in these two minutes! Not far off there was a church, and the gilt cupola was glittering in the bright sunshine. He remembered that he stared with terrible persistency at that cupola and the rays flashing from it; he could not tear himself away from the rays. It seemed to him that those rays were his new nature, and that in three minutes he would somehow merge with them. . . . The uncertainty and feeling of aversion to that new thing which would be and was coming at once was frightful." But there was a more dreadful sensation. He was tortured by the thought of what life would be if it were given back to him, of the eternity that would stretch out before him, of all that he would pack into it, of the fullness with which he would live it. At last the thought made him so furious that he wished they would shoot him at once.

Inevitably one imagines that Dostoevsky was here transcribing emotions that he had lived through. At the last a feeling of utter indifference came over him. He was not sorry to die. Perhaps the sheer intensity of his experience brought him momentarily to the point of emotional exhaustion. Everything seemed insignificant beside the terrible moment of transition to the unknown, to darkness. He embraced Pleshcheyev and Durov. There was momentary comfort in the warm contact. He had some five minutes more to live. He thought achingly of Mikhail.

Meanwhile the men tied to the posts had their hoods shoved over their eyes. Dostoevsky watched them with a kind of composure. A sense of the inevitability of the end blunted his agony. The command rang out smartly: "Ready. Aim!" Fifteen rifles swung into position. There was a rumble of drums like doom. At the sound, the rifles were tilted upward, the men at the posts were unloosed, a Government courier leapt from his carriage with a paper in his hand. The terrible comedy was over. It was a reprieve.

Capital punishment was commuted to terms of hard labour in Siberia. At the news two of the men threw themselves on their knees in prayer, one of them crying out: "The good Tsar! Long live our Tsar!" Grigoryev, who had just been unloosed from the posts, was raving. Another of the reprieved men said bitterly: "It would have been better if they had shot us." Several men felt so —the blow to their human dignity implied in this sham execution was crushing. Dostoevsky was incapable of either joy or indignation. The stupor of indifference still held him. He had lived through something so terrible that now nothing mattered.

In the meantime the guards were busy with the convicts. They helped the men remove their shrouds—Dostoevsky kept his as a souvenir, and gave each a convict's cap, a sheepskin coat, and a pair of felt boots. In the biting cold the warm clothing was a godsend. Petrashevsky was clapped into irons right there on the platform with his own aid, and, after he had embraced and kissed every one of his comrades, was sent off directly on his long journey to Siberia. The rest were taken back to prison. When Dostoevsky found himself again in his cell, whole and alive, he was at last able to surrender himself to the joy of resurrection. He strode back and forth, and from the depths of his shaken being came something that was almost a song.

IV

So this was what he had to face—four years of hard labour in Siberia. And then, for an indefinite period, the black lot of a soldier in the ranks. But he would not look so far ahead. The main thing was that he was alive, a human being among his kind. Life was a gift, a single moment could be like the widow woman's cruse. He felt conscious of an untapped reservoir of spiritual energy. It fairly seethed in him. Not to be brutalized, to remain a human being under the most degrading circumstances—he must stick to that now. He had come to an end, but that meant actually a beginning. He would be reborn. The head that had been busy with ideas and images, that head was off his shoulders. To love, to suffer, to pity, to remember—wasn't that enough? The hopes of youth were torn out of his heart. He was done with writing. But was he really? Perhaps when he had served his term there would be a chance for it. But there would be years when the images that he had conceived and nourished would either fade out of his mind or, dying there, fill him with the poisons of decay. Yes, he will go under if he can't write. And even if his spirit holds out, won't his body go to pieces under the strain? No matter! He had been about to die: he was alive. What had he to fear?

He poured out his heart thus to Mikhail in a letter that he wrote the day of the reprieve, after permission to see his brother was refused. He charged him to live quietly, with prudence and foresight. His commissions were few. Mikhail would probably receive his books and papers, the draft of a play and of a novel and the manuscript of *A Fairy-Tale for Children*—all he had written in prison. He should make certain to return to the old lady Maikov her own copy of her late son's book, which Dostoevsky had borrowed. Mikhail would find the right words in which to give that old friend his last greeting. He should press the hands of the young Maikovs, of the good Yanovsky, kiss brother Kolya, send a word to Andrey, to their sisters, to uncle and aunt. He assured him that there was no bitterness in his heart, and that all he wanted was to be able to embrace some one of his own people.

This wish was finally granted him. He was allowed to see his brother two days later, a few hours before his departure for Siberia. It was Christmas Eve. With Durov, he was taken to the commandant's house, where the investigating commission and the court-martial had held their sittings. In a large room on the ground floor, lighted dimly by a single lamp, he saw a familiar figure. Yes, it was Mikhail. Dostoevsky was wearing a sheepskin coat and felt boots, in readiness for his long journey. Of the two brothers, it was the convict who was the calmer, and it was his part to comfort the one who remained at home.

The farewells were over quickly, and Dostoevsky went back to his cell. Shortly afterward he left it again for the last time. It was precisely midnight, the hour that ushered in the birthday of his Saviour, when he was clamped into irons. They weighed ten pounds and made it hard for him to walk. It was usual for convicts to tramp the long trail to Siberia. Dostoevsky, with his comrades, was spared this ordeal. He left the fortress seated beside a gendarme in an open sleigh. There were two more sleighs, holding Durov and another convict, with a courier leading the way.

It was mild and clear, and the air must have throbbed with the booming of innumerable church bells. The holy night was upon Petersburg. Dostoevsky's heart was heavy; small anxieties pricked him. But the fresh air and the swift soft movement were easing the aches and longings. A kind of calm elation filled him He looked with steady intentness at the houses that he knew by heart, each lit for the festival, at the passing streets that were part of the life he was leaving behind: they were familiar and strangely different. He said a mute good-bye to each. His way lay past Mikhail's lodgings and Krayevsky's apartment. Behind those gayly lighted windows were Mikhail's wife and children—they had been invited, his brother had told him, to the Christmas party. As his sleigh glided past the house, his heart was cruelly squeezed. Now it was out of sight. He must wrench himself away from it all, though it broke him.

CHAPTER EIGHT

CONFESSIONS

SUPPOSE the reprieve to have arrived too late and Dostoevsky to have been cut off from life at the age of twenty-eight. He would then have been remembered as a minor writer, having to his credit a handful of stories, a novelette, and one unfinished full-length novel—the fruit of less than half a dozen years of feverish labours. Actually he is remembered by work of far wider scope, greater complexity, and deeper significance. Yet these early writings deserve attention not only because they hold intimations of his later achievements, but also in their own right. They are not merely promise, but achievement.

Poor Folk, the work with which he opened his career, lacks the obvious autobiographic cast which is common to first novels. It deals with a gentle copying clerk of middle age who takes upon himself the rôle of guardian of a young girl whom he might have married, had he been less miserably circumstanced. He is utterly lost when the girl, in her weakness and despair, becomes the bride of a well-to-do, coarse landowner, able to give her the creature comforts that are beyond the poor clerk's power to bestow. George Moore summed up this romance with his usual felicity thus: "Makar [the clerk] is one of life's convicts, Varvara is the mouse that comes for crumbs; and the end is the same: a better filled hand is extended to the mouse, and the mouse returns no more to cheer the cell's loneliness!"

The hero is not a projection of the author's self, nor is the milieu one that he knew from first-hand experience. Here are none of the earmarks of a young man's production. This is a work of pathos rather than of passion. The characters live not the life of the senses, but of the sentiments. For a love story, it is curiously sexless. The attitude of the poor clerk toward his correspondent—the tale is told in letters—is half avuncular, half maternal. Indeed, it is not surprising that a contemporary reviewer thought he saw in it the hand of a young lady. There is something vague and soft about it, and in spite of sordid details, it leaves the impression of a pastel in lavender and grey. The competence with which the characters are realized is the chief token of the young novelist's genius.

Dostoevsky followed up *Poor Folk* with a work of a totally different cast: "The Double." The first is transparent and shallow; the second has its opacities and profundities. Of the two pieces, "The Double" is the more original, if the less readable. It is a study in mental derangement—maniacal psychosis, to be exact—and as such the marvel of the psychopathologists. One Golyadkin, a Government clerk in a subordinate position, invites himself to a dinner party given by his chief, and upon being refused admittance, steals into the ballroom for the dance that follows, only to be shamefully ejected. He does these things half against his will, compelled, as it were, by a malevolent force. Then, as though symbolizing his divided state, his double appears on the scene. This double is in some respects the image of what Golyadkin would himself choose to be: a man possessed of *savoir-faire,* a free and easy fellow, able to insinuate himself into the good graces of his superiors. From the beginning Golyadkin is naturaly the butt and victim of this figment of his imagination. Suffering from a growing delusion that the world is in league against him, he comes to believe that his double is his most dangerous rival and the chief tool of his persecutors. After a series of adventures, half real, half illusory, Golyadkin, as the tale concludes, is helped by his double into a carriage which takes him to a lunatic asylum.

The compulsive behaviour of Dostoevsky's hero, the relation between his sense of insufficiency and his delusion of grandeur, the progress of his persecution mania—all this is handled with remarkable understanding. This story by a young man of twenty-five reveals an uncanny knowledge of the working of a diseased mind. It is hard to say how much of this knowledge was the fruit of self-knowledge. He did speak of "The Double" as "a confession." The theme of the story—that of a man in conflict with his double —may have been suggested to him by his reading, particularly Hoffman. The story, however, was less the product of literature than of experience, reflecting as it did the dangerous movements of a soul bent, Narcissuslike, over itself. It is a subject from which a man of Dostoevsky's temperament might well have shrunk. The fact that he was able to delve into these matters and even to inject some of the classic humour of the situation into his tale argues that when he occupied himself with it he had the requisite degree of mental stability. It is noteworthy that he only attempted it after he was heartened by the enthusiastic reception of *Poor Folk*. Further, it is probable that the writing of it helped to sustain him, and postponed the breakdown which he suffered later. Having projected certain abnormal tendencies of his own, he was, if only for a time, free of them. In fine, "The Double" tapped a deeper level of the author's mind than its predecessor did, and was more clearly prophetic of his powers as a master of psychology.

Dostoevsky recognized the shortcomings of his story. It was tedious in the telling, and hallucination and reality were not made to dovetail sufficiently well. At the same time he knew that in "The Double" he had hit upon a theme of true originality and importance. Many years afterwards he planned to rewrite the piece, so as to bring out its latent possibilities. He did not carry out his intention, but variations on the theme run through his mature work.

In his next piece, "Mr. Prokharchin," he worked the same vein that he had explored in "The Double." Here too the character around whom the lugubrious story revolves is a petty clerk, an utterly insignificant, utterly lonely creature, cut off from his kind. He is even more humbly circumstanced than the man pursued by his double and, indeed, ostensibly possesses nothing but a box with a German lock. The box contains only rags, but his dirty mattress proves to be stuffed with coin. His hoarding grows out of his morbid fear of want, and the money is doubly precious to him, as it is a crutch for his tottering ego. Malicious waggery on the part of his fellow-roomers throws him into a panic about the little security that he has. In his delirium, his latent sense of guilt asserts itself. His reason goes, and death follows his mental collapse. The glint and clink of gold are seldom absent from Dostoevsky's pages: as he was constantly plagued by the need of money, so too he was haunted by the idea of its peculiar power, here for the first time a dominant note.

II

Shortly after the completion of "Mr. Prokharchin," Dostoevsky, as will be recalled, attempted a new story, which he called "The Shaved Whiskers," but gave it up in disgust, as a mere repetition of what he had previously done. For a while he tried his hand at journalism, publishing four feuilletons in the daily, *Sanktpeterburgskie vedomosti* (St. Petersburg Bulletin). The genre, then flourishing in France, was becoming popular in Russia. What attracted him to this type of writing was its informal, intimate tone, its easy freedoms, the opportunities it offered for setting down random opinions, observations, fantasies. He was to return to it in later years, enlarging his scope.

When he returned to fiction, it was to start out on a new tack. His next work, "The Landlady," is quite unlike the writing that preceded it in its departure from the realistic method. It is a melodramatic tale, teeming with madness and mystery. Ordynov, a young recluse, who lives with his books and his dreams, is drawn out of his self-communings by a weird amorous adventure. The beautiful creature who is the object of his ecstasies is under the spell of an old man gifted with occult powers and subject to epileptic seizures. She, too, has strange fits caused by her belief that she is responsible for the death of her parents. And as for Ordynov, he passes from one sinking spell to another. Is the wild story of her life, as she relates it to the half delirious Ordynov, the invention of a madwoman? Is her aged husband the quondam brigand and assassin that she makes him out to be? Did the old man actually try to shoot Ordynov, and did Ordynov really attempt to knife the old man? It was not the author's intention to furnish an answer to these questions. There is a constant confusion of fact with the stuff of revery. The story concludes with the parting of the young people, and Ordynov is abruptly thrust back into the state of self-centred brooding in which he was first found. What had drawn him had been not a true light but a will-o'-the-wisp; robbed of it, he sank back into a deeper shadow.

Belinsky said of the story that it was "a monstrosity," and that there was not a word in it that was not false, stilted, and artificial.

One cannot agree with this harsh judgement. Looking closely at this strange narrative, one finds here and there a hint of power, a token of startling insight. There is something at once original and authentic in the description of Ordynov's delirium. One is brought up short by the girl's confession that at bottom she cherishes her shame—an attitude of which more will be heard later—and by the old man's casual remark that freedom is an unendurable burden to the weak spirit, an idea to which Dostoevsky will return. Indeed, both Ordynov and the young woman, with whom he falls in love, exemplify the tragedy of the faint heart.

The author was shrewd enough to recognize that the romantic vein exploited in "The Landlady" was foreign to him. In his next story, "Polzunkov," he returned to his first manner and offered a character study of great inwardness. The central figure is a man who habitually makes a clown of himself in order to borrow a few roubles from the people whom he amuses. At the same time he feels shame for those whom he provokes to this ugly laughter and snatches eagerly at any fig leaf to cover his moral nakedness. His effort, while making a butt of himself, to win a grain of respect from those who jeer at him is a disturbing and pathetic spectacle. The protagonist of the story may have been related to the drunkard who haunted the Petersburg suburb in which Dostoevsky spent the summer of 1847. When other sources failed, the wretch would canvass the cottages, offering to flog himself for a consideration. Dostoevsky took up a collection for him.

In the tale that followed, "A Faint Heart," Dostoevsky is again dealing with insanity. Once more the main character is a humble copying clerk, a young man with a gentle spirit and a sad flaw in his make-up. Feeling himself a nonentity, he is literally overwhelmed with gratitude for what he conceives to be undeserved good fortune and by his inability to express that gratitude. His mind breaks under the strain, not of suffering, but of happiness.

Unlike most of the early stories, "An Honest Thief," which appeared next, deals not with petty officials or intellectuals, but with a man of the people. The tale is told by a veteran who has turned tailor to support himself in his old age. It has to do with a drunken derelict whom the tailor had taken in and allowed to live on his charity. The wretch repaid this kindness by stealing a pair of riding-breeches his benefactor had made for a customer, and did not confess until remorse brought him literally to his death-bed. Here is another broken soul that has no power to mend itself. In the original version the narrator appends a moral to the tale: that the death of the poor devil attested to the human dignity that he had all but forfeited by his crime, and that vice is not a native element of human nature. Dostoevsky wisely omitted this post-script in the later editions of this well-rounded and moving story, probably realizing that the tale itself pointed the moral with suffi-cient clarity and force. As for the successor to this piece, "A Christ-mas Tree and a Wedding," which exposes the ugly character of a schemer who manages to marry an heiress young enough to be his daughter, one might be inclined to neglect it altogether as a bagatelle, were it not that these few pages carry, however lightly, the suggestion of that sexual interest in a child on the part of an adult which recurs not infrequently in his mature writings.

"White Nights," the last of his early stories, if one excepts the piece he wrote in prison, presents a situation similar to that retailed in "The Landlady." The difference is that here the action is within the range of the usual and the characters are within the range of the normal. The hero, as in the other story, is a daydreamer, un-fitted for life, who falls in love, only to lose his lady, and retire again into himself. During the brief period of his happiness it is as though the mists of fantasy had melted from before his eyes and he feels himself at last a man among men. The ghost, having, as it were, drunk of human passion, is about to take on flesh. But no! The girl, who loves another from whom she has been sepa-rated, is beginning to reciprocate his affection when her beloved returns and carries her off. What seemed to have the heat and colour of reality proves a mirage. The experience leaves the young man sadder but not sourer, and the piece ends on a note of gentle resignation that is in key with the wistful tone of the entire story.

I I I

If that winter morning on Semyonov Square had been Dostoev-sky's last, we should have had no full-length novel from his pen, but only the torso of one, namely, the ill-fated *Netochka Nezvanova*.

He began to hatch the plan for a big novel soon after the publication of "The Double." Before long he was speaking of a novel in four parts which was ripe in his mind and which he expected to write in Italy. It gave him no rest. The final issue of *Fatherland Notes* for 1846 carried an announcement that "*Netochka Nezvanova*, a novel by Dostoevsky" would run in the magazine the next year, and indeed he obligated himself to deliver the first instalment of the work on January 5, 1847. But it did not materialize, and the final issue for that year again contained a notice promising it to the subscribers the following year. The first instalment which included two parts, did not appear until 1849, and at the time of his arrest he was up to his neck in the writing of another instalment. The third part appearing without his signature while he was in prison awaiting sentence, he read it in his cell with some misgivings, since he had not seen it through the press. There were to be at least three more parts, but presumably since too much had happened to him in the interim, when he returned to literature he did not take up the work where he had been forced to drop it. Neverthless, he allowed a revised version of the incomplete novel to appear in his collected works. The revision was chiefly in the nature of cutting, an entire incident being omitted from the text.

In *Netochka Nezvanova* he attempted an ambitious work with a complicated plot. Originally the novel had as its sub-title "The History of a Woman." It is a somewhat loose-jointed affair and, indeed, even in its present fragmentary shape contains three distinct themes. The first is the tragic story of a musician with a great talent which through a fatal weakness in his nature he allows to go to waste. The second theme is the childhood of his little stepdaughter, Netochka, who is morbidly attached to him, and who, when he dies of "acute mania," is adopted into an aristocratic family, where she forms a passionate affection for the small daughter of the house. The third has to do with the consequences of a suspected infidelity on the part of the lady who is so tenderly bringing up the waif. Here for the first time Dostoevsky uses a mysterious letter as part of the machinery of his plot. The procedure is clumsy, and in every respect this third part is the weakest.

The tale is chiefly remarkable for the illumination of the emotional and imaginative life of children, its intensity, sensuality, and paradoxical ambivalence. Netochka, as a little girl, loves her step-father with a strange passion grounded in pity. All her joy is to think of him. She imagines him to be a harassed sufferer, abused by her mother, and accordingly conceives a deep hatred for that unfortunate woman. She is driven in upon herself, gradually loses contact with reality, and moves in a world of fantasy. Her relation with the proud little princess, like that with her father previously, is in the nature of a love affair having all the tokens of adolescent passion. The little princess, too, adores her own father, has strained relations with her mother, and feels a violent affection for Netochka, although this love for some time disguises itself as hatred.

Originally Dostoevsky intended to give Netochka a male counter-part. The passage in which this character was introduced figures only in the text of the novel as published serially, having been omitted from the revised version. Like Netochka, he is a poor orphan, a crushed and terror-stricken little creature rescued by the prince from a life among hostile strangers. With great difficulty Netochka wins his confidence, and he tells her that at the bottom of his misery is the unbearable thought that he is partly responsible for the death of his parents—they died within a few days of each other. He confesses to Netochka that out of sheer selfishness he had practically tormented his father and mother to death, but the little girl sees more deeply into the situation. She understands that he really loved his parents, but out of a desire to realize fully their devotion to him, he perversely made them suffer on his account. At the same time his confession awakens her to the consciousness of the suffering that she had caused her own mother, and arouses in her a like feeling of guilt.

At the outset Dostoevsky had spoken of the novel as "a con-fession." In the story of the unfortunate musician with which it opens there are passages which have an autobiographic ring. It is more probable, however, that in portraying the inner life of Net-ochka, of the little girl with whom she was in love, of the little boy who was to be the hero, he was unburdening his heart of the tan-gled emotions that belonged to his own early years. Certainly he could not draw upon observation. While he was writing the story he was living outside of a domestic circle, and most of his friends were young unmarried men like himself. He saw little of Mikhail's children and had been separated for years from his own small brothers and sisters. It is hard to see how he could have written some of these pages without an extraordinarily clear retrospective view of his own childhood.

Netochka Nezvanova reveals such an interest in, and understanding of, both childhood and early adolescence that it is not surprising to find "The Little Hero," the piece which he wrote in the fortress, dealing with a similar theme. "The Little Hero" is the story of an eleven-year-old boy's first experience of falling in love, an experience which, alike in its raptures and its agonies, held a troubling foretaste of maturity. A wistful note steals into the narrative toward the end, but the setting is a country house where elegant ladies and handsome men are gathered for a festive occasion, and a brightness appropriate to the tale, if unusual with the author, lies on the story like a bloom. The introduction, which was omitted from the final version, is in the form of a monologue, in which the narrator, sitting before the fire of a wintry night, while the storm drubs the pane "with bony fingers," soliloquizes on the kind of tale that he is going to offer his companion, a girl on the threshold of womanhood. It is to be a story not so long-winded as to allow her to lose interest, not so moving as to draw tears, or yet so amusing as to rouse laughter, not frightening, because last night she had had bad dreams—in short, something quiet, soothing, and withal fascinating. As he delimits the tale in this fashion, one imagines Dostoevsky himself setting forth the requirements as to the kind of fantasy that he dares play with in his lonely cell. The narrative thus seems to have offered the author a refuge from his own sorry situation, but this in no wise detracts from its significance as a study of the awakening of the senses in a young boy.

IV

It is fairly clear from these early stories what were the literary influences that worked upon Dostoevsky. The major force in Russian letters at this time was the romantic humorist, Gogol, who ushered in the age of prose that followed Pushkin's death. It should be rememebered that Turgenev was still a mere budding author and Tolstoy, a lad in his late teens, was occupied with the studies and amusements of an undergraduate. In dubbing Dostoevsky "a second Gogol," his contemporaries were referring to certain tricks of style, but more particularly to the fact that he chose to deal with those humbly stationed characters who were the stock figures of the so-called Natural school. It is not difficult to discover traces of the foreign authors that he devoured so greedily—the fantast, Hoffman, as well as the sensational and sentimental writers of both France and England. But it is harder to catch him in the act of paying the tribute of imitation to his youthful idols, Schiller and Balzac.

Superficially less of the stuff of Dostoevsky's personal history found its way into these stories than is usually the case with a man's early writings. Many of the things that filled his hours are absent from his pages. Thus, one would not guess from them that he had ever studied military engineering, or that most of his acquaintances were cultivated, and some comfortably situated people. That he kept out of his work the dangerous social and political ideas that were bandied about at Petrashevsky's and elsewhere is not surprising. Under Nicholas I such notions could not find their way into print. At the same time there were means, for those who sought them earnestly, of expressing, if indirectly, a protest against social evils, and indeed, many of those who read *Poor Folk* in Nekrasov's miscellany saw in it an indictment of the social order which produces such wretchedness. Yet with each successive story Dostoevsky made it harder for his readers to see in his work anything approaching criticism of the system under which he was living.

It is only when one looks closely at the writings of this first period, that one discovers here and there settings and situations that are directly traceable to his own experiences. The gleaming field of the frozen Neva; the black canals with their lean lampposts along the embankments; the Petersburg streets in all seasons and all weathers, but chiefly at dusk, and when the granite is wet underfoot and the sooty houses loom dark and bulky on the riverfront; damp, filthy, ill-smelling stairways leading to rooms with grimy green walls which exude a putrid odour—these made the familiar framework of his own days. It is not implausible that the match in *Poor Folk* had some distant connection with his young sister's marriage to the middle-aged Karepin, especially as the situation repeats itself in Dostoevsky's later work. Ill health, particularly nervous ailments, is the lot of several of his characters, as it was his own. They suffer from severe depressions and have moments of ecstasy when their consciousness is almost unbearably intensified— states that he also knew. The *flâneur* in "The Landlady" who "did not miss a single impression and looked with thoughtful eyes into the faces of passing people, watched the characteristic aspect of every- thing around him, and listened lovingly to the speech of the peo- ple, as though verifying in everything the conclusions that had been formed in the stillness of solitary nights"—this *flâneur* walked in the shoes of Fyodor Dostoevsky. One cannot escape the feeling that the delirious dream of this character is based upon the author's actual experience. The narrator in "White Nights" who knows some houses in Petersburg so intimately that they seem to him almost human is also no other than Dostoevsky: is he not said to have walked miles just to see a particular building in a certain light?

The hero of "White Nights," as well as the hero of "The Land- lady," resembled him in a more fundamental respect. Like these creations of his, he too was a man who wasted himself in daydream- ing. But unlike them, he recognized the dangers he incurred and was able to overcome them, though perhaps not as fully as he believed. Maturity, tardy and incomplete though it was, brought him a saving sense of reality. The very bitterness with which he harped upon this theme indicates how deeply he had suffered from the ravages of fantasy. Both "White Nights" and "The Landlady," it will be remembered, are stories of men who shipwrecked on the coast of dreams. In each case, the failure of the young man to win a woman seems to be symbolic of his fatal inability to become suffi- ciently attached to anything outside of himself. At the time when Dostoevsky was busy with the latter tale he was writing to Mik- hail about the risks involved in a surrender to fantasy, and the necessity for establishing a balance between the inner life and that other existence in which one must cope with the actual world. It was evident that he knew whereof he spoke. One of his feuille- tons mentioned above offered an anatomy of daydreaming that he later incorporated into "White Nights" in an expanded and slightly altered form. He was undoubtedly helped in this dissec- tion by his gift for self-analysis.

The dreamer, he wrote, is a man with a lust for life but with a weakness in his make-up that hinders him from satisfying his appetites. They come to depend for food upon his imagination. His fantasy is nimble, mercurial, febrile. It seizes upon a hint, a nothing, and builds an airy world, staging melodramatic conflicts within it on a heroic scale. Space shrinks, time abdicates. No fabulous island is too remote for the dreamer's habitation. He packs a lifetime into an hour. Thrilled and soothed by his reveries, he craves more and more these insubstantial excitements, without allowing himself to become aware of the poisons his self-indulgence is distilling. With the exaltation of a lover yet with the self-absorption and instability of a child, he leads his inane existence. Gradually, he loses his sense of the actual, and that moral instinct which holds reality inviolate. Life wears a hostile look for him. He walks through it with averted eyes, dreading every new situation, fearful of having to meet the world on its own terms. Fancying himself in a golden nook, the haunted troglodyte does not see that he is living in a dingy corner.

Dostoevsky came to believe that it was something in the nature of a sudden illumination that freed him from the dangers of idle revery. Only yesterday he had been living among ghosts, fancying himself a Pericles, a Marius, a Christian martyr, a knight riding into the lists, a hero out of Walter Scott. And suddenly men and women of flesh and blood swam into his view—ordinary people with whom he rubbed elbows, but who were none the less fantastic creatures. It was as though in a flash he understood that a simple clerk, a poor student, was as remarkable, as strange, as absorbing, as any figure in history or romance, if one but tried to plumb the secret of his being. His imaginative passion now fastened not upon the figments of his youthful fancy, but on the lodger next door, the child on the wooden pavement below. He shook off the stupor of the daydreamer, and gained a foothold on the common earth. His fantasy had been like a plant with aerial roots; now it was gripping the soil.

The episode that he thought marked this crucial point in his development occurred in his early manhood. He described it in the course of a chatty essay he contributed to a magazine many years later. The description, oddly enough, includes a passage on the appearance of the Neva in the winter dusk lifted bodily out of his early story, "The Faint Heart." On a bitter January evening as he was hurrying home, he halted on the river-front to watch the sunset sky. The smoke was building an ethereal city above the snow-locked streets and the glittering river, and the real city looked as insubstantial as a dream. It was one of those moments when the world sets the senses vibrating so exquisitely that they seem to be keyed to a truth beyond their grasp. Ambiguous though his report of the experience is, the implication seems to be clear: he was startled into a perception of the mysterious, the fantastic, quality of reality itself. From that wintry sunset on the Neva—he called the moment a vision—he dated the beginning of his "existence": his birth as a writer.

Dostoevsky's first story does appear to be the work of a man who suddenly becomes aware of the humdrum life around him, not as something to eschew, but as something to marvel at and pore over. Yet the impulse behind most of his early work was not so much a desire to retail the circumstances of the lodger next door and the child on the wooden pavement below. What worked itself out here was a curiosity about the naked self, particularly in a diseased state. Underlying his understanding of others was his insight into certain dispositions and emotional mechanisms of his own. From the first, literature was for him not escape from himself, but rather a form of confession. He used that term in speaking of at least two of his more important stories.

At this early period the avowals are indirect, veiled, ambiguous. One is struck by the fact that many of these tales deal with humble, helpless people, people with a weak hold on reality, personalities so defective that they break down readily under strain, so stunted that they are doomed to solitude. It is conceivable that in identifying himself with these dwarfed, thwarted souls Dostoevsky was gratifying his secret sense of his own insufficiency. His interest in the theme of "The Double"—an interest that was to remain with him to the last—may have fed on an awareness of the duality of his own nature. A sick soul, divided against itself, may project its division in the form of a "double," which assumes a distressing reality for the sufferer; the artist, tormented by a similar split in his nature, follows a similar process, but is able to reduce his double to a mere symbol and to confine it within the bounds of a work of the imagination. As has already been indicated, these studies of men wrecked by their inability to meet life on its own terms had for him a therapeutic value. That they should conclude with remarkable disclosures of what lies in the hearts of children seems only natural. It was as though Dostoevsky in trying to understand himself was moving up the stream of his memories to its source.

CHAPTER NINE

BURIED ALIVE

THE SLOW frosty dawn of a brilliant winter day was just breaking as the little caravan of sleighs approached the town
of Schlüsselburg. The travellers had made the forty miles
from Petersburg in a night. The trip in the open air had given a
sharp edge to Dostoevsky's appetite, and he attacked his breakfast as though he had gone without food for a week. The heart-
ache he had felt on leaving Petersburg had somehow been eased by
the journey, and the brisk weather and the glimpses of Christmas
trees heartened him. The sun shone on the clean snow and brought
out the colour in the scarlet sashes of the grey-kaftaned drivers—
they changed at every station. What with the holiday, food at the
roadside inns was plentiful, and through the generosity of the
Government courier, a friendly old soul, they were provided with
good meals. The sleighs glided on, past snowbound villages and
forlorn towns, first in a southerly direction, and then straight east,
against the sun. Choosing the less frequented roads, they followed
virtually the very route traversed by those aristocratic convicts, the
Decembrists, a quarter of a century earlier. As the days wore
on, the cold became unendurable, and they were transferred to
covered sleighs. In spite of this Dostoevsky froze "to the heart."
In the province of Perm one night they struck Arctic weather
—forty degrees below zero. He did not know how he lived through
it.

As he put home further behind him, his mood sagged. The party
was in the Ural Mountains, crossing the borderline between the
two continents, when it was caught in a snowstorm. The sleighs
stuck in the drifts, and the convicts had to clamber out—a clumsy
job, what with the heavy irons on their legs. While the drivers
were struggling with the horses and the vehicles, Dostoevsky stood
still and peered into the tossing night. Behind him lay Europe and

his past, before him stretched Siberia, as dark as his future. His eyes filled.

He did not get a taste of the life that awaited him until he reached Tobolsk. It was then mid-January. The Tobolsk prison was a cross between a clearing house of crime and a hostelry for transient convicts. Before being assigned to their respective places of confinement or exile, all the condemned spent a brief period in these vile, congested, dilapidated cells. Dostoevsky and his two comrades were first taken to a large chamber, crowded with prisoners of both sexes and all ages. Some were having half of their heads shaved, as was prescribed, some were being clapped into irons, others, ready for the march to their final destination, were being chained in groups to an iron rod. In the foul air, against the grimy walls, these grotesque heads, these branded brows, these brutish snouts, were frightening to behold. Yet for Dostoevsky there must have been, as an antidote to his horror, that mixture of tenderness and curiosity that he had always felt in the presence of the humbled. Soon he would be one of them. Did the thought carry with it an overtone of bitter satisfaction?

There was little time for reflection. Dostoevsky and his companions were searched, a process during which he was relieved of all the money he had on his person, and then the three of them, half frozen and dog-tired, were locked into a cold cell together. Durov lay down on the bench that served as a bed. Dostoevsky and the other man, Jastrzembski, crouched on the dirty floor. It was a black hour. Jastrzembski spoke of suicide. Dostoevsky tried to put heart into him—of the three he was the least depressed. Finally, solace came in the shape of hot tea and a candle. Jastrzembski had been deprived of the rum he had bought at Kazan, but Dostoevsky still had a few cigars in his pocket, and what with the hot drink and the light and the tobacco, there was a kind of conviviality in the foul, narrow room.

The half dozen days that he had to stay here were not utterly bleak. Some of the Decembrists had settled in this Siberian town with their families, and the womenfolk, who with such high fortitude had followed their exiled husbands into the wilderness, made an opportunity to mother this new generation of political prisoners. Dostoevsky, like the five or six other members of Petrashevsky's circle who were temporarily confined here, received food at their hands, and warm clothing, of which he was in sore need. Above all, these contacts gave him the feeling that there were people beyond the walls to whom the prisoners were still human beings. These ladies—they were the wives and daughters of aristocrats—engineered a meeting with the prisoners at the warden's house. They tried to encourage the men, offered them practical advice, and gave each a copy of the New Testament, the only book permitted in prison. They took occasion to warn Dostoevsky—together with Durov he was to do his term at Omsk—that the warden there, a Major Krivtzov, was an ugly customer, whose viciousness was as limitless as his power over the convicts, and he was an autocrat of the prison. It was a cheerless prospect, and such glimpses as Dostoevsky caught of the men with whom he was to spend the next four years of his life chilled him to the bone.

One of the ladies who was especially kind to the Omsk convicts was Natalia Dmitrievna Fonvizina. She had high connections, being related to the Governor General of Western Siberia, and was therefore in a particularly happy position to help Dostoevsky. When the time came for him and Durov to set out for Omsk, Mme. Fonvizina, with a friend, saw the two of them off. It was an irregular procedure, but the ladies made sure that the escorting gendarmes should be complaisant. One of them was to transmit a letter from Mme. Fonvizina to an influential friend at Omsk, in which she begged him to take an interest in the two prisoners. In a bitter frost, the two women waited on the high road, several miles from the town, having taken care to leave their sleigh a good distance behind them, so that there should be no witness to the meeting. The *troikas* bearing the convicts halted, and with some clanging of irons the men climbed out to say their last farewells. Compared to Durov, with his regular features and black beard just then covered with icicles, Dostoevsky, in his heavy sheepskin coat and fur cap with earlaps, looked rather homely, frail, slight, and young.

II

When for the first time he lay down on the bare planks that for four years were to serve him as a bed, covering himself as best he might with his short sheepskin coat, he was fairly sick with the impressions of the day. It was afternoon when they had driven into the town of Omsk, a three days' journey from Tobolsk. They had at once been taken before the major of whom they had been warned. The pimpled purple face with eyes that glared maliciously through spectacles made Dostoevsky think of a spider about to pounce on a fly. The man was all he had been painted. Before dismissing them he promised them the lash for the slightest misdemeanour.

At the guardhouse Dostoevsky was shaved on one side of the head in the fashion prescribed for civilian convicts. All his own clothes were taken away from him—the major had told him plainly that a convict had no property—and he was given a parti-coloured suit of grey and black, with a yellow diamond on the back, a cap to match, and a new sheepskin coat. He was to change his linked fetters for irons made of rods, which were worn under the trousers and were less clumsy for work, but this was to wait till the next morning.

The short winter day had already turned to dusk when he passed through the sentinel-guarded gate and found himself within the high prison enclosure. The convicts were returning from work under escort and falling in, preparatory to roll-call. A bewhiskered non-commissioned officer opened the door of the prison barracks, a long, low log house, and Dostoevsky got his first sickening whiff of prison air. All at once the low-ceiled room, dark except for the light of a few tallow candles, filled up with men, and the stench thickened. Then the doors were locked for the night. Dostoevsky, like everyone else, had three planks on which to stretch his body, soaked with iodine and mercury. Until sleep released him, he must struggle to breathe this air, heavy with the smells of unwashed bodies, of vile smoke, and of the uncovered night-pot in the ante-room, must watch with scared greedy eyes the haggard branded faces, the ragged grimy figures, and, even when he lay with closed lids, must listen to the oaths, the guffaws, the thin clank of irons.

He awoke in the dark, shivering with cold. A drum beat the reveille at the prison gate, and the doors were being unlocked. The air was chilly and intolerably foul. The convicts stretched and yawned, sullen with sleep. They crowded around the two pails of water. Each one took the dipper, filled his mouth with water, and washed his face and hands from his mouth. There was wrangling over the single dipper. Breakfast consisted of bread and *kvass*. To get it, Dostoevsky followed the other prisoners across the yard in the grey light of dawn to a neighbouring building, which was at once kitchen and messroom. While the others were mustered out to work beyond the walls, he was sent to the smithy to have his fetters changed. The first three days a convict was allowed to rest from the fatigues of the journey, and so he returned to the barracks. He got there near mess hour, when some of the prisoners were already coming back from work.

In all his comings and goings he was conscious of hostile eyes furtively watching him, this newcomer, this "gentleman." But there were a few convicts who, smelling money on the "gentleman"—he had indeed succeeded in smuggling in a few roubles in the binding of his New Testament—made up to him, showing him how to wear the fetters, procuring a box with a lock on it for his clothes, helping him to get a teapot of his own, as many of the prisoners managed to do. After mess, when he had gagged over the cockroaches in the cabbage soup, he was able to comfort himself and Durov with a pot of tea. The two of them were sitting quietly over their cups when a convict, a slouching hulk of a man, furious with drink, lumbered into the messroom, followed by an entertainer in the shape of a little fellow with a fiddle, also a convict. At once the giant, Gazin by name, began taunting the two tea-drinkers, for whom the prison fare was not good enough. Dostoevsky and his companion thought best to ignore the bully, and this enraged him further. He snatched up the first weapon that came to hand—a huge, heavy tray. The rest did not move a finger to defend the newcomers. For a breathless second it seemed as though the two of them would have their heads bashed in. A sudden shout from the passage: "Gazin, your vodka's stolen!" diverted his attention at the crucial instant and saved them. That evening after dusk Dostoevsky walked beside the fence, and with a sick heart pondered the day behind him and the years ahead, until the drum summoned him back to his second night in the barracks.

The adjustment to his new surroundings was painful in the extreme. He suffered cruelly in mind and body. Soon after his arrival in the prison, authorities there had been informed that it was the emperor's will that both Dostoevsky and Durov should be shown no leniency, but should be treated as convicts "in the full sense of the word." Major Krivtzov, "Eight-Eyes," as the inmates called the warden because of his eyeglasses, needed no such injunction: spiteful, vengeful, unrestrained, he behaved as though all the prisoners without distinction were his natural enemies. He would have a man flogged for sleeping on his right side, because, he said, Christ slept on his left, and so everyone should do likewise. True, several influential persons were disposed in Dostoevsky's favour, but they were practically powerless in a town crawling with sycophants and self-appointed spies. At one time some officers on guard duty went out of their way to spare him certain hardships, but he seemed to resent their kindness. It was as though he took a bitter pleasure in his sufferings. For a while he did clerical work in the prison office, but this did not last long. He bore the full brunt of penal servitude. He was doing his term in a fortress prison, which, being subject to a strict military régime, was worse than the Siberian civil prisons connected with mines or mills. He was always in the prison motley, with half-scraped head, always in irons, always under guard, always under lock and key when not at work. The prison population was a mixed crowd, in which practically every type of criminal and every section of the immense country was represented. With the exception of Dostoevsky and Durov and a few Poles, who were also political offenders, all were common criminals—burglars, counterfeiters, murderers. "The devil must have worn out three pair of shoes before he brought us all here," they would say of themselves.

They were herded in two decrepit log houses, long since condemned as unfit for habitation. The ward to which Dostoevsky was assigned held about thirty men. Here they lived "all in a heap," as he put it. The roof leaked, and the walls were draughty. The wooden floor was rotten through and through and slippery with filth, though a convict was delegated to scrub it. As for the men, they got baths only on the eve of high holidays, and the dirty, steamy, crowded bath-house made Dostoevsky think hell must be something like that. The inmates stank "like swine," as he wrote to Mikhail, adding: "They say they can't help being swinish, for they're 'living human beings.' " In winter the tiny windows were always dimmed with thick frost, and the place was so cold that the water in the pails froze. The convicts did their laundry indoors, and the room was flooded with slops. The stove, for which only six logs were allotted at a time, gave off not so much heat as poisonous fumes, which at best produced a sick headache. The warm months were even more difficult to bear. The work day was longer and harder, and the nights were agony, what with the stifling air, and the sleeping-platform alive with fleas, lice, bedbugs, and cockroaches that murdered sleep.

III

Now he knew what it meant to be buried alive. It was as though the oldtime fears that had haunted the couch of the promising young author were realized. He was walled in, weighted down, encompassed by a darkness that was all the more terrifying because it could not be struck at or wrestled with. Sometimes it was not the darkness of the grave but that of the jungle. He was surrounded by the faces of men like beasts. And what added to the nightmare quality of the experience, they were like one face, depraved, spiteful, cunning, cruel.

Slowly his eyes grew used to the heavy gloom. The faces became distinct one from another, and began to look human. Here, it dawned upon him, were men much like himself. Were they not Russians? Were they not his brothers? He felt a strong curiosity about them, a deep kinship with these guilty ones. On the whole, the men behind the prison walls were no worse than those who remained outside. Indeed, he discovered among these jail-birds men of great spiritual strength, and some capable of the purest compassion. Under the ugly exterior there was a native human excellence. There were criminals who commanded his respect, there were those who won his reluctant affection.

Life in the prison was life still. It asserted itself in this bleak place like grass thrusting its way between slabs of granite. The brutal severity of the prison regimen was to some degree corrected by an equally incredible laxity and disregard of the rules and regulations. The convicts were not permitted to do any work for themselves or to own money. Nevertheless, as soon as the doors were locked for the evening, the barracks would turn into a humming workshop.

Many pursued a craft, some engaged in buying and selling and in financial transactions of sorts, and there were even those who hired themselves out to their mates as entertainers, lookout men, and factotums. Everybody managed to earn something, and with the aid of the money secured some semblance of the amenities. They ate other than prison food. Cards, tobacco, and vodka were strictly forbidden, yet they gambled, smoked, and got drunk—and the more enterprising got themselves women.

It is uncertain whether or not Dostoevsky learned a craft well enough to ply it in prison. He did, however, generally have a little money in his pockets, and so lived up to his comrades' notion of him as a "gentleman." Like the others, he understood that money here was not merely a means of obtaining a few pleasures, but was doubly precious as a symbol of freedom, the dream even of the "lifers." The convicts sweated for money and seized upon it greedily, but they also used it in the most spendthrift fashion, fearing it would be snatched from them before they could enjoy it.

Of course, all infringements of discipline were made under peril of reprisals. "Eight-Eyes" would descend like the wolf on the fold. Goods and money would be confiscated, and the offenders flogged. The high holidays, Christmas and Easter, were the rare occasions on which relaxation of discipline was, if not sanctioned, at least connived at by the prison officials. Sometimes even amateur theatricals were allowed, and then, if ever, the convicts forgot their fetters.

Forced labour was the least harassing feature of the situation. Work, though compulsory, was in itself a purposeful and, to an extent, satisfying activity. True, occasionally one had to work in the open, exposed to the rain or to bitter cold. But generally, the conditions of labour were tolerable. Having no trade, Dostoevsky was listed in the prison register as a "common labourer." When he was with a gang, his fellows, out of spiteful contempt for the "gentleman," would try to prevent him from taking part in the common task, such as the wrecking of an old barge. What irked him was the thought that the prisoners who could not possibly believe in a *barin's* readiness to get callouses on his hands were mistaking his zeal for an attempt to make up to them, and were thus justified in despising him. But he insisted on his rights to work, and in the end won out. He baked and pounded alabaster, turned a lathe in the prison workshop, carried bricks as a mason's apprentice, shovelled snow. In his eagerness to work he was guided by a healthy instinct. He was obeying a lusty will to live. The rough physical labour toughened his body and saved him from too much brooding. To get away from the prison, to catch a glimpse, on the shores of Irtysh, of the prairie under the open sky and the smoke-blackened tent of a nomad, merely to be out of sight of the fortress, with its oppressive buildings, its sentinel endlessly pacing the earthen wall, this was to taste, in some measure, relief, to be strengthened against misery.

There was one other escape. Occasionally, at night when sleep would not come, his imagination led him out of the foul gloom of the barracks. Scenes enacted themselves, characters wearing their fate like fetters worked out their destiny before his closed eyes. He elaborated certain ideas and trends of thought. Some of these imaginings had the quality and evanescence of dreams, but even though he could set nothing down, much of his mature work must have germinated in the darkness of those prison vigils. One night while he was lying on his hard planks, sunk in a mood of depression and self-analysis, he conceived the idea for a great and profound novel. It was to be, of course, his "confession" and, at the same time, his supreme and final work. Was it the vast narrative that he outlined later under the title of *The Life of a Great Sinner?* There is a bare possibility that he even set down some notes on paper, but if he made any at all, they must have been few and scattered. What tormented him was the fear that his passion for the subject would have evaporated when he came to execute it. Not to be able to do more than think and plan was a terrible ordeal.

His mental sufferings were aggravated by the implacable hostility of his fellow convicts. A man of the people arriving in prison found himself among equals and was without question admitted into the confraternity. As a "gentleman," Dostoevsky was an outcast among outcasts. At the end of his prison term, it seemed to him that he had lived all the time encompassed by an unyielding wall of hatred. "They would have devoured us if we had let them," he wrote Mikhail of himself and Durov. " 'You, gentlefolk, have iron beaks, you've pecked us to death; you used to be masters and tortured the people, and now you're lower than the lowest, you're one of us!'—that's the theme on which variations were played for four years. A hundred and fifty enemies couldn't tire of persecution —it was their pleasure, diversion, occupation." This was painting the picture blacker than the reality. As a matter of fact, there were several of his fellows there who grew to be fond of him, and whose liking he returned. But even these always looked upon him as different from themselves, a member of another class. The chasm between the classes was never so clearly present to Dostoevsky as in this place and at this time.

For his own part, he was eager to get close to these people. One Easter day, to escape the drinking, gambling, and fighting that marked the holiday in prison, he lay down on his cot, pretending sleep, and sank into memories of childhood. He remembered vividly the moment in the copse when he had been frightened by the cry of "wolf" and had run to the peasant Marey for protection. And as he sat up, roused by the remembrance, and looked at his fellow convicts, his hatred of them dropped away, and he asked himself if his shorn, branded neighbour hoarsely shouting a drunken song was not perhaps another Marey. It is doubtful, however, whether at this time he had that conviction of the virtues of the common people which was to become so firm an article of his creed. In any case, he could form no ties with his fellows. For one thing, he was unwilling to surrender any of the manners and opinions of a cultivated man. He had, too, a sullen, forbidding demeanour that perforce made a solitary of him. Durov's companionship was no help— in fact, as time went on the two men came to hate each other as only those forced to live together can.

Because of the unfriendly atmosphere, the lack of privacy was particularly trying. Never had he imagined the horrors inherent in this prison communism. There were times when he bitterly hated everyone around him, feeling that these forced companions were stealing his life from him. To be alone was as fundamental a need with him as the craving for food. He knew he was wrong, but he could not overcome his repugnance.

There was one place of refuge, the military hospital located outside the fortress. There was filth even there, in spite of a superficial tidiness, there were lice, there were the eternal fetters—they were

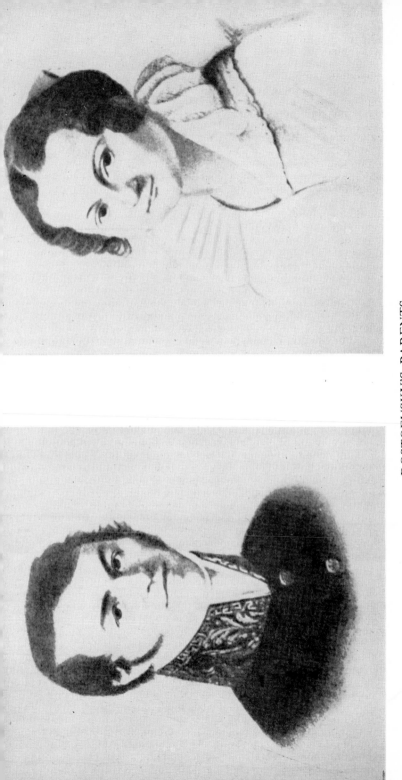

DOSTOEVSKY'S PARENTS

Drawn in pastel in 1823 by Popov

removed from the convict only after death—there was the tainted depressing air of the sick room. The days dragged on, long, dismal, monotonous, and the nights lay heavily on the sleepers and the sleepless alike. Yet, with the connivance of the doctors, who were equally kind to sick prisoners and to malingerers, Dostoevsky went there often. It was a change. There were new faces, the discipline was less severe, the food was less disgusting, and, above all, it offered an escape from the spite, the envy, the enmity. The prisoners were treated more like human beings, and behaved more like them. All kinds and conditions of men were gathered here; local convicts, men on their way to other prisons, men who had just been sentenced, civilians and soldiers who were awaiting trial, prisoners from the disciplinary battalion. Men talked to each other more freely than they did in the barracks, and Dostoevsky hung greedily on every word. He made the most of this opportunity for sinking himself in the life of the people, he stored up mental notes.

Sometimes toward evening a man half dead from a flogging would be brought into the ward. The attendant would at once try to remove the splinters from the back of the victim, which was a mass of bleeding wounds, and then cover it with a cloth soaked in urine—this was supposed to reduce the pain and the inflammation. At such moments Dostoevsky, trembling with excitement and horror, would hover about the attendants. Everything connected with this savage punishment had a tremendous fascination for him. He would beg the attendants to save the man's life: it was not seldom that convicts died after having been treated to the sticks. For one of the male nurses who was particularly merciful, Dostoevsky made a clothes-brush in token of his gratitude.

The story goes that he himself was subjected to a flogging and that it was in consequence of this that he became an epileptic. This must be dismissed as a legend. True, it was while he was in prison that he recognised for the first time that he was suffering from epilepsy. He believed that he contracted the falling sickness during his first year there, and had no memory of the seizures that preceded his arrest, nor did he connect his ailment with anything that happened to him in his earlier years. This bears out Freud's statement that a neurotic's account of the course of his ailment is apt to be untrustworthy: "Experience shows," he writes, "that their memories introduce falsifications designed to break down an unpleasant casual connection." A week after Dostoevsky was discharged from penal servitude he was writing to Mikhail: "My bad nerves brought on the falling sickness, but the attacks are rare." He added that he also suffered from rheumatism, but that the hysteria of the preceding years was gone. Most unexpectedly, he proved equal to the rigours of prison life. In a sense they benefited him: they cured him of his melancholia and hypochondria. He did not imagine ills any more.

Miseries of body and mind were of the essence of his situation. What more natural than that he should cry out from the depths to the Christ of his childhood? His only reading was the New Testament. Every time he returned to it he found another word of solace. It affirmed the divine character of every human being that breathed, irrespective of his fortunes. It spoke of mercy to the sinner, it spoke of comfort to the sufferer, it promised beatitude to the humbled, the persecuted, the hated, the outcast. It offered life more abundant to the living, and to the dead, resurrection. He read of the raising of Lazarus (was he not himself entombed?); of the casting out of the devils (had he not been among the possessed?); of the changing of water into wine at the marriage in Cana of Galilee (would joy yet be poured out for him too?). The phrases and parables that had been the common-places of his early days, the older familiar stories of the miracles, must have taken on for the convict a new meaning, an astonishing reality. Dostoevsky put into the mouth of a character in his last novel the words: "It is impossible for a convict to be without God." He felt that the criminals among whom he lived, though they were abandoned by the Church and crushed by the State, were deeply conscious of their sinfulness and clung all the more firmly to God, and he eventually came to believe that he had himself received the God he had all but lost, from the hands of these rough peasants, these thieves and murderers. It may be that they had robbed him of that faith in man's essential goodness and ultimate perfectibility which is the basis of humanitarianism, and it was thus that he had been compelled to rely more heavily upon divine aid. There is reason to think that his conviction of sin was part of his make-up; his imprisonment, then, could only have heightened his sense of guilt, and also, by punishment, assuaged it.

Furthermore, this very sense of guilt, which had its roots in his morbid character, made him long for atonement and inclined him the more strongly toward religiosity. Whatever peculiarities of his personality made him reach out for religion, his experience in prison strenghtened them.

Not that even now his faith was naïve and simple. His need to believe was terrible. He knew that while he lived he would not be free from doubt. All the more violently did he stamp upon his own thoughts. Where was his Saviour? The cross was real enough, the mob was real, the darkness real—but what of the resurrection? Yet somehow his very agony begot serenity. He knew moments of spiritual poise. In those moments he loved yes, even these oppressively close neighbours of his, and felt that he was loved in return. This was the peace that passeth understanding. It must come from God. Not so much God the Father as God the Son, an intimate, a humanized Deity, a divine Brother. If reason refuted him, perish reason! "In such moments," he wrote to the devout Mme. Fonvizina, referring to the intervals of grace, "I have composed within myself a confession of faith in which everything is clear and holy for me. This confession is very simple. Here it is: to believe that there is nothing more beautiful, more profound, more sympathetic, more reasonable, more manly, and more perfect than Christ. And I tell myself with jealous love that not only is there nothing, but indeed there can be nothing. Furthermore, if anyone proved to me that Christ was outside the truth, and it really was a fact that the truth was outside of Christ, I would rather remain with Christ than with the truth." Here is ostensibly a confession of simple faith, a reiteration of Tertullian's *"Credo quia absurdum."* From the point of view of Christian orthodoxy, this credo has a serious flaw. It is not without a tinge of blasphemy in admitting that he who said: "I am the way, the truth, and the life" could be in conflict with the truth. For the believer the conflict is unthinkable. Dostoevsky's plight was, one suspects, that to the end of his days he was unable wholly to reconcile Christ and the truth or to renounce either.

In *The Brothers Karamazov the* condemned man is warned that he may not be able to bear the cross of life in prison, that he may "cry quits," and become savage or embittered. Dostoevsky did not write this out of his own experience: he did not cry quits. Over and above his brief periods of serenity, which he took as gifts from Heaven, and in spite of his occasional rebellion, he accepted penal servitude with a resignation that argues aquiescence in the justice of his fate. Did he perhaps obscurely feel that he was getting his deserts, not for the trivial offence that he had actually committed, but for a monstrous crime that he had willed secretly, without his own knowledge? Certainly there was one element in his situation that gave him a strange and subtle pleasure. This was the humiliation to which he was subjected. He was among the lowest, one of those to whom even the poorest peasant referred as "an unfortunate" and offered alms. A Polish convict who was in Dostoevsky's ward, upon being tendered such an offering, proudly refused it: he was no common criminal, he exclaimed, but a political offender. Not so Dostoevsky. Early in his prison days, as he was returning to the barracks one evening under guard, he passed a simple woman with her little daughter. The child whispered something to her mother, who stopped and fumbled in her pocket for a coin. The child snatched it and ran after Dostoevsky to thrust it into his hand, saying: "Here, poor man, is a farthing, for Christ's sake!" He treasured this first alms a long time and afterwards regretted that he had not kept it.

IV

As the end of his term drew nearer, life in prison became more tolerable. This was not because of the removal of "Eight-Eyes," which happened at the beginning of Dostoevsky's third year, or because the prison itself shortly afterwards underwent a nominal change of régime. Rather it was because habit had eased the hardships of the place. Incredibly, it had become a kind of home. Then, too, he enjoyed certain unprecedented liberties. He established contacts with some friendly townspeople and was able to borrow books. He read *David Copperfield* and *Pickwick Papers* in the hospital. One night, after the doors were locked, he actually found himself with a magazine in his hands. He drank in the words as a man parched with thirst drinks water. He scanned it hungrily for news of the world from which he had been snatched. It was his first chance of such a glimpse. The one person who might have written to him—

Mikhail—sent him not a word during his entire stay in prison. How utterly cut off he was! How hard it would be to get back!

Exactly four years after he had entered the fortress his fetters were knocked off by the prison blacksmith, and he walked out of the gates, a free man. Free? According to the terms of his sentence, he was now to serve as a private in Siberia, and he knew that in exchanging the convict's motley for the soldier's uniform, he was altering his appearance rather than his condition. In the meantime he enjoyed a brief respite between the two kinds of servitude. The town of Omsk he found to be dirty, dissolute, and infested with soldiery. Still, it held several good friends who did all they could for him, even to lending him money. He stayed for a short time at the home of the son-in-law of a Decembrist, where he was treated like a member of the family.

He was chagrined to discover that he had been assigned to a battalion stationed in Semipalatinsk, also on the Irtysh, but hundreds of miles farther south. What could he look forward to in that hole, lost in the depths of the Kirghiz wilds? To go there was to suffer yet another wrench, to be farther away from home, to be abandoned by that friendly ghost of his past which, toward the end, had visited him at Omsk.

Yet as he faced this change in his life, the curious half-acknowledged serenity that had supported him in prison turned to a kind of exultation. He was like a convalescent after a long, dangerous illness, who, having come near to tasting death, relishes living all the more. He felt that he was on the verge of the great crisis of his existence. He was ripe for the event. If fate cheated him now, everything was lost. He was satisfied with his life, he wrote to Mikhail, his mind was at rest, his future was spread out before his eyes. The only thing he dreaded was that the burden of a soldier's life under some bully of a sergeant would be too much for him.

To reassure him, friends were telling him that at Semipalatinsk he would be among simple-minded people. But experience had taught him that he had more to fear from the simple than from the sophisticated. Still, he consoled himself, human beings were human beings everywhere. He begged Mikhail for two things: books and money. "Books," he cried, "are my life, my food, my future." He must have magazines—he had had to do without them for so long—histories, ancient and modern, Greek and Latin classics, the works of economists, the writings of the Fathers of the Church, the Koran, Kant's *Critique of Pure Reason,* and particularly Hegel's *History of Philosophy;* also a German dictionary. He will soon take up his pen again, but he must first do much reading. As for money, it is vital to a private as to a convict. If only Mikhail will keep him until he is permitted to leave Siberia and publish his work! What is spent on him will not be lost. These years have not been wasted. For one thing, he has learned to know the Russian people as few men do. He cannot write drivel now.

The single high road that connected Semipalatinsk with the world crossed a bare plain. Occasionally, during the journey that Dostoevsky's little party made largely on foot, they would pass the nomad's black tents, or encounter leisurely caravans of camels. Overtaking a string of carts, he got a lift for some miles, and jogging along, seated on a coil of rope, with the broad sky over him and a sense of freedom in his heart, he felt lighter in spirit than he was ever to feel again. On March 2, 1854, he tramped into the town and laid his eyes for the first time on its drab, wooden one-story houses, its endless fences, its unlit, unpaved streets. As at Omsk, the soldiers' barracks were located in a fortress, or rather in the ruins of one. The town—it was really only an overgrown village with a population of five or six thousand—had once been a military outpost of the expanding empire, and although it was now merely the administrative centre of a thoroughly subdued region, it was not sufficiently removed from the border to have lost its military air altogether.

Again he was one of a crew of wretches in uniform, again he was sleeping on a plank bed, only slightly softened by a thin felt mattress that he had to share with his neighbour, again he was messing with an unsavoury lot, this time scooping the cabbage soup with his wooden spoon out of a common bowl. But there was no clank of chains, no grating of keys in locks, one could breathe the air without choking and eat the food without gagging, and one was not continually followed by a guard with a gun. His companions here were, however, not so different from the people he had been thrown with in prison. Some were serfs who had been drafted into the army at the instance of their masters as punishment. There were, too, desperate characters who had sold themselves as substitutes for other men. The air was thick with threats and curses, the sound of whacks, the groans of those who had been flogged.

Among the privates there were lads in their teens, who like Spartan boys had been taken from their parents in childhood to be raised as cannon-meat. One such boy, by the name of Katz, occupied the planks next to Dostoevsky's. The two became friendly, Dostoevsky playing the big brother. Katz, who did a bit of tailoring on the side, managed to provide himself with a samovar, a luxury he shared with his mate. Many years later Katz recalled him as a taciturn, unsmiling man whose few words were uttered in a soft, slow, clear voice, and who in his free moments would sit alone lost in thought or poring over his one treasured book, the New Testament. But leisure was rare, what with reviews, sentry duty, and constant drill—he had to learn over again practically everything he had been taught at the military school. He was so busy he hardly found time for sleep. All that was required of him he performed punctiliously and eagerly. One of his superiors remembered long afterward how quick he had been to salute, and how his behaviour had always been marked by a deep humiliity. In July he was able to write to Mikhail that he was as good a soldier as the next man and that his superiors were satisfied with him. He had attained this at the cost of heavy exertions, "but," he added, "I do not complain, it's my cross, and I deserve it." He had yet another cross to bear in the shape of strange seizures which, in his opinion, "resembled epilepsy and yet were not epilepsy."

The winter brought him a godsend in the person of a young man fresh from law school who had been assigned to the post of district attorney at Semipalatinsk. He arrived from Petersburg in November, bearing with him a letter from Mikhail, another from Apollon Maikov, some linen, books, and fifty roubles. The young Baron Wrangel—he was only twenty-one—was an exception to the usual run of civil servants who found in Siberia their happy hunting-grounds: alert, sensitive, sincere, bursting with good intentions and high ideals, he was the sort of person with whom Dostoevsky could feel at ease. And since he came from Petersburg and from Mikhail, he was a piece of home. Wrangel, of course, knew the story of this morose man with the sallow, freckled face, the fair closely cropped hair, the husky voice, who, though a person of his own class, stood before him in the uniform of a private. Their friendship was christened with tears. At their first meeting the young man wept with homesickness on Dostoevsky's rough grey shoulder, and in his turn, Dostoevsky cried over the letters from home.

v

An intimacy soon sprang up between the young district attorney and the political exile. In writing home, the youth described his friend as a man of deep religiosity and an iron will. He loved him as a brother and respected him as though he were his father. Dostoevsky was grateful for this affection, though he could not fully reciprocate it. He would spend with Wrangel as many hours as he could, drinking numberless glasses of tea, smoking cheap, stinking Majorca tobacco in a long pipe, reading and studying. Indeed they were planning to undertake together the translation of Hegel's *Philosophy (sic)* and of *Psyche: zur Entwickelungsgeschichte der Seele,* by C. G. Carus.

Their talk sometimes turned on politics. There was nothing in the opinions of the political exile to grate upon the respectable young district attorney. Dostoevsky spoke as a patriot and a loyal subject of the tsar. Indeed, he had expressed himself in that vein while he was in prison, much to the disgust of the Polish politicals who were confined with him. He had harped on the rôle of the aristocracy, insisted on Russia's right to Poland and the other annexed provinces, looked forward to the entry of Russian troops into Constantinople, and enlarged on the supremacy of the Russians, in comparison with whom the other nations were mere caricatures. He may have exaggerated his ideas partly to annoy the Poles, whom he heartily disliked. But plainly these were overstatements of what he actually felt. In fact, shortly after he was out of prison, stirred by the events of the Crimean War, which was being fought thousands of miles away, he composed a poem in a violently jingoistic strain, assuring Russia's enemies that his country would be saved by the Cross and the Throne, and prophesying that the two-headed eagle would press on toward "Tsargrad" (the old Russian name for Constantinople).

What had landed him in prison now seemed to him a fatal misunderstanding. In a letter to his old friend, Maikov, whom he had vainly tried to interest in the setting up of the secret press, he referred to the affair as "hardly more than an accident," and went on to picture himself as one who had always been "a true Russian," devoted to "the Russian idea," and believing in the holy mission of his fatherland. Before his arrest he had associated with both conservatives and radicals. He had been nourished on conservative sentiments, he had had more than a nibble of radicalism. In the isolation imposed on him by his exile, his leanings toward the established order asserted themselves. It was his belief that he owed this "change of convictions" to his prolonged contact with the masses: they had taught him to honour the tsar as they had taught him to worship Christ. It is permissible to doubt that he understood himself thoroughly in this matter. His nature was too rich in contradictions to allow of any simple explanation of his attitudes. One cannot help wondering, however, whether it was dread of the power for evil that he had seen in the criminals around him and that he suspected in his own heart, that dictated his professed adherence to law and order. It is at least plausible that his Siberian experiences impressed him with the need for restraint, for discipline, in the form of Church and State, and that fear of the very strength of his anarchical self-will gave his opinions the colour of conservatism.

Orthodox though Dostoevsky's views were, it argued some courage on Wrangel's part to allow himself to be seen in the company of this common soldier, so recently a convict. But Wrangel went further than that. He introduced his new friend everywhere. He even took him to the military governor's, and after that all doors were open to him. Dostoevsky now counted among his acquaintances the élite of the town and was "loved and respected," as he wrote to his brother, by his superiors. Some of the ladies, officials' wives, took an interest in this private with a past. One of them showed him the verses she wrote. He became a frequent visitor at the house of his battalion commander, a little pot-bellied man who was always drunk and who was ready to give away his last shirt to the first comer. Though Dostoevsky was often seen at the home of a Cossack officer, which was the scene of much gambling, he seems not to have yielded to that temptation. Nor did he drink.

Wrangel only once saw him slightly under the influence of liquor. He had the peculiar slant on a company that was almost always drunk of a man who remains sober.

For some time he had been in private lodgings, having been permitted to live outside the barracks. He roomed with a soldier's widow, the mother of two daughters whose youthful and not inconsiderable charms were her chief source of income. Her lodger, unlike the natives, could not take this kind of thing as a matter of course. Occasionally he would be roused to remonstrate with the woman. She would silence him by arguing that sooner or later the girls would give themselves to a common sergeant for two cookies or a pound of nuts, whereas if she introduced them to fine gentlemen, there was both profit and honour. In spite of the public character of his landlady's household, he was enjoying privacy for the first time in five or six years. When he walked from the parade ground, through the waste of sand and briers where were scattered the wooden houses of the Russian section of the town (so-called to distinguish it from the Cossack and Tartar neighbourhoods) and, having opened the wicket gate, stepped behind the tall fence, past the watchdog on his chain, entered the old log cabin, and at last found himself in the low grimy room, crawling with cockroaches, he had the long-denied comfort of being at home. There he would make his meal of the cabbage soup, *kasha,* and black bread that he had brought from the barracks.

His soldierly duties were no longer so onerous. There was some leisure. He employed it to make a few copecks by tutoring. While he taught, he kept on his cloak, so that his pupil should not see how threadbare his trousers were. As usual he was penniless and in debt. There was, of course, Mikhail to appeal to. Mikhail had given up literature and turned to business. During Dostoevsky's third year in prison, his youngest brother having come of age, the family estate was sold and the proceeds divided among the heirs. Mikhail used what he received to open a cigarette factory. This change did not materially improve his fortunes, so that Dostoevsky had less to hope for from his brother than he realized. It will be remembered that he had forfeited his own share by accepting a lump sum in advance.

However much he had gained in knowledge of human nature

during his prison years, there were certain things that he had lost, and he was now trying to recover them. He was suddenly overcome by a desire to improve his mind and fill the gaps in his education. This ambition was not to last long and indeed, in a formal way, he never achieved more than a shallow culture. He enjoyed the exemption from dependence on mere learning, which is the privilege of genius. Naturally, the most important thing that his leisure gave him was a resurrection of the old figments, a surrender to the new images that haunted him. The writer was reviving.

CHAPTER TEN

FIRST LOVE

THE SENSE of release that the hardships of his life as a soldier could not smother was heightened by a friendship that was flourishing before Wrangel arrived on the scene. It was, in fact, more than a friendship. For the first time a woman entered Dostoevsky's life. A few months after his coming to Semipalatinsk he fell in with a petty official who, like most of the Siberian bureaucracy, hailed from Russia. This Isayev, a sweet-tempered, high-minded, improvident fellow, in spite of some talents and education and the responsibility of a wife and son, drank heavily and could not keep himself in hand. He was then, as often, out of a job, and the little family was in severe straits. The wife, a woman of about thirty, would have stood out even in a less crude society. Marya Dmitrievna was a fragile blonde, with small, irregular, pleasant features and an eager, cultivated mind. A spirited creature, with a deep sense of injury, she felt keenly the indignities of her situation, and her poor health—like Dostoevsky's mother she carried within her the seeds of consumption—fed an irritability that could melt into a startling tenderness.

Dostoevsky was constantly at the Isayevs'. He tutored the little Pasha and spent long evenings with his parents, particularly the lonely mother. For the first time in five years he had found a woman to whom he could talk. She was kind to this exile in the uniform of a common soldier. Life had trampled on her, too. Their very quarrels—the friendship of such a pair could not always be serene—endeared her to him the more. There were nights when he left the house in a state bordering upon ecstasy.

It was probably before he became absorbed in her that he had a brief intimacy with a girl to whom Marya Dmitrievna would not have bowed. All that is known of the affair is that this Liza was a striking beauty, that she sold bread in the Semipalatinsk market place, thus supporting her orphaned brothers and sisters,

126

and that Dostoevsky wrote her more than a score of letters which she, though only half-literate, answered. Unfortunately, the correspondence has been lost, but it is reported that in his letters he urged her to continue taking care of the family, even if it meant sacrificing her own happiness. As a matter of fact, she never married, though she lived to a ripe age. It is doubtful whether any trace of Liza is discoverable in Dostoevsky's writings, and she left no mark on his life. It was quite otherwise with Marya Dmitrievna. As the months went by, she meant increasingly more to him. But she was the wife of his friend. His feeling for her must remain as secret as it was hopeless.

Suddenly this ambiguous relationship was threatened. In May, 1855, Isayev was appointed to a post at Kuznetzk, nearly five hundred miles away, and there was nothing for the family to do but to pull up stakes and go there. The money necessary for the removal was supplied by the obliging Wrangel, although nominally it came from Dostoevsky. When the time for departure arrived, he accompanied the Isayevs several miles beyond the city limits. He said his good-bye to Marya Dmitrievna under a pine tree that added its pungency to the heartbreaking sweetness of the spring night, while Isayev lay in the carriage, overcome by the Veuve Cliquot with which Wrangel had plied him. It was daybreak when Dostoevsky was in his room again, relieved to be rid of the kindly but intrusive baron. He paced the floor in misery for a long time.

Soon a letter came from Kuznetzk. He answered promptly and eagerly. What distance prevented them from saying to each other they confided to paper. Unfortunately, all that has been preserved of the correspondence is his first letter. He writes that their departure has left him orphaned. He can only compare this loneliness to what he felt when he was arrested and shut away in the fortress. Both Marya Dmitrievna and her good husband had loved him, had treated him as one of their own. Were it not for them, his spirit would have perished, but they made a human being of him again. Now that they are gone, he doesn't know what to do with himself. Even Wrangel tries him—he can't help contrasting the man with her. Does she remember Wrangel's summer cottage? The garden is the same as ever, even to the bench they sat on. He is worried about the Isayevs' circumstances. They expect an inheritance from

her grandmother, but this means that they'll be burdened with the
old lady and that Marya Dmitrievna will have to wash her lap
dogs. They must not take her in, unless she pays a thousand roubles
a month for her keep and offers a written guarantee that she will
die in three months. Dostoevsky concludes by embracing Isayev as
a friend and brother, and wondering if he will ever see Marya
Dmitrievna again.

The letters that kept coming from Kuznetzk were upsetting.
Marya Dmitrievna was ill. She was lonely. Isayev was in a bad way,
as usual. Dostoevsky lived in a fever of anxiety. He was temporarily
sharing the baron's summer quarters, a spacious, dilapidated house,
with mushrooms growing through the rotten flooring. Externally,
he led a bucolic existence, feeding the pigs and chickens or, clad
in a faded pink cotton vest, working in the vegetable patch. But he
was miserable. His superstitious streak got the better of him, and he
visited fortune-tellers. Wrangel tried to distract him, but in vain.
He carried him off to visit neighbouring mining towns. He took
him along when he went shooting. Dostoevsky was bored by the
sport and, as even under happier circumstances, utterly indifferent
to natural scenery, however full of dramatic surprises.

Absence had sharpened his feeling for Marya Dmitrievna.
Wrangel laid himself out to arrange a meeting of the two in a town
midway between Semipalatinsk and Kuznetzk, but was not successful. Meanwhile events were developing rapidly. Early in August
Isayev died, leaving his widow and seven-year-old son penniless in
a strange town. There was not even enough for the funeral expenses,
and the widow was practically driven to accepting alms. The news
made Dostoevsky frantic. He borrowed from Wrangel to help her.
Somehow she scraped through the autumn and the following winter
at Kuznetzk. The letters she was now receiving from Dostoevsky
were no longer those of an affectionate friend, but of a passionate
lover.

They exchanged vows. But how could they think of marriage?
Aside from the fact that he was five hundred miles away from his
beloved, he was still a private, relying largely for his living expenses
on rare and meagre remittances from Mikhail. Furthermore, the
devoted Wrangel had left Siberia in December, and the friends who
remained were not so dependable. The worst of it was that he

couldn't be sure of her. At Kuznetzk she was surrounded by meddle-
some matrons bent on arranging a match for her there. She might
be forced to take shelter under her father's roof in Astrakhan. Not
that this would write finis to Dostoevsky's hopes. He was ready
to wait for her, if it meant five years.

Life was hell. He suspected that she was not writing the whole
truth. Knowing his jealous nature, she was, he told himself, afraid
to be frank with him. His suspicions seemed justified. In March
he was overwhelmed by a letter in which she said that she had
decided to speak plainly and put this question to him: suppose a
man, well along in years, but of sterling character and with an
assured future, say, a civil servant, were to offer her his hand,
should she say yes? He must consider the matter carefully like the
true friend that he was and answer her without delay. She was alone
with her child at the end of nowhere, her chief support being her
old father. What would become of her if he died? She ended by
telling her correspondent that she loved him and that this was all
a mere notion.

The mere notion threw Dostoevsky into a faint. He recalled a
rumour that she had promised to marry someone in Kuznetzk, which
he had carelessly dismissed. He sobbed over her letter all night.
Before dawn he wrote to her. He threatened, pleaded, poured out
words of tenderness. He would die if he lost her. But she must tell
him the whole truth, and spare him nothing.

He spent two weeks in torment. Strange that he was still alive.
He did not condemn her for a moment: she could not be expected
to marry a private. He could not, he could not give her up. He
would go mad, he would throw himself into the Irtysh. But suppose
he were standing in the way of her happiness? No, she loved him,
he was sure of it. She could not be happy with anyone else. She
was capable of selling herself to give her child bread. His pitiful
darling was so kind, so easily deceived. Curious, that he should
be in the boots of the wretched hero of his *Poor Folk*—it was as if
he had prophesied his own fate. Come—he had a claim upon her
that could not be dismissed. At his time of life, love was no light
fancy. This affair had been going on for two years now, and the ten
months of separation had only exasperated his passion.

He was ready to walk to Kuznetzk (just to see her once more, and then let come what might. The ghost of hope restrained him from doing something desperate. He was certain that should his affairs take a favourable turn, he would be preferred to any and all of her suitors. At last a letter from her lifted the darkness from his heart. It had all been a ruse. Some time previously he had written her that during Carnival week he had attended a dance, and she got the idea that he was beginning to forget her. She became panicky. Resenting what she took to be his defection, she had written in a chilly tone. Finally, to discover where she stood, she made up the story of a suitor. Reassured by his agonized reply, she put her cards on the table. As for the rumour of her marriage, it was such a piece of gossip as commonly flourished in Siberian towns.

I I

In spite of this happy conclusion to the episode, the situation remained painful in the extreme. Marya Dmitrievna was constantly ailing. He too was ill. His attacks, which generally occurred at night, were not frequent, but alarming. He told Wrangel that each seizure was preceded by an "inexpressible voluptuous feeling." For two or three days after the attack he felt broken in body and spirit. The uncertainty of their situation was maddening. She could not stay on at Kuznetzk much longer. Should she go to her father in Astrakhan? Should she tell the old man she was about to be married? To whom was he to be married? On what? Everything depended on whether or not Dostoevsky could better his position. If only he were transferred from the military to the civil service! Even in the lowest rank, with the pittance of a salary. Or else, if he were allowed to take a position with a private employer. The director of the Altai mills was ready to give him a berth. He could get ahead. Siberia was the place for making money. If he had a little free cash, he could double it in a year by clever speculating. Any job would tide him over until he came into his own again by getting permission to publish.

For six years he has been fighting against hell. Has he come through all this only to fail in supporting a wife? He will soon be thirty-five. He will die if he loses her. He's not cheating her by asking her to wait. By September he will have a novel ready that will outdo *Poor Folk*. If the worst comes to the worst, he can publish anonymously and pocket the cash all the same. With time they may even put something aside. He is counting on his pen. He is a man who has something to say.

What heartened him was the knowledge that several people in Petersburg were exerting themselves on his behalf. Wrangel, before he left Semipalatinsk, had already begun prodding his influential relatives to do something for his friend. Once in the capital again, the baron was beseiged with desperate appeals to act promptly. And Dostoevsky had yet another cause for hope. Mention has been made of his ode on the Crimean War, written in 1854. Now he penned another ultra-patriotic poem on the occasion of the birthday of the Dowager Empress, in which he lamented the recent passing of her august spouse. He had handed it to the commander of the Siberian Corps who happened to visit Semipalatinsk with a request "to lay it at the Empress's feet." Whether or not it had reached her, he was promoted to the rank of corporal.

Encouraged by this advancement, which occurred in November, 1855, and urged on by his need, he took a further step. On March 24, 1856, he wrote to General Eduard Todleben, the Sebastopol hero, whom he had known in happier days and whose younger brother had been his schoolmate. He begged the general to intercede with the Emperor for a poor and ailing exile who had repented the error of his ways. Admitting that he had been justly punished for having intended to act against the government, he stressed the fact that he was now suffering for opinions that he had repudiated. No longer did he believe in "theories and utopias," as he had done in his youth. He wished to serve his country, but not as a soldier. Civil service would be less uncongenial, but his most earnest wish was to be permitted to publish his writings. He had always considered the writer's calling to be the noblest and most useful. A measure of literary ability was his sole possession. Perhaps he, a corporal, was rendering himself guilty of insubordination by daring to write to an adjutant general, but he committed himself to the mercy of his superior.

The communication was to be handed to the general by the most devoted, the angelic, the priceless, the invaluable, the irreplaceable Wrangel. He could make it plain to Todleben, who would in turn be able to impress it on the Emperor, that Dostoevsky would hence-forth be a loyal subject. Perhaps Maikov, too, could put in a word for him with the general. If only the young Todleben could be reach-ed! He would throw himself on his brother's neck and implore him to save his old schoolfellow.

Simultaneously Dostoevsky gave Wrangel another commission. He was to find out what had become of Mikhail. Had he forgotten that he had a brother? Had he given himself over to money-grubbing altogether? Why was he letting eight months go by without a word? An urgent request for money sent the previous December had gone unheeded. Of course, Mikhail might be in straits, but then he must have known that as for him, he was in the last extremity. Now he must beg him for money again: he encloses the letter. There may be a chance to visit Kuznetzk, which means no small outlay. Again, he ought to insist on Marya Dmitrievna's accepting some money from him. Only once in a lifetime does a man need money so desperately. He cannot ask anything of Wrangel: he is too deep in debt there already. Nor does he want alms from Mikhail. He would rather the two of them should go under than accept anything like that. He wants a brother, not money. Perhaps, like relatives in novels, Mikhail is jealous of Marya Dmitrievna. Does he forget that his brother is a man of thirty-five, with enough good sense for ten people? Wrangel must persuade Mikhail to come to his rescue at this critical moment of his life. For seven years life has been gall. He is not made of stone. There is a limit to his endurance.

Todleben showed himself to be the man Dostoevsky thought him. At any rate, according to Wrangel, the wheels had begun to turn. The exile is filled with hope and overwhelmed with grati-tude, particularly to the young monarch whom, he says, he adores. He sends Wrangel an ode of his on the coronation and the conclu-sion of the Crimean War, begging him to see that it reaches the emperor. He entrusts another copy to the governor-general, who is going to Petersburg for the ceremonies, and who may get him per-mission to publish it. He had previously started an essay on Russia, but he had given it up when he noticed that it was turning out to be a political pamphlet: certainly the Government would not allow him to re-enter the literary world with such a piece, despite its patriotic tone. He had then started a paper on a safer subject: art and Christianity, which was the precipitate of ten years' meditation, and which he had thought out to the last syllable while he was still in prison. He hopes to be allowed to dedicate it to Her Highness, Maria Nikolayevna, the President of the Academy of Arts, and to publish it anonymously. As a matter of fact, all these efforts to get permission to publish were really for the sake of the novel that he had under way, and which was his refuge from his troubles. Neither the political nor the esthetic essay is heard of again.

And now came reassuring news of Mikhail. In a long letter he explained and justified his conduct. He had preserved silence during the four years of Fyodor's incarceration because he had failed to get permission to write, and he was afraid that secret correspondence would work his brother harm, and though he did not admit as much, since he had a large family and small courage, he yielded all too readily to the dictates of prudence. He insisted that he was as devoted as ever. But even when he was free to write, he was paralysed by the knowledge that his messages were read by strangers before they reached his brother, and so his letters were few and far between. He had not so much as said that the previous summer the family had been increased by twins, so that he was now the father of five children. As for his business, though it was expanding, it was just then going through a crisis, and so he could send no more than a hundred and fifty a year. He was perfectly sympathetic with regard to his brother's love affair, but just because Fyodor was no mere boy and because marriage involved no end of petty cares, he begged him to wait until his situation was more settled. He must have patience: many influential people had his cause at heart. Mikhail ends his letter with the assurance that he has not turned into a bloated business man—if Emilia has taken on weight, he remains lean and pale, the last of the romantics.

III

With the approach of Dostoevsky's third summer at Semipalatinsk the outlook became distinctly brighter. There was in the offing a transfer to civil service or perhaps an army commission. Suddenly he was crushed by the knowledge that even if there should be a change for the better, it would come too late. In June he realized his dream of seeing Marya Dmitrievna. He had a ten days' leave to go to Barnaul, a neighbouring town, and he risked going on to Kuznetzk. It meant a large expense and the danger of being court-martialled, but no matter. "I saw her," he wrote to Wrangel. "What a noble, what an angelic soul! She cried, she kissed my hands, but she loves another."

The other was Nikolay Vergunov, a youth of twenty-four, a native of Tomsk, a teacher in a country school with a prospect of one hundred roubles a year, a person with little culture and less experience of life. It was plain to Dostoevsky that a union between the two was madness, He argued with her. He pointed out that she would be buried in this hole the rest of her life, with a litter of children, and nothing to look forward to. She was five years the boy's senior: how long would it take before she would have to suffer her young husband's reproaches for having ruined his youth? Was it not likely that he would wish her death? And in any case, was this half-educated little Siberian schoolmaster a fit companion for a woman who had lived, who had suffered, a woman of her refinement and culti-vation?

She was not impressed by his arguments, she could not expect him to like the prospect. He knew this, and it made it harder for him to speak. But there she sat, agonized by the picture he painted. He took pity on her. He began to defend her young lover. This touched her to the quick. She began in her turn to pity Dostoevsky. She became tender. Her heart turned toward him now. If he had not been devoted to her, body and soul, already, he would have fallen in love with her then; she was so animated, so full of common-sense and delicious folly, so kind, so quixotic. She was the very woman to throw herself away.

She introduced Dostoevsky to his rival. The two became friendly. He reasoned with the young man and reduced him to tears. The youth seemed able to do little more than weep. After two days of mingled torture and bliss, Dostoevsky left Kuznetzk with a heart in which hope still fought despair. Towards the end the widow seemed to be swinging round to him. In parting she asked him to write to the young man frankly and fully.

He addressed a long letter to both, repeating practically the same

arguments he had advanced against the marriage by word of mouth.
He made every effort to take a point of view which was completely
disinterested. What was his dismay to discover that his attitude was
thoroughtly misunderstood! Her reply was an indignant defence
of the young man, although nothing had been further from Dostoevsky's mind than to attack him. As for Vergunov, he took offence,
tried to rouse Marya Dmitrievna against his rival, and generally
behaved like a fool and a cad. But characteristically, without waiting for Dostoevsky's response to her first outburst, she veered
abruptly round and made overtures of peace. Her later letters,
however, made him feel that to be out of sight was to be out of mind.
She fretted, she grieved but the other man meant more to her. How
would it all end? He did not know, but he was bent on working for
her happiness, whatever it might entail for him. He was like a man
who had lost his mind. This wound would never heal. If he could
only tear out his heart and bury it!

What must have kept him from collapse was the fact that his
soldierly duties were particularly exacting just then. Also he was
busy trying to be of practical assistance to the lady. Petitions had
to be written and various people approached, so that her son could
get a scholarship in one of the military schools. And then there
was all the red tape connected with securing her pension. He
trembled at the thought that she might forfeit it by remarrying
before it came. Finally, he must exert himself on behalf of his rival:
in addition to other commissions, he urged Wrangel to sing Vergunov's praises to the governor general and to put in a word for
the young man with another high official in the hope of getting him
a promotion that would double his salary. If she did marry him,
she must at least be spared certain privations.

As for himself, he was up to his ears in debt. Should his officer's
commission eventuate as expected, there would be unavoidable
additional expenses. Again he must ask help of Mikhail and of
Wrangel. If he gained permission to publish, he would certainly
repay them by the New Year. Wrangel must bear with him, for
Christ's sake. He was at the end of his tether. He was in a state
where a man takes to drink, or drowns himself. If only he could
see her, were it but for an hour.

The manifesto published on the occasion of the coronation of

Alexander II in August, 1856, vaguely promised relief to political prisoners of the class to which Dostoevsky belonged. Whether because of this amnesty, or owing to the intercession of influential persons, or thanks to his patriotic poems, on October 1, Dostoevsky was promoted to the rank of *praporshchik* (ensign), the lowest commissioned officer in the army. "The Lord grant our angel monarch a long and prosperous reign!" he cried. This promotion meant the restoration of his status as a noble. It was also a step on the road to freedom. To retire from the service altogether and be permitted to write for publication—that was his heart's desire. What sort of a military man was he anyway, with his strange attacks? Every time they left him with weakened faculties and would, he feared, eventually lead to insanity.

One good thing about his new position was that leaves were more easily obtained, and so he might see her. "I am an unhappy madman," he wrote Wrangel. "Such love is a disease. I feel it." Every week he received long letters from her, bearing all the signs of deep, sincere affection. But did she love him? He did not know. Sometimes she called him "brother." Her marriage to his rival was temporarily in abeyance, apparently for financial reasons. He felt that there was no hope, but he remembered his visit and persuaded himself that then he had, after all, won her back. Hope or no hope, he must see her. She had caused his resurrection; she was the light of his life. "She is one of God's angels," he told Mikhail, "whom I met on my way, and suffering bound us together."

His salary as an officer being a mere pittance, and his equipment expensive, he was now deeper in debt than ever. He assured his brother that his straits were not due to his sharing what he had with Marya Dmitrievna: she was not the sort to accept anything. As far as he was concerned, he stinted himself "like a Jew." He managed, however, to get to Kuznetzk toward the end of November.

The visit was decisive. On December 21 he wrote to Wrangel that, God willing, he would be married before Carnival. She loved him. She had loved him all along. And he hadn't a copeck. Mikhail was not to be counted upon. His one hope was his wealthy uncle in Moscow. He would write him and, meanwhile, borrow from a newly acquired friend. If he thus ventured further into debt, it was because he had a thousand roubles worth of manuscript. It was therefore of supreme importance to him to obtain permission to publish. If it should be withheld another year, he was lost. He was, of course, willing to write anonymously or under a pseudonym. In all his life he had never faced such a crisis. Wrangel must leave no stone unturned to get him that long-coveted privilege. He should also do what he could for Vergunov. The boy was taking an examination for promotion, and wires must be pulled so that he would be sure to get it. He deserved this and more. Vergunov was dearer to him than a brother. He was ready to beg for him on his knees.

The following day he wrote to advise Mikhail of the important event. He told his brother that the decision was final, and he was not to be argued out of it. His future wife was a woman in a thousand. If, as he hopes, "the adored being who rules us" will permit him to publish his writings, their livelihood is assured. Literature will yet hear of him. His mind is clearer and steadier, and he has laid up a rich fund of material. As for the worries and troubles that married life carries with it—well, she is dearer to him than the whole world, and he cannot abandon her, helpless and suffering as she is. If Uncle refuses to advance the necessary money, he will have to depend solely upon himself, God, and "His angel, our monarch." He knows that Mikhail's financial assistance is out of the question at this time, but he has one favour to ask of him. Will he not please send an Easter bonnet, two caps with blue ribbons, some silk material in a fashionable colour for a dress—his bride is tall and has a fine figure—a mantilla, perhaps of velvet, a lace kerchief, and half a dozen fine linen handkerchiefs. There was nothing decent to be had at Semipalatinsk and what could be bought, was frightfully expensive.

Until then Mikhail had been the only one he had taken into his confidence, and he had warned him to keep the love affair a secret, since he wanted no counsels of prudence from the family. The time had come when he must tell them. On the day that he apprised Mikhail of the step he had decided to take, he wrote to his sister Varya, who had a good deal of influence with the Kumanins. He painted the situation in a rosy light. The lady was six years his junior and came of an excellent family. Her father, who held an important post at Astrakhan, was a descendant of a French nobleman who had fled to Russia during the revolution. She was a charming and highly educated woman, devout, sensible of her duties, and he loved her more than his life. They were a perfect match. They understood and respected each other and had the same likes and dislikes. Of course, his pay as an officer would not keep them, but she had had to manage on little before this, and she was a good housekeeper. Besides, sooner or later, he would be permitted to publish his work and so make a living by his pen. In the meantime he would borrow the money he needed to get married on, in the hope that Uncle would pay off this debt. He relied on Varya to break the news to Aunt, to assure her that he considered her his "guardian angel," and to get her blessing for him. Varya should also hand his letter to Uncle at the right moment and, with Aunt, bring him to see this marriage in the right light. As a political offender, he was under surveillance and would probably, and deservedly, long remain suspect. Now, wasn't the Government more likely to trust a settled married man than an unattached bachelor without responsibilities? It was essential for him to be in the good books of the authorities, and marriage would be a step in that direction. Perhaps Uncle would see the force of that argument. In any event, Dostoevsky concluded, he had made up his mind and nothing would swerve him.

If he considered his poor health an obstacle, he made no mention of the fact. He did consult local physicians, only to be assured that his attacks were mere "nerves" and that his marriage might improve matters. To the last, however, he was harassed by uncertainties: would he be able to borrow the money? Could he get to Kuznetzk, be married, and return before the end of his leave which was only for fifteen days? Any one of a dozen things might interfere with the wedding. The enterprise involved a trip of a thousand miles by carriage.

Finally, more than the six hundred roubles which he had mentioned in every letter as his minimum requirement was in his pocket, and he could proceed to rent a flat and buy the household necessaries—all he owned was a mattress and a pillow. Alas, his officer's equipment was still to be gotten. Before long he realized that he would be left with nothing on his return to Semipalatinsk.

But he could wait no longer. He decided to take a chance—he had a feeling that luck was with him in all the critical moments of his life. He went to Kuznetzk and everything passed off smoothly. The wedding took place on February 6, 1857. It was a modest yet respectable affair. Nikolay Borisovich Vergunov stood sponsor for the groom. The local chief of police and his wife gave the bride away, and the officiating cleric was present at the feast.

Time was pressing, and the couple had to set out for Semipalatinsk as soon as the ceremony was over. On their way they stopped off at Barnaul. Here Dostoevsky suffered a violent seizure. The physician who was called in diagnosed the case as epilepsy, and when Dostoevsky insisted on knowing the worst, told him that in the course of such an attack he was bound to die of asphyxiation resulting from a throat spasm. The period of the new moon, he added, was particularly dangerous for him.

The news was crushing. It struck him that, had he known the truth, he would have given up the thought of marriage. Whether or not he was overestimating his own prudence, regrets were vain. What if he were to have a seizure while on duty. Strapped in the tight uniform, he was sure to choke to death. Marya Dmitrievna either had not suspected the nature of her husband's attacks or had never been present at one. In any event, she was horribly frightened and also took sick. The newlyweds arrived in Semipalatinsk in a lamentable state. Of course, things were at sixes and sevens in the flat he had rented from a postman. And to make matters worse, the brigade commander arrived, and there was a parade, with all the fuss and fatigue it entailed. Their married life was beginning under ominous circumstances.

CHAPTER ELEVEN

TRAVELLING STANDING STILL

THERE was something in Dostoevsky that fought depression. He had a blind faith in the future. It was as though his sufferings had yielded a residue of courage and optimism. The Barnaul doctor, he told himself, may have made a mistake. The bureau drawer held 250 roubles: Uncle Kumanin had behaved handsomely, and this sum was left after Dostoevsky had paid a small part of his debts. As for his Masha, the past had left its traces on her, and she was incredibly moody and difficult, but, he wrote Mikhail a fortnight after their return to Semipalatinsk, "she never ceases to be kind and high-minded, I love her dearly, she loves me, and for the time being all goes well." After the stormy months that had preceded their union, the two tasted something like peace. Her anxiety melted away in the atmosphere of affection with which he surrounded her and her child—his judgment of the boy's character was flattering rather than perspicacious. He was happy in loving, she in being loved. They lived quietly, saw few people, and held on to the money, which nevertheless had a way of slipping through their fingers. If only he could earn his bread!

In May he was notified that his rank in the gentry had been re-stored to him, and he took this to be another token of his monarch's graciousness. Could the Government withhold from him much longer permission to return to Russia and to publish his work? He saw himself in Moscow before the year was over. It was essential for him to go there to consult physicians. Since April his attacks had been more frequent, and he had to take a leave of absence to recuperate. The seizures occurred while he was on sentry duty, as he had feared, and in his sleep. The after-effects were hard to bear. His condition did not remain a secret from his relatives by marriage, and when one of his sisters-in-law sent him a nostrum against the falling sickness he assured her that he would use it, for he was not opposed to "sympathetic and magnetic cures" and believed in the efficacy of folk remedies.

His whole existence centred on the expectation of leaving Semipalatinsk. The Siberian air stifled him. There was something demoralizing in the life of this frontier settlement, overrun with petty officials as with locusts. The absence of civilized amusements—there was but one piano in the whole town—and of reading matter was stultifying. The men drank, gambled, and gorged themselves. The women, of whom there were few, had nothing with which to relieve their boredom except gossip. The whole region was a godforsaken wilderness into which the dregs of Russia had been drained.

There was one redeeming feature in the situation: his anxieties did not prevent him from writing. He had nothing finished to show for the work that he had done before his marriage, although as the year 1856 was drawing to a close he had been telling everybody that he had a thousand roubles' worth of manuscript ready for the press. Most of it existed in his imagination. During the long oppressive nights in prison he had spun out of his head what he conceived to be his "great and final tale." When he was released he did not commence it, though, by his own account, "everything was in readiness," because, for one thing, his affair with Marya Dmitrievna deprived him of the necessary peace of mind, and rather than risk spoiling the material, he decided not to touch it. Instead, he began a comedy, which pleased him so much that in order to follow his hero's adventures in greater detail he turned from the dramatic to the narrative form.

As the work proceeded, not only was the form altered, but the tone as well. In the early winter of 1857 he had on his hands a bulky, serious novel, half of it actually written, though in a rough state. It was going splendidly. And he had to give it up: The thought of finishing it in a hurry made him sick. He could not possibly complete it to his satisfaction in time to sell it before the year was out, and by that time he would need no less a sum than 650 roubles, to pay off the debt contracted just before his marriage. His creditor, who had promised to wait indefinitely, began to dun him three months after the wedding and made his life miserable. Besides, he would soon be without a copeck for his daily needs. He would put his hand to something less ambitious, that could be just dashed off and would bring immediate returns. Katkov, the editor of the Moscow review *Russky vestnik (The Russian Messenger)*, had already approached him for a contribution. He would do a story and a novelette, both pieces that he had worked at earlier, and these would present no difficulties. Now that he had put aside the big novel, he felt as though he had grown wings. What with the recompense for one of these projected pieces and a tidy sum from his friend Pleshcheyev out of an imminent inheritance, he was sure to be on his feet by April. Meanwhile, Mikhail must for the last time come to his rescue.

Mikhail did so by securing him an advance from the publisher of *Russkoye slovo (The Russian Word)*, a review which was about to be launched. But this was insufficient to cover his debts, and by March, 1858, he was again anxiously asking himself where the next rouble would come from. This time he was saved by an advance he received from Katkov. He planned to give *Russkoye slovo* his story —a fragment had detached itself from the long novel he had abandoned—and *Russky vestnik* his novelette. After the lapse of all these years he was once more putting himself in bondage by selling his unwritten work, as he had repeatedly sworn not to do.

II

The work on his first commission, the short story, had been going badly. He hinted that he was hindered by circumstances other than the arrival of a new commander. Perhaps what he was thus guardedly referring to was trouble at home. With little Pasha placed in a school at Omsk and no greater household concerns than were given her by their four-room flat, his wife had little to do but brood over the marriage she had just made. What with her unstable temperament and his peculiarities, the uncertainties of their finances and of their health, there was much to disturb the conjugal harmony. Gossip had it that the situation was aggravated by her jealousy. There seem to have been scenes over a beautiful Polish girl, one time Dostoevsky's pupil, and so wild a creature that her elderly husband, before going out, secured himself against cuckoldry by closing a bureau-drawer on her long hair and locking it. The unhappiness that attended Dostoevsky's married life may have begun in those early days. Eight months after the wedding he was writing to his sister-in-law that he had a foreboding of death, not, he insisted, a hypochondriac notion, but a matter-of-fact feeling: he had experienced everything possible, and life had nothing more to offer him.

What life did offer him was a repetition of a state of affairs with which he had been well acquainted before he went to prison: money worries, illness, writing against time, the feeling that, thus driven, he was botching his work, and this when he was practically making his second début. There was yet another spoke in the wheel: in January, 1858, he tendered his resignation from the army on the score of ill health, at the same time requesting the privilege of residence in Moscow. To his petition he attached the following certificate signed by "Yermakov, physician," on December 21, 1857:

"I have examined *Praporshchik* Fyodor Mikhailovich Dostoevsky in the presence of Captain Bakhirev and ascertained that he is 35 years old and of middling physique. In 1850 he suffered his first attack of falling sickness (*epilepsia)* with these manifestations: outcry, loss of consciousness, convulsions of extremities and face, foam at the mouth, stertorous breathing, small, fast, abbreviated pulse. The attack lasted fifteen minutes. Followed general weakness and return of consciousness. In 1853 he suffered another attack, and since then they occur at the end of every month. At present Dostoevsky complains of general weakness and a run-down condition, also of frequent facial neuralgia due to an organic ailment of the brain. Although during the last four years he has been almost constantly under treatment for epilepsy, he has had no relief, and for that reason cannot continue in His Majesty's service."

For over a year he was kept on tenterhooks waiting to have his resignation accepted. In February he learned that *The Little Hero*, the tale he had written in the fortress while waiting to be sentenced, had been published the previous year, in the August issue of *Fatherland Notes*—news from home travelled slowly. This was disconcerting, for he had wanted to rewrite the piece. Still, there was comfort in the reflection that, though the story had been printed anonymously, the Government was lifting the ban on his work.

He had expected to finish the tale for *Russkoye slovo*—it was *Uncle's Dream*—on December 15, 1857; actually it was completed more than a twelvemonth later, and published in March,

1859. The work agitated him so much that he had to take his time over it, goaded though he was. When Mikhail chided him for his tardiness he replied with some heat that though he usually set a scene down in the first flush of inspiration as was right, he afterwards spent months and years polishing it. What kept him from getting on faster with the story was his feeling that in being re-introduced to the public with *Uncle's Dream*, he was not putting his best foot forward. Indeed, the tale shows no evidence of the maturity that time and suffering should have brought. It might well have been written before fate had cast him down. That he wrote it with one eye on the censor may account for its utter inoffensiveness. He himself was to describe it as "a trifle of dove-like gentleness and remarkable innocence." It is a farcical piece with a note of tragedy, peopled with caricatures and lay figures. In the background is the character made familiar by his early stories: the young dreamer who through some fatal flaw in his nature loses the woman he loves. The provincial setting alone is obviously the fruit of his Semipalatinsk experience, and he must have been paying off many old scores when he wrote that the provincials, because of their constant spying on each other, ought to be psychologists and specialists in human nature, but that instead they were mostly asses.

All the while he was going on with novelette for *Russky vestnik:* "The Village of Stepanchikovo" (known in English and hereafter referred to as "The Friend of the Family"). Not that he liked it any better than the other, but it had to be finished. He had good things in his head, but they were all in the nature of long novels. There was one in particular that he was set on, but he couldn't write it to order, and besides he had to be in Russia to work on it. It was his fate to write for money. "It is a wretched trade," he sighed, "that of a penniless author." On December 12, 1858, he said that he was sending off the novelette in a few days, but six months passed before he dispatched the final instalment to Mikhail.

"The Friend of the Family" is a meatier piece of writing than its predecessor, more complex in design, and, though the narrative lags occasionally. shows a more sustained power. As in most of his early stories, the character dominating the action is a man who for years had eaten the bread of humiliation, his dignity outraged and trampled upon. Dostoevsky takes a new tack here by placing him in a position where he is the master, revered, pampered, adulated, and watches his antics as the absurd creature gives free rein to his limitless conceit, lords it over everyone in his neighbourhood, and smothers all in unctuous rhetoric. The author achieves his effect through overstatement, hyperbole, excess, until one sees his Foma Fomich, larger than life, the embodiment of a monstrous vanity that is merely his overcompensation for insults previously endured. The other characters, all of whom revolve around Foma and dance to his piping, are drawn in less detail, with the possible exception of the nominal master of the house, a man with a heart of gold, a naïve soul whose boundless kindness is matched only by his reverence for ideals. This story, with its genial tone, its happy ending, bears little evidence of having been written by an ex-convict. One might perhaps see some trace of Dostoevsky's bitter experience in the fact that he chose to draw a slave in power, tyrannizing over his betters, while the pure in heart is something of a gullible fool. It took long years for the emotions and ideas germinated in the darkness of the prison to ripen and bear fruit in his writings.

He was making his final preparations for the event that had for so long been the centre of his hopes—departure from Siberia. His resignation was accepted in March, 1859, and he was permitted to return to Russia, though he would have to live not in Moscow as he had wished, but in the provinces. He chose as his residence the city of Tver, which is situated on the railway line between Moscow and Petersburg. The money for the trek of twenty-five hundred miles came in the form of an additional advance from *Russkoye slovo*. But the sum would not keep him after they reached Kazan. For the last time Mikhail must save him by sending a remittance *poste restante* to that city, or he would find himself stranded in a strange place.

III

They bought a *tarantass* in which to make the trip, with the expectation of disposing of it at the end of the journey. They sold whatever they could, including Marya Dmitrievna's hats, presumably because they would be too outlandish to wear at home. The great day, July 2, 1859, dawned clear and fine. The farewells were long and effusive, and there was much clinking of glasses before the late afternoon hour at which they set off.

A postillion accompanied them all the way, and they changed horses and drivers at each posting station. The weather was admirable and the road smooth. Their first stop was Omsk, that place of bleak memories. Here they picked up Pasha and went on their way. The weather continued fine, and though the road grew worse, the carriage held out bravely, nor was there any delay in getting fresh horses. Aside from two attacks during the early part of the trip, Dostoevsky kept well. The only fly in the ointment was the staggering prices they had to pay for food and other necessaries at the stations: it got so that on being told the cost of this or that article the traveller would look fearfully into the eye of the vendor to see if the man was in his right mind. Yekaterinburg (now Sverdlovsk) was the exception, and there, tempted by the cheapness of the goods displayed, they bought all manner of knick-knacks to take home as presents.

One glorious afternoon towards five o'clock they came to a forest clearing where a tall post marked the borderline between Asia and Europe. They all clambered out. His feet once more on native ground, Dostoevsky crossed himself. Before him, by the Lord's mercy, lay the promised land. It was ten years since he had stood in the snowy darkness, fronting in the opposite direction, and saying a mute good-bye to Europe and his youth. These years had tempered and toughened him. They had robbed him of something forever and brought him strange and terrible gifts in exchange. But this was not the time for reckoning profit and loss. The vodka flask in its wicker basket came out, and everybody, not forgetting the faithful postillion and the coachman and the veteran who guarded the post, drank to the hour. Then Dostoevsky, with an unaccustomed sense of freedom, wandered off with Masha and the child, to explore the woods and pick the wild strawberries that dotted this beloved earth.

When they set out again it was to travel through virgin forests so splendid that even one as indifferent to natural beauty as Dostoevsky could not but be enchanted and lifted out of his current anxieties. They seized him again when he reached the Volga and found himself in Kazan, as he had foreseen, without enough money to complete the trip. A tedious and expensive wait of ten days followed.

DOSTOEVSKY IN 1847

Drawing by Trutovsky

Then the remittance came from Mikhail and they went on, catching a glimpse of the great fair at Nizhny and stopping to visit the Troitzky monastery to which as a boy he used to be taken by his mother. He was less moved by its associations than amazed by its treasures and monuments: the Byzantine chapels, the rich jewels, the old books, the needlework of tsarinas, the garments of Ivan the Terrible. And then came the domes and gables of Tver, the goal of the long journey.

At Tver they were "settled on a pin-point." They would soon be moving on to Petersburg, but how soon? The uncertainty was nerve-racking. They were travelling standing still. The promised land was proving no nearer the heart's desire than the wilderness. Indeed, Tver was the most hateful city in the world, a thousand times worse than Semipalatinsk: no interests, no life, bleak, cold, stony—a prison. He was so close to, and yet, considering the wretched postal service, so far from his friends and relatives in the two capitals. And here they had to set up housekeeping, spend their last few roubles on such essentials as a samovar, and wait. Of course, everything was very expensive, and there was no buyer for the Siberian chaise, the family's sole capital. Masha, being without a bonnet, was confined to their furnished flat, which did not improve her disposition.

At once disaster swooped. Katkov, after some hemming and hawing, turned down "The Friend of the Family" and told the author that he could get his manuscript as soon as he refunded the five hundred roubles that had been advanced to him. Far from being sunk, Dostoevsky was buoyed up by the familiar waters of calamity. His faith in the little novel was unshaken: if it was long-drawn-out and bad in places, it had moments of high comedy. When, therefore, at the end of August, Mikhail came to embrace the brother from whom an evil fate and long years had divided him, Dostoevsky was able to persuade him to redeem the manuscript and try to place it elsewhere. They had five days in which to renew their intimacy. It was a difficult business, but they made a start. At last there was somebody to whom Dostoevsky could unburden himself, to whom he could speak freely of his plans, to whom he could retail the plots of the novels that he was revolving in his mind. When it came to the question of getting permission to live in Petersburg, they decided to do nothing until after September 8, when he might come under the amnesty that was expected on a state occasion.

Mikhail set off at once to secure the manuscript and, having obtained it, offered it to *Sovremennik*. Dostoevsky was out of sympathy with its liberal outlook, but it was an important review, and he was anxious to see his name in it. His situation was desperate, but when Nekrasov, who had privately decided that Dostoevsky was played out and would not come back, offered him less than the figure he had set, he instructed Mikhail to refuse it. They must put a good face on a bad business and hold out for the right price. They must bargain, they must haggle, they must pit one editor against another. What he wants is not glory, but money. After much manoeuvring and many worries, the novel was bought by his old employer, Krayevsky, at Dostoevsky's figure and appeared in *Fatherland Notes* at the end of the year.

The sale of the manuscript saved the situation, and with a little help from Mikhail and his sisters, he was able to face the future. If only he could collect his writings and publish them in book form, either on his own or through a bookseller. This would keep him going and allow him to concentrate on a big piece of work. It was October when, after some hesitation, he decided to turn his hand to writing an account of his prison days. He assured Mikhail that he would finish it in six weeks. Then he planned to settle down to his great novel. It was the work that he had conceived in prison, his "confession," the thought of which had been with him constantly. He would put his heart's blood into it. He felt that he was now ripe for it, that it would be his definitive utterance. It would be a trilogy, and would allow him to work in a story of passion, the idea for which had come to him later and which he had never used. With his incurable optimism as to his speed, he gave himself three or four months to finish the first part.

In spite of his fine intentions and his courageous mood, he could not keep his promises to himself—his situation was too difficult. His illness persisted, and what was the use of going to provincial doctors? They were either young men just out of school or old fogies who had forgotten all the medicine they had ever known. Also, he was finding a few more creases in the marriage bed. Masha was uneasy. He could not help feeling that she feared he would die here in Tver and leave her and her child in the same position that his predecessor had left them. And there was always the oppressive uncertainty as to how soon they could leave this miserable place. The eagerly anticipated eighth of September left matters unchanged. Something had to be done.

Dostoevsky was not without friends in Tver, and though social life in the provinces was something of a nuisance, it had its uses. He was in fact received socially by the governor himself, and this high official undertook to transmit the petition which Dostoevsky decided to address to the emperor. It was an abject missive in which he requested permission to live in Petersburg in order to get the medical attention which would, he trusted, prevent his attacks from ending in death or insanity. He also put in a request for a scholarship for his stepson Pavel in a secondary school or cadet corps. In conclusion he compared the emperor to the sun shining on the just and unjust alike, and declared himself ready to give up his life for him. He also wrote in a similar strain to General Todleben, who had responded to his appeal on a previous occasion, and to Prince Dolgorukov, the Chief of the Gendarmerie. In fact he wrote to so many possible benefactors at once that he thereby delayed his release from the Tver captivity. In November he slipped off to Moscow for a short visit to the relatives there and returned more resentful of his confinement and more fretted by the uncertainty of his lot than ever. His delivery came in the middle of December, and the Christmas Eve that marked the tenth anniversary of his departure for Siberia he was able to spend in Petersburg with Mikhail.

CHAPTER TWELVE

RESURRECTION

Like birth, resurrection is traumatic. Back home, Dostoevsky had not only to rediscover his friends, to re-establish himself in literature, to plunge from the stagnant backwaters of Siberia into the quick current of metropolitan life, but to adjust himself to an altered world, to an age that had a different complexion from that which he had known ten years earlier.

Some intimations of the change had reached him in his isolation. But now he had to take the full impact of the serious sixties. In the distant days before his exile, a few earnest souls used to come together and explore possible roads to Utopia and talk, under the rose, about the need for the correction of public evils. Now the Government itself was pushing great reforms, chief of all the liberation of the serfs, and official corruption had been so freely and loudly denounced at every dinner-table, in the press, on the stage, that the subject had become tedious. Russia, in the words of an underground leaflet of the day—one of the first of its kind—had entered upon "the revolutionary period of its existence." The Crimean campaign had had the usual effect of a disastrous foreign war: it had lowered the prestige of the Government at home. The death of the iron Nicholas in the midst of defeat had brought to the throne a monarch bent on giving the country a new deal. Men were not only responsive to ideas of change, but, what was unprecedented, they were eager for a practical programme. The Westernist orientation had a greater following than Slavophilism. The younger generation of both sexes was hard-headed, blatant, cynical, materialistic, or at least liked to think itself as such. This harsh temper was in part due to the fact that there was an increasing number of commoners among the intellectuals. They scorned fine sentiments as they did the fine arts, turned their backs on old-fashioned morality trod upon conventions, threw religion overboard, made a fetish of science. Because of their eagerness to deny all accepted values, these young people were soon to win for themselves the name of nihilists, though the term, which owed its popularity to Turgenev's use of it in *Fathers and Children*, eventually came to be applied by the general public, especially the more conservative element, to all extremists, particularly those who were politically-minded. The latter were not disarmed by the concessions that Alexander II's government granted. In this freer air the spirit of opposition grew and flourished. Before long it would identify itself with the faith and works of revolutionary socialism.

One thing was clear to Dostoevsky: he could not be with these rebels. They were ready to welcome a political prisoner returning from exile, but in those ten years he had lost all touch with the young man who had attended the Petrashevsky Fridays, had read Belinsky's letter before a responsive gathering and had had a hand in setting up a secret press. He would not carry one brick to the socialist edifice. It was another tower of Babel. He stood with Christ. He was a faithful communicant; he was a loyal subject.

He fell in naturally with people of a conservative temper. They were his contemporaries, or slightly younger than he, interested, like himself, in public affairs and trafficking in social and political ideas. It was not, however, a particularly distinguished circle, its members being mostly lesser lights in the world of letters, with a scattering of the other professions. He found some familiars here, such as Apollon Maikov and Yanovsky. He found some strangers too. Mikhail's house was one of their meeting-grounds, and of course Dostoevsky took a leading place. There was something attractive about this pale, big-browed man with the military moustache and the look of a aplebian; his history—of which he said little— was unusual, his mind original, his talk simple, vehement, pregnant. He spoke freely in the presence of his old friends and he was stimulated by the presence of such new ones as the lovable drunkard, Apollon Grigoryev, and the detached young philosopher, Nikolay Strakhov.

But though no longer thrown back upon his own resources, it was not easy for the ex-convict to find his bearings in the confusion of the new era. For so many years he had been forced to hold his peace. He had so much to hear; he had so much to say. No wonder that when he began to speak, he stammered a bit and sometimes contradicted himself. He wasn't, moreover, content with the rôle of a writer of fiction: there was an urge in him to reshape the actual world not merely in his imagination, but also in fact. Before he left Siberia he had been nursing the notion of having a corner in some journal where he could express the ideas that had been bottled up within him, and could comment on what he would find going on around him. In Tver the notion had crysallized into a project for founding a review with his brother. Mikhail, for his part, was also anxious to get into the publishing business and, indeed, the previous year he had secured a permit to issue a weekly. Dostoevsky, in this at least the same man he had been a dozen years before, was sure that with their abilities, the two of them could easily make a fortune.

They decided to launch a large review. While Mikhail, the owner, was business manager, Dostoevsky undertook the editorial duties and was generally the one to determine the policy of the magazine. Strakhov and Grigoryev were among his steady collaborators. The first issue of *Vremya (Time)*, as the periodical was called, appeared in January, 1861.

The field was by no means a crowded one, though on the other hand, the reading public was extremely limited. *Fatherland Notes*, Dostoevsky's old market, though still under the same management, had gone downhill. *Sovremennik*, on the contrary, was flourishing under the direction of the radical Chernyshevsky, upon whom the mantle of Belinsky had fallen. The new magazine, *Russky vestnik*, was coming to the fore. It was then progressive, in accordance with the spirit of the times. A more recent arrival on the scene was *Russkoye slovo* which was soon to become the organ of the nihilists. And there was yet another publication, not advertised, not indeed, publicly mentioned, but perhaps more avidly read, *Kolokol (The Bell)*, published abroad and smuggled into Russia. Its editor, Alexander Herzen, was the most prominent and influential of the expatriates who were beginning to cluster in London, Paris, and Geneva, and there work for radical reforms and, indeed, revolution at home.

To be successful in Russia in those years, a magazine had to be the organ of a cause. *Vremya*, Dostoevsky decided, could not align itself either with the Westerners or the Slavophils. His review would fly its own flag. The magazine, he announced, would seek to bridge the abyss that Peter the Great had opened between the educated classes and the common people. There was no obstacle to a union between the intellectuals and the men of the soil, because, he insisted, quite forgetting what his lot as a "gentleman" had been in prison, Russia, unlike the West, knew no class antagonisms. Along with this "silent revolution" must go recognition of Russia's distinctiveness. "Our task is to create for ourselves a new form of our own, indigenous, taken from our soil, deriving from the national spirit and national principles." One of these was autocratic government, the political expression of an essentially monolithic people. Another was "panhumanism," an instinct which enabled Russians to identify themselves with people of alien cultures and which suggested that it was Russia's mission to unite mankind by combining the ideals of the separate nations in a living synthesis. Dostoevsky was to reiterate this idea without making it plausible.

He was thus setting up on a pedestal the traditions he had once dared to question. He was obviously trying to connect the two phases of his existence: the Western culture that he had absorbed as a young man and the appreciation of the people that had come to him in prison in his contacts with his fellow convicts. He had known an intellectual life, he was knowing it again, but on the other hand, he had lived alongside the plain folk, with the worst of them, and he wanted to bring those two halves of his experience together.

These confused nationalist and populist ideas carried an intimate meaning for him, but they were not fruitful as a programme for the magazine. Its pages reiterated the doctrine that salvation lay in the soil and the people. But what this salvation implied in practice and what steps must be taken to achieve it, remained something of a mystery. There was some talk of the abolition of ranks and the moral regeneration of the classes, but one practical step *Vremya* advocated was the spread of literacy among the masses, a measure favoured by all but the blackest reactionaries. The editors' nationalist bias should from the first have drawn them to the Slavophils, from whom Dostoevsky borrowed many of his ideas, notably the theory of Russia's "panhumanism." Indeed, eventually he would find himself with this group. For the present, however, he held aloof.

There was that in their attitude which went against his grain. Their snobbishness irritated him. It was obvious in everything they said that they were comfortable gentry, with lands and houses and, only a little while ago, serfs. He had nothing but his pen between him and starvation. Indeed, the scorn of the literary proletarian for the privileged breaks out more than once in his writings.

Liking the Westerners even less than he did the Slavophils, unwilling to identify his magazine with either, believing, indeed, that both were played out, he attacked now the one, now the other. Yet in some respects *Vremya* was an organ of liberal opinion, and was looked at askance by the authorities. It stood for the great reforms of the period, advocated the emancipation of women, flaunted democratic sentiments, rapped those who idealized medieval Muscovy, printed contributions from Nekrasov and other acknowledged radicals, and once took an enlightened stand on the Jewish question. In an editorial note appended to a translation of Hugo's *Notre Dame,* Dostoevsky wrote: "The basic idea of the art of the nineteenth century is the rehabilitation of the oppressed social pariah, and perhaps toward the end of the century this idea will be embodied in some great work as expressive of our age as the *Divine Comedy* was of the Middle Ages." The materialistic element in the liberal complex was one thing that he could not stomach, and yet he was capable of saying on at least one occasion that while he didn't think he came out of a retort, he could nevertheless see that one might believe that wicked nonsense and yet be a good man. When, in the fall of 1861, certain university students were thrown into prison for protesting against the Government's attempt to restrict their liberties, the editors of *Vremya* expressed sympathy with the rebels by sending them a huge roast beef, prepared in Mikhail's kitchen, along with a bottle of cognac and one of red wine. During that winter Dostoevsky figured together with Chernyshevsky on the programme of a literary soirée which was designed as a parade of progressives, and which resulted in the deportation of one of the speakers. Although at heart he did not feel himself a wronged man, he was not averse to making capital of his martyrdom as a political prisoner.

One morning in May, 1862, Dostoevsky, like many other people in the capital, found at his door a leaflet entitled *Young Russia,*

the work of several Moscow students, secretly printed and issued
in the name of the Central Revolutionary Committee, a fictitious
organization. This was the leaflet mentioned earlier as having declared that Russia had entered the revolutionary period of its existence. It called for total destruction of the existing order, expressed
assurance that Russia was destined to be the first "to realize socialism" and ended with the words: "Long live the Russian social and
democratic republic!" By chance the appearance of this blood-
thirsty proclamation coincided with a series of fires that ravaged the
capital as well as other cities. Consequently, it was rumoured that
the conflagrations were a case of revolutionary incendiarism.

Vremya was one of the few organs of the press that tried to dis-
credit this theory and to absolve the student body as a whole from
responsibility for the *Young Russia* proclamation. The editor intended to run an article on the subject, but two versions of it were
forbidden by the censor and the magazine barely escaped suspen-
sion for its "harmful tendency," in the words of the chairman of the
commission that investigated the fires. On the other hand, when
the fires first broke out, Dostoevsky apparently gave credence to
the idea that they were the work of revolutionaries. He rushed to
Chernyshevsky and implored him to use his good offices with the
young hotheads so as to keep them from further excesses. Chernyshevsky, who was scarcely acquainted with his visitor but knew
him to be an epileptic, was amazed by the absurd request and, fearful lest argument make him violent, gave him every soothing re-
assurance.

The concessions to the liberal point of view prevailing at the
time may have been made with a view to securing more subscribers.
In his usual blunt fashion Apollon Grigoryev said that *Vremya*
was trying to serve both God and Mammon. More probably, the
ambiguity of its position reflected the confusion in Dostoevsky's
mind on the leading issues of the day. He had a feeble grasp on
political realities. Either because he was always provocative, no
matter how muddled his thinking might be, or because he was a
skilful editor, *Vremya* achieved a remarkable success. In the second
year of its existence it had more than four thousand subscribers,
and was practically a rival of *Sovremennik,* the most influential
progressive review of the period.

II

Dostoevsky wore the editorial yoke with a will. He selected material for several departments, he revised and annotated manuscripts, he read proof, he contributed serious essays and light pieces, he engaged in controversy—polemics was the life of the magazines of the day—he wrote exhibition notices and book reviews, he had a hand in the section on current events, he composed the annual advertisement calculated to catch the subscriber. He admonished, prophesied, jeered, entertained. He was in his element. Newspapers and reviews had always constituted a large part of his reading. Although he was outraged by the current idea that literature was merely a tool of social betterment, he was anything but content with an ivory tower. He was always ready to climb down and travel the dusty road of journalism. To be in the thick of things, to comment on the passing scene, to form public opinion—this was a satisfaction second only to that of his main business as a novelist.

The transition from being turned inward upon himself, in a place where the latest paper was a month old, to heading a large national review, was a dizzying experience, and one which fed his sense of power. No wonder, then, that he plunged into the work with a kind of frenzy. But here was this wretched unmanageable body of his. It was always on the point of playing him false. In March, 1861, when the April issue was being prepared, he was struck down by an epileptic seizure of unusual violence and lay unconscious for nearly three days. It was his fate to have to work by fits and starts.

Gradually life fell into as much of a routine as the attacks allowed. He was temporarily released from the iron vice of poverty. Shortly after returning to Petersburg he succeeded in getting a bookseller to issue a two-volume edition of his collected works, and when, the next year, Vremya made its appearance, there was always a little money to be had. His rooms were on an unkempt street in a poor, crowded neighbourhood, a few blocks away from Mikhail's house, where the editorial offices were located. Nearby was Strakhov's lodging. Dostoevsky usually reached the office around three o'clock, having just breakfasted on a cup of tea. At the first opportunity he had reverted to his habit of working at night, and accordingly slept late. At Mikhail's he would generally find Strakhov, and perhaps one or two others; they would look over the mail together, read the papers, discuss the news, and then go for a stroll until dinner time. Petersburg was a dreadful place—the look of it depressed one, the climate killed one. But, after all, everybody who lived the life of the mind was there. Often he would drop in on Strakhov again at seven o'clock and have tea with him. There were many things about this man to attract Dostoevsky: his wide culture, his anti-mechanistic stand, his critical acumen. Himself interested in fundamentals, he liked to philosophize with Strakhov, who had had the formal training he had missed, and who had enough of the pedagogue in him to enjoy delivering little lectures on biology, on the limits of knowledge, on modes and substance.

During their long hours together Strakhov observed his friend closely. He found in him "a peculiar duality": Dostoevsky was capable of giving himself up to certain thoughts and feelings, but his surrender was not complete; a part of his mind played the rôle of an unconcerned onlooker. It was from the deep, secret chamber of the self where the beholder was stationed, Strakhov suggested rather unreasonably, that the energy came that flowed into his art. Dostoevsky was himself aware of his habit of watching his own reactions; as though in a single body there were an actor and an audience of one.

Because Strakhov had the philosopher's serenity without his dullness, Dostoevsky was glad to have him by during the fits of dejection which so often assailed him, as well as when he was recovering from the throes of an epileptic attack. Strakhov left an account of one seizure which he witnessed in 1863. It was Easter Eve, near midnight, and the two were alone at Strakhov's deep in talk. "He [Dostoevsky] was saying something that was full of exaltation and joy. When I supported his thoughts with a remark, he turned to me with the face of one at the peak of ecstasy. He hesitated a moment as though seeking for a word, and had already opened his lips to pronounce it. I looked at him with keen attention, feeling that he was about to say something extraordinary, that I would hear some revelation. Suddenly, a strange, long-drawn-out, meaningless moan issued from his mouth, and he dropped to the floor unconscious. . . . The body was rigid with convulsions and foam appeared at the corners of the mouth." It was common for the attack to be preceded by an instant of such ecstasy as Strakhov noticed on his companion's face. "For a few moments," Dostoevsky used to say, "I experience such happiness as is impossible under ordinary conditions, and of which other people can have no notion. I feel complete harmony in myself and in the world, and this feeling is so strong and sweet that for several seconds of such bliss one would give ten years of one's life, indeed, perhaps one's whole life."

In *The Idiot*, there is a detailed account of Prince Myshkin's epileptic aura. "The sensation of life, the consciousness of self, were multiplied almost tenfold at these moments, which lasted no longer than a lightning-flash. His mind and his heart were flooded with extraordinary light; all his vexations, all his doubts, all his anxieties were laid to rest at once, as it were; they were all resolved into a lofty calm, full of serene, harmonious joy and hope, full of reason and ultimate comprehension. But these moments, these flashes, were only a premonition of that final second (it was never more than a second) with which the fit began. That second was of course unendurable." The moment is further described as giving "a feeling, unheard of and unsuspected till then, of completeness, of proportion, of reconciliation, and of startled devotional merging with the highest synthesis of life." Dostoevsky has his hero reflect that this moment of ecstasy, of "being at its highest," is but part of his disease, and yet Myshkin arrives at the paradox that this "extraordinary strengthening of the consciousness of self," however abnormal in origin and destructive in effect, remains a real, a supreme value, and is indeed "worth the whole of life." Dostoevsky does not mention in this passage the depression which followed the fit and which was as acute as the premonitory bliss. What dominated him in this black mood was an unaccountable feeling that he was an evildoer, that he had committed a terrible crime which had gone unpunished.

III

His relations with his wife after his return from Siberia are something of a mystery. At first they shared living quarters—Strakhov caught a glimpse of her one day and long remembered her delicate pleasing features and her pallor. Later on she stayed alone, at least part of the time, in Tver or Vladimir, where the climate was less unfriendly to a consumptive than in the capital. Before long she was reduced to the existence of a bed-ridden invalid. So little is heard of her that it was as though Dostoevsky were leading the life of a bachelor. If he did not, like his brother Mikhail, "the last of the romantics," keep a mistress, he may well have allowed himself sexual adventures outside the marriage bond. It is not impossible that the lurid incident retailed in "Notes from the Underground" derives from experiences of this period. He was moving in a circle where, according to Strakhov, people were tolerant of "all kinds of physical excesses and abnormalities" and where, though "spiritual vileness was judged strictly and subtly, carnal vileness did not count at all." Such an attitude toward sins spiritual and carnal was peculiarly congenial to Dostoevsky. The evidence of his own indulgence in the excesses and abnormalities, which is incomplete, must be discussed elsewhere.

It is certain that his marriage had not proved a happy one. From Tver he wrote to Wrangel: "If you ask me, what shall I say? I've taken family cares upon me, and I bear the burden." He confided the nature of their private difficulties to at least one person, a woman, and discreet. He had met her during the first year of his stay in Petersburg, at one of Mikhail's modest evening parties. She was a fascinating little actress who had taken his old friend Yanovsky as her second husband. She was estranged from him at this time, partly because he objected to her continuing on the boards. Dostoevsky sided with her, and she was naturally delighted to find a champion in a friend of the doctor's who was also a writer of note. Dostoevsky, for his part, relished the society of a charming woman, who was bathed in the glamour of the stage and whose grace and good humour relieved him from the tension in which he habitually lived. There was some talk of dramatizing *Netochka Nezvanova* and giving her the lead, but that came to nothing.

She was playing in Moscow when he went there for a glimpse of the old city in the spring of 1860, and it was during one of his visits that he opened his heart to her on the subject of his own domestic circumstances. When his return to Petersburg made it impossible to talk to her, he wrote to her, thereby arousing Yanovsky's lively suspicions. Dostoevsky saw that the man was suffering from two kinds of jealousy: that of love and that of self-love, and said so in a letter to the actress. He also took occasion to assure her that he himself loved her too disinterestedly, too fervently, to be in love with her. Either because she had no use for his affection, or because he had exaggerated its fervour, she seems to have dropped suddenly and completely out of his life. Yanovsky, too, practically disappears from the picture. As a successful administrator—he ultimately won the rank of general—he felt that it did not become him to mix with mere scribblers.

I V

Dostoevsky was scribbling away at a great rate. In addition to his publicist writing, there was his fiction. The opening issue of *Vremya* carried as its chief attraction the initial instalment of a full-sized novel from his pen, under the title, *The Humbled and Insulted*, known in English as *The Insulted and Injured*.

This was not the great and final work he had been planning to write as soon as he returned from exile. Of that nothing further is heard. In fact, this "feuilleton novel," as he called it, is so far from being his projected masterpiece that one must scan it closely to find in it traces of his genius. He had written it in a hurry, because the review was in need of a novel, he said by way of excuse, and of necessity had filled it with puppets. The excuse is scarcely acceptable. He seems to have taken considerable time over it, and even if that were not the case, some of his best work was written in haste. Be that as it may, there is much in the book that is either derivative—his models ranging from Sue to Hoffman—or half thought-out and faulty in execution. The pages drip with thick, syrupy sentiment, and many of the characters and situations are the stock-in-trade of the mystery tale and such dusty appurtenances of melodrama as the implacable father who refuses to forgive a daughter abandoned by her lover.

And yet this narrative is the work of an unconventional novelist. His signature is unmistakable on the pages devoted to the immoralist, Prince Valkovsky, and on those in which he deals with the fourteen-year-old Nelly and her unhappy mother. The two are figures in a secondary plot. This parallels the main fable, which is an unusual version of the eternal triangle and treats an order of emotions not generally exploited in melodrama. Four persons are involved: Vanya, loving Natasha, does everything in his power to promote her happiness with Alyosha; the latter, an irresponsible youth, includes in his affections both Natasha and Katya; each of the two girls is prepared to surrender her own happiness to that of the other. One recognizes Dostoevsky's hand in the concern with these emotional complications and one discovers some of his own features in Vanya. He is an ailing man, a writer whose literary début is practically a transcript of Dostoevsky's experience and whose rôle is not unlike his creator's when he all but assisted his future wife into marriage with another.

If the story has a meaning, it lies in the contrast between the love that "seeketh not itself to please" and the lust of the man who knows no law but that of his own appetite. It is clear that the author is on the side of the angels. Yet he allows virtue to be its own, and only, reward. The insulted and injured go unavenged, while the unconscionable Alyosha gets Katya, and the unspeakable prince, favoured by fortune in every respect, is left in secure possession of his ill-gotten gains and about to marry a young heiress. The novel excoriates starry-eyed idealism and contains an angry caricature of the Petrashevsky coterie. It may be taken as a farewell to the Utopian dreams that haunted Dostoevsky's youth.

If he had the unhappiness of knowing that his first ambitious effort since his return to literature was, for all the welcome it received from an undiscriminating public, a mediocre piece of work, he had reason to feel that it was merely a misstep. He had something to say and he would yet find a way to say it. For the present, he had another iron in the fire: his prison memoirs. He had begun jotting down reminiscences of his life as a convict shortly after his release. He may have started writing them even before his chains were struck off. It is certain that he had brought back from Siberia a notebook containing scraps of prison argot and barrack talk which he had set down on the spot. It was during the hard weeks in Tver, when he seemed to be neither bond nor free, that the work took definite shape in his head. He was calling it *Notes from the Dead House* (known in English and hereafter referred to as *The House of the Dead*), and though he planned to make it impersonal, he was

sure it would be a gripping thing, full of stuff that was new to literature. Besides, a liberal audience—and what part of the reading
public could not be so described in those days?—would lap up
the story of the life in prison of a former political convict. He expected to have it ready by December 1. Actually it was serialized
in *Vremya* two years later, in 1861-2, after the appearance of the
early chapters in a newspaper the previous year.

In spite of the thin pretence of being the memoirs of a man who
had served a ten-year sentence for killing his wife, *The House of
the Dead* is so patently woven of Dostoevsky's own experiences as
to furnish practically a complete record of his prison days. Nevertheless, the book is for the most part impersonal, as he had wished
it to be, and always gripping. The author, as might be expected, does
some psychologizing. He accounts for the convicts' drinking bouts
and such splurging as was possible for them, their extreme touchiness and bragging, their sudden outbursts of violence, by their unconscious longing, branded and fettered as they were, to assert
themselves, their terrible need to taste at least an illusion of freedom. Time and distance had softened and enobled the faces that
looked so coarse and vicious when he had first come to live among
them. In fact, he is not free from a tendency to idealize his fellow
prisoners. He describes two or three of the convicts as examples
of moral excellence. "Perhaps," he ventures, referring to the criminals, "they are the most gifted, the strongest of our people," and he
speaks of the mighty energies that have been wasted within the
prison walls. On the other hand, several monsters stalk through
these pages. Men of immense strength of will, they are inaccessible
to repentance and look down on the common herd, those who
honour the moral code whether they observe or break it. Prison
gave Dostoevsky an insight into the nature of evil which violently
shook his faith in man's native goodness. "The characteristics of the
executioner," he remarks casually, "exist in embryo in almost
every man of to-day." Both gnomic utterances and psychological
observations are, however, merely parenthetical in this account of
convict life, as straightforward as it is masterly.

In some respects this book stands apart from the entire body of
Dostoevsky's work. It differs from the rest as a drawing differs
from a portrait in oils. The dispassionate observer stands between

the characters and the reader, and prevents that intimate contact with them that Dostoevsky's fiction affords. It is the situations, not the people, that are memorable. Here is not a work of imagination, but what may be called a "documentary." It lacks the feverish, troubling, subversive quality that is his hallmark, and one is not surprised to find Tolstoy, who was out of sympathy with Dostoevsky's most characteristic work, placing this wholesome book at the head and front of his confrère's performance. Behind the prison walls there is no one who doubts that life is worth living if one is free, no one who asks whether freedom is ever difficult or dangerous. It is curious that in *The House of the Dead,* which is obviously autobiographical, the author's inner life should remain out of the picture, while in his fictional writing, one constantly detects his lineaments in the features of his imagined saints and criminals.

CHAPTER THIRTEEN

"REVOLT OF THE PASSIONS"

I N THE last century Western Europe exercised the same fascination over the Russian mind that it still does over the American. "To the Russian," Dostoevsky has a sympathetic character in one of his later novels observe, "Europe is as precious as Russia; every stone in her is cherished and dear. Europe was as much our fatherland as Russia. Oh, even more so! It is impossible to love Russia more than I do, but I never reproached myself because Venice, Rome, Paris, the treasures of their arts and sciences, their whole history, are dearer to me than Russia. Oh, those old, alien stones, those wonders of God's ancient world, those fragments of holy wonders are dear to the Russian, and are even dearer to us than to the inhabitants of those lands themselves."

Dostoevsky had no memory of the time when he had not been dreaming of visiting that part of the world, particularly Italy. If only he had a chance to tread that fabulous soil while there was still some vigour and heat and poetry left in him! Finally, in the summer of 1862, the wish was realized. He had completed *The House of the Dead* and it was running serially in the magazine. Moreover, he had sold the rights to its publication in book form for the substantial sum of twenty-five hundred roubles. *Vremya* was going well enough for him to leave it in Mikhail's hands with only a few qualms for thus shirking his responsibility. He found reasons, though not very adequate ones, for leaving his wife behind.

His heart leapt as the train crossed the frontier at Eydtkunen. He was excited, and he was puzzled. What was the secret of Europe's pull upon the imagination? How was it that the cultivated among his own countrymen, while owing everything to Europe, still remained essentially Russian? Was there some curious chemical reaction between the human spirit and the soil in which it was rooted? Whether these thoughts kept him awake, or whether he

164

meditated thus because he couldn't sleep, he came to Berlin in no mood to like the city or its inhabitants and decided in disgust that it looked and smelled just like Petersburg. He had a happier glimpse of the Rhineland, and in the middle of June found himself in Paris. The weather was nasty. There wasn't a soul he knew in the city. In the two miserable weeks that he spent there he formed a violently hostile opinion of the Parisians and of the French people generally. They were polite and venal, solemn and false, and as servile in fact as they were noble in appearance. This nation of shopkeepers believed that the whole duty of man was to make money and accumulate possessions, all the while crooking the knee to honour, virtue, high ideals. The female of the species had every mark of the kept woman: greediness, vivacity, vacuity, depravity. The principles proclaimed by the great revolution had failed. Liberty—what was it but the freedom to do what you pleased? But under the Second Empire, you could do what you pleased only if you had a million. And since not everybody had a million, there was no liberty. Equality too was non-existent. As for fraternity, how was that possible among a people with individualism, aggressive and predatory, in the blood? Fraternity could only exist where the individual was ready to give himself into the hands of the community without question or reserve, and where the community was intent on insuring the personal liberty of the individual, while guaranteeing his security as a member of the group. This was the true socialism, a system based not on rational self-interest, but on brotherly love. In 1848 Karl Marx had predicted that the bourgeois order, "with its classes and class contrasts," would be superseded by "an association in which the free development of the individual is the preliminary condition for the free development of all." He had expected that the change would come about through violent revolution, whereas Dostoevsky relied upon Christian altruism. As no such spirit was discernable in the West, he wrote, socialism could never come about there. When he was thus arguing with himself in public —he gave an account of his trip on his return home in a series of rambling feuilletons, which he called *Winter Notes on Summer Impressions*—he said only by implication that Russia was a more fertile ground for the seed of Christian communism.

It is likely that he discussed these views with Alexander Herzen, the celebrated expatriate, when he crossed the Channel to spend a week in London. Strange, how he was drawn to these socialists! Herzen found his visitor a naïve, somewhat muddle-headed person, but very likeable, and filled with that faith in the Russian people which was a tenet of this radical's own creed.

London struck Dostoevsky at once as different from the French capital. It was on a grander scale. The streets were more crowded, the parks more magnificent than anything in Paris, the slums more horrible, and there was no effort to conceal or disguise the sores of the city. Was this the final answer to the riddle of how man should live with his fellows? He went to see the Crystal Palace at Sydenham and thought he was in Babylon. The structure filled him with horror. Was it for this that man had worked and suffered through the centuries—this epitome of soulless materialism, this apocalyptic monster of iron and glass?

One Saturday after midnight he lost his way and found himself walking through Whitechapel. The gas flares shone weirdly on the sullen faces of men sodden with drink, women with the voices of harpies, and ragged waifs. For three days afterwards he was tormented by the memory of what he had seen. In the Haymarket he watched the prostitutes in and around the cafés, saw girls barely in their teens soliciting, and mothers bringing mere children for the trade. The poor, the desperate, were jostling one another in the darkness into which their brothers had carelessly thrust them. As for the ministers of religion, they were plump, dignified gentlemen, catering to the wealthy classes, sending missionaries to convert the African heathen and ignoring the savages at home. This vast agglomeration of men and things seemed to him to be governed by an unclean spirit, arrogant and blind.

Winter Notes on Summer Impressions is a scathing critique of the bourgeois order, and by implication a prophecy of its downfall. In these pages he dealt exclusively with Paris and London, ignoring the remainder of his journey, which had taken him to Italy via Switzerland. In Geneva he met Strakhov and the two went to Florence, where they spent a leisurely week. They walked into the Uffizi and despite Strakhov's protests promptly walked out again. Except for the "Madonna della Sedia," Dostoevsky was bored by the canvases. The other monuments of the ancient, splendid city meant

no more to him. As a traveller, he was interested above all in the
new faces that he saw about him, the private conflicts that he could
read in them. He had no eyes for landscape and cared for the
sights of the town only as a backdrop for the human drama. They
spent their days walking the streets where the crowd was thickest,
and in the evening they would sit over a glass of the local red
wine and talk. They did not go to Venice, and so Dostoevsky had
no opportunity to drift in a gondola in the arms of a young Venetian, as he had playfully anticipated when he was planning the
trip. Nor did they go to Rome. Instead, they recrossed the Alps,
and he returned home.

He had gone abroad with that reverence for Europe which was
common to Russian intellectuals, but, without fully realizing it,
he had carried with him a complete set of prejudices against the
more recent phases of Western civilization. The eight or ten weeks
that he spent in Europe served only to intensify his hostility. He
came home all but convinced that the people of the West were
incapable of living together in Christian brotherhood, and were
doomed to go down in a war of all against all. At the same time
his faith in his own countrymen had been strengthened. These
convictions, which he retained to the end, he eventually erected
into a doctrine. The *Winter Notes* exude a petty venom against
the French and English which makes it look as though, unwilling
to consider the beam in the Russian eye, he went all the more
ferociously about the business of casting the mote out of the foreign eye. In his stories and novels the weaknesses of both the
Russian soul and the Russian system are manifest. Yet his publicist
writing exhibits a tyrannical inner check against giving vent to any
thoroughgoing criticism of the fatherland.

II

Once home again, Dostoevsky took up his life where he had
dropped it. He had reason to be heartened by the turn affairs were
taking. He had brought back with him material for his travel
sketches. His *House of the Dead* was having a great vogue. The
review was forging bravely ahead. If it held its own for another
year or two, they would be able to pay off all the debts they had

incurred in connection with it, and it would become a profitable enterprise. True, his editorial duties left small leisure for the kind of writing that he most wanted to do. Nevertheless the November issue of the magazine carried a story over his signature. It was "An Unpleasant Predicament," a coldly satirical account of the disasters that ensue when a would-be benign superior condescends to fraternize with his humble subordinates. The story, which is more skilfully wrought than most of his minor pieces, is a thrust at the false brand of humanitarianism in a day what that virtue was given lip service everywhere.

The year 1863 began inauspiciously with the Polish rebellion. After some hesitation the general public allowed itself to be overwhelmed by a wave of patriotism. Politics was not the strong point of Dostoevsky's review, and some months passed before it ran an article, from Strakhov's pen, on the Polish question. The editor liked the piece, the censor passed it, and it appeared duly in the April issue. And then the blow fell. A jingoistic Moscow paper raised a hue and cry against the article as pro-Polish. Strakhov's style was so abstruse that it was possible to put this interpretation on his words, although nothing was further from his mind than to give aid and comfort to Russia's hereditary enemy. The ill-starred article was soon the talk of the town, and the matter came to the Emperor's ears. "All Moscow is indignant about it," he observed one morning to the Minister of the Interior. The latter promptly responded that the review had been suppressed. The diplomatic lie sealed *Vremya's* fate.

Here was a piece of ill luck. The magazine was the innocent victim of a misunderstanding. Its suppression was hard on all those connected with it and was a disaster for Mikhail. Shortly before the crash he had sold his cigarette factory, which had been steadily going down hill. Now he had debts amounting to twenty thousand roubles and nothing to fall back upon. For Dostoevsky it was the old story of defeat, disappointment, endless anxiety. His wife was ill, and he was again short of money. The sums that had come to him during the past year or two he had somehow been unable to hold on to, and for the present he had no prospects. Yet in the midst of it all he found himself preparing to go abroad. He borrowed the money for the trip from the Fund for Needy Authors, the loan being secured by the copyright on his books. How could he take such a step at such a time? He had his reasons.

There was his health. His falling sickness was getting worse. His memory was failing rapidly, and the depression that followed each attack was so severe that he feared he would ultimately be driven mad. The Petersburg doctors gave him such contradictory advice that he felt he must seek counsel elsewhere—from Ramberg in Berlin and Trousseau in Paris. His seizures occurred at least once a month and sometimes twice in one week. There was another motive for his journey than the need for consulting physicians, though it is doubtful if it was a conscious one at the outset. The gaming-tables of the German watering-places offered him the chance of mending the family fortunes by a rapid stroke of luck. The gambler in him had long been waiting his chance, and now he leapt at it. He reached Berlin about the middle of August, and from there went straight to Wiesbaden, one of the four towns where roulette flourished under the aegis of the law.

Here he succumbed to the fever that was to burn in him for years. Watching the men and women at the tables, he discovered the secret of winning. It was very simple. Fate was in his grip. He worked out a system. The thing was to follow it faithfully and keep cool whatever turn luck took. He had two difficulties: he couldn't stick to his system: he couldn't keep cool. He applied his system, won over ten thousand francs, and locked them up, determined to leave town the next morning without looking into the casino again. The next morning he was back at the tables. He failed to follow his system, lost most of his winnings, returned again in the evening, followed his system, won three thousand francs, and was able to leave Wiesbaden the next day with five thousand francs in winnings.

If, in spite of the fact that he believed in his system and that he had money in his pocket to back his belief, he left the place for Paris after four days, it was because he was obeying another, stronger pull. He was off to keep his rendezvous with Polina.

III

Dostoevsky may have come to know Apollinariya Prokofyevna Suslova—Polina or Polya to her friends—the second year after his return to Petersburg. She contributed a story to the September issue of *Vremya* for 1861, and indeed her literary ambitions may have brought them together. He soon began to visit the house, where he met her younger sister, Nadezhda, with whom he became very friendly. Both sisters, though daughters of a former serf, were well educated, and exemplified the "emancipated woman" who had emerged in the early sixties, that era of feminism. They belonged to the nihilist generation which at once repelled and fascinated him. Nadezhda, the first Russian member of her sex to become a physician, was of the rigoristic, puritanic type, Polina, under the composed, matter-of-fact exterior that was the fashion, concealed an emotional instability that was to work havoc with her life. Hers was a fiery nature, impetuous, intransigent, impatient of restraint, avid of experience, and not without a streak of cruelty. When Dostoevsky met her she was an extremely attractive girl in her early twenties.

They were friends. They were lovers. It is said that she took the initiative in declaring herself. Both by nature and conviction she was careless, in fact scornful, of the proprieties, and she had no inhibitions regarding physical intimacy. It was her first affair, and she took it seriously. Yet the celebrity may have meant to her more than the man. He—at forty—was thrilled to find this girl half his age in love with him, but he failed to live up to her idea of what a passionate relationship should be. Either because he showed a disconcerting lack of loverly abandon or because she felt humiliated by not coming first with him, indeed by being treated as a convenience, she repeatedly spoke of breaking with him. Many years later she was able to tell her husband that she had not been able to forgive Dostoevsky his unwillingness to divorce his wife on her account. As a matter of fact, to protect Marya Dmitrievna's peace of mind he went to great lengths to hide his liason from her, and he succeeded.

In the spring of 1863 Polina went to Paris, as so many of her compatriots did, to breathe the free air of the West, to study, to live. Perhaps at moments the trip seemed to her to be in the nature of a flight from her entanglement with Dostoevsky. Nevertheless, it was understood that he would join her in Paris and that together they would go to Italy. His unfaithfulness to Marya Dmitrievna was no secret to Mikhail, and what is more, his wife's sister knew of it and apparently did not condemn him.

He reached the French capital on August 26, 1863, and his note announcing his arrival was answered by a letter from Polina telling him that he had come "a bit late." He used to tell her that she would be slow to surrender: he was wrong. She had given herself to another "at the first call, without a struggle, without assurance, almost without hope of being loved in return." This other was a handsome young Spaniard—a medical student—with whom she had plunged into an affair on her arrival in Paris. To this new lover she meant no more than a week's pastime, and by the time Dostoevsky came it was fairly clear to her that her Spaniard was through with her, but that could not lessen her passion. There was nothing to do but tell Dostoevsky how she felt. She had feared his coming, while half desiring it. She pitied him and yet anticipated the pain she was to give him with half-acknowledged malice.

Before her letter had time to reach him, he came straight to her room, barely recovered from the fatigues of his journey and from the slight attack that he had had en route. What then passed between them is retailed in her diary.

She was taken aback: "I thought you wouldn't come, after my letter."

"What letter?" he asked.

"Telling you not to come."

"Why?"

"Because you are too late."

His head sank: "Polya," he said after a short pause. "I must know everything. Let's go somewhere. Tell me everything or it will kill me."

They left the room and got into a cab. They did not look at each other, He clung to her hand, now and then squeezing it convulsively. "Don't, don't," she tried to soothe him. "I am here." He did not open his lips except to shout to the driver in a voice of despair: "*Vite, vite!*"

When they were alone in his room he fell at her feet, and clasping her knees burst out crying.

"I have lost you. I knew it."

As soon as he could master himself, he began to question her.

The other man—was he young, was he handsome, was he clever? Had she given herself to him? The last query roused her: it wasn't right, she said, to ask such questions.

"I don't know," said he, "what's right and what's wrong."

As she went on talking it became clear that she was terribly in love with a man who no longer loved her. Dostoevsky clutched his head. Only two weeks ago she had been writing that she was ardently in love with *him*. His worst fears were realized. She was bound to turn to another. She had only fallen in love with him by mistake, because her heart was roomy. But this other—it was a purely physical attraction. There might be hope for him still.

He was resigned now, and quiet. Better to have had the gift of her love for a while than never to have known it at all. He told her so. They must remain friends. They had planned to travel in Italy as lovers. Why not let him take her there, anyhow? They would be as brother and sister.

Oh, yes, she could believe in his ability to maintain such a relation! He would have his novel to occupy him. She spoke thus, perhaps not because he had given her reason to believe him cold, but because she was somewhat piqued by the rapidity with which he had accepted the new state of affairs. Her words hurt him. Didn't she know how hard it would be for him to get over this?

When they separated, she promised to come and see him the next day. She felt better after having spoken to him. He understood her.

The following day Polina received news that her Spaniard had typhus and could not be seen. Dostoevsky tried to hearten her. Two mornings later he was roused from sleep by a knock at his door. It was Polina, red-eyed and white-faced, come to ask him to visit her as soon as possible. Then she left.

The previous day she had run into her supposedly stricken lover on the street in the best of health. It was all over. She had locked herself in her room and stayed awake all night, crying. She had made up her mind to kill her deceiver. But first she went to ask Dostoevsky to come to see her. She dared not remain with him, for she hoped against hope that her faithless lover would yet come to make amends.

He did not, and in fact ignored her ever afterwards. Dostoevsky was there promptly. He listened to the story, sympathized, dismissed the whole affair as an ugly accident, and told her to give up all thought of avenging herself—he had previously said that on such creatures one used insect powder.

Dostoevsky now found himself in a situation all too much like that which preceded his marriage. Again he was the displaced lover comforting the woman he had lost to a younger man. Polina continued to confide in him fully and lean on his advice. Consumed with the fury of a woman scorned, she seemed to have no thought for him. Would she or would she not join him in his trip south? She did not keep him long in suspense. She had the courage to tear herself away from Paris and the cruelty to let him take her to Italy. He was relieved to shake from his heels the dust of this magnificent, abominable city, where the only things one didn't tire of were the fruit and the wine; but the whole adventure was madness. He was going off on an ambiguous, expensive journey as though he were free of worry about either health or money, as though there were no brother in desperate straits, no sick wife, no troublesome stepson to consider.

IV

The trip thrilled and exhausted him with the fever of balked sensuality. Having just emerged from a passionate affair and plainly still burning with the agony of it, Polina was doubly desirable. If he had gone out of his way to contrive a situation abounding, for a man of his make-up, both in subtle torment and in that perverse pleasure which he sucked out of pain, he could not have done better. She had consented to become his travelling companion, as had originally been planned: might he not yet succeed in persuading her to become his mistress once more? Her behaviour was not such as to make him despair, but, on the other hand, she said nothing to give him hope. As a matter of fact, she was determined not to return to his arms.

They were both unhappy, but they pretended to each other and themselves that they were off on a lark, and his tension and anxiety expressed itself in an exaggerated gaiety. They travelled via Germany and when, on September 5, they reached Baden-Baden, they engaged two connecting rooms. They had tea in her room—it was about ten o'clock in the evening—and then, feeling tired, she slipped out of her shoes, lay down, dressed, on the bed, and asked him to pull his chair closer. She took his hand and held it in hers. He said he liked sitting that way. She told him she had been harsh with him in Paris and had seemed to be thinking only of herself, but indeed, she had been thinking of him, too. Did she guess what was going on within him? Suddenly he got up, stumbled over her shoes, and sat down again. He explained that he had wanted to close the window, but, no, he confessed that what he had really wanted was to kiss her foot. She was embarrassed, almost frightened, and tucked her feet in, but invited him to stay on. He stared at her till she hid her face in the pillow. Finally she dismissed him, saying that she wanted to go to sleep. He lingered on, then kissed her good night, all too warmly, and went out with a smile, but returned, ostensibly to close the widow, and advised her to get undressed. She said she would do so as soon as he left. He did not close his door until, under a flimsy pretext, he had come back once more.

The next day he apologized profusely for his unbrotherly behaviour, saying that he had been drunk, but she passed the matter over in a manner that left him as uncertain as ever where he stood. Didn't he have a gambler's chance of winning her? His attention during their Baden stay was divided between this hazard and the gaming-tables. Perhaps, under the circumstances, his gambling was in the nature of a substitute for another form of excitement. He spoke of his gambling-fever as a "damned revolt of the passions."

He made no progress with the lady, and he lost practically everything at roulette. In his first quarter of an hour at the Baden tables he won six hundred francs; his Wiesbaden "system" was working. But he could not stick to it, and disaster followed. How could he keep away from the tables? He needed money for Mikhail, for his wife, for his literary future, and for the immediate expenses of the trip. Hadn't he gone abroad for no other purpose, as he wrote to Mikhail, than "to save you all?" Far from playing the saviour, he was reduced to begging for help. He had to write to Mikhail to remit what he had sent him from the Wiesbaden winnings for safe-keeping, and to his wife to return part of the money he had sent her. The thought that this might cause her inconvenience, ill and needy as she was, only added to his torments: after a fashion, he loved her. Meanwhile, in the hope of recovering something, he took as many as he dared of his last francs, won a considerable sum with them, staked it all on one throw, and lost the whole. There was nothing for it but to leave Baden-Baden at once. At Geneva he pawned his watch and Polina her ring. This enabled them to go on to Turin, where the remittances from home were to reach him. He lived in daily terror that the hotel bill would be presented and he would not be able to meet it—the scandal of the situation would be terrible. As soon as the money reached them they made for Rome, and from there went on to Naples. There they ran into the Herzens' whom Dostoevsky perplexed by introducing Polina vaguely as a relative, while flaunting his intimacy with her.

She took pleasure in provoking him, but now and then repented her cruelty. There was a day in Turin when she was affectionate towards him. He responded so eagerly that she redoubled her tenderness and ended by crying on his bosom. He did not know what to make of her. Sometimes her resistance seemed mere coyness. In allowing certain intimacies without yielding to him, was she leaning toward surrender or was she denying his manhood? Was she making him the scapegoat for her Spaniard, or was she avenging herself on him for his own sins against her in the past? Was it just heartless coquetry? When, one day, he told her that she must not keep a man cooling his heels too long or he would bolt, she smiled. Was she still thinking of "the Peninsula," as he called her Salvador? She denied this, but only with her lips.

There must have been moments when his passion for her was mixed with intense hatred. Occasionally he would allow himself to taunt her. One night in Rome he did so with a peculiarly offensive gaiety. He did not try to keep it up. He was having a bad time of it, he confessed. Everything presented itself as an onerous duty, a tiresome lesson to be learned. At least he was trying to divert her. She was touched, and threw her arms around his neck. But he was not deceived and told her sadly that she was on her way to Spain Abruptly he began to joke again, and when he left her—it was one in the morning and she was in bed undressed—observed that it was humiliating to have to leave her thus: "Russians," he concluded with a military flourish, "never retreat." And he retired.

Polina, being subject to the literary itch, used this phase of her relations with Dostoevsky as material for a story. It is the kind of fiction that is only a very thinly veiled transcript of truth. The hero who plays Dostoevsky's part in this narrative relieves the ennui of the lady in the case by relating to her his adventures with a prostitute. When this form of entertainment disgusts her, he ventures that such low pleasures serve only to heighten the transports of exalted love. So closely does the story follow the record of the affair in her diary that although this incident does not figure there, it is highly probable that she invented it. If the conversation did indeed take place, he may have talked as much to vex as to amuse.

Toward the end, Polina's story moves rapidly. The heroine discovers more things to dislike in her companion, their relations become intolerable, and she drowns herself. Actually, the end of the trip on which the lady went with Dostoevsky was less dramatic. From Naples they retraced their steps to Turin, where he must have received money from Russia—he had written Strakhov that when he reached Turin again he would be flat. There they separated peacefully enough, she going back to Paris, he making his way home. They had been together a little less than two months. He stopped in Homburg sufficiently long to lose everything he had at the gaming-tables, and having exhausted all other resources, was forced to appeal to Polina. She raised a small sum to send him, even pawning her watch, rather relieved that she could thus pay off some of the money he had spent on her. She could not bear to feel obligated to this man whom she had once idolized, but whom she was now beginning to hate.

CHAPTER FOURTEEN

ENDS AND BEGINNINGS

IT WAS October before Dostoevsky was home again. He found himself in a cheerless situation. Marya Dmitrievna, who was staying in Vladimir, had grown much worse. She could not brave a Petersburg winter, so he took her to Moscow and stayed there with her. It must have been clear to him that her end was coming, and pity, that had been potent in drawing him to her at first, kept him beside her at the last. His own health was deplorable: either he had not profited by the advice of the European physicians or, in the stress of his affair with Polina, he had not consulted them at all. The change of air and scene had wrought an improvement, but it was short-lived. And then, although it was understood that Mikhail would be allowed to resume the magazine under another title, permission was slow in coming and the uncertainty was harassing. The sole comfort was a legacy of three thousand roubles from Uncle Kumanin, which Dostoevsky received in November and which meant a temporary surcease of money worries.

Finally, the authorities relented, and in 1864 *Epokha (The Epoch)*, as the new review was called, materialized. It was started under the most unfavourable auspices and failed to achieve the success of its predecessor. To begin with, the permit came so tardily that the January issue appeared only late in March, when the subscription season was over. Even the established reviews were doing poorly, the reading public being in an apathetic mood. The first issue had some claim to distinction, containing as it did a story by Turgenev and the initial instalment of a remarkable contribution by Dosto-evsky: "Notes from the Underground." But the make-up of the new magazine was shabby and the contents of the subsequent num-bers singularly flat. This was partly due to the hostility of the censors, who mutilated the contributions which they did not kill. Mikhail had little cash to invest in the enterprise and, as he was far

177

from well, could not bring to the business the energy and shrewdness it demanded. To crown it all, Dostoevsky, who was expected to edit *Epokha,* could not be of much help, since he was absent from Petersburg most of the time and absorbed in his private affairs.

It became plainer to him every day that Masha's state was hopeless. Like his mother, and like several creatures of his imagination, she was the victim of consumption. She was virtually wasting away, now lamenting her end, now making wild plans for years she was never to see. Her irritability grew extreme, and at times her mind was unsettled. She had a mania for winding up clocks until the springs broke. She would imagine that the sick-room was full of devils—the doctor had to chase them out of the window with his handkerchief. For days, for weeks, for months, Dostoevsky had no respite from this misery.

His one refuge was the house of his sister Vera, the only member of the family in Moscow whom he cared to see. Nothing could have been in sharper contrast to the sick-chamber than this happy household, bubbling with the activities of eight children, the youngest an infant in arms, the eldest, Sonia, a girl of eighteen. Dostoevsky grew quite fond of his brother-in-law, the excellent Dr. Ivanov, who was treating Masha, admired the little ones, and made a favourite of Sonia. He had noticed her on his previous visits to Moscow, but it was only now, on looking at her closely, that he recognised what a whole-hearted, exquisite creature she was.

But for all the comfort that Vera and her family afforded him, he felt that his burden was more than he could bear. Masha was dying. He kept having attacks and, in addition, was again suffering from piles. What with his debts and the expenses of his wife's illness, the legacy was soon gone, and when the spring thaws came, he had to go on wearing his heavy goloshes and his winter overcoat for want of the price of seasonable apparel. By nightfall his nerves were in tatters, and he would sit down to his desk stale and sick. He had all kinds of tempting ideas for articles, but he couldn't manage to write one of them. And the thought that he was useless to the magazine at this critical time—the first issues were decisive—tormented him. At least he was able to go on somehow with that queer, savage story, "Notes from the Underground." It was slow work at best, and it was bound to suffer a dismal interruption. He was labouring over the brutal details of the story to the sound his wife made in the next room over the business of dying. He wrote to Mikhail that he had never been in a worse state. The Tver lodgings, the barracks, the prison, the cell in the fortress—these were shadows: only his present hell was real.

Before going abroad, Dostoevsky had installed a tutor in his Petersburg rooms to take charge of his stepson, and the two were still living there. Pasha, who was now in his teens, already showed signs of being a bad egg. Toward the end, Dostoevsky sent for him, but the impossible boy was no consolation to his mother. In fact, she showed him the door, saying she would summon him when she felt that she was dying. When that event seemed imminent, Dostoevsky wrote Mikhail to be sure to ship the boy to Moscow for the funeral and get him a black suit, cheap.

Finally the fretting and the coughing were over, and even the solemn bustle of the death-chamber hushed. It was the evening of April 15. The following day Dostoevsky snatched time from the unfinished "Notes from the Underground" and found composure of spirit to make a long entry in the small brown leather notebook in which he recorded expenses and jotted down passing thoughts.

"Masha lies on the table,"* he wrote. Will he ever see her again? Can one truly love another as oneself? Christ alone was capable of obeying this commandment. His example had made it plain that personality at its highest means nothing but the readiness to surrender one's ego to each and everyone, with the selflessness of perfect love. Such love is the very law of man's ideal, and yet it runs counter to human nature, and will only be realized when that nature is transcended, when the mould of mere humanity is broken, for the nature of God is in direct opposition to the nature of man. The atheists are wrong when they argue against Christianity on the grounds that men still suffer and that there is no brotherhood among them. The Christian ideal cannot obtain on earth, where man is in a state of transition. He is on the way to the attainment of a divine state, which is the end and aim of all development. This new being, so different from the old Adam that he may not even bear the name of man, will live in a timeless, but otherwise unimaginable paradise. All that is certain concerning these godly crea-

* Before placing the body in a coffin it was customary to lay it on a table.

tures is that they "will neither marry nor be given in marriage, but live as the angels of God." They will not require the selfish, separate union between man and woman; each, while preserving his identity and differing from others—for in my Father's house are many mansions—will merge with all in the divine synthesis. The family is sacred, because only through the succession of generations can the spiritual goal be attained, and, too, it is in children as well as in the memory of one's friends that one finds personal immortality. But in the name of the ultimate ideal, the family, with its exclusive ties, must be discarded. No, in heaven there will be no marrying nor giving in marriage. But in the meantime, one who fails—as he and Masha had failed, as man inevitably failed —to sacrifice the self lovingly for another's sake must know that he has sinned and suffer accordingly. Yet what joy in the approaches, however limited and uncertain, to the goal! Such are the contradictory elements in the earthly equilibrium. He concluded with an outburst against materialism, that unripe fruit of paltry knowledge, that principle of death, as opposed to the teaching of true philosophy, which meant God and life, abundant and endless.

There are few passages in Dostoevsky's notebooks more illuminating than these elliptical and incoherent jottings, made on the impulse of the moment, presumably for no eye but his own, to satisfy some inner need for self-clarification. He had once asserted that, if the choice must be made, he would stand with Christ rather than with truth. It is not surprising to find him now standing with Christ against human nature, but he oversteps the bounds of orthodoxy when he insists that the Christian ideal can only be realized when man shall be man no longer, but shall have become as the angels of heaven. What could this mean but that he was bidding Utopia farewell, and further, that in setting up Christ as the pattern of humankind, he was setting before himself an ideal he knew to be poles removed from his own native impulses? The family must ultimately be transcended. He had married; nay, more, he had committed adultery. He might do both again. He looked forward to a state in which man should live free from the lusts of the flesh. He knew himself hopelessly driven by them. The clearest point in these confused reflections is Dostoevsky's will to keep the integrity of each individual, while all attain to a selfless communion.

He was writing in the detached, reflective strain of a somewhat fuzzy-minded Christian philosopher, meditating on things earthly and paradisal, rather than in the tone of a bereaved husband with the death-rattle still in his ears. That at such times he should reflect on the limitations of earthly love points to the tragic flaw in the relation to which death had put a period. If he felt remorse for sin, it was that against Christ, rather than that against his late wife. If he spoke of heaven, he seems not to have been concerned with his meeting Masha there, and he was content with such shabby immortality for her as was afforded by his remembrance of her and the continued existence of her good-for-nothing son. It was as if he had long since accustomed himself to the idea of being without her. As far as possible he had provided for her physical needs and cared for her son, yet she seems to have faded out of the picture long before her end. He had behaved like an unattached man even in the Petersburg days when they were living together. She bore him no children. Hard words were frequently exchanged—it is said that in her rages she did not hesitate to throw up to him the fact that he had been a jailbird. He seems not to have kept their incompatibility a secret from his intimates, though only one revealing reference to the subject has been preserved. It occurs in a letter to Wrangel. Nearly a year after his wife's death Dostoevsky was writing to the man who had witnessed his frantic wooing: "Oh, my friend, she loved me boundlessly. I, too, loved her without measure, but we did not live happily together. I shall tell you everything when we see each other. Now I shall only say that in spite of the fact that we were positively unhappy together (because of her strange, suspicious, and morbidly fantastic character), we couldn't stop loving each other. In fact, the more unhappy we were, the stronger our attachment grew."

One imagines their life together to have been a succession of stormy quarrels and equally stormy reconciliations. This marriage appears to have been presided over by a passion that now took the aspect of love and now that of hatred. Such a relationship is all the more plausible since we find Dostoevsky's imagination playing perpetually and illuminatingly upon the ambivalence of emotion. Moreover, this love that feeds upon mutual unhappiness fits into the picture of a man who had a curious faculty for turning situations against himself, for sucking pleasure out of pain. That he could love his wife sincerely while at the same time being passionately attached to another is intelligible enough. He had, as he had said of Polina Suslova, and as could be said of many of his characters, "a wide heart." When, in his novels, he drew one such roomy-hearted figure after the other, he may well have been creating them in his own image.

The character of Dostoevsky's first wife was assailed by his daughter Lubov (Aimée), the child of his second marriage. In her life of her father she makes out her mother's predecessor to have been a deceitful, dissolute woman who, on the very eve of her wedding, spent the night with a lover, and not only made a cuckold of Dostoevsky afterwards, with the same insignificant youth, but taunted her husband with it later. This version of the matter, like so much else in the book, is untrustworthy. It is barely possible, however, that in this case the biographer was embroidering, in her prejudiced and sensational manner, upon fact. Perhaps Marya resembled her husband in this—that she was capable of continuing to love the one to whom she was unfaithful. In any event, his daughter's malevolent words are contradicted by his own remark in the letter to Wrangel quoted above: "She was the most honest, the most noble-minded and generous-hearted woman that I have ever known in my life." Nearly ten years after her death, when he was married a second time, and happily, he described her to a new-found friend, in whom he discovered a resemblance to her, as "a woman with the loftiest, most rapturous soul . . . an idealist in the fullest sense of the word, yes, and at the same time as pure and simple-hearted as a child." This must be the last word on the subject.

II

Losing no time, the widower returned to Petersburg and to his editorial work. He was back in his old apartment with Pasha— he had sworn to his wife on her deathbed that he would never abandon the boy. His first disagreeable duty was to evict the tutor who, it transpired, had maltreated and starved his pupil, had debauched the fifteen-year-old boy by bringing women from the street into the flat, and ended by carrying off a pair of his employer's sheets.

A little older, a little lonelier, Dostoevsky resumed his former way of life. His immediate task was to complete "Notes from the Underground." This he did, and the final instalment appeared in the April issue of the magazine which came off the press in June. The financial situation was not as acute as usual. Before leaving Moscow, he had sent his brother explicit instructions as to the proper means of squeezing some money out of their godmother, and thanks to his strategy, Mikhail had secured ten thousand roubles from Aunt Kumanina. Furthermore, he had borrowed six thousand roubles from Dr. Ivanov. The sum was sufficient to allow Mikhail to set up a printing establishment as a prop for the review. There were heavy odds against them, but it looked as though, if they worked hard, they might yet put *Epokha* on its legs.

And then Fate struck again. Mikhail took to his bed. His illness was of short duration. On July 10, a little less than three months after burying his wife, Dostoevsky stood beside the lifeless body of his brother.

"I loved my brother infinitely," he wrote to Wrangel, and to Andrey, a fortnight after the blow had fallen: "He loved me more than anyone in the world, more than his wife and children, whom he adored." Dostoevsky was using the hyperbole of bereavement. In his grief he forgot that during his four years of prison Mikhail had let prudence get the better of affection and sent him not a single word, and that there had been a sad scarcity of both letters and remittances during the years of exile. There had been occasions when he had grave doubts of Mikhail's devotion. But no matter. Mikhail had shared his earliest memories. They had grown up together in the same house. For years they had attended the same school. They had lived together. They had worked together. With Mikhail gone, to whom could he confide his anxieties and disillusionments, his hopes and ambitions? Death had never trod so close to him. He had lost a part of himself.

But grieving was a luxury for which he had no leisure. Mikhail's estate consisted of three hundred roubles which went to cover the funeral expenses. In spite of the money sunk in it, the liabilities of the magazine, in the shape of debts that Mikhail had incurred to run it, far exceeded its assets, so that the family was left without visible means of support. The widow and her children, all of them minors, gathered around Uncle Fyodor, their sole hope, and wept. He shouldered the responsibility.

Two courses were open to him. He could abandon the review to its creditors, take the widow and the four orphans—one of the children had died that year of scarlet fever—into his own household, and slave at his pen to support them all, his stepson, and himself, not to mention his dead brother's mistress and her child. This would leave the blot of bankruptcy on Mikhail's memory—an intolerable thought. Although he was himself an incurable borrower, indebtedness always impressed him with a sense of more than merely legal obligation and seemed to him somehow to involve the very personality of the debtor. The other possibility was to continue with the magazine, in the hope of ultimately paying its debts and turning it over to the family as soon as it was a profitable enterprise. After taking counsel with himself and with all concerned, he chose the second course—to his sorrow.

The deceased had been able to run the review partly on credit. Dostoevsky needed cash. Perhaps Andrey would lend him something, at ten per cent interest. But the little brother was not a prey to generous impulses. There was yet another hope: Aunt Kumanina. He had never yet asked anything of her. He would not be asking for himself now—it was to save Mikhail's stricken family that he would swallow his pride. When, a few months previously, he had advised his brother how to get around the difficult old lady, he had mapped out a detailed plan of action: there must be no preliminary skirmishing, a bold attack, thus: "You have a fortune, ten thousand roubles will not ruin you. If you do not come to the rescue, your godson and nephew, and his helpless babes, will be lost! You have one foot in the grave—how will you appear before Christ, and before your late sister?" One must work on her conscience, on her piety, on her family feeling; she would be torn between fear for her money and the dread of taking a sin on her soul; she would wave her hands, she would cluck, she would groan; she would yield. The strategy had worked once, and he may have used it this time. As he sat in the drawing-room of the sprawling Moscow house that he had known since childhood, confronting the quaking, whimsical old woman, was he pierced by the injustice of it all—that he, with his health broken, his work still to do, a mounting load of responsibilities on his shoulders, should be at the mercy of this foolish, useless relic, squatting on her moneybags?

Whatever he may have done or thought, he returned to Petersburg with ten thousand roubles from good old Aunt Kumanina. The sum, like the similar amount Mikhail had received from her, was in the nature of a loan, which was never repaid and which was reckoned as his share of his inheritance from her. With this he could make a start. After some casting about, he found a figurehead to act as nominal editor, since, as an ex-convict, he could not serve in that capacity, and so set *Epokha* on its way again. Legally he had no share in the enterprise, the review being the property of Mikhail's heirs.

He wanted to build up a journal of opinion, a political organ, sensitive to the trend of the times. In *Vremya* he had made some attempt to reconcile the liberal and conservative points of view. In *Epokha* he broke with the Westerners and took a definitely conservative and Slavophil stand. The recent Polish rebellion had started reaction in big places and among the public as well. The incipient revolutionary movement suffered a setback, but the ferment remained at work. Dostoevsky was out to give battle to "the nihilists," with their crude materialism, their harsh, cramping, "Quakerish" attitude. They asked art (when not rejecting it altogether) to limit itself to copying the barren fact. They denied all the poetry and colour and music of life, forgetting that music was the language of things so profound that the mind had not yet grasped them. Worse: theirs was a way of blind violence. As though the blood and thunder of revolution were not always futile! Freedom was not something to be imposed. A nation would take as much as it was capable of enduring, for freedom was a burden. These socialists wanted world citizens, all alike. What a bore! They fancied that if you altered economic conditions, you would have a new human being to deal with, one who would have no need of God or of his own hearthstone. Western poppycock! Nothing can be changed until the soul of man is changed. The brotherhood of man

—here spoke the tenacious Christian socialism of his youth—will be achieved only by love.

One didn't use plain words like socialism and revolution in the public prints. Dostoevsky confided these reflections to his private journal and his letters. He also tried to have them covertly set forth in *Epokha*. He regarded the review as a weapon with which to club the radicals. They returned the blows with interest. *Epokha* got decidely the worst of it. Its opponents were lustier and cleverer. The adversary in Dostoevsky's eyes was *Sovremennik*, which was as aggressive as ever, although it had lost the captaincy of Chernyshevsky, who was by now serving his term as a political convict in Siberia. Dostoevsky saw the long arm of that powerful review in every mishap that befell his own.

All during the autumn and winter he was in continuous fever. He haggled with the printer, he ran to the censor, he placated subscribers, he begged for contributions, he edited manuscripts, he read proof, he borrowed money, he paid some of the bills, he borrowed more money. By the end of 1864, he had all but succeeded in making up for the delay of the earlier issues. He did it by bringing out two numbers every month, but he had to sacrifice the quality of his material. He had high editorial standards, but he had to print what he could get, which wasn't very good. One of his best contributors, Grigoryev, had died shortly after Mikhail did. The turn of the year brought no change in the magazine's fortunes. The subscribers numbered only thirteen hundred, as contrasted with *Vremya's* four thousand. He slaved twelve, thirteen, nineteen hours a day, but he could only work intermittently. He made promises. He couldn't keep them. He tore his hair over his mistakes. He committed them again. He worked furiously, but all he produced was confusion. He brought out one issue. He brought out another. And then the cash box was empty. Not a copeck with which to pay the paper-manufacturer, the printer, the contributors. He made a few feeble efforts to save the lost cause and then surrendered. *Epokha* was done for.

I I I

Dostoevsky's work on *Epokha* had been chiefly editorial. In all he contributed to the magazine a grotesque skit, "Crocodile," in which contemporaries saw some thrust at Chernyshevsky, and "Notes from the Underground." The personal element had been absent from *The House of the Dead*. In "Notes from the Underground" it returned with a vengeance. One is back again in the confessional. In fact, the original title of the story seems to have been "A Confession." But the man to whom one listens does not merely beat his breast. He sticks out his tongue, he argues, he spits, he struts, as his disquieting, irritating, absorbing soliloquy unfolds.

This creature of the underground—one has encountered him in Dostoevsky's pages before, if under different circumstances and in a different guise. A homeless child, early humiliated by the relatives upon whom he is dependent, he is repulsed by his more fortunate schoolfellows. One suspects that in describing the boy's hatred for his coarse, stupid companions, and his exacting demands upon his sole friend, Dostoevsky was to some extent recording his own experiences at the engineering school. Reduced to a proud solitude that is increasingly difficult for him to bear, the boy becomes a daydreamer, a lotus-eater, a victim of his own fantasies, like so many characters of the early stories. But while those were gentle anaemic souls, the undergroundling is a creature full of gall and venom. His imaginings make up for the meanness, the gloom, the savagery of his actual life, and allow him to go on squatting in the mud undisturbed. After a stretch of dreaming in which he poses as the mighty hero serving the cause of "the good and the beautiful," he plunges all the more greedily into the nastiness of petty, furtive, shameful debauchery.

As the years go monotonously by, this opiate all but loses its potency for him. On the other hand, he remains an unintegrated personality, torn by the conflict of opposed tendencies, unable to give himself wholly to one emotion or the other, agonized by the helpless inconsistencies of his own character. "I did not know," he says, "how to become anything: spiteful or kind, a rascal or an honest man, a hero or an insect." Thin-skinned in the extreme, he alternates between a sick sense of his own shortcomings and a complete arrogance toward the rest of the world. He craves the approval of the people he despises. A morbid self-esteem exposes him to constant fear of humiliation, yet he courts the thing he fears. Incapable of action, he insists that it is the habit of reflection, his overdeveloped intellect, that arrests his impulses. Having thus excused himself to himself, he withdraws into a corner, nurses his wounds and sulks. His humiliation, his injuries, his imagined revenge, his very impotence, becomes a source of perverse pleasure, a poisonous food for his starved ego.

The undergroundling reveals himself completely in his attempt to emerge from his den and participate in normal life. In a moment of abysmal loneliness he forces himself upon a group of former schoolmates, knowing that he is not wanted, and joins in a farewell dinner tendered to a man whom he abominates. Things go from bad to worse. His companions wipe the floor with him but he sticks to them, and when they all go off to a brothel he borrows money from one of them and follows them. Waking in the small hours, he proceeds to paint for his bedfellow a fearful picture of the future that awaits her, contrasting it with the happiness she has forfeited by leading a life of shame. His eloquence brings a lump into his own throat. But he understands that in talking thus he is enjoying the display of his own rhetoric and, what is more fundamental, he is making up for the mortification he had suffered by outraging the girl's soul after having outraged her body. He reduces her to contrite tears and, having impressed her with his inner nobility, leaves her, feeling that he is a hero to this poor bawd, if to no one else. Out of gratitude, perhaps, he invites her to his lodgings.

The next few days he alternates between magnanimous, sentimental dreams in which she eventually becomes his adoring wife, and fear of what will happen should she accept his invitation to come to him in his shabby rooms. Indeed, when she finally does turn up one evening and surprises him in the midst of a humiliating scene with his servant, he is so enraged at her having caught him thus that he tells her that during their night together he had merely been making game of her. She, feeling that he is not so much vicious as wretched, is swept toward him, crushed though she is, on a wave of pitying love. Even as he responds to her embrace he is stabbed by the realization that the tables have been turned and that she is the heroine of the situation, while he has become the object of her compassion—that she had love to give, while he had nothing. His envy of her whipping up his spite, his hatred kindling a sudden passionate desire for her, he commits the final outrage: he deliberately turns her gesture of pure affection into a prelude to an act of lust such as is the routine of her trade, and presses the insult home by cramming money into her hand as he shows her the door.

The story is a perfect anatomy of the neurotic temperament, with its compulsions, its inhibitions, its emotional ambivalence and consequent discords, every expression of a disruptive maladjustment. In telling it, the undergroundling clings to the fiction that he is setting it down without thought of the reading public, simply to get rid of an oppressive memory. Before he makes his confession, however, he delivers himself of a rambling philippic directed against imaginary opponents, his voice now crackling with sarcasm, now choking with hysteria. There is self-analysis here, there is philosophizing, there is revolt.

Plainly this tormented soul has much in common with his creator. If Dostoevsky did not necessarily share the undergroundling's experience, this rebellion is his, these ideas are of a piece with his thinking. Indeed, the undergroundling's outpourings can best be understood in connection with the polemics in which Dostoevsky had engaged on the pages of his reviews. The "new men," for whom Chernyshevsky was the chief spokesman, believed that human beings were governed by enlightened self-interest. Dostoevsky saw things otherwise. Human nature, his hero insists, is not so simple. Man is at bottom an irrational creature. He loves not only creation, but chaos and destruction, not only well-being, but also suffering; he loathes the mechanical, the predictable, the final. Reason is but a part of the self; it knows what it has succeeded in learning, and some things it will never learn; all that's certain about history is that it has little to do with reason.

A belittling of the intellectual member is not surprising in a man who proclaimed himself ready to side against truth, if he could not have Christ on other terms. Was he afraid of reason? It threatened his faith. It challenged traditions and allegiances to which we will find him clinging with increasing fervour. Worse: that cold light, directed upon his own soul, might reveal a disorder there distressing for him to contemplate, might dispel a darkness that soothed him.

The Christian, Dostoevsky had said to himself in the chastened mood that followed his wife's death, should be ready to surrender his ego. But who could attain to that ideal? No, argues the man

from the underground, strip the personality of all its perquisites
and at the core you will find not the intellect, but the will. What
man wants is not to act rationally and to his own advantage but to
act as he chooses, following his own sweet foolish impulse, no
matter what the consequences may be. And if it be proved beyond
the shadow of a doubt that the will is an illusion, that man is a
mere mechanical device, obedient to laws external to himself? What
if science reaches a point where the behaviour of a given individual
may be calculated fifty years in advance? The undergroundling does
not deny such a horrible eventuality—which, incidentally, science
in our own day has seriously called in question—but he believes
that man would "kick over the whole show," would go mad, rather
than accept such an orderly, completely rational deterministic
scheme of things.

Chernyshevsky and his kind believed that the good of the individual, rightly understood, is one with the good of the community,
and so looked forward to a perfect society established on the basis
of a rational egoism or what a later thinker was to stigmatize as
"intelligent greed." Already in his *Winter Notes on Summer Impressions* Dostoevsky had inveighed against this brand of socialism
as a product of the individualistic West. Seeing that the spirit of
brotherhood is wanting, he argued there, the European socialist
seeks to persuade men that it is to their interest to live a communal
life. He reckons the gains and losses entailed thereby, and the
balance is unquestionably in favour of his plan. There is just a
mere trifle on the debit side: the loss of a fraction of personal
liberty. But to the beneficiary this is the fly in the ointment, and
he will have none of it. The socialist will call him a fool and say
that the man hasn't the sense of an ant, who accepts her place in
a rational scheme. The undergroundling, speaking here for Dostoevsky, definitely sides with this fool in rejecting the socialist
millennium. In *What's To Be Done?*, the novel Chernyshevsky
wrote while imprisoned in the fortress of Peter and Paul, the heroine
dreams of a palace inhabited by the happy communists of the
future, a structure of iron and glass that she cannot describe except to say that a hint of it is conveyed by the Crystal Palace at
Sydenham. It is the very building that had so horrified Dostoevsky
during his London visit. It is this Crystal Palace the underground-

ling reviles, declaring it to be actually an ant heap, a sheepfold, a prison. Let my right hand wither, he cries, before I carry one brick to such a building!

He delivers himself of this protest in the course of Chapter Ten, which Dostoevsky had told Mikhail, embodied his central idea, but which had been hopelessly garbled by the censor. "Oh, these censors, these swine, where I mocked everything and sometimes simulated blasphemy, that they let stand, but where I deduced from all that the necessity of faith and of Christ, that they cut! What's the matter with those censors? Are they in a conspiracy against the Government, eh?" One readily imagines that this central idea was of a piece with the meditation on Christ, which he set down in his journal between the writing of the first and second parts of this narrative. Dostoevsky had used the story to attack the positivists, the utilitarians, the rationalists, who had not reckoned with the nature of the creature destined to inhabit the palace of their design. On the other hand, merely to rebel against a mechanistic universe and to cling to one's private whim, as the undergroundling does, was death. What he said in his meditation, what presumably the censors would not let him say in his story, was that the only way out was the way of Christ, the surrender of one's will in the name of love. Unfortunately the passages expunged from the "Notes" have not been preserved.

At the climax of the story it is the prostitute who shows herself capable of a genuine and generous love, while the man from the underground, who has nothing to give, tramples on her precious offering. At this crucial point he is seen as totally deficient, cut off from the sources of "living life." He is here conceived as an example of what it is to have nothing to lean upon, nothing to give oneself to, to be torn from the moorings of tradition, in a word, to be one of those divorced from "the soil," the symbol of every value in Dostoevsky's social philosophy. Not that this conception of the undergroundling is sustained. Dostoevsky spares no effort to strip this "anti-hero" naked and show him in all his shame, and yet he does not compass his end. The wretch's very capacity for rebellion, for pain, shows that life is still hot in him. He may be "the nastiest, stupidest, absurdest, and most envious of all the worms on earth" his behaviour may be base and spiteful, but it is felt to be the warped expression of impulses that are of fundamental worth. He spits upon the good and the beautiful, but it is in the mood of one who calls the grapes sour. And so it is not astonishing when this worm says to his imaginary opponents, the sane, normal men who carry on the world's work beyond the walls of this cave: "There is perhaps more life in me than in you." Nor is it surprising that Dostoevsky makes him, to some extent, his spokesman. A decade later the novelist was to jot down in his notebook an ambiguous apologia for the undergroundling. He is aware of his own baseness and indulges in self-punishment, yet is convinced that no one is any better than himself. "What is to support the will to reform?" Dostoevsky asked. "Reward? Faith? But there is no one to hand out rewards, no one to believe in." One more step, and you have extreme debauchery, crime (murder). That is "the tragedy of the underground," and Dostoevsky prided himself on having been the first to reveal it. "The underground, the underground, the poet of the underground!" he concluded. "Feuilleton writers harp on it, as though it were something humiliating for me. Fools! This is my glory, for it is the truth."

The importance of "Notes from the Underground" is out of all proportion to the size of the piece. The ideas of which it is the vehicle are essential to his later, more massive works. It is the prologue to his novels.

CHAPTER FIFTEEN

LUCKLESS SUITOR

LIFE had snapped in two. He was left alone. He had nobody, nothing, to live for. Masha was gone, Mikhail was gone. The magazine was bankrupt. Existence was a dismal, inane bustling in a vacuum. To establish new contacts, to form new ties—the very thought was an abomination. He felt sterile, he was empty of everything but despair. As he looked back to the past he saw only its warm, familiar, homely aspects, the comradeship it had held, the love, the rewarding work. The future was a blank in which the sole certainties were loneliness, epilepsy with its threat of madness or sudden death, old age.

Shortly after Mikhail's death Dostoevsky expressed these sentiments to Andrey. He reiterated them to Wrangel months later, after the review had gone under. He said the same thing to Polina Suslova's sister. And yet—it was absurd!—at the same time he had the paradoxical feeling that life was just beginning for him. He had, he said as much in earnest as in jest, the nine lives of a cat. There were in him reserves of vitality larger than he guessed. They had not failed him in previous crises; they did not fail him now. He had neither rebelled against nor been crushed by imprisonment and exile. Now fate was punishing him again, and again disaster gave him the sense of release and renewal that comes with expiation. His feeling that life was beginning for him had a far sounder foundation than his feeling of having come to the barren end of it. He was indeed on the threshold of a period in which he was to discover the satisfaction of married happiness and of fatherhood, and in which he was to reach his full stature as a writer.

As a matter of fact, there was not as wide a gulf between his past and his present as he sometimes imagined. There were bridges across the chasm. He had told Wrangel that the two who died were the only ones he had ever loved, and that he could not love again, nor did he want to. At the same time he was writing to Polina's sister that he still loved Polina. Furthermore, he was occupied less with this desperate old attachment than with more recent ones. Unthinkable as new ties seemed, the need for them asserted itself, and that in the months which immediately followed the funerals. Of one bizarre relation which engaged Dostoevsky at this time little is known beyond what is revealed in a bundle of letters dating from December, 1864, and January, 1865, and signed "Marfa Brown."

Her Anglo-Saxon surname notwithstanding, the woman was a native Russian of the lower middle class, her maiden name being Panina. Dostoevsky had come to know her through a certain Gorsky, who contributed stories of life in the slums to both *Vremya* and *Epokha*. At the time she was living with this man, a wretched drunkard, having been passed on to him by another literary hack with whom she had sunk to the depths of destitution. Her youth and such looks as she may once have possessed had vanished. Dostoevsky took an interest in this wreck of a woman and, as she was familiar with English and possibly with other Western languages, he offered her work as a translator. She fell ill and was admitted to a hospital. He may already have known something of her past, but it was through the somewhat incoherent letters which she wrote him from her sick-bed and those which she asked him to read before transmitting to her lover, that he learned some of the details of her extraordinary history.

Her easy virtue consorted with a roving disposition. By her own account, she is "a pauper and a universal vagabond," and she lives for the moment: "I have always been of the opinion that life is made for impressions . . ." For logic she has no use. Her early career is a blank. She has been in Russia for two years. Before that she had been roaming Western Europe. One of her letters contains an extraordinary account of her wanderings, ending with her marriage in England to a sailor from Baltimore, who seems to have given her his surname, if nothing else. How much was fact and how much fantasy in this story? Whatever the answer, she refused to make literary capital of her adventures, though Gorsky kept insisting that she do so.

Had it not been for him, she might sooner have left the hospital

to which her checkered career had brought her. Gorsky, penniless,
homeless, jealous as a cat, feared that on leaving the infirmary she
would take up with any man who could give her a place to lay her
head, and so he would come drunk and storming to the ward and
make a scene, demanding that she stay on, by malingering. Dostoevsky, from whom she seems to have hidden nothing, also came to
see her there, gave her money, gave her sympathy. At one time
he advised her to stay with Gorsky. Again, in the teeth of the man's
jealousy, he suggested that she come direct from the hospital to his
own flat. Did the lost creature attract him as a woman, as she had
so many other men? In her last letter to him, which is formal in
tone, if not in content, she thanked him for all his kindness, saying:
"In any event, whether or not I shall succeed in satisfying you
physically, and whether there will be that spiritual harmony between us upon which the continuation of our acquaintance will
depend, believe me that I shall always remain thankful to you for
having honoured me, for at least a moment or for some time, with
your friendship and favour." She was happy, she went on, to have
met, after all her sufferings, a man like Dostoevsky, "possessing
such serenity of spirit, tolerance, commonsense, and candour. . . ."
She concluded: "It is all the same to me whether our relationship
lasts a long time or not, but I swear to you that far beyond any
material advantage, I prize the fact that you have not scorned the
fallen part of my nature, that you raised me above the level on which
I stand in my own estimation." With this letter Marfa Brown re-
treats into the obscurity whence she came.

So little is known about this strange incident, about the character of the woman and the nature of her relations with Dostoevsky,
that it is impossible to speak with any certainty of the part she
played in his life and the imprint she left on his work. Perhaps some
memory of her went to the creation of those of his women who
have left the path of conventional virtue without truly degrading
themselves.

II

Perhaps the enigmatic Marfa faded out of the picture because
Dostoevsky's attention was diverted by the appearance of a girl
who had everything that she lacked—youth, beauty, health, spirit,

and who, moreover, came of a distinguished and well-to-do family. If Marfa, in her pitiableness, bore some faint resemblance to his poor wife, the newcomer was like a younger and lovelier Polina. Like Polina, she had swum into his ken as a contributor to his review. Soon after Mikhail's death forced him to take over *Epokha*, he had received first one and then a second manuscript from an ambitious novice by the name of Anna Korvin-Krukovskaya. He wrote encouragingly to the authoress and printed both her stories.

In January, 1865, she came to the capital from her country home and on February 28 she sent him an invitation to call on her at the home of her aunts, whom she was visiting. When he reached the mansion on Vasilyevsky Ostrov and was admitted to the drawing-room, he discovered that his contributor was a Lorelei of a girl with golden hair and green eyes, in her early twenties. They were not alone. Her mother and her little sister, a sharp child of fourteen, sat with them during the entire visit, and two elderly aunts kept peering in at them at odd moments, staring at him as though he were a wild beast. Disconcerted by all these supernumeraries, the pretty bluestocking maintained a stubborn silence. The mother exerted all her social gifts to relieve the situation. In vain, Dostoevsky, no less vexed than his young hostess, answered rudely in monosyllables, kept plucking nervously at his thin blond beard and biting his moustache. He looked old and ill, as always when he was not at ease. After half an hour of this misery, he got up, bowed awkwardly, and, shaking hands with no one, made his exit. Anna burst into hysterical tears. To have anticipated for months this first encounter with the great writer who had set her on the road to fame and to be thus spied on, babied, and thwarted! It was intolerable! The mother joined her tears to the daughter's, and everyone was wretched.

For the young authoress, Dostoevsky's visit was more momentous than he could have guessed. Aside from anything else, it put a seal on her declaration of independence from her family. Their attitude was such that she had had to keep her literary venture secret from them. When one of his letters, enclosing a remittance, had come by accident into the hands of her father, there had been a terrible scene. General Korvin-Krukovsky was a gentleman of the old school, who looked forward to seeing his lovely daughter shine at court balls, and who had a particular horror of lady authors. "You begin by selling your writings," he shouted at Anna, "and you will end by selling yourself." Nevertheless, the culprit was allowed to read her story to the domestic circle. The general was so moved by it that he relented to the extent of granting Anna permission to meet Dostoevsky on the family's next visit to the capital. Of course, her mother must be present when the journalist and ex-convict came to call.

A few days after Dostoevsky's first unhappy visit, he called again. He had to. He had fallen in love with his fair contributor at sight. This time he found the two sisters alone, and, freed from constraint, both he and Anna were different persons: he, youthful, amiable, brilliant; she, eager, interested, gay. The ice once broken, he kept on coming to the house, rather too frequently. And yet he was made to feel at home, even by the mother. Except when there were other visitors, he was quite at his best, thrilling his sympathetic listeners with monologues delivered in his broken, passionate whisper. Showing no reserve before the two sheltered young girls, one of them in her early teens, he outlined to them the plots of his projected novels, including details that were to prove unprintable, and described episodes from his own life, such as his first epileptic attack. The mother must have become genuinely fond of him to continue putting up with him.

Although he was so much of a social liability, she had the rashness to invite him to an evening party at which she was entertaining all her most fashionable acquaintances. He came, in an ill-fitting dress suit, and proceeded to embarrass his hostess in every way. He would respond to an introduction by mumbling unintelligibly and turning his back on the guest. The worst of it was that he monopolized Anna, holding her hand, whispering in her ear, repelling every intrusion upon their privacy, and, when her mother finally succeeded in separating them, almost by main force, he sat sulking in his corner and glaring at the company. The particular object of his angry regard was a handsome young colonel, a cousin of Anna's, who was quietly but firmly courting her. Dostoevsky decided that the family was bent on marrying her off to this wealthy fop with the epaulets and the shapely legs, and the only time during the whole evening that he opened his mouth, it was to utter a broad hint about mothers who were eager to find rich husbands for their daughters.

That evening was the beginning of the end of Anna's infatuation with the great man. He found himself at a disadvantage: a middle-aged man in love with a young vixen. Feeling that he was losing her, he came more frequently, he exacted accounts of how and with whom she spent her time in his absence. She was out, she was dancing, she was with her cousin—and this while he had been struggling with chaos in the *Epokha* office. He fairly invited her to tease him, which she did with the cruelty of youth. One way in which she taunted him was to flaunt her radicalism. She must already have been something of an unbeliever and a socialist. He scolded her for a little nihilist. They argued. They quarrelled. He left, saying that he would never see her again. He returned the next day.

Anna's little sister Sonia was generally on the scene, drinking everything in and watching her sister's suitor with worshipping eyes. She was rather pleased to see them quarrel. The cooler Anna grew, the more serious became Sonia's transports. Dostoevsky fell into the habit of holding her up as a model to the frivolous Anna. He praised her earnestness, her looks, her manners. A warm word from him about her playing set her to securing a good teacher at once and to spending hours at the piano every day. She was at particular pains to learn the *Sonate Pathétique* because he had once said that it stirred up in him a whole world of forgotten emotions. He was ordinarily deaf to music, but in the right mood he could be shaken by Beethoven as well as by a barrel-organ tune.

One night, toward the end of their stay in Petersburg, Dostoevsky came to the house to find the two girls alone. The hour, the impending departure, the unexpected privacy, all wrought them up. Sonia was not long in sitting down at the piano and starting her *Sonate Pathétique*. Ignoring her sister, she played for an audience of one, trying to wake in him that "world of lost emotions." She did not look up from the keys until she lifted her hands from the last chord, to discover that she was alone. With a heavy heart she wandered from one room to the next and, lifting a portière, saw Dostoevsky sitting on a sofa beside Anna, holding her hand, his face pale and distraught, and heard him telling her in a shaken whisper how passionately he loved her. Sonia rushed off to her own room to hide her shame and sorrow, dreading nothing more than she would be summoned—she knew they had heard her—and that she would have to face those two. For the first time she became aware of the nature of her feelings for Dostoevsky. The pages from her diary that described those moments might have come from one of his novels. She got into bed and lay there sobbing. As the hours passed, and no one called her, her dread changed to indignation at such neglect. She hated them both. No one could have understood her emotions more fully than the man who had roused them. But he was not concerned with Sonia just then. Anna had refused him.

As she confided to her little sister the following night, she could give this genius her respect, her admiration, even her affection, but she could not marry him. With astonishing insight she realized that he needed a wife who would have no life of her own, but would devote herself wholly and cheerfully to his needs. She was not that sort; even now she was constantly irritated by not being herself in his presence. The prospect of being "sucked into" him, and lost, terrified her. In rejecting her suitor she must have told him these hard truths. He came only once more, to make his farewells.

The episode in which the two sisters figured so romantically is set down in Sonia's reminiscences, written many years later. She adds that some six months after their departure from the capital Dostoevsky wrote to Anna that he had fallen in love with "a wonderful girl," who had agreed to marry him. The betrothal occurred in November, 1866. It has therefore been generally assumed that the memoirist committed an error, speaking of six months instead of a year and six months. A suggestion has recently been made that the novelist proposed to Anna not in the spring of 1865, but in the winter of 1865-66 when the Korvin-Krukovskys were again on a visit to the capital. It is certain that in 1865 and 1866 the two kept up a desultory correspondence and that he expressed a desire to visit the family at their estate.

According to her successor in his affections, Dostoevsky was actually betrothed to Anna and they parted because of the incompatibility of their views, but he loved her enough to wish her a mate who would share her crooked opinions. She did indeed marry a socialist, and a Frenchman to boot. They were both active in the Paris Commune, and a secretary of the Russian embassy in the

French capital described her as a Megaera. After the fall of the Commune she saved her husband from the scaffold by escaping with him to Russia. There Dostoevsky, then a married man, met her again, and the two families became friendly. He also saw a good deal of her sister. She had married a certain Kovalevsky, whose name her mathematical genius made internationally famous.

III

He was a bankrupt lover. He was a bankrupt publisher. He had sunk his legacy from Aunt Kumanina in *Epokha,* and the failure of the review left him not only penniless but, since he had taken over Mikhail's obligations, saddled with debts amounting to thirteen thousand roubles, or perhaps it was fifteen thousand— he was hazy on the subject. What would become of the widow and the orphans? There was his work to fall back upon, but he was in an awkward position with regard to marketing it. He had perforce to offer it to editors of reviews that had been reviled in the pages of *Vremya* and *Epokha.* His first step was to obtain a loan from the Fund for Needy Authors. He had indicated in his application that he was threatened with debtors' prison, where, in his present state of health, he could not write. He then turned to his old employer, Krayevsky, and asked an advance on a novel, *The Drunkards,* to be delivered in the autumn, but met with a refusal.

Suddenly immediate payment was demanded on some of his overdue notes. Debtors' prison loomed all too close. Matters went so far that he was visited by a police officer. He got into talk with this man and was soon listening interestedly to all manner of details about the work of the police. The bits of information supplied by this casual friend were stored away and eventually put to good use in the writing of *Crime and Punishment.* The officer did not have to discharge the unpleasant duty of carrying him off to jail. At the psychological moment Stellovsky, a Barabbas of a publisher, came forward with a shameful contract that Dostoevsky promptly signed. It allowed the man to bring out an edition of all of Dostoevsky's previous work, and further provided that he should receive an unpublished novel on or before November 1,

1866. Failure to deliver this manuscript on time gave the publisher the right to issue, without payment to the author, everything he would write within the next nine years. In consideration of all this, Dostoevsky received three thousand roubles. Two-thirds of this sum went toward the payment of the protested notes. He did not then know that the money actually reverted to Stellovsky: the IOU's on which immediate payment was demanded were in possession of this shark, who had quietly bought them up for a song. Early in July, with a small residue in his pocket, hardly enough to live on for any length of time, Dostoevsky went abroad.

He had long ago decided to spend three months in every year out of Russia. He was lonely abroad, and the alien surroundings disgusted him, yet, oddly enough, he felt better and worked better away from home. This time he had some hope of seeing Polina Suslova again. The previous year she had written him that they might meet at Spa and upbraided him for writing a cynical story quite out of character, by which she meant "Notes from the Underground." But Mikhail's death had kept him at home. There was also the lure of the gaming-tables, and there may have been the added urge to escape the scene of his present embarrassments.

As though he were ever able to escape! He fell from the frying-pan into the fire. The trip was a disastrous one. True, there was a letup in his attacks, but at the beginning of the journey he caught a chill, and the fever clung to him relentlessly. From Berlin he went to Wiesbaden, where he found Polina.

One can only surmise what happened between the two during the few days they spent together. At the time when *Epokha* was still a going concern an acquaintance had jokingly suggested to her that she marry Dostoevsky and turn the review into a radical organ. She would not hear of it: "What kind of Iphigenia was she?" she wrote in her diary, with more self-knowledge than classical learning. She told herself that she hated Dostoevsky—he had caused her needless suffering, he had killed her faith in men. In the angry letters that she had sent him she accused him of sadism, coarseness, cynicism. His answers have not been preserved but in a letter to her sister, dated April 19, 1865, he denied Polina's accusations. She had been offended, he wrote, because he had at long last dared to talk back. "Her egoism and amour-propre are colossal," he added "She demands *everything* from people, never forgives anyone a single imperfection and exempts herself from the slightest obligation to others . . . There isn't any humanity in her relations with me. She knows that I still love her. Why, then, does she torture me!" The Wiesbaden meeting apparently did not improve Dostoevsky's standing with her. She continued to treat him contemptuously and pitilessly. Yet she did not put an end to their relationship, and when she left for Paris they parted amicably.

As before, she brought him bad luck at the tables. At the end of five days he had lost everything, was reduced to pawning his watch, and owed money at the hotel. He was still sick and was worried about Polina, who had left with so little cash that he feared she might be stranded at Cologne, and starving. The servants did not answer the bell, didn't clean his shoes, were altogether wanting in respect for him. He kept as quiet as possible, sitting and reading most of the time, so as not to get up an appetite.

Knowing that Turgenev was in Baden, he appealed to him for a loan. And he disliked the man, all the more intensely since she had once been in love with him. One of the first books he had read on coming out of prison was *A Sportsman's Sketches,* and it had filled him with delight. When Turgenev's *Fathers and Children* appeared, the same year as *The House of the Dead,* Dostoevsky wrote an enthusiastic letter to the author, and was assured that he was one of the two men who understood the novel. As an editor, he had had some friendly interchanges with Turgenev and, indeed, had coaxed a story, "Phantoms," out of the literary lion for the first issue of *Epokha.* In discussing this piece with Mikhail privately, Dostoevsky had said that it was "fairly decent," but that there was "much trash in it, something nasty, sickly, senile, impotent, and so without faith—in a word, the whole Turgenev with all his convictions." Yet here he was, making a clean breast of his shameful predicament to this objectionable creature, and even saying that it was morally easier to turn to him because he was more understanding than others. Turgenev did indeed send half the amount requested—a debt which was not to be repaid for eleven years—but this was only a drop in the bucket.

Dostoevsky also turned for help to Herzen, who was then in Geneva, and even to Polina, saying that if she had reached Paris and could raise some cash, she should send him one hundred and fifty gulden forthwith. Herzen was silent. Herzen was dismissing him as a disorderly wretch who didn't deserve help—was that it? To think of this socialist upholding middle-class morality! He was forgotten by God and man. And this intolerable idleness, this waste, this uncertainty! He hated the town and its last inhabitant. He had struck bottom: If there was anything lower, he had no knowledge of it. For three days he had gone without dinner, but what was worse than hunger was the meanness of the servants in refusing him a candle in the evening, if he had so much as an end left from the night before.

Finally there was a kind letter from Herzen, but no money. Again he appealed to Polina. Another fortnight passed, and his situation was unchanged. Then he confessed everything to Wrangel and begged for money with which to pay off his debts and go to Paris. There was no reply and he wrote again. He was threatened with arrest; there was no question of Paris now, he must go home. But on what? He was in utter despair. At least, he was idle no longer. He was working day and night on a story, a new version of the piece refused by Krayevsky. He had a thousand roubles' worth of manuscript and would surely be able to repay his friend within a month.

At last, a hundred thalers! Wrangel was to be counted on. But the hotel-keeper got most of it, and he was just where he had been before. It was now the end of September. His one hope was Katkov, the editor of *Russky vestnik*. He had had the happy idea of offering him the work he had under way, asking an advance of three hundred roubles on it. He soon realized that instead of a short piece he would be able to finish in a fortnight or a month at most, he had a long novel on his hands. The story grew, not only in volume, but in depth. He felt that he was at work on "the best thing" he had ever written. Not that writing was easy, for his health was wretched. His epileptic attacks had let up, but he was wasting away with fever.

Finally, the local Russian priest came to his aid, giving security for him on what he owed the hotel-keeper, and advancing him the fare home. On the way he stopped off at Copenhagen to see Wrangel. Early in October he was back in Petersburg.

The very first night home he had a violent attack. He had
hardly recovered from it when he was struck down by one that
was even worse. Within six weeks he had four seizures. The one
bright spot in the gloom that enveloped him was the fact that
Katkov accepted the novel he was busy with, and sent him the
advance he had requested. But what was three hundred roubles
when he had just added two more creditors, in the persons of Wrangel and the Wiesbaden priest, to his long list, when he had not only
himself to support, but his stepson Pasha as well, when he had his
sick brother Kolya to help, and when Mikhail's widow and her
children were hanging on his neck like so many millstones! Emilia
made it plain that she considered him obliged to support them.
Hadn't her poor husband kept sending him remittances when he
was in Siberia? Hadn't he founded a journal to give him a place to
print what other reviews rejected? And hadn't he, Dostoevsky, in
the end wrecked the enterprise that should have kept them all?

Before the week was out the money was gone, partly into the
widow's pocket, and he had to borrow another hundred to live
on. Where should he turn next? If he could only get a Government pension for Mikhail's family, or if he could revive the magazine! But he dared not think of any new venture until he had brought
his name before the public again by finishing his novel.

He had not been home long when Polina arrived in town. As
indicated above, he had written her sister in the spring that he still
loved her, if against his better judgment. Now, in the midst of these
desolate, harassing days, he threw his better judgment to the
winds. Perhaps they could still make something of life together. He
pursued her as before. They quarrelled as before. While abroad
she had been moving in radical circles, and intellectually they were
further apart than ever. Knowing his weak spot, she poked fun at
religion. He reminded her ungallantly of her previous complaisance:
"You cannot forgive me the fact that you once gave yourself to me,
and so you take revenge on me." On November 2, 1865, she made
this entry in her diary: "He (Dostoevsky) has long been offering
me his hand and heart, but he only makes me angry by it." Some
three months later she left Petersburg. The break was now final.

CHAPTER SIXTEEN

A RUSSIAN TRAGEDY

THROUGH all the vexations that met him on his return home Dostoevsky kept steadily at his novel. He was not going to spoil it. He started putting it in the form of a confession, and gave it up. Next he tried writing it in the shape of a diary kept by the hero, a murderer, after he had committed his crime, and gave that up. Both drafts have been preserved, at least in part, and published. Finding these methods cramping, he did not hesitate, in November, to cast all he had done overboard and rewrite the novel in the objective manner which is that of the final version. It was this ability to destroy and build anew, this constant exhausting labour, that held for him moments of intense joy and an indestructible sense of power. The frustrations of sickness, the want of affection, the indignities thrust upon him by poverty and indebtedness, could not rob him of that. By the end of December he had just a fraction of the manuscript ready. Nevertheless, Katkov was rash enough to begin the publication of *Crime and Punishment* in the January number of *Russky vestnik* for 1866, and thereafter, for a whole year, Dostoevsky raced against time to furnish copy for each successive issue. Luckily for him, the review never came out on time.

His winter was bitterly lonely. His sole companion in the disordered rooms was Pasha. He lived like a hermit, saw no one, went nowhere. No sooner did the epileptic attacks abate than he was laid up with piles—nothing new, but more virulent than ever. The worst part of it was that his ailment made writing impossible, so that when he recovered he had to sweat to make up for lost time. And then the seizures commenced all over again. He had fits of irritability that exceeded all bounds. There were constant money worries. He pawned his clothes. He sold his books. He borrowed right and left. He lived in the shadow of debtors' prison, horrified by the thought that it would wreck his novel. The more he paid his creditors, the uglier they got. He was killing himself for Mikhail's family, and the children didn't even bow to him. He was so wretched that as he looked back to the period before his brother's death, it seemed a time of peace and plenty.

And yet, after enumerating all his troubles in a letter to a friend, he concluded: "But do not imagine that I am much tormented. No, there have been many happy moments. Life and hope have not ended for me yet." Although his seizures meant intermittent traffic with death, his mind was naturally turned toward life. As usual, he thrived on punishment. He was somehow quickened and energized by it. To Strakhov he had the jaunty appearance of an eligible on the lookout for a wife.

Indeed, the sad state of his health and of his finances notwithstanding, the thought of marriage was always there. He had been refused by Anna and by Polina. He was not discouraged. In the early spring he went to Moscow to get an advance from Katkov. This time he stayed with his sister Vera and was in the unaccustomed position of being a member of a large, jolly family. On Easter Eve the whole household went to church for the midnight service, but he remained at home in the company of a young thing, a friend of his twenty-year-old niece Sonia. The girl made up for what she lacked in looks by her gaiety and vivaciousness. When the family returned in the small hours, she laughingly confided to Sonia that her uncle had actually proposed to her and that, in turning him down, she had teased him with Pushkin's verse about " an old man't heart the years had petrified."

His sister Vera, seeing the matter in a sober light, sought to engineer a match more suitable to his age and circumstances. The lady she fixed upon was her own sister-in-law. Yelena Pavlovna Ivanova. True, Mme. Ivanova was not free, but her husband, Dr. Ivanov's brother, had been ill for years, and his death was hourly expected. Dostoevsky lent himself to Vera's plans for him so far as to ask the prospective widow some months later whether, if she had her freedom, she would marry him. She would not say either yes or no, so that he felt himself nowise bound.

He had intended to go to Germany in the spring and finish his novel there in peace, but this proving impossible, he spent the summer with the Ivanovs in the country just outside of Moscow. He occupied a room in an empty cottage, but he went there only to work and to sleep, taking his meals with his sister's family. It was delightful to be with them all again, particularly Sonia. The more he saw of her, the more he loved her. He admired in her a restraint, a clear intelligence, a native dignity, an inability to compromise, precisely those features, as he was to tell her one day, that he found lacking in himself. One seems to glimpse something of Sonia in those strong and compassionate, virginal and warm-hearted women who move through some of his pages.

The Ivanov house was overflowing with young people, the children, already numbering nine, and their friends, so that there would not seldom be twenty sitting around the dinner-table. In this holiday atmosphere Dostoevsky relaxed and soon found himself taking part in the moonlight walks, the games, the charades, the practical jokes, with the best of them. He was even more careful of his appearance than usual, his shirt well starched, his blue jacket and grey trousers neatly pressed. He had long since given up shaving his chin soldier-fashion, and the thinness of his beard touched his vanity, a fact his young companions were not slow to discover. They teased him about it, admitting among themselves that he looked younger than his forty-five years.

"When I write something," he had once said, "I think of it while I dine, while I sleep, while I am engaged in conversation." For all his immersion in his work, he could turn from the writing of *Crime and Punishment* to the composing of a piece of nonsense verse. He was apt, nevertheless, to leave his young friends abruptly and go to his desk, and the servant who was sent to sleep near him, so that he would not be alone during a seizure, came back one day refusing to spend another night with the master: why, he had a murder in his mind, he walked the floor all night talking about it aloud to himself.

The autumn found Dostoevsky again in Petersburg busy with the last part of *Crime and Punishment*. It was not until Christmas, however, that he turned in the final instalment, but since the review was late, as usual, he was still able to see the concluding chapters appear in the December issue.

II

Originally he conceived the story which developed into *Crime and Punishment* as a short novel dealing with the drink evil—a topic that was then in the public eye. Thus the narrative would have a bearing on a current social problem, a consideration that never ceased to count with this quondam disciple of Belinsky. And then abruptly he decided to make something totally different of it. The drunkards, who were to have given the title to the story, receded into the background, eventually taking a wholly subordinate place, and the novel became "a psychological account of a crime," as he described it in offering to *Russky vestnik*. The plot of this Russian tragedy remained virtually as he outlined it in his letter to Katkov: an impoverished university student—to be called Raskolnikov— kills a worthless old pawnbroker and her sister into the bargain; chance favours him—he commits the murder without leaving any tell-tale traces behind him so that he is beyond the reach of justice; but in the end an inner compulsion brings him to confess. It was early in Dostoevsky's Wiesbaden captivity, just after he had gambled away his last thaler, perhaps as he was strolling under the trees or lying sleepless in his unpaid-for room, that his imagination first seized upon the idea of Raskolnikov's crime. Here was something to weigh in the balance against his losses.

Raskolnikov is a spirited youth, high-minded, with generous impulses and more than a touch of the Schilleresque about him. At the same time he lacks that integration which makes for moral health—his very name connotes schism. He is akin to the fantasts and brooding recluses who haunted Dostoevsky's imagination in the days before his exile. Like them, he is one of life's expatriates, leading an unreal, solitary, cerebral existence. And the student's rags smell of the foul air of the underground. He has in him something of the venom that the troglodyte secreted in his dismal cave; he takes the undergroundling's vindictive pleasure in his humilia- tions. Yet in one respect he differs radically from the dreamers and the inhabitants of the underground: their conflicting impulses para- lyze the will and leave them incapable of action; his inner seething must sooner or later precipitate an explosive deed. It is thus that Dostoevsky takes the great stride from pathos to tragedy. /

How could those sensitive hands bring down the axe and rummage among the bloodstained trinkets? Repeatedly the murderer asks himself, in anguish of soul, what moved him to his fateful act. His self-probing is most rigorous and acute in the scene of his confession to Sonia, the saintly prostitute who plays so important a rôle in his history.

Why did he kill? For plunder. But that wasn't it. If Napoleon, say, could not have begun his career without killing and robbing an old pawnbroker, would he have hesitated? But never mind Napoleon. There he was, ground down by poverty, with the prospect of endless drudgery, and virtue as its sole reward. He had only one life to live. With the wretched old usurer's money he could make something of himself, save his mother from penury and his sister from a loveless marriage or worse. Then he would give himself to the service of humanity. One tiny crime in exchange for thousands of good deeds! One death for a hundred lives! Shall a man stand by while people suffer, for fear of spilling a little blood? But what nonsense! He didn't murder to help his mother. He didn't murder to gain wealth and power and become a benefactor of mankind. He was urged on by something altogether different. He might have plodded, slaved, achieved something that way. But he would not. He lay in his dusty den like a spider, and sulked, brooded. Perhaps he was a little mad. Perhaps it was sickness. At any rate, a new, a compelling idea took possession of him. Men are what they are, and nothing will change them. But there are two kinds of men. There is the common run, who live within the law and cannot do otherwise. And there are the Caesars, the masters, those who have a new word to say and therefore have a right—with the sanction of their own conscience—to shed blood, those who abrogate the law and renew it thereby. Power lies ready for the daring one to take. He killed simply to test himself, to find out and quickly, whether he was a man who had the right, as well as the daring, to transgress. What he raised his hand against was not a human being, but a principle—the moral principle. But the very fact that he needed to test himself was proof enough that he was not one of the strong. Furthermore, with a part of his mind he had known all along that he was not made of heroic stuff, and that indeed he would be admitting as much to himself after the murder. Perhaps he swung the axe merely to escape debating with himself about it any longer.

Here is a tangled skein! In unravelling it one gets little help either from the prosecutor, who is shown to have an extraordinary insight into the criminal's character, or from the author himself. Dostoevsky early recognized that ambiguity in accounting for the crime would work confusion in the story, and he made a note to the effect that he must explain it "either this way or that way." That he did not bring himself to do so is a tribute to his understanding of the complexity and elusiveness of motives.

The deed once done, the murderer is seized by emotions he had not reckoned on. He feels himself cut off from mankind "as with scissors." It is as if he had suffered an immitigable excommunication from the body of his fellowmen. As the days go on, his loneliness is made more terrible by an anxiety that sometimes touches panic, sometimes yields to the apathy of exhaustion. In the end, unable to bear his sufferings, he gives himself up to the authorities.

Although the motivation of the murder remains uncertain, the rôle played by cerebration is stressed. Raskolnikov's is a crime of the intellect, of "a heart unhinged by theories," as the astute investigating officer diagnoses the case, the act of a man capable of killing another or himself for the sake of an idea. While the criminal's responsibility is not called in question, nevertheless he is presented as having acted in a compulsive way. In spite of his uncompromising intelligence and his habit of introspection, Raskolnikov is ignorant of what moved him to his deed and can only offer rationalizations. He commits the murder half against his will. He walks to the crime as though "not on his own legs," and goes through with it "as though the hem of his coat were caught in the wheels of a machine and he were drawn into it." His turnings and twistings, his return to the place of the crime, his circling round the investigating officer "like a moth round a candle," his dealings with Sonia—all point to an irresistible urge to confess. His behaviour proclaims a craving for punishment in order to placate his offended conscience. Yet if he is feverishly busy analysing his reactions, he fails to see clearly into the workings of his own psyche. Punishment gives him a sense of release in a fashion incomprehensible to him.

DOSTOEVSKY IN 1858

Photograph taken at Semipalatinsk, Siberia

In some respects Raskolnikov answers to the description of a type of transgressor termed "the neurotic criminal" by a leading psychoanalyst. Such an individual transgresses under the pressure of an unconscious drive and is far from deterred by punishment.

Raskolnikov makes his confession in the same compulsive manner, not quite knowing why, under the urgency of a force that seems outside of himself. He goes to Siberia unrepentant. Not once does there escape from his lips anything like the cry: "Here's the smell of blood still!" All the anguish the murder has brought upon him does not compel him to acknowledge it as a crime. He continues to cling to his "gloomy creed": the *moral* right of the superior person to bloodshed. What gnaws at him is that he has failed the test. No, he is not one of the strong. He insists that what he suffers from is wounded pride.

At the end of his first year as a convict Raskolnikov finally undergoes a spiritual rebirth. It is partly due to Sonia's compassionate love for him—she has gone with him to Siberia. This prostitute is the image of chastity and an exemplar of simple faith, humility, self-immolation. She has gone on the streets to feed her father's second wife, a consumptive, and her children whom the man's drinking have reduced to destitution. Sonia is the perfect foil for Raskolnikov. And yet if he is irresistibly drawn to her and if it is to her that he first confesses, it is because he feels a similarity in their fates, and that not merely by reason of their both being outcasts. She had sacrificed herself; he had sacrificed others. But in so doing he had been experimenting upon himself and offering, as it were, his own throat to the knife. The peculiar kinship and the abyss between them are nowhere so strikingly suggested as in the scene wherein the prostitute reads aloud to the murderer the Gospel passage concerning the raising of Lazarus. None but these two who have put on corruption could be so stirred by the promise of resurrection. Sonia is clearly the seed that, having died, will bear much fruit, and it is not astonishing that in the end she is the instrument of Raskolnikov's salvation.

III

While the novel was still in embyro Dostoevsky had written to Katkov that Raskolnikov commits the murder under the influence

of "certain odd *unfinished* ideas which are in the air." He was referring to the irreligious, materialistic, rationalistic trend that he
discovered on his return from Siberia—in short to nihilism. He
had attacked it in *Notes from the Underground*, he was attacking
it again. He felt that nihilism was weakening the moral fibre of this
compatriots, and it was, in a sense, to medicine the times that he
had written the tale in which earthly and heavenly justice is visited
upon the evildoer. His intention was to show the criminal as the
spiritual child of unbelief. Raskonikov belongs to an erring generation. "You turned away from God," Sonia says to him, "and God
has smitten you, has given you over to the devil."

Lacking the discipline of religion, and with nothing but reason
to guide him, he falls prey to the hideous *idea* that there is an élite
having a *moral* right to crime. In the epilogue to the novel Raskolnikov has a delirious dream. A dreadful new plague is spreading
over the earth. Attacked by a mysterious virus, whole cities go mad,
each of the madmen in a frenzy of intellectual arrogance believing
that he alone is in possession of the truth. Men cannot agree among
themselves as to how to perform the most ordinary tasks. The very
distinction between good and evil, right and wrong, is lost. Men kill
each other senselessly. Fire and famine stalk through the land. Were
it not for a few pure spirits destined to found a new race, mankind
would perish from the earth. The dream is a confused vision of a
world falling apart because people depend on reason alone to hold it
together. Significantly, the dream comes to Raskolnikov when he is
at last on the verge of his repentance. It is as though an understanding of his own folly were struggling to reach his consciousness.
Had he not himself been possessed by this disease of the intellect?
"Life took the place of dialectics." It is thus that Dostoevsky indicates the nature of Raskolnikov's regeneration.

A few days before the appearance of the first instalment of *Crime
and Punishment*, the newspapers carried the story of a Moscow
student who had committed a murder remarkably like the one depicted in the novel. Dostoevsky was quite proud of this mark of
his astuteness. Here was proof that Raskolnikov's act was no mere
figment of a writer's fantasy, but rather a symptom of the disease
ravaging a rootless generation. Impulsive young men were ready
for monstrous deeds. In fact, when only a small portion of the

novel had been printed, on the afternoon of April 4, 1866, one such young man, a member of a student circle, fired at the Tsar. Dostoevsky, rushing to Maikov to tell him the shocking news, was pale and trembling, hardly able to express his horror at this attempt upon the father of the Russian people, to whom every subject owed filial love and obedience. Everywhere he saw signs of the moral chaos to which educated people were a prey.

Some ten years after the appearance of *Crime and Punishment* its author had an opportunity to pass judgment on a man who had committed an offence under circumstances similar to those in the imagined case of Raskolnikov. Dostoevsky received a letter from a former journalist who had turned bank clerk and been imprisoned for embezzling a large sum of money. Depending on a miserable pittance and with no assurance of keeping his position, he had decided to embezzle exactly three per cent of the bank's annual profit in order to support his old parents, secure the future of his brothers and sisters, his motherless children, his young fiancée and her immediate family, and to assist, he concluded his apologia, "many other insulted and injured, without doing any substantial harm to anybody." He was a close reader of Dostoevsky, and it is not impossible that he had been moved to the act partly under the influence of Raskolnikov's logic; like Raskolnikov, he remained impenitent. Dostoevsky found it in his heart to absolve the thief, or almost. "I look upon your crime," he wrote in response, as you judge it yourself," adding with emphatic humility that he was no better than his correspondent. He told the offender, however, that he did not quite like the fact that he felt no compunction. "There is something higher," he concluded, "than the arguments of reason and the force of circumstance—before that everyone must bow."

To be guided by the intellect alone is to fall from confusion into mortal sin. Such is the lesson of *Crime and Punishment*. Morality rests on a transcendental, religious foundation. Man cannot be good, indeed, he cannot live, without God—the cry reverberates throughout the body of Dostoevsky's fiction. For the transgressor salvation lies in atonement through suffering. At one time he considered making the thesis that suffering is the price of happiness the central idea of the novel. "Man must earn his happiness," runs an entry in his

notebook, "and always through suffering." He erects this into "the
law of our planet." Furthermore, he sees no injustice in such a dis-
pensation: since the gain is so great there should be no quarrel with
the cost.

I V

One need not take to heart either the moral that is explicit in
Crime and Punishment, or any that may be extracted from it, in
order to respond to its impact. The virtue of the book lies in the
body and pressure of the story. One ignores the moments of bathos,
the unlikely coincidences, the awkwardness, and yields to the power
of a work that has the urgency, the tension, the seriousness of high
drama, without abandoning the large privileges of the novel.

The settings help to create an atmosphere of gloom and desola-
tion: a coffinlike den that "cramps the soul and the mind"; a base-
ment tavern, with the click of billiard balls from the rear and a
hurdy-gurdy sounding through the window; a market place in the
slums; the overly neat flat of the old pawnbroker. They are sketched
in deftly and with a realistic concern for the precise detail, such
as the glass of "yellow" water handed Raskolnikov in the police
station (in the sixties drinking-water in Russia's capital was not
purified). Against this dismal background one witnesses scenes that
speak of life's cruelty and man's depravity and weakness, but also
scenes that stir one because they show a drunkard, a sensualist, a
prostitute, a murderer, in utter abasement or despair straining after
something that will give a transcendent meaning to existence. Such
is the passage in which that derelict, Marmeladov, Sonia's father,
unburdens himself to Raskolnikov as the two sit over their glasses
in a pot-house. There are few pages in Dostoevsky that so abound
in pathos and pity and so amply attest his ability to find words that
touch the heart.

It cannot be said that one has the same sense of hearing a living
voice when Sonia speaks. There is something obviously contrived
and not a little that is mawkish about her. Svidrigailov, who has a
leading rôle in a secondary plot, is a kind of double of Raskolnikov,
a projection of the latter's lower self, a man beyond good and evil
and so beyond life. Although a substantial figure, presented in
realistic terms, at times he gives the impression of being a halluci-

nation of Raskolnikov's. The nightmarish episode of his suicide is among the great scenes in the world of fiction.

Others move through these pages, playing their parts in the subplots. But these are all tributary to the main action: the drama of Raskolnikov. He is drawn with extraordinary imaginative power. Dostoevsky's avowed intention was to champion the ethics that holds inviolate every human soul as divine in origin and of infinite worth. Yet he presents with considerable persuasiveness Raskolnikov's *idea*, which argues relativity of good and evil and anticipates Nietzsche's doctrine of the superman. He plays the devil's advocate too ably not to have had some lurking sympathy for the devil's viewpoint. A preliminary note for the novel is illuminating. In response to the detective's reference to the moral law binding upon all, Raskolnikov says: "Well, but suppose conscience doesn't accuse me—I seize authority, I get power, whether money or might—not for evil. I bring happiness. Well, and because of a miserable fence, to stand and look over it, to envy, to hate and yet to stand still. That's base!" On the margin opposite this jotting Dostoevsky scribbled: "Devil take it! He's partly right."

Indeed, right and wrong are not neatly docketed and pigeonholed in this novel. They are allowed to merge into each other and become their opposites. The author is plainly partial to the extremist, the one who goes the limit whether in good or in evil. It is the Laodicean, middle-of-the-road temperament that he abominates. The one wholly repulsive character in the novel is not the murderer, or that lost soul, Svidrigailov—before he makes his exit he gives evidence of a generous humanity—nor yet those whom Luzhin denounces as "unbelievers, agitators and atheists," but rather that comfortably circumstanced, self-important, meanly prudent man himself.

Raskolnikov's story affects the reader like a record of an actual experience, made by a man labouring under the compulsion to relive it in all its poignancy. Every movement of the murderer's body and mind, every detail in the interplay between his physical sensations and his psychic states, the thrusting and dodging in the duel between him and the detective—all that is set down with complete authority. Hence the effectiveness of the book. One suffers, thinks, feels, dreams, with Raskolnikov. Vicariously the reader commits the crime and endures the punishment. Without having to pay Raskolnikov's price, he, too, achieves some modicum of grace. One recalls Freud's intimation that to Dostoevsky the criminal was almost a saviour, who by his act frees his fellows from the necessity of obeying the murderous urge common to the children of Adam.*

Be that as it may, the novelist's sympathy with Raskolnikov seems to go beyond an author's indentification with his hero. It may be asked why Raskolnikov chose this bloody way of breaking through from the underground to "living life." Does the clue perhaps lie in the character of his creator? It is possible that through this fiction and several that were to follow, Dostoevsky was projecting obscure criminal impulses stronger than flesh is generally heir to? The close relation between epilepsy and crime is said to be a matter of statistical record. At all events, the inwardness with which Raskolnikov's feelings after the crime are depicted probably owes much to the sense of guilt that was the deep undercurrent of Dostoevsky's emotional life. If unconsciously he craved punishment, he must have been satisfied in no small measure by the ordeal of setting down Raskolnikov's experience so unflinchingly.

---

*A noted psychologist testifies to the novel's extraordinary power by citing the case of an obdurate murderer who became accessible to repentance "under the overwhelming influence of Dostoevsky's *Crime and Punishment.*" (Theodore Reik, *Geständniszwang und Strafbedurfuis,* Leipzig, 1925, p. 116).

CHAPTER SEVENTEEN

A LITTLE DIAMOND

THE LONG months devoted to the writing of *Crime and Punishment* held for Dostoevsky, in addition to the usual burden of money worries, ill health, and loneliness, yet another cause for vexation: the novel he had contracted to deliver to the robber Stellovsky. It will be recalled that it was due November 1, 1866. He pleaded for an extension of time; he begged Stellovsky to take a promissory note instead of the manuscript, but the man was adamant. He would have his pound of flesh. And how could Dostoevsky wrench himself away from the work which was then wholly absorbing him? But there was something attractive about performing the impossible. He would write two novels at once: to one he would give his mornings, to the other his nights. Was there ever a writer who worked like that? The mere idea would kill Turgenev.

Not that Dostoevsky acted on this notion. By July he had no more than a plan for the piece, and the wretched business was spoiling his waking hours and haunting his dreams. October first came and went, and not a line was written. A little group of his friends suggested that he farm out the novel among them. But he wouldn't consider it. He did, however, fall in with the extraordinary suggestion that he hire a stenographer and dictate the story. He began dictating the evening of October 4, and in twenty-six days the novel was completed and Dostoevsky's part of the contract fulfilled.

He originally called the story *Roulettenburg,* but, at the instance of the publisher, changed the title to *The Gambler.* It is probable that he did some work on it before those hectic October weeks. Certainly he had had the subject in mind for a long time, perhaps ever since he had first haunted the tables. In September, 1863, while he was travelling with Polina, he wrote down on little scraps of paper a sketch for a story about a Russian living abroad who wandered from one gambling resort to another, completely possessed

217

by a mania for roulette. He hoped to repeat his success with *The House of the Dead* by a description of another kind of hell that he also knew intimately. The hero is a cultivated person, but, as Dostoevsky put it, "half-baked in every way, a man who has lost his faith, but dares not disbelieve, a man rebelling against the authorities, yet fearing them. He comforts himself by saying that he *has nothing to do* in Russia and he excoriates those who summon our expatriates back home. . . ." The novelist also saw the story as an opportunity to set forth his observations on his countrymen abroad—a topic then widely discussed in the press. This tale of a gambler was the subject he seized upon when, three years later, he found himself in need of a theme that could be worked up quickly and at no great length.

The rather limited space at his disposal did not prevent him from burdening himself with a fairly complicated plot and a number of characters. The setting afforded him a welcome chance to spill his venom upon the French, polished and hollow, and the Germans, grasping and dull. His mouthpiece is his protagonist, Alexey Ivanovich, a young man employed as a tutor by a Russian family living in "Roulettenburg." Probably because he wrote in such haste, this central character is not sufficiently elaborated, while the *femme fatale* who is the heroine of the story remains something of an enigma, her behaviour subject to various interpretations. At least one of the secondary characters, notably the wealthy old *babushka* upon whose death the family's prospects wholly depend, is superbly drawn.

Greed and lust dominate these pages. The leading theme is the tutor's passion for his employer's step-daughter, significantly named, Polina, who is involved with two suitors, a rich English industrialist, and a titled French bounder, her lover at the time. It is an exasperated, sado-masochistic feeling compounded of love and hate. The tutor sees the erotic relationship and the sensual pleasure it involves as dependent on the slavery and abasement of one partner and the complete domination of the other. He has something to say about both aspects, on one occasion echoing a line from *The House of the Dead,* thus: "A human being is a despot by nature, and loves to be a torturer." Dostoevsky will keep coming back to this ambiguous emotion, the *odi et amo* of Catullus, in his later writings, and perhaps present it more subtly but never in firmer outline.

Just as the gaming tables figured in his curious journey with Polina Suslova, so here too Dostoevsky links love with gambling, intimating, as it were, a hidden connection between the two. In the story, Polina's French suitor and lover, casting her off, outrages her by an indirect gift of fifty thousand francs. She had always shown the tutor contempt and sometimes hatred, and had appeared not to prize her limitless power over him. Now she goes to his hotel room, resolved to give herself to him. Does she hope to wipe out the affront to her pride by thus proving to herself that she is not to be bought? Here as throughout her behaviour leaves room for speculation. She lets the tutor read the Frenchman's insulting letter, and, in a frenzy, he leaves her in his room and rushes off to the tables, ecstatic with absolute self-confidence. He will win fifty thousand francs, and Polina can throw them in the face of the despicable Frenchman. He returns in an hour with four times that sum. While he was making his phenomenal kill, the woman for whose sake he was playing was obliterated from his mind by the excitement of the game. Memories of that excitement, flooding in upon him after his return to her, momentarily make him forget her presence. The two spend the night together.

Morning brings a revulsion of feeling on her part. She demands the fifty thousand francs as her pay, flings them in his face and leaves him. One thinks of the scene in which the protagonist of "Notes from the Underground" turns on the prostitute when he realizes that their relative positions have been reversed. Having lost Polina, the tutor squanders his fortune with a *cocotte* in Paris and returns to the tables as if blindly seeking to recapture the great moment when he had brought both chance and the inaccessible lady to their knees. He becomes utterly and hopelessly a slave to roulette. Not even the knowledge that Polina loved him all along and still loves him after a lapse of two years can save him from his obsession. That knowledge, which is disclosed at the end of the tale, comes as a surprise to the reader as well as to the tutor. The theory has been advanced by an American critic that the idea of the novel is the connection between the protagonist's failure as a lover and his fatal shortcomings as a spiritual being, one lost between belief and disbelief, a man suffering from "metaphysical impotence;" but if Dostoevsky intended to bring this home to his public, he failed to do so.

When his stenographer expressed her scorn for the gambler, the author took his part. He assured her that "many of the young man's feelings and impressions had been his own." Indeed, his own experiences, especially his affair with Polina Suslova, are plainly reflected in *The Gambler*. He was to know more of the gambler's hell in the years to come. In this respect the story was not a farewell to the past, but rather an anticipation of the future.

I I

Dostoevsky scarcely saw the girl who walked into his study that bright October morning to take dictation on *The Gambler*. He talked of this and that, unable to get down to work, and finally declared that he could dictate nothing then and that she must come back in the evening. He was glad at least that the stenographer was a woman: a man would have been sure to go off on a spree sooner or later. In the evening he continued to put off the unfamiliar business of dictating, but managed to get the novel started, and arranged for her to return the next day.

She was late. He was in a panic. He had forgotten her name and had failed to take down her address. He knew he had been difficult. Perhaps she would not show up at all. But she did, full of apologies for the extra half hour she had taken to make a handsome copy of what he had dictated and for the next several weeks the efficient, imperturbable creature, looking the graver in her neat mourning, appeared regularly and punctually.

It had taken some courage for her to return. She had been so elated over this first job of hers, more especially since her employer was to be the celebrated author whose name had often been on her late father's lips, and who was the object of her girlish adoration. And her first impression had been so painful. His flat was shabby and gloomy, and he himself looked old, ill, and queer, with his odd eyes, the pupil of the right one dilated with ratopine (he had injured it during an attack). And he behaved strangely. He was nervous, irritable, abrupt. He kept forgetting her name. He smoked continuously and repeatedly offered her cigarettes, though she had said she thought the habit unwomanly. Almost directly on seeing her he had told her that he was an epileptic and had had a fit only recently. In the evening he showed an even greater lack of reserve, describing to this stranger, among other things, his sensations as he stood on the scaffold on Semyonov Square waiting to be executed. When she left him at the end of that first day, her disappointment and bewilderment were tinged with pity for a man obviously lonely and unhappy.

As the days went by, Dostoevsky found dictation less of a strain. Decidedly the little stenographer suited him. She showed herself not merely self-effacing and methodical, but heartily interested in the work. His friends offered advice, reproached him for having entered into this arrangement with the cursed Stellovsky, commiserated with him in his predicament. Anna Grigoryevna Snitkina— he did learn her name at last—was helping him out of it. The pile of manuscript was growing daily. She kept assuring him that they would finish the thing in time, and it actually looked as though she were right. He came to take comfort in his contacts with this demure, dependable, cheerful girl. If she was plain, she had—it eventually dawned on him—pretty grey eyes and a pleasant smile. If her judgments were naïve and shallow, she took the book seriously. Fictive characters were real to her. Indeed, her first love had been the hero of his *Insulted and Injured*. When she confessed this to Dostoevsky, he said that he had only the vaguest recollection of what the novel was all about, and promised to reread it.

While they sipped tea or munched pears out of a paper bag, he would unburden himself to this sympathetic listener. He complained about his money troubles—she had seen for herself the table set with wooden spoons when the silver was at the pawnbroker's—he reminisced, he told her about his luckless affair with Anna Korvin-Krukovskaya, he showed her his late wife's portrait, a gloomy one, made the year before she died. But Polina Suslova was scarcely mentioned. His happy moments? He had none to tell her about, and yet . . . he still hoped for happiness. In time he made a habit of recounting to her where he had been and what he had done while they were apart. On one occasion he told her that there were three ways open to him: to settle in Constantinople or Jerusalem, to go abroad and give himself up to roulette, or else to get married. What should he do? Would any woman have him? Of course, the girl answered, and marriage was the step for him to take.

Gradually he learned some things about her—she had lost her awe, and spoke to him as to an uncle. She was only twenty. Her father, a civil servant with a taste for literature, the theatre and old china, had died in the spring, leaving in modest but comfortable circumstances a family consisting of her mother, who was of Swedish descent, herself, a married sister, and a brother, now a student at an agricultural college. She had taken up shorthand not so much because she needed to earn her living as because, like many a young miss in the sixties, she wanted to be independent. She was a girl of the period also in her objections to having her hand kissed and being helped out of a cab, but her unconventionality stopped there. She neither bobbed her hair nor affected spectacles; she was a respectful daughter and an observant Christian. She had two suitors, she told Dostoevsky, but intended to accept neither—she would wait until she could marry for love.

He caught himself thinking of her ever so often. As their sessions drew to an end, the idea that he would no longer see her regularly filled him with regret, and it was plain that the prospect of parting distressed her. She had received his confidences with such a friendly, even a motherly, air. She had taken his occasional brusqueness with perfect good nature. She was eager to come and so sorry to go away. A man did not have to be a novelist to see how it was with her. Perhaps that way some makeshift happiness awaited him.

It was his forty-fifth birthday, October 30, when she brought him the clean copy of the last instalment. The sight of her, looking taller and more graceful than usual in a long lilac silk dress she had put on in honour of the occasion, brought a flush to his cheeks. His pleasure in the visit was, however, abruptly checked by the entrance of Emilia Fyodorovna, who either out of arrogance or because of an intuitive grasp of the danger to herself in the situation, chose to snub the little stenographer. He was mortified and, finding that he could not persuade the girl to remain, saw her to the door and pressed her to name the day when he might call at her home.

He came, as appointed, four evenings later, met her good mother,

to whom he tried to be attentive, and found Anna Grigoryevna herself more responsive than ever. He told them that within a week he
was going to start work on the last part of *Crime and Punishment*,
and in that connection he would want her services again. Three days
later—it was Sunday—he paid a second call, this time uninvited.
Before he left, she promised to come on Tuesday to arrange for the
dictation.

On Monday night Dostoevsky had a dream. He was rummaging
among the papers in an old rosewood box, given to him in his
Siberian days, in which he kept manuscripts, letters, and objects
that had a sentimental value for him, when he noticed something
twinkling and vanishing among them. The thing caught his attention, and he went after it. It proved to be a small, sparkling
diamond. When he awoke he could not recall what he had done with
it, but he felt that the dream was of good omen. Wasn't he at last
going to come upon a tiny brilliant that would light his days? He
was still under the spell of his dream when Anna Grigoryevna came
in, a little tardily, from the bright frosty street, and he told her about
it at once. On her remarking that dreams went by contraries, his
mood dropped. But with her usual tact, she tried to cheer him up
and began asking him what he had been doing since she had seen
him last.

He had been busy, he said, with the plot of a new novel. The end,
which hinged upon the psychology of a young girl, somehow eluded
him, and she must help him with it. He went on to outline a story
which even her modest intelligence easily discerned to be a disguised
version of his autobiography. It had to do with an artist, unsuccess-
ful, ill, lonely, burdened with debts and responsibilities, who had
fallen in love with a girl less than half his age. So as not to call her
the heroine, he called her Anna, "a lovely name," he observed,
although on a previous occasion he had said that he disliked it,
having found all Annas dry, reserved creatures. This Anna was
gentle, sensible, and cheerful—not a beauty but not bad-looking
either. The oftener the artist saw her, the more convinced he grew
that she would make his happiness. Did Anna Grigoryevna think
it psychologically possible that such a girl could return the love of
such a man? Of course it was possible, she asserted hotly. He bade
her, in a voice that shook, put herself in the girl's place and him in

the hero's, and imagine that he had asked her to be his wife: what would she say?

"I should answer that I loved you and would love you all my life."

III

Anna's mother made no objection to the match. The groom's relatives, however, behaved quite differently. When Pasha heard the news—they were able to keep the engagement secret only a week— he came to his stepfather's study and made a scene. He was astonished and outraged, he stormed, not to have been consulted in a matter which touched him so nearly. He reminded Dostoevsky that he was too old a man to think of beginning life over again, and, besides, he had other duties and responsibilities. Nor did Emilia Fyodorovna and the other relatives conceal their disapproval. Indeed, they went so far as to try and frighten the young fiancée out of the marriage by malicious gibes and hints. And there were some among Dostoevsky's friends who, for disinterested reasons, warned him against this rash step. But his determination remained unshaken.

Not that the twenty-five years' difference between him and his betrothed failed to weigh upon him. He even teased himself, and her, too, by impersonating the would-be-youthful senile ruin of a man from his story, "Uncle's Dream." Anna did her best to quiet him on this score, promising him to age quickly, and trying, by her dress and demeanour, to appear older than her years. As for him, he acted the part of the conventional fiancé, calling on her every night, bringing her sweets from Ballet, taking her, on one extravagant occasion, to the theatre. Yet he had his misgivings, tinged, doubtless, with self-contemplative irony.

What with the distraction incident to his matrimonial project, Dostoevsky let *Crime and Punishment* ride. At the end of November it suddenly dawned on him that the instalment of the novel for the month's issue of *Russy vestnik* was still unwritten. As the magazine regularly appeared a month late, the delay was not fatal. With characteristic firmness, Anna, who from the first regarded herself as his helpmeet in every sense of the word, took matters in hand.

He must lock himself in every day from two to five and work, and when he came to her in the evening, dictate the final version. In this fashion the last part and the epilogue were completed in reasonably good time. This part includes the scene between Svidrigailov and Raskolnikov, in which the middle-aged roué gloats over his coming marriage to a sixteen-year-old girl, whereupon the young man observes: "The fact is this monstrous difference in age and development excites your sensuality! Will you really make such a marriage?" One wonders what Dostoevsky felt as he dictated this passage to his prospective young bride.

Christmas he spent with his sister Vera and her family in Moscow. The great news had not reached them yet. He confided it first to his favourite, Sonia, who rejoiced at it. Then he told Vera and the others. The sister-in-law to whom she had hoped eventually to marry him off was there, apparently no nearer to widowhood than before and more unhappy than ever, but holding nothing against Dostoevsky, which rather relieved him. Among the giggling girls was the vivacious young thing who had rejected him the previous Easter. The house was full as usual, everybody wished him well, and on New Year's Eve at midnight the head of the family raised his champagne glass in a toast to the newly affianced pair. But in spite of the good will and general gaiety, there were often times when he was the victim of an unaccountable gloom—the familiar oppressive feeling like the consciousness of having committed a crime.

The purpose of his Moscow visit was to see his publisher. He wanted Katkov to give him a substantial advance on his next novel. Indeed, without it, they would have to postpone the wedding. On January 2, 1867, he was able to write his "priceless and eternal friend, Anya" the good news that Katkov had proved obliging: he had advanced one thousand roubles, promising another thousand within two months, so that nothing stood in the way of their union.

As soon as he got home, however, the money began to melt away so rapidly that only by placing part of it in Anna's hands for safe-keeping could he be sure of the wedding expenses. Preparations for the event were begun at once. Anna was if anything the more eager of the two: she could scarcely wait for the time when she would be entitled to take such care of him as she felt he needed. Once they were married, his fur coat would not be pawned to help his relatives-in-law, as had happened during the courtship. With her modest dowry she assembled a trousseau that he insisted on seeing as it came from the dressmaker's. With the same money she furnished the new home—they rented a five-room flat in the neighbourhood of his old apartment, which he turned over to Emilia Fyodorovna and her family. On the fifteenth of February, the very month of his first wedding, Dostoevsky went through the marriage ceremony for the second time.

The marriage was solemnized in the Trinity (Izmailovsky) Cathedral at seven o'clock in the evening. They could not afford a wedding trip, but Dostoevsky invited the company to the new apartment, where champagne flowed freely until midnight struck the signal for the guests to leave the couple alone.

Whether or not Dostoevsky remembered the violent attack that had followed quickly upon his first wedding-day, he must have wondered nervously how soon his young bride would see him in a fit for the first time. They were married about a week when he had a sudden severe attack during an evening they were spending at her sister's house. His first wife, on a similar occasion, had been terribly frightened. Anna was made of different stuff. Her sister went into hysterics, and the rest of the household devoted itself to her. But the bride kept her presence of mind. She held his head on her knees all through the convulsions and did not break down even when he had a second and worse seizure an hour after recovering from the first one. The ordeal of that night, with no one to help while he lay screaming with pain or muttering like a man out of his mind, tried Anna and found her not wanting. Even in the evil mood that followed the fit he must have recognized that he had married a woman whose strength was equal to her devotion. Before he had ever proposed to her, he had asked her whether, if he married again, he should choose a kind or a clever woman. For himself, he thought it should be a kind one, so that she might love and pity him. He could not hide from himself that, at bottom, that was his reason for marrying Anna. The time was over now for the storms of passion that marked his relations with Polina Suslova. He was seeking a safe haven. With this girl, who respected him as she would her father, and pitied him as she would her child, he would find it. It was not a step to be particularly proud of, but there it was.

I V

The first few weeks of married life were a period of relative peace, in spite of the alarming frequency of his attacks. The public that not so long ago had relished Turgenev's *Fathers and Children*, and was even now being regaled with the first part of Tolstoy's *War and Peace*, was going mad over *Crime and Punishment*. The novel had brought the magazine five hundred new subscribers and was immediately published in book form. Dostoevsky had not yet embarked on any fresh venture, and meanwhile he was free to savour his new life and discover what leisure was like. Now he had a companion on his walks. On one of them he led Anna into a deserted courtyard he had described in *Crime and Punishment*, and showed her, off in a corner, the stone under which Raskolnikov had buried his loot.

He was glad to see that Pasha was attentive to his young stepmother; indeed, it looked as though her presence had a refining influence upon the boy. Emilia Fyodorovna was giving Anna the advice of an experienced housewife. The nieces and nephews who used to pay him stiff, infrequent visits were now running in at all hours and often staying for meals. This was just the companionship Anna needed. True, with all the entertaining, expenses were mounting. Besides, the constant stream of guests was rather tiresome and quite put a stop to those long intimate hours he had enjoyed with Anna before they were married.

One night he returned home from a visit to the Maikovs and found the house dark and Anna lying in bed and crying. But why? What had happened? Between sobs the story came out. She couldn't stand it any longer. She had done her best, but it was useless. Life in his house was no longer endurable for her. Emilia Fyodorovna kept loading her with admonitions and drawing invidious comparisons between her and Pasha's late mother. But it was chiefly Pasha who was making things impossible for her. He was continually heaping insults on her. He made fun of her housekeeping in front of guests, when it was he himself who, out of sheer spite, had emptied the cream-jug before his father's breakfast, made off with the matches, sent the maid on a wild-goose chase, so that she didn't have time to dust the study. That very morning he had told her that his father had made a mistake in marrying her, that she was a poor housekeeper, that she spent too much of the family's money, that his father's attacks were getting worse all on her account. And wasn't Pasha setting her husband against her? Fyodor scarcely talked to her any more. Indeed, when they were together, with this crowd of silly young people filling the house? He couldn't have cared, this master psychologist, this seer into the human heart, if he hadn't noticed what they were doing to her!

Dostoevsky listened to this outburst in amazement. It had never entered his head that things were at such a pass. He assured Anna that he loved her as deeply as ever, but the more he comforted her, the more freely her tears flowed. When she was finally quiet again, he told her that he had been thinking of going to Moscow. Now he would surely do so and take her with him. He would persuade Katkov to give him an additional advance, and they would go abroad on the money. Hadn't that been one of their dreams?

Two days later he was introducing his bride to his sister Vera and her family. He noticed that the young people, with the possible exception of Sonia, received Anna somewhat coldly. The truth was they were cross with her for having upset their plans for marrying off this favourite uncle to their favourite aunt, Yelena Pavlovna, as soon as she should become a widow. The ice was broken, amusingly enough, by the very girl who had rejected Dostoevsky's suit the previous spring. Before the Moscow visit was over, Anna was on good terms with the whole household, and if he had ever doubted the strength of his affection for her, he now proved it by finding himself an excessively jealous husband. They left the city, feeling that the week they had spent there had been their real honeymoon and carrying with them a thousand roubles from Katkov. The trip abroad seemed assured.

Of course, both Pasha and Emilia Fyodorovna set their faces against such an extravagance. What would they live on while the couple were making a summer's jaunt? Besides, there were the creditors. The seven thousand roubles he had received for the separate edition of *Crime and Punishment* had gone into their pockets.

But this only whetted their appetite. Again they were threatening to attach the household effects and put Dostoevsky in debtor's prison. It occurred to him that this last might not be so bad. It might even give him the stuff for another *House of the Dead* and bring in four or five thousand roubles. But, of course, even if there were not Anna to consider, he might not be able to write in the stuffy cell during the hot summer months. Europe offered itself as a refuge. He needed a trip abroad for his health: he was in a state of intolerable nervous tension. And yet the more he thought of it, the more he felt that under the circumstances, the journey was out of the question. Emilia's notion of their taking a house in the country together, with her to spare Anna the trouble of house-keeping, was not so bad. They would stay home; Anna would adjust herself; everything would be all right.

Two days after they came home—he had already decided to abandon the trip—Anna took a walk with him. At her suggestion, they stepped into a chapel to say a prayer before the icon of the Virgin. And then, after some little hesitation, she drew for him a fresh picture of her situation. They must have at least a month or two of peace together, she pleaded. Their married life was at stake. If she was to be constantly at the mercy of Pasha and Emilia Fyodorovna, a separation was inevitable. They must go abroad to save their happiness. Didn't he see it? She broke into tears on the street. If she had but a taste of undisturbed comradeship with him, their union would grow strong enough to withstand strains and shocks. Money? There was the new furniture, the piano, the silver, her jewellery, and some securities of hers, too. If they pawned it all, there would be enough for the trip and something for Pasha and Emilia Fyodorovna to live on, as well. She had spoken to her mother, who had approved the plan. Her tears were her strongest argument. Before Dostoevsky had done comforting her, he agreed to her scheme. They went at once to apply for a passport. Here was a woman of action. Three days later, on April 14, at five o'clock in the afternoon, they entrained for Berlin.

CHAPTER EIGHTEEN

ROULETTENBURG

AFTER a day or two in Berlin, where Dostoevsky enjoyed a Russian bath, the couple settled in Dresden in a furnished flat of three rooms. Why Dresden? It didn't really matter to him where he was. At any rate, now they were completely alone: there was no one to interfere with their privacy, no one to sow dissension between them. Yet it was not an idyllic existence. Even when he did not have one of his frequent attacks, he would be likely to wake up in an ugly mood. There were days when nothing pleased him; he grumbled at the food, at the landscape, at the layout of the streets. The Germans annoyed him intensely. The attractions of the city—the open-air concerts, the galleries—gave him only shallow satisfaction. They had practically nowhere else to go except to the post office, where they were always being disappointed, and to the library, where there were a few musty Russian books. The pair quarrelled perpetually: over her soiled gloves, over the sunset, over the right way to handle an umbrella, over the brewing of a cup of tea. He would scream at her; she would tremble with rage. He had always thought, he said, that a wife was her husband's natural enemy. But they made up. Their fallings-out were of the kind that all the more endears. There were, too, many moments of jollity and intimate companionship, particularly in the small hours of the morning when, after a night's work, he would wake her to say a lingering good night.

The precarious conjugal peace was sometimes shaken by gusts of jealousy. Anna had reason to be anxious. Her husband's affair with Polina Suslova had not remained a secret to her, and in Dresden she discovered that he was keeping up a correspondence with the woman. Finding a letter from Polina on his table, she read it with the unscrupulousness characteristic of her where her affections were concerned, and was thrown into a storm of jealous tears.

She would have been even more enraged had she seen his answer which he penned almost as soon as they were settled. Polina knew nothing of his marriage, and Dostoevsky was under the necessity of breaking the news to her. He did so in a manner that was slightly apologetic. When he had finished dictating *The Gambler*, he wrote he noticed that his stenographer, "a young and rather attractive girl . . . had fallen sincerely in love" with him, and for his part, he "liked her more and more." His brother's death had left him depressed and lonely, and so he had proposed to her. In spite of the frightful difference in their years, he was increasingly convinced that she would be happy: "She has a heart and is capable of love." Then he broke off abruptly to discuss his financial situation, but closed on a personal note, addressing Polina in the words he had used in writing to his fiancée from Moscow, as his "eternal friend." He knew that it was difficult for her to be happy: "Oh, darling, it is not to a cheap, *necessary* happiness that I invite you. I respect you, and always did, for your exacting nature, but how well I know that your heart cannot help demanding much from life, and people seem to you either infinitely shining or else utter scoundrels and vulgarians."

Cheap happiness, a makeshift, a compromise—was that what he had achieved? Polina would have lifted him to the heights and cast him down into the depths. Anna, the kind one, seemed capable of giving him the tenderness, the comfort, the protection that were necessary to a man broken by years of suffering—but that was all. This must have been one of those moments when a vague shame, a slight rebellion crossed his contentment.

Polina's reply to Dostoevsky's letter arriving ten days later, in his absence, Anna again did not scruple to open it, read it, and seal it up. She had the bitter satisfaction of seeing how he received it. He took a long time over the first page and, as he went on reading, his face flushed and his hands trembled. She pretended to think the letter came from his niece and asked for news, but he said briefly that it was not from Sonia, and smiled forlornly. He was absentminded the rest of the evening and could hardly grasp anything his wife said to him. The next morning he reread the letter, pacing up and down the room as though looking for something he had lost, and for days afterwards he was out of temper.

Anna had, however, nothing further to fear from her husband's former mistress. Late in May there was another letter from Polina, apparently the last one. She is known to have opened a village school the following year, but the authorities closed it on the grounds that she bobbed her hair, wore blue glasses, and never went to church. In a police report dated 1868, she was accused of having "close relations with persons abroad hostile to the government." Later she tried her hand at literary work, translating a biography of Benjamin Franklin—she had long been interested in America—and for a while she attended the first university courses in Russia thrown open to women. In middle life she married a man many years her junior. An ardent admirer of Dostoevsky, this Vasily Rozanov in time wrote commentaries on the novelist and composed other miscellaneous works in a mystical and retrograde vein. Before long Polina left him. It is said that she fell in love with a student, who spurned her, whereupon she denounced him to the police as a revolutionary. Perhaps she had already undergone the change of heart which eventually landed her in the camp of black reaction. According to another report, she drove a foster-child to suicide. In *The Insulted and Injured* Rozanov found a description of a woman that, he declared, fitted Polina perfectly: Prince Valkovsky's sketch of an ostensibly cold and unapproachable beauty who secretly savoured a depravity so monstrous that she could have given lessons to Marquis de Sade. He also likened her to the instigator of the Massacre of St. Bartholomew. Her father spoke of her in less literary terms as a she-devil.

These characterizations help to support the impression that she contributed something to the creation of those sinful, passionate women who figure in Dostoevsky's major novels. It seems, too, that the lacerations these two inflicted upon each other helped to shape the novelist's conception of "the great constringent relation" between the sexes. His daughter, an unreliable witness, recounts how one day in the late seventies a veiled woman clad in black came to see the novelist, refusing to give her name, and, in answer to his query as to her reason for coming, simply threw back her veil and looked at him. Dostoevsky stared at her without a flicker of recognition, and only after she had swept out of the room in mute pride it flashed upon him that this woman whom he had failed to recognize was Polina. Perhaps it was precisely by stepping out of his life that she made so firm a place for herself in his art.

II

The couple had scarcely been a week in Dresden when Dostoevsky began to get restless. He was idle, he was bored, he was getting fat! He stood it another week, and then he succumbed to the old fever, taking the train for Homburg and the tables. He had to spend several hours at the Leipzig station, and as he paced the huge waiting room full of smoke and the smell of beer he asked himself how he could have left his young, innocent, patient angel alone and friendless in a strange town, while he was going . . . where? On what fool's errand? It was sheer madness. The reason that offered itself readily was the money he hoped to win, the money he needed to live on, the money with which he must pay off his creditors. On previous trips abroad he had offered a similar excuse for his gambling. But the author of *The Gambler* must have understood that it was not hope of gain alone that was sending him to the tables. At the moment he was not in urgent need, though his funds were low. He may well have been driven by the desire to challenge fate, by the craving for risk, and for the anguish, the humiliation that such an experience held for him.

He intended to stay away no more than four days. They stretched out into ten. He still firmly believed in his "system": if you keep cool and calculate your moves, you are bound to win. The trouble was that he couldn't keep cool for more than half an hour at a time, and yet he did not leave the tables for longer than it took to smoke a cigarette. Gambling was never meant for a nervous man like himself. And so in the end he always lost. Oh, it was vile, sordid, contemptible! But he needed this fever. His nerves were ragged with the excitement, and he was tired from sitting still so much, but his health was excellent and there was no thought of an attack.

Every day he poured out his hopes and fears to Anna in a letter full of self-reproach and affection. God had given her to him that he might expiate his enormous sins by guarding and preserving this young soul in all its purity, and now perhaps he was injuring it irreparably. But she must continue to love him. Only now that he was away from her he realized how he loved her; they were becoming truly one. When he was with her he hid his tenderness under sullenness and irritability, but that was his wretched character. Would she ever forgive him all the torture he had caused her? And how could she ever respect him again? He had appealed to her for the fare home and had immediately gambled it away. She must send him another remittance, but she mustn't dream of coming to fetch him. Such want of confidence would kill him.

As soon as he received the money, he went back to her, having wasted the staggering sum of three hundred and fifty roubles and left his watch in the hands of a Homburg pawnbroker.

Anna received him without a word of reproach, and they settled into a placid, if somewhat dismal, routine. They looked in at the post office, they went to the library, they roamed through the museums, they stopped for a cup of coffee and an ice or for a try at the shooting gallery. After dinner they strolled in the gardens and listened to the orchestra; in the evening he read or tried to work: he was then busy setting down his reminiscences of Belinsky, but with little success. Meanwhile she was assiduously filling her notebooks with mysterious hooks and dashes. What could she be writing there? She refused to tell him. She had promised her mother, from whom she was absent for the first time and for whom she was frightfully homesick, to write down every detail of her life abroad. And so she was doing this, as she did everything, dutifully, patiently, with an unmitigated interest in trifles and a total lack of discrimination. She recorded the changes in the weather and in Fyodor's moods, his quarrels with waiters, librarians, and post-office clerks— German words, which ordinarily failed him, came in a flood when he was furious. She retailed his frequent absurd quarrels with her, their reconciliations, and the exchanges of loverly nonsense that lightened their dull existence and made her supremely happy. She listed everything each of them had to eat and drink and never omitted to mention the exact cost of everything they bought and some things they didn't buy, and how the price compared with the price of the same items at home.

One night early in June she had something important to tell him: she suspected she was pregnant. They both rejoiced when the sus picion became a certainty. If it were a girl, they would call her Sonia, for the heroine of *Crime and Punishment*, and his favourite niece; they rather hoped for a boy—then there would be no need for a dowry, and in that case they would of course call him Mikhail. Now there was something pleasant to tease her about, and a new source of worry. It looked as though they would have to stay abroad much longer than they had originally intended, a good deal to Anna's relief, since, however home-sick for her mother she might be, she dreaded the return to Petersburg, where she would again be at the mercy of her relatives-in-law.

But what would they live on? And what would become of Pasha and Emilia Fyodorovna and her children? The money they had taken with them was rapidly melting away, and there was not a word from Katkov, to whom Dostoevsky had written for an additional five hundred roubles just after the Homburg disaster. Moreover, toward the end of their Dresden stay he had a most alarming experience. In the state of irritability which always followed one of his seizures he had a tiff with a clerk at the Russian consulate, and in the midst of it he had a hallucination: Mikhail suddenly appeared, head and shoulders, in the doorway. Was he going mad? As he looked back upon the weeks just before he left Russia, it seemed to him that he had then been in a state verging on insanity. Now, at least, his attacks were less frequent.

Homburg had cured him completely of his gambling fever, Dostoevsky thought. He had really benefited by the adventure. The lesson was cheap at the price. But the day after writing this to Anna he made up his mind that his great mistake had been in not taking her with him: then he would have been mentally at ease and able to take advantage of his system. Back in Dresden this idea grew upon him: the thing for them to do at the first opportunity was to go together to some gambling resort for an extended stay. Anna let herself be persuaded. It did not matter where they lived, provided he was with her, and besides she might conceivably exercise a restraining influence upon him.

In spite of the boredom, the sense of waste, the anxiety that these Dresden days held, they affected what the two had hoped of them: they cemented the union. Dostoevsky's cruel nerves gave his young wife moments of childish panic and despair, and at times she was ready to throw herself out of the window, but when, late in June, the money from Katkov arrived and they were leaving the city, Anna wrote in her diary: "Good-bye now, Dresden. . . . How happy we have been here together; I don't really count our little differences one bit, as I know Fyodor loves me, and the cause of it all is nothing but his irritable, volcanic nature; even for that do I love him beyond all words."

III

As soon as they had the fare, the couple took the train for Baden. True, when he had been in this gambler's paradise with Polina he had had a run of bad luck, but going with Anna, it would be a different story.

They arrived in Baden on July 4, and for the seven miserable weeks that they remained there their existence revolved around the gaming-tables. He would work spasmodically at his article on Belinsky, which was still far from finished, and without putting anything on paper he was brooding in the night hours over a project that he hoped to make a bigger thing than *Crime and Punishment*. But he was not free to give himself to these occupations. He was a man possessed. It was an illness, a mania. He cursed the game, he cursed his luck, he called himself a weakling and a scoundrel. But as long as there was anything to stake, he was in a fever until he got to the gambling-rooms.

At first, gains and losses alternated, but the former were always modest until, on the twelfth day, he won heavily. It was a stormy evening, and by the lightning-flashes the couple counted out a fortune of three thousand francs. The next day luck turned against him, and thereafter smiled on him intermittently and briefly. He continued to hope, in vain, that he would repeat his coup. When he did win, there was a feast: fruit, berries, wine, pastries. More frequently he lost. Two fairly large remittances from Anna's mother were promptly gambled away, and gradually her brooch, her ear-rings, her lilac dress, her fur coat, her lace scarf, a pair of his trousers, his old hat, their wedding rings found their way into the pawnbroker's shop, only to be redeemed with his winnings, and pawned again. He had to slink out of the house with his bundle concealed from the landlady's eye, cool his heels in dingy rooms, waiting for some shady trafficker in secondhand goods, receive such characters in his own lodging, run from one moneylender to another, and when he finally got his man, there was disgusting begging and bargaining.

As if there were not enough to make their heads ache, they were roused early every morning by the thumping boots of the smith's apprentices in the attic overhead and kept awake by the hammer and bellows below stairs. It was to this wretched lodging that Dostoevsky would return from the casino, so often empty-handed, to face the girl whom he had married less than six months previously and who was now carrying his child. He shouted that he was to blame, he cried that he hated her, he threw himself at her feet, he beat his head with his fists, he sobbed—and he went back. The thing was stronger than he. How would he take care of Pasha and the others? How would he ever pay off his debts? He screamed, he wrung his hands. He would go mad or shoot himself! And what if Katkov should suddenly die? He was full of whims. He worked himself into a frenzy over trifles. There was constant wrangling, no less bitter for being absurd. He was ruled by superstitious fancies. He blamed his losses on a Pole who stood next to him at the tables, on a Russian woman who chattered too much, on an Englishman who reeked of eau de Cologne, on Anna who had refused to take a walk with him. She continued the patient Griselda: she bore with his ugly temper, his unjust reproaches; she soothed him; she hid her own tears from him; though she tried to shield him from himself, she let him have his way.

She had her moments of inward rebellion at his egotism, his lack of kindness and understanding. She could bear to trudge to the pawnbroker's for him, to wash his shirts, to nurse him during his seizure, even to watch him as he stood at the tables, his face flushed, his eyes bloodshot as though he were drunk, but she was enraged at the thought that he was more concerned about Mikhail's widow and orphans than about his own wife and their unborn child. She told herself that all their sufferings were for the sake of strangers and that she herself meant nothing to him. But these were only brief and transient moods. A tender word from him, a gesture of affection would dissipate them.

The very miseries of their situation drew the two together as prosperity and pleasure could not have done. When he would come in white-faced and then dazzle her with the gold he had won—he had a habit of showing a woebegone face in good fortune, as though to propriate jealous Fate—there would be flowers and wine and delicacies, and life would have a sparkle. But even when his pallor was unfeigned, when their things were in pawn, the rent unpaid, the coffee and candles got on credit, the news from home devastating, the future frightening—even then they would turn to one another with a smile or a kiss, and feel that where all else tottered, their affection was secure. So many entries in her journal concluded on a confession of complete conjugal bliss. At the end of one of their most dismal days, when they were wondering how they would go on at all, she wrote in her diary: "It seemed to me that all this trouble was a kind of atonement for the tremendous happiness that had come my way in marrying Fyodor." Was she repeating something that her husband had suggested to her in one of their midnight talks? Was it thus that he accounted to himself for his irrational and ruinous passion?

IV

The pair were the more dependent upon one another because they lived in complete isolation, too poor and too absorbed in their predicament to be aware of the glittering life of the resort, let alone take part in it. But even if they avoided the promenade by daylight because Anna had nothing to wear (and the couple had certainly not come to drink the waters in the company of pampered fashionables), Dostoevsky could not help chancing upon Russian acquaintances among the cosmopolitan crowd at the casino. The very first Sunday he ran into Goncharov, already the renowned author of *Oblomov*. A solid citizen and a state councillor, Goncharov was at first somewhat abashed at being caught gambling, but seeing Dostoevsky's matter-of-fact acceptance of the situation, he admitted that he was playing, and the two drifted into talk. Among other things, Goncharov said that Turgenev, who was then a resident of Baden, had noticed Dostoevsky at the casino the previous day but, knowing that gamblers dislike being interrupted at play, had not accosted him.

What a nuisance! He still owed Turgenev the money he had

borrowed when he was stranded in Wiesbaden two years earlier, and now he would have to go and call on him, or the man would think he was being avoided. He knew how it would be: Turgenev would pretend to embrace him, but only offer his cheek to be kissed. He had the manners of a fop, of an aristocratic trifler. His latest novel, *Smoke,* with its paean to Western civilization, was enough to turn the stomach of any Russian. And to think that this man, with his ample income, was paid at a higher rate than he, with all his responsibilities and burdens, could hope for!

It was Wednesday morning before Dostoevsky forced himself to call on Turgenev—a duty all the more disagreeable since he was not in a position to pay his debt. The visit lasted an hour or so. Straight from the quiet house on Schillerstrasse he went to the casino. He won a considerable sum of money and after a sumptuous dinner returned to the gambling-rooms, but luck turned against him, and though he went back to the tables three times the same afternoon, he always lost. He became so irritable that, there being nothing else to complain of, he worked himself into a rage because it took so long to get dark. It was in this angry mood that he told Anna, over their evening tea, about his visit to Turgenev. The man was embittered by the failure of *Smoke* and kept returning to the sore subject, but he, Dostoevsky, had said nothing about it. He had, however, advised Turgenev to get himself a telescope and train it on Russia, otherwise he could not hope to understand what was going on there. He had also told Turgenev frankly that he was not the realist he thought himself. Before taking leave, he could not help venting his animosity against the Germans, saying that they were stupid and often deceitful. Although this had offended his host, who declared that he had become a German himself, the two managed to part with a show of friendliness.

The following morning Turgenev, who wished to save appearances, returned Dostoevsky's call, but at an hour when he knew he would not be received. When, later, they ran into each other at the casino, neither bowed.

Nearly two months later Dostoevsky gave a fuller account of his visit to Turgenev in a letter to Maikov. The conversation, he wrote, had first centred on *Smoke,* and Turgenev had been shameless enough to say that the main point of the novel was that mankind would lose nothing if Russia were to sink through the ground. And of course he was an atheist: he had said so flatly. Good God! Religion gives us the incomparable beauty, the serene ideal of Christ, while all these Turgenevs, Herzens, Chernyshevskys—the whole Belinsky progeny—present nothing but a spectacle of emptiness, vanity, and abominable self-love! Turgenev pretended to love Russia, but he hated and made a mock of everything original there. Among other things, he had said that the Russians "must crawl before the Germans," that civilization was the one common and inevitable road, and that any attempt on the part of Russia to go its own gait was "swinishness and folly." He was going to put all these ideas in a pamphlet he was writing against the Slavophils. It was at this point that Dostoevsky had mentioned the telescope. Here was a home thrust, and it annoyed Turgenev accordingly. The rest of the account agrees with Dostoevsky's report to his wife.

The story of the quarrel was soon common gossip in literary circles. A copy of the passage relating to it in the letter to Maikov was sent anonymously, probably by Strakhov, to the editor of *Russky arhiv* ("Russian Archives"), a historical review, with the request to preserve the document for posterity. Before the year was over, Turgenev learned of it and, believing that Dostoevsky had been responsible for this step, hastened to write a letter to protest to the editor, Bartenev. He said that he could not possibly have expressed his intimate convictions in the presence of his visitor, for the simple reason that he thought the man "not wholly in possession of his mental faculties, an opinion shared by many other persons." Dostoevsky, he went on, "sat with me no more than an hour, and retired after having relieved his heart by ferociously abusing the Germans, myself, and my latest book. I had neither the time nor the desire to argue with him. I repeat, I treated him as I would a sick man. The arguments which he expected from me must have presented themselves to his deranged imagination. . . ." A few years later, writing to a friend about the affair, Turgenev said: "He [Dostoevsky] came to me . . . not to pay the money he had borrowed off me, but to upbraid me for *Smoke* which, according to his notion, should be burned by the hand of the executioner. I listened to his philippic in silence, and what do I learn? That I expressed within his hearing criminal opinions, which he hastened to communicate to Bartenev. . . . It would have been simple calumny, if Dostoevsky weren't crazy—which I don't doubt in the least. Perhaps he hallucinated."

It is not probable that Turgenev listened to Dostoevsky "in silence," but it is more than probable that Dostoevsky, in his wrought-up state, distorted and exaggerated whatever his host may have said. Just at that time he was locking the door on those aberrations of his youth he identified with the name of Belinsky. Turgenev, appearing to him as the spiritual son of the dead heresiarch, drew down upon his own head all the lightnings Dostoevsky intended for Belinsky. More than likely he attributed to Turgenev not the opinions he heard, but the opinions he expected to hear from that quarter.

V

August found the fortunes of the couple at low ebb and Anna's patience almost gone. A remittance from her mother relieved them slightly. With part of this sum in his pocket, Dostoevsky went to redeem Anna's ring, brooch, and ear-rings, but before he reached the pawnbroker's he found himself at the casino, where he gambled the money away. He came home in a desperate state, crying, and calling himself a worthless scoundrel. This was the last drop. They would leave this accursed place the next day. No longer able to trust him, Anna accompanied him to the pawnbroker's to redeem her trinkets. The following morning—it was August 23—he was again at the tables, having pawned his ring, and lost again. As before, he came home agonizing, calling himself a blackguard, and entreating Anna's forgiveness on his knees. As these losses left them without enough money for the journey, the ear-rings went back to the pawnshop. An hour before the train left, he managed to gamble away a few more thalers. That day Anna closed the entry in her diary thus: "I will even forbid my children ever to come here, so much have I endured in this place."

There could be no thought of going home. He was afraid the creditors might have him arrested forthwith. He and Anna must, therefore, winter abroad. They had planned to go either to Paris or Italy, but this being too expensive, they went to Geneva instead, so that Dostoevsky was again following the route he had previously taken with Polina. On their way they stopped off at Basle, where they did some sight-seeing. At the museum here he stood in fascinated horror before Holbein's "Dead Christ." Anna in her oversensitive state, refused to look at it, and when she rejoined her husband after a quarter of an hour she found him still standing before the canvas as though chained to it, and with that slightly frightened expression on his face which frequently betokened an approaching attack. She led him away, and he became quiet, but as he left the museum he swore that he would return to look at the picture again.

The impression the canvas made upon him he transcribed in the bitter testament ("An Essential Explanation") of the consumptive Ippolit in *The Idiot*. If the transcription, as is likely, is a faithful one, this realistic picture of the corpse of Christ came as a challenge to his faith, a dark echo of his doubt. "When you look at this picture, nature appears to you as an immense, merciless, dumb beast, or more correctly, much more correctly, speaking, though it sounds strange, in the form of a huge machine of the most modern construction which, dull and insensate, has senselessly clutched, crushed, and swallowed up a great and priceless Being, a Being worth all of nature and its laws, worth the whole earth, which was created perhaps solely for the sake of the advent of that Being! This picture expresses and involuntarily suggests to one the conception of a dark, insolent, unreasoning and eternal Power to which everything is subject." How could men see this corpse, and believe? "These people surrounding the dead man . . . must have experienced terrible anguish and consternation on that evening, which had at once crushed all their hopes, and almost their beliefs. They must have parted in the most awful terror, though each one carried away within him a mighty thought that could never be wrested from him." One imagines Dostoevsky looking at this dead body and paraphasing Scripture: Blessed are they that have seen, and yet have believed.

The couple's circumstances when they arrived in Geneva were dismal. They had only a few francs left and nothing to expect but a paltry fifty roubles from home. It was terrible for Dostoevsky to think of the straits Pasha and the others must be in. If only he hadn't burdened himself with all those debts! He must throw him-

DOSTOEVSKY'S FIRST WIFE

Photograph probably taken in 1863

self on his friends again. He begged Maikov to lend him a small sum, turning part of it over to Pasha. Maikov's response allowed them to keep their heads above water for a while. To add to his troubles, his attacks became more frequent: horrible as those seven weeks at Baden had been, he had suffered only two seizures there. At Geneva there was hardly a week without an attack, and for days thereafter he lay stupefied. How, under such conditions, could he work? And yet only work could save them.

The setting of his days was changed, but it was no less foreign. If the people around him were not Germans, he found them just as alien, repellent, chilling. Russia was further away than ever. And return was indefinitely postponed. He was like a fish out of water. True, there were some Russians in Geneva, but they were professional revolutionists, expatriates, and so there was no question of commerce with them. They only helped to make him feel that he was a castaway, living on an uninhabited island. Oh, for Russian faces, Russian speech, Russian interests! He longed for them, he needed them for his writing.

His writing? He had nothing black on white to show for the summer. He had carried no manuscript with him to Geneva. All he had was an idea for a novel. It would be a big thing. "I love it terribly," he was writing to Maikov a few days after his arrival in Switzerland, "and I shall be writing it with joy and anguish." But he must first be quit of the essay on Belinsky. He had been working at it on and off all summer, and now at last, before September was half over, he completed it. It had been a ticklish job. He couldn't face squarely the issues involved in any discussion of Belinsky and still hope his article would pass the censor. He felt like a man walking on eggs. He wrote, he tore up, he rewrote, and finally produced a piece that was neither here nor there, much to his own disgust. As the manuscript was never published and has been lost, irretrievably it appears, one can only guess at what he actually said. It must have been a farewell to the short-lived radicalism of his youth, a renewed attack on socialism and unfaith.

Just about the time that he was putting the finishing touches to this ill-starred essay, the International League for Peace and Freedom was holding a congress in Geneva, in the hope of averting an impending Franco-Prussian conflict. The shades of opinion represented ranged from a pallid liberalism to communism and the most violent anarchism. If Dostoevsky was among the crowd that packed the huge Palais Electoral at the first session, the afternoon of September 9, he heard the wild applause that greeted alike the address delivered by the representative of the Workers' International and the more sentimental eloquence of Garibaldi. It is certain that he went with Anna to get a glimpse of the proceedings the next day. One of the first speakers at that session protested against Garibaldi's declaration of the previous day that the congress should adopt "the religion of God," even though what he meant was the religion of reason. Far from creating a new religion, the orator argued, reason should destroy those that exist. Churches, no less than barracks, must be razed to the ground. This sentiment elicited loud applause, in which Garibaldi himself joined. Then a shaggy, unkempt, toothless giant, wearing a nondescript grey cloak with a red flannel shirt showing from under it, made the steps of the rostrum creak under his elephantine tread. It was the veteran revolutionist and apostle of anarchism, Bakunin. His programme was simple and bold. The Russian Empire must go. All the other monarchies of Europe must go. The false principle of nationalism must go. Peace and freedom would come only through a spontaneous federation of communes. A United States of Europe must rise upon the ruins of the existing empires. May Russian arms suffer every defeat, may the power that rests upon them suffer every humiliation: this was his wish as a liberty-loving Russian.

Other speakers followed. So here they were in the flesh, these European socialists, these prophets of the new order, who had been only disembodied names to Dostoevsky until now. The whole thing turned his stomach. After two more days of speechifying, the congress disbanded. If he did not attend all the sessions, he must have followed the reports of them in the papers. The departure of Garibaldi, before the opening of the third session, removed a restraining influence, and during the final days the socialist faction and its opponents were at it tooth and nail. To Dostoevsky the congress was one continuous squabble, a babel, a bedlam. What was there to hold these saviours of mankind together? They wanted to achieve peace by fire and sword; they wanted to get men to share their possessions fraternally—by decree. Naturally, they

would abolish Christianity. And to think that these wretches were
stirring up the unhappy workers! Thus he set down his impressions
of the congress in letters home. The moments of enthusiasm, of
glorious accord, the noble gestures, the universal reverence for the
Italian hero and the exalted principles he stood for—all this went
unnoticed. All Dostoevsky could see was that these members of the
League for Peace and Freedom were dangerous fools who did not
understand that peace could not be legislated and that the only
safeguard of freedom was religious faith.

CHAPTER NINETEEN

THE IDIOT

AT LAST he was able to take his novel in hand. It was high time to get to work. Aside from the old debts, there were all those thousands of roubles he had taken from Katkov. And the people at home had to be provided for. He would share his last shirt with Pasha, the poor dear boy. As for themselves, soon there would be the additional expenses of Anna's confinement and, please God, another mouth to feed. The novel was his only hope. And it stubbornly refused to take shape. Images, ideas, situations were churning in his head, but the characters somehow kept slipping away from him, and in consequence the plot was always shifting.

His point of departure was the character of "the idiot," a youth hated by his mother, who had given him this nickname and the reputation of an idler, although he actually supported the whole family; as a child he had been abandoned by his parents. The only thing that this boy has in common with the hero of the novel in its final version is his sobriquet. He first presented himself to Dostoevsky's imagination as the embodiment of a self-love so passionate and extreme that it was akin to madness. In some way the Idiot is to come into conflict with his opposite, also a passionate soul, but a selfless Christian. The Idiot is in love with an unhappy young girl, Mignon. She was to be modelled partly on the heroine of a sensational trial which was going on at home just when Dostoevsky began planning the novel in earnest—a fifteen-year-old girl so cruelly treated by her parents that she tried to commit suicide and repeatedly set fire to the house. It is curious that just when he was joyfully anticipating the arrival of his own first-born, he should have been haunted by the idea of a child suffering from the unnatural hostility of its parents.

He made one "final" draft after another, changing the plot,

shifting the emphasis, introducing new characters. He was like a man groping in the dark. His fancy, dwelling amid scenes of wild generosity and insane jealousy, in an atmosphere of rape and incest, of love that was hatred and hate that was love, kept summoning up half-formed shapes of men and women. But whither was this chaos of sensuality moving, and how was it to be redeemed? Perhaps precisely because the Idiot sank to the depths of selfishness and evil he might touch the peak of grace. Even that notion brought Dostoevsky no further.

It was already November, and all that his labours had resulted in was a pile of notebooks crammed with contradictory jottings. Suddenly he was seized by a new idea. His central character would be not a passionate sinner but, instead, a man caught in a tangle of mad passions, yet preserving a childlike purity and sweetness— the Idiot of the published novel. Here was a complete, a mastering image. Now there need be no more hesitation. He sat down to write.

A week after he fastened upon his theme, on November 17, he abandoned the manuscript on which everything depended, and his darling Anna, and in a few hours reached the little watering place of Saxon, the only resort in Switzerland offering the attractions of Baden-Baden, Homburg, and Wiesbaden. This was not the first time he had visited Saxon. He had been there six weeks previously and come home with empty pockets, having left his wedding ring in pawn. And now against every persuasion of reason, he was there again. This time Fate must relent!

Anna had offered no resistance: she knew that to oppose him would be only to fan the flame. She stayed behind in their dingy furnished room and waited for tidings of disaster. They came in the form of a letter announcing that he had lost everything, that his overcoat and his wedding ring were in pawn, and that he was condemned to stay in the accursed place until she sent him a remittance. Never, never again would he go near the tables! Never again would he steal her money "like a low, dirty thief." He would yet win her respect. But she must love him as he loved her, "infinitely, eternally." She must not grieve over the loss—he would borrow from a compatriot in Geneva and ask Katkov to double their allowance (the publisher had agreed to send him one hundred roubles a month). He would make her happy. A new life was beginning. If his pockets were empty, his heart was full of hope. The novel, the novel would save them!

Strange, how the ruinous adventure left him with a sense of well-being! Back at his desk, he attacked his work with new energy. For two weeks he laboured steadily. And then he tossed aside everything he had written. The thing was worthless. He had made another false start. December was already under way, and the first instalment of the novel was due for the January issue of the magazine. He had taken an advance of forty-five hundred roubles and had not a page to give in return. In a panic he began to plan anew. His head was a mill, grinding out six different schemes every day. That he did not go insane was a marvel to him. The room was like an icehouse—these brainless Swiss in the midst of forests didn't know how to heat their houses—and he sat at his desk in his overcoat. He tried to keep that out of pawn. And in addition there was the unbearable thought that Pasha, to whom he had not been able to send a copeck, might be starving.

After a feverish fortnight he began the actual writing again. Although the central figure remained the Christlike Idiot, so changed was the setting that he was really attempting a new novel. By dint of half killing himself he was able to dispatch the first instalment in time for the January issue, which, luckily for him, was late as usual. But it was a bad business. Here he had sent off the first seven chapters of the novel, but he had only the vaguest notion of how the action would develop. Furthermore, even the central figures had not matured in his mind. Two or three of them were fairly present to him, but the Idiot, the chief character, the one upon whom the whole significance of the novel depended, was far from clear. To have dispatched the first chapters under these circumstances was a sheer gamble, was staking everything on the next turn of the wheel. It was a good thing Katkov did not know this: he had told him a deliberate lie to the effect that much of the novel was written in the rough and he only had to polish it off. The one comfort was that the first part was more or less in the nature of an introduction and allowed him a free hand later on. Would it whet the appetite of his audience as he intended it to? Anna liked it but, as he wrote to Maikov, she was no judge of his business.

The new year brought word that Dr. Ivanov, the husband of his sister Vera and the father of ten children, had suddenly died. Dostoevsky wrote tenderly to Sonia, telling her how much he loved them all. They must form one big family. And she must not believe that life ended so abruptly and meanly. No, it went on —there were other worlds than this. But we must be worthy of the final communion of all souls. She must believe not in death, but in resurrection.

Ivanov had left his family practically destitute, and this concerned Dostoevsky nearly: he had gone surety for Mikhail when the latter had borrowed six thousand roubles from Ivanov, a sum that had never been repaid. He immediately wrote to Vera to say that he held himself responsible for the amount, and would pay it as soon as possible. This practically doubled his indebtedness, but there were more immediate matters to worry about: how to make both ends meet from day to day while he was trying to get on with the novel. He was missing Anna's help, now that she was no longer able to take dictation steadily or to copy for any stretch of time. She spent long hours sewing baby-things. Meanwhile he kept steadily at work, and by the end of February he was able to send off another instalment, the last nine chapters of Part One. There were some fine things in what he had written, but he was still uncertain as to the rest of the plot, and some of the characters continued to be in a state of flux.

I I

At the end of February the weather, which until then had been excellent, abruptly changed, and it stormed every day. This further irritated his nerves. He had two seizures in rapid succession. This was the price, he thought, of the tumultuous scene with which the second instalment closed. On March 3 he went to bed at seven p.m. in a befogged state. Some time during the night he felt Anna's hand on his shoulder and heard her say: "I think it's beginning: I am in pain." "My poor darling," he murmured drowsily, "how I pity you!" The next thing he knew it was daylight. Anna was suffering severely. It happened that the landlady and the servant had left them alone in the house, and Anna had not renewed her attempt to rouse him for fear that he might have another attack. She had spent the whole night in an agony of pain and dread, listening to the wind and the rain beating against the window, and comforting herself as best she could with prayer, while her husband slept heavily beside her.

Fully awake now, Dostoevsky rushed for the midwife. For thirty-three hours Anna was in labour and was only delivered at dawn on March 5. The baby was a girl, large, healthy, and, in her father's eyes, pretty. The terror of those endless hours, and then the sense of having partaken of a mystery, having witnessed a miracle, were unforgettable. Dostoevsky set them down years later in a passage of *The Devils,* (known to the English-reading public as *The Possessed* and hereafter referred to under that title). "There were two and now there's a third human being," says the husband, "a new spirit, finished and complete, unlike the handiwork of man; a new thought and a new love . . . it's positively frightening. . . . And there's nothing grander in the world."

He doted on little Sonia. He couldn't tear himself away from the baby, rocking it, crooning to it, helping with its bath, and pinning it into its swaddling-clothes. She looked remarkably like him, he found, even to the wrinkles on her little forehead, and as she lay in her crib he could have sworn she was composing a novel. He communicated the great news to his family, although he had no illusions as to how they would take it. His sister Vera would be the only one to share his joy. To the others the baby's arrival was something of a disaster. Indeed, Maikov urged him to make his will without delay, for if anything happened to him, the Petersburg relatives were capable of trying to snatch the inheritance from his widow and orphan.

It was all very well to talk about wills and bequests, but just now all that he had to leave his family was debts. The baby's coming had only piled them up higher. She was not two weeks old when everything they could possibly raise money on was in the pawnshop. His epilepsy was getting worse, and what if the baby or her mother took sick? He had asked Katkov for a further advance, so there was still hope. But even that well might conceivably dry up. What then? And to crown it all, the excitement, the distractions, and the sleepless nights had prevented him from touching the novel!

Katkov's kindness knew no limits. He granted the advance, so that Dostoevsky could ease his conscience by helping Pasha and Emilia Fyodorovna once more. He had been excused from contributing to the March issue, but here was April and not a line written, and he had given the good Katkov his solemn promise to send copy in on time for the April issue. He was under the most pressing obligation. He must not lose a moment's time. He must work as he had never worked before. He kissed Anna and the baby, and with a portion of the advance in his pocket, boarded the train for Saxon and the tables.

Within a few hours of his arrival he was writing to Anna for money with which to redeem his ring and pay his fare back. He had taken the bread out of the mouth of his wife and baby. His baby? What kind of a father was he, anyhow? He didn't deserve to have a child. He was doomed to torment those whom he loved most. He had done an abominable, an inexcusable thing. But it had taught him a lesson. And it was not without a good side. Perhaps the Lord in His infinite mercy had led him to the tables again in order to save him, "dissolute, low, petty gambler" that he was. For the disaster had left him with an amazing idea which was bound to prove the salvation of them all. It had come to him as he was walking in the park at night after he had gambled away the last franc; it was just as in Wiesbaden when, in the same desperate state, he had lighted on the idea of *Crime and Punishment* and at the same time conceived the extraordinary notion of offering the novel to Katkov.

Here was his remarkable plan: he would write to Katkov to help them move to Vevey! This is what he would say: Mikhail Nikiforovich, you have been my Providence; you made my marriage possible; you've been my support through all these months; now you must do one more thing; Geneva doesn't agree with us; Vevey, on the contrary, is rural, quiet, cheap; my attacks will cease in that wonderful climate, which will also benefit my wife and baby, and, with all of us well, my novel will march; by autumn at the latest you shall have it complete, and your generosity will be fully repaid; only now do send me the three hundred roubles we need for the removal. He outlined this plan in a letter to Anna from Saxon, adding that in the autumn they would return to

Russia via Italy, which he must show her. If only she knew how full of hope and confidence he was now.

He was no sooner back in Geneva than his elation gave way to despondency. He worked doggedly, indeed he forced himself to write directly after a severe attack, in a state that he described to Maikov as insanity. But the thing refused to shape itself properly, and in the end he had only two ragged chapters to send off. Geneva seemed windier and gloomier than ever, and the only thing that made life bearable was the baby. Even his joy in her was embittered when he thought of the future.

In the middle of May his mother-in-law joined them. Her coming heartened Anna, made both of them feel less forlorn, and was a blessing for the baby. It was part of the daily routine for it to take its nap in the *Jardin Anglais*. One afternoon a treacherous *bise* blew up, and the child began to cough. The cold developed into pneumonia. For a week the doctor came every day and assured them that the baby would recover. Nevertheless, Dostoevsky, uneasy and unable to do any work, hung over the crib constantly. The morning of May 24 the doctor told them that the baby was much better. At the usual time Dostoevsky left the house for the café to look through the Russian papers. Two hours later little Sonia was dead.

The light, the warmth went out of the world. He thought he could not bear the pain of it. A small creature, scarcely three months old, hardly human yet, one would think, strange that she counted so heavily with him! They would have to bury with her so many hopes, so many dreams. She had already begun to smile, to recognize him, to quiet her crying when he came close. She had been a person, a separate spirit. And where was she now? There was no comfort for him anywhere. Some weeks previously, writing to his niece Sonia on her father's death, he had spoken to her of the continuity of life, of spiritual communion, of other worlds than this, of resurrection. There was no echo of all this in the words in which he announced his sad news to Maikov. He begged his friend to keep it from the family for a while. They were capable of being pleased, rather than otherwise, at the baby's death, and this thought was intolerable.

From the first he had disliked Geneva, finding it a grim, gusty place, thick with Calvinists and drunkards. Now he had good reason to hate it. These vile winds, that stupid doctor, the careless nurse—they had taken his Sonia from him. And where else would one find neighbours who would knock at the door and ask a bereaved mother not to sob because it annoyed them?

On a warm cloudy day that suited their heavy mood, Dostoevsky went with Anna to pay a farewell visit to the little grave, and from the cemetery they went straight to the steamer that was to take them across the lake to Vevey. Yes, they were indeed going there, but under what heartbreaking circumstances! As they glided over the quiet waters mirroring the enchanted landscape, all the cruelties that life had shown him, from his mother's death, through prison and exile, the harassments of his first marriage, the vexations of his literary career, his unhappy loves, down to this last desolating grief, rose up to crush him.

That summer among the cool beauties of Vevey was the bleakest the pair were ever to know. They avoided the streets so as not to see other people's children. There was nothing to distract Anna from her sorrow, and night after night she gave herself up to the luxury of tears. But she was sustained by the hope of being a mother again—this was her constant prayer. As for Dostoevsky, he wanted Sonia. If another child came, he asked himself where he would find love for it in his heart. Time only sharpened his anguish. He could not forget how the baby's eyes had followed him on that last day when he went off to read the newspapers. That memory was a wound that would not heal.

By contrast with his mood, the serene charm of the town was painful. Where was the demi-Eden he had imagined Vevey to be? Why, it was worse than Geneva. True, the scenery was incomparable, and the place was free of the *bise* that had robbed him of Sonia. But the air he discovered to be enervating in the extreme, as did Anna, as did her mother, who, having come to help care for the baby, now found her occupation gone. The natives here were just the same dishonest, mean, filthy imbeciles they were elsewhere—indeed, he asserted irritably, the Kirghiz in their *yurtas* were cleaner in their habits than the Swiss. A vile place, this republic, bourgeois to its rotten core! Like all Europe. No, for true high-mindedness, simplicity, and understanding, you must go to the Russian masses. They want not comfort, but goodness. They have preserved through all adversities the Russian idea, which is inseparable from the Orthodox faith, and which within a hundred years will regenerate the world. Such, he had written to Maikov some weeks earlier, was his "passionate belief." That this high mission might be accomplished, Russia must reign supreme over all Slavdom. She must prepare for the great conflict to come and keep out of European struggles. Her strength, her future were bound up with the people's love for the tsar. All this the wretched radicals could never get into their heads. The filthy nonenities swollen with self-importance! He abused them in unprintable language. For himself, he had become a "complete monarchist."

Dostoevsky had thought that at Vevey he would feel better and work better. He was mistaken. His health was worse. During May, the month of little Sonia's fatal illness, he had succeeded in writing but a paltry two chapters, and in the summer months that followed he managed to squeeze out of himself only driblets. He noted with horror that his powers were failing. He could no longer work at his old speed. The last instalment of the second part did not appear until the July issue. If only he could break the evil spell and make something good of the rest of the novel, he might yet revive, otherwise he was lost. To add to his distress, he could not get a Russian paper to read. And, after a long painful silence, a letter from Pasha saying that he had lost his job sent his stepfather further into debt for his sake. Dostoevsky lived for letters from home, especially Maikov's, and he began to suspect, justifiably, that his mail was being tampered with. Certainly the letters he wrote were read by the police—its long hand reached even to Geneva, where the Russian priest was in the secret service. And to think that he, Fyodor Dostoevsky, a nationalist, a patriot, a man adoring his sovereign, a man who was with the Government to the point of "playing traitor," so he said, to his "former convictions," was held suspect. It was almost enough to turn him from his allegiance.

They had stayed over a year in this hateful Switzerland, and another winter there was unthinkable. Both of them were literally sick of it. By September they were in Milan—their money would not take them farther south. The journey refreshed him; the Lombard peasants reminded him of muzhiks. The climate of Milan agreed with him, and the sights, particularly for Anna, were diverting. But living was more expensive; it rained a great deal, and again there was not a Russian face, not a Russian book or newspaper. They were bored, they were gloomy, they had not left their grief behind them at Vevey. And his prospects were as uncertain as before. How could they return home? And how could he live away from it? The novel kept to its slow pace. It was already November, and he still had the whole of the fourth and last part to write. Indeed, this was to be the crown of the work, that portion for the sake of which he now believed that he had written the whole. If only he could have had the chance to revise it all before publishing any of it! Now that he was on the last lap, the conviction grew upon him that he had never touched a richer subject than this of the Idiot, and that, Heaven help him, he had come near botching it. At any rate, he could not rush the last part so as to publish it before the year was out. In order to avoid carrying it over into the January number for the following year, Katkov would have to issue the remaining chapters separately as a supplement, and Dostoevsky, to make up for the expense and inconvenience, would waive payment for that part. And how he needed the money!

This unusual arrangement was actually carried out. The last chapter is dated January 17, 1869. Toward the end he was delayed by two severe attacks coming in swift succession. He finished the novel in deep anguish of soul.

I I I

When *The Idiot* was finally under way, Dostoevsky told his niece Sonia, to whom he was dedicating the novel, and his friend Maikov that his intention in writing it was to portray what he called "a wholly admirable human being." He had cherished such an idea in secret for a long time, and yet it was not fully ripe even now, so that he felt that in his desperation he was rashly plucking a green fruit, which should have been granted a longer summer to mature. The thought made him ache. He knew, besides, what a difficult problem he had before him. He was setting himself the task of presenting an image of perfection. This meant, of course, an image touched with the light of the infinite suffering, divinely compassionate face of Christ. There, he said to himself, was the only perfect man the world has ever known. But could he offer a convincing imitation of Christ to an age of drift and confusion? True, the attempt to represent moral excellence in literature was not new. There was, he reflected, Don Quixote; there was, to take a very different instance of goodness lovable by reason of its very absurdity, Mr. Pickwick. There was Jean Valjean, that man of sorrows, who attracts sympathy by his sufferings. How could he make his own hero ridiculous, how could he make him pitiable, and thus save him from insipidity?

In the notes for the novel its hero is referred to as "Prince Christ." The finished work retains only a few traces of this conception. Prince Myshkin's face, with its large blue eyes, hollow cheeks, thin blond beard, is suggestive of the face on the icon. He suffers little children to come unto him and befriends a woman who is an outcast—this in a sickeningly mawkish passage which is the nadir of Dostoevsky's art. The novelist is careful, however, not to stress the protagonist's Christlike features. The problem before him, he knew, was how to depict a man, not a god. His instinct as a writer told him that he must humanize his paragon by a degrading touch of nature. He solved his problem by making his hero an "idiot." The wine is precious, but the vessel is flawed. If his "principal mind," as one of the women who love him puts it, is extraordinarily fine, his other mind, the subordinate one, is defective. Prince Myshkin's lineage goes back to Ivanushka the Simpleton, or rather to the *yurodivyi* (the saintly imbecile), the Russian equivalent of the Teutonic "pure fool."

As the novel opens, the guileless young nobleman, who has spent most of his life abroad, is returning to Petersburg, without any visible means of support and practically no connections, to make his home there. He shows few traces of the obscure mental ailment from which he had been suffering since childhood, but, like his creator, he is subject to epileptic attacks, and he behaves so oddly that people at first blush dismiss him as "an idiot." He has not been in the capital a day when he finds himself fatefully involved with half a dozen men and women he had never seen before. The development of these entanglements forms the substance of the novel. Its structure shows a symmetry unusual for Dostoevsky. It begins with Myshkin sitting opposite Rogozhin in a railway carriage and receiving his confidences regarding his passion for Nastasya Filippovna. It ends with Myshkin sitting on the floor beside Rogozhin; the body of Nastasya, whom he has just murdered, lies in the next room. But the main plot is overlaid by a mass of subplots and digressions, the narrative teeming with the stock characters and situations of melodrama, the surprises, coincidences, and climaxes of the thriller. Not infrequently the action halts, and there are comic interludes, especially when General Ivolgin, a grotesque quasi-Dickensian figure, appears on the scene. Nevertheless, the novel as a whole is marked by urgency and tension, moving as it does through a series of crises to a dimly foreshadowed tragic denouement.

Throughout, Myshkin's motives are in sharp contrast with the greed, the sensuality, the vanity, the meanness, the sheer perversity that rule the men and women whose destiny is caught up with his. He is gifted with candour, gentle gaiety, true courtesy, the wisdom that comes from the heart, a pitying love that, understanding all, pardons all. He knows himself generally inadequate and confesses to having "double thoughts," in which a high motive is coupled with a base one. The fact that he invariably acts upon the former does not mitigate his feeling of unworthiness. He asserts his self by yielding it. Innocence is another of his virtues, but his chief characteristic is meekness. One cannot imagine him chasing the money-changers out of the temple. He is poles apart from Don Quixote, whose figure haunted Dostoevsky while the novel was in process of gestation. The hidalgo fights, even if sometimes only against windmills, the prince is apt to remain a passive bystander. Implicit in his behaviour is the proposition that all coercion, whether of body or mind, is an attempt upon the freedom to choose between good and evil, which is the token of being human.

On one occasion he does show an intransigent spirit: he startles the aristocratic guests at a soiree by launching a passionate tirade against the Catholic Church as the betrayer of Christ and the mother of atheism and socialism. From these plagues, he prophesies, mankind will be saved by Russian Orthodoxy. Here Dostoevsky was making his hero a mouthpiece for one of his pet ideas. Sensing that it was out of character for the gentle Myshkin to express himself thus vehemently, the novelist has him go beyond himself in this fashion when he is on the brink of an epileptic seizure. An account of the twilight state preceding another of his attacks is one of the most remarkable, and exacting, passages in the book.

Dostoevsky uses the novel as the vehicle of other convictions of his own. On the fantastic night when Myshkin's friends celebrate his birthday with wine and talk that outlasts the dawn there is a debate in the course of which the materialistic trend of the age is denounced and utilitarian ethics indignantly repudiated. Curiously enough, the author allows these cherished sentiments of his to be voiced by a drunkard, cheat and lick-spittle, Lebedev. There are other thrusts at the nihilists. A group of them figure in the novel as comrades of a young man who, on the grounds of being the illegitimate son of Myshkin's quondam benefactor, claims part of the inheritance that the prince suddenly falls heir to. They are a shabby, dirty crew, cloaking a youthful timidity with an equally youthful arrogance. Dostoevsky started to caricature these boys, but could not sustain his satiric tone. The young blackmailers turn out to be nothing but ill-bred yet fundamentally good-hearted children, who end by bowing to the force of Myshkin's moral superiority.

Indeed, all but the complete worldlings, and these play only a minor part in the novel, are open to the influence of Myshkin's radiant personality. Though he babbles of preserving the leading rôle of the caste into which he was born, his humanity transcends class divisions—he unbosoms himself as readily to a servant as to a high dignitary. Involuntarily he draws both men and women to himself. From the first the violent Rogozhin takes a brotherly interest in him, and the very day of his arrival in the capital two ravishing beauties, utterly different in character and circumstances, fall under his spell. One is Aglaia, the general's daughter, an impulsive, spirited creature with something delightfully fresh and virginal about her. The other is Nastasya Filippovna. Carefully brought up for his pleasure by a wealthy roué who made her his mistress in the first bloom of her youth, the sensitive, passionate woman carries about with her a burning sense of degradation, which drives her to wilfully shameful behaviour. She has a compulsion to keep her festering wound open. Of her two suitors, one has been bribed by her seducer to marry her; the other, Rogozhin, desires her with a blind lust that can only bring destruction. The

prince offers her marriage to save her from her suitors and herself.
His love could perhaps have made her whole. But all he is in a
position to give her is pity; oddly enough, he does not realize that
this can only confirm her feelings of being beyond redemption. She
rejects him, though or perhaps because she is in love with him. Yet
Aglaia is instinctively jealous of her and Rogozhin sees in the prince
a baffling rival.

The destinies of the two men are strangely linked. From the
beginning they are attracted to each other. In one of the early drafts
of the novel they figure as brothers. A significant passage of the
final version shows them exchanging the crosses they wear, in token
of spiritual kinship. Is it the kinship between the divided halves of
one personality, the higher and the lower self? Is it the equivocal
brotherhood of body and soul? One is tempted to read such symbo-
lism into the novel, although it is doubtful whether Dostoevsky intended it.

Myshkin's first interest in Aglaia develops into a strong attachment,
which nevertheless does not become a normal passion. It remains
a diffuse, gentle, discarnate if profound, emotion. True, he asks
her to marry him, almost, it appears, because everyone expects him
to do so, yet all he demands of the relation is companionship. He
had previously offered to marry Nastasya, indeed, the very evening
of his arrival in Petersburg, at the stormy gathering at her home.
This was an act of pure compassion. Pity remains the major element
in his love for Nastasya, even when, forced by the two contending
women to choose between them, he leaves Aglaia for her. That
choice, to his grief, is imposed upon him by the world. For himself,
he sees no reason why he should not, after his own fashion, love
both women at the same time.

More than once Dostoevsky projected characters whose affections were thus inclusive—"wide-hearted" he called them. But in
Myshkin he imagined not an inherently polygamous man—rather a
man who offered a love clear of all that makes it a selfish, exclusive
passion, locking lover and beloved within a private chamber. Here
he was embodying that ideal contrary to man's nature, the love
that makes men "as the angels of heaven," on which he had meditated the night his first wife lay dead. The woman in the novel, on
the other hand, love him in a earthly, possessive way, though Nasta-

sya is ready to give him up for fear of making him unhappy. At the very end of the book Myshkin is told: "Aglaia Ivanovna loved you like a woman, like a human being, not like an abstract spirit. Do you know what, my poor prince, the most likely thing is that you've never loved either of them!" This is the opinion of a man of the world. The novel, while emphasizing the radiant fullness of Myshkin's love, which goes out to all whom he meets, nevertheless lends colour to the worldling's view. Repeatedly it is hinted that the prince is sexless and that his chastity is a matter of physical deficiency. Is this angel perhaps a eunuch?

Certainly the angel has no flaming sword, no protecting pinion—at best he is an ineffectual one, beating his wings in the luminous void in vain. Raskolnikov had had a vision of an elect group of pure spirits who were to save distracted mankind and found a new race. Myshkin is one of those pure spirits, but, significantly, he has no issue. He enters the novel a young man, just emerged from the shadow of mental illness; he leaves it, his mind deranged beyond recovery. This exemplar of the Christian virtues has brought only destruction, not simply upon himself, but upon practically all with whom he comes in intimate contact. An embodiment of living grace and serenity that all the evil seething round him cannot quite submerge, he is himself an instrument of calamity. Nastasya is brutally murdered by Rogozhin. Myshkin foresaw the crime, but did not prevent it. Aglaia gives herself in marriage to a wretched impostor, a Pole to boot, and embraces Catholicism—as low a fall as Dostoevsky could conceive. Was this train of disasters all that best of men could bring about? Generally, Dostoevsky sees grace as the ultimate gift of sin and suffering. Myshkin has come by his virtues gratuitously and his anguish is no atonement for either his own or anyone else's sins.

The novelist threw out the suggestion that the "fantastical" quality of the Idiot, his inability to cope with reality, was natural in one belonging to a social class that had no roots in the native soil. Myshkin's case, then, would be, like Raskolnikov's, symptomatic of the disease which, in Dostoevsky's opinion, was ravaging Russian society. But the novel scarcely bears out such an interpretation. The reader is more apt to perceive in Myshkin's failure the inevitable defeat of an impossible ideal by the world and the flesh.

In *The Idiot*, as elsewhere, Dostoevsky is seen making an anguished effort to side with Christ against what he had once called "truth." He had never needed faith more desperately than during the bleak months when, in a strange and hated land, harassed by all his usual anxieties and, worse, bereaved of his first-born, he composed this work. The image of Myshkin must have been a light in his darkness, a shield against the powers of evil in his own soul. But he could not make it as fully present to others as to himself, and it wavered sometimes in his own mind. He was not ripe, as he admitted at the start, for the great task he had set himself. The book betrays the doubts, emphatic and unrefuted, crowding the author's heart. The novel is not wanting in the suggestion that the divine prototype of Myshkin also failed. Nature is represented as Christ's victorious enemy. Dostoevsky allows one of the characters to describe, in terms shocking to the religious sentiment, Holbein's picture of the dead Christ, which so disturbed him when he himself saw it in Basle. The agony of facing death is a theme that recurs here, now as the experience of the condemned the moment before execution, now as the frantic rebellion of a boy in the last stages of consumption. Nowhere is there the remotest hint of the consolations of the Christian faith.

This tumultuous, perplexing, profoundly ambiguous book is not the *Imitatio Christi* that its author had apparently intended it to be. But, with all its defects, it is a work exhibiting great psychological acumen, an astounding grasp of character, and, as a foil for melodrama, genuine tragedy and awkward dialectics it offers moments of high comedy. Above all, Myshkin's personality sheds a warmth and a radiance that make the book shine, however fitfully, like a good deed in a naughty world.

CHAPTER TWENTY

THE SECOND EXILE

S O OFTEN the completion of a piece of work left Dostoevsky with a sense of failure. He felt acutely how far his imagination outstripped his craftmanship. *The Idiot* was a case in point. The novel didn't express a fraction of what he had wanted to say, but there was no helping it now. How was his public reacting to it? What were the critics writing? In his isolation he could not know. As a matter of fact, they were content to say little about a book that puzzled and discomfited them. The most ominous thing was that the publishers were in no hurry to bid for the rights to a separate edition.

The one good thing the new year brought them was the discovery that Anna was again pregnant. But how would they meet the expenses of her confinement, and what would they live on in the meantime? He was still in debt to Katkov, and he had no other source to look to for money. Besides, after all the many months of labour entailed by *The Idiot,* he needed a fallow period. And Emilia Fyodorovna was asking for a regular allowance, instead of casual remittances. That ancient enemy of his couldn't get it out of her head that he was obliged to support her and her family.

By the time he had sent off the last part of the novel, they had been settled in Florence for two months. He had pleasant memories of his visit there with Strakhov, and it proved a more congenial place than Milan, not so much because of the chance of seeing again his beloved "Madonna della Sedia," as because of the Russian books and papers. The Florentine winter was mild: in February roses were blooming in the Boboli Gardens. But the damp, warm air was enervating, and he held it accountable for his frequent attacks. Soon he would be facing the second anniversary of his European exile. This was worse than Siberia. There had been no such sunlight, no miraculous works of art at Omsk, but there, in the Asiatic wilderness, he had been at home, among his own people. He was not afraid that he would become assimilated, like Turgenev: he hated foreigners. But away from home he felt that he was losing the little strength, the little talent he possessed.

By March things had come to such a pass that they had pawned their underwear, and if he had not been able to borrow two francs from a stranger, they might have perished in this foreign city. Maikov, the one man who could have kept him in touch with Russia, had stopped writing altogether. There wasn't a living soul on whom he could count. They had been forsaken by God and man. Again Katkov saved the situation by a remittance. But the money he sent was as usual insufficient, and Dostoevsky soon found himself appealing for more in payment for a new novel, which the review could start running in 1870. He had yet another prospect. Strakhov had become the editor of a new magazine, *Zarya (Dawn)*, and Dostoevsky promised to give him a short piece, which could be tossed off without much effort and would not interfere with the larger work. He liked the notion of contributing to a periodical which, from the first, struck a clearly nationalist, anti-radical note. The advance would enable them, he thought, to leave Florence for some place where they would at least be familiar with the language, possibly Germany.

It was spring now, and the city was getting hot. But the publisher of *Zarya* was dilatory, and they were forced to stay on and on. July came, and they were still stranded there. In Switzerland Dostoevsky had known the rigours of cold, now he was tasting the torments of heat. He could only compare Florence to a Russian steam bath. The three of them, for Anna's mother was still with them, were crowded into one small room. The windows looked out on the stone arcades of a market place which at midday was like an oven. At night they were kept awake by people making merry in the streets, and with the dawn came the babble of market women and the braying of asses to keep them from sleep. Work was out of the question. As he watched the tourists parade the blazing streets—the city seemed to him much more crowded than when he had been there with Strakhov seven years previously—he marvelled that, having the price of the fare in their pockets, they stayed in this hell. Torn between boredom and irritation, he looked at everything with the eyes of a caged beast. What was this flower of cities but a prison? And a foul prison, too: twice he had the horrible experience of catching a tarantula in their room.

Katkov came to the rescue once more, and the three were finally enabled to flee Italy. To break the journey, they stopped off at Venice, where Anna lost her fan, a mishap that made her cry like a child, and at Vienna, which he preferred to Paris. They had hoped to settle in Prague, where there would be a chance for him to get in contact with the Slav world, but lodgings proved too expensive, and so, early in August, they found themselves back in Dresden again, almost precisely two years after having left it (he was entered in the police records as "a retired Russian lieutenant and *rentier*").

Away from Florence, Dostoevsky discovered that he had been unjust to it. Why, the heat had actually benefited him. Here in Dresden his epilepsy was worse, and he suffered from fever. It was already September, and he had not done a stitch of work either on the piece for *Zarya* or on the novel for *Russky vestnik*. Further more, Anna's second pregnancy was a difficult one: she was in, nervous, and terrified of dying in childbed. When he thought that they would have to expose the second baby to the Western methods of child rearing that had killed the first, he was in despair. No, no, they must go back to Russia, for the child's sake, for their own future, for his work, his work! Better debtors' prison at home than this empty freedom abroad.

I I

On September 26 the child was born—a big, healthy, pretty baby. When he was registering his daughter's birth, he amazed the clerk by being unable to remember the mother's maiden name. It was plain that he was losing his memory. In announcing to Maikov the good news of the little Lubov's arrival, he confided that there were less than ten thalers in the house, and that neither the doctor nor the midwife had been paid. He dared not appeal to Katkov again, and so he turned to the publisher of *Zarya*. He could not let himself think what a refusal would mean. He would have to sell his overcoat, his suit, his underwear. Pasha and Emilia Fyodorovna would suffer too—mentally he had already set aside part of the money for them.

There was yet another humiliation for him to swallow at this time. They were scarcely settled in Dresden when a letter from Maikov brought word that Aunt Kumanina had died, leaving a bequest of forty thousand roubles to a monastery. The exciting side of the news, as retailed by Maikov, was that, in the opinion of the executor, the will could be successfully contested, since it had been made when the old lady was of unsound mind. This would mean ten thousand roubles for Dostoevsky and an equal sum for Mikhail's family. Maikov advised immediate action. Dostoevsky wrote at once to the executor for further information. He also sent the news to Sonia, saying that he considered her his conscience and asking what she thought it would be right for him to do in the matter.

In due time he received a letter from Sonia telling him point-blank that she disapproved of this move. Further, there came a letter from his brother Andrey, the aunt's guardian, declaring that the old lady had no such fortune to bequeath, that there was no such clause in her will, and that, although she was quite off her head, she was otherwise hale and hearty. He said further that the annulment of the will would undoubtedly benefit all the Dostoevskys, but it was not to be thought of. Andrey's words, too, implied that his brother was an unscruplous schemer. Apparently all the relatives had been apprised of the affair, and the wildest rumours concerning him were in circulation. A pretty kettle of fish! Here he was painted as a monster of greed and selfishness, ready to snatch the bread out of the mouths of orphans, when he had been weighing so carefully the ethics of the step! True, he had told Maikov that if he did decide that it was right to act, he stood ready to bring suit on his own account as well as on that of the others—certainly he needed money sorely enough. But what had been his first thought? Mikhail's orphans. He had sacrificed the share of the inheritance he had received earlier, to save the review for Mikhail's family. To pay their debts he had robbed his own wife and child. And what thanks, he asked himself privately, did he get for it? To be despised as their slave and hated as the author of their ruin. And so Sonia was looking down on him, too. This was a pleasant thought to brood on.

A series of misunderstandings, as well as carelessness on the part of the publisher of *Zarya*, delayed some six weeks the arrival of the money Dostoevsky had asked for. In the meantime they were starving. Anna, who was nursing the baby, had to pawn her last warm skirt, with the snow already on the ground, and in order to get two thalers to send an urgent telegram to the publisher he had to raise money on his trousers. He could not bring himself to disclose all the shameful details of their situation. But worse than all these humiliations at the hands of strangers was the affront to his dignity from a man who knew who he was. The swine of a publisher was treating him like a flunkey. His heart was swollen with indignation. And after this, he wrote to Maikov, "people demand of me art, pure poetry, without strain, without poison, and point to Turgenev, to Goncharov! Let them look at the conditions under which I work."

He did work in spite of everything, and when the worst period of stress was over, life fell more or less into the old lines. He rose at one o'clock, managed to do a little writing in the afternoon, went for a stroll through the gardens to the post office, which he so often left with empty hands, came home to dinner—there was one most of the time—and then took another walk to the library, where he devoured three Russian papers down to the last word. Not seldom the reading left him with the unhappy impression that things at home were not all that they should be. But he consoled himself with the thought that at this distance he was bound to misjudge the situation.

From half past ten at night to five in the morning he was at his desk. He cursed this story he was writing—he had conceived a hatred for it from the beginning—but he kept at it. Early in December it was finished, months late and five times as long as he had originally intended it to be. At least he had the comfort of being able to revise the manuscript as a whole. He had to wait for additional money from the publisher before he could send it off: he wasn't able to pay the postage.

He regarded *The Eternal Husband* as a diversion from his more serious literary pursuits. Indeed, the story, or rather short novel, travels light. A provincial official discovers after his wife's death that she had had a series of lovers, one of whom, Velchaninov, fathered the little girl he has brought up fondly as his only child. The cuckold is presented as the uxorious, henpecked husband born to be deceived. The lover is the typical gay deceiver caught, however, in a moment of physical and spiritual distress that ill befits his character as Don Juan. The interest centres upon the husband. His habitual self-restraint gone, he arrives in Petersburg with the child, ostensibly on business, but actually on an errand of vengeance. He tracks down Velchaninov, and there ensues a psychological duel between the two men, which forms the substance of the narrative. The thrusts made by the cuckold, the parries of the lover, all the moves they execute in obedience to their ambiguous impulses, make an absorbing spectacle. There are few passages in Dostoevsky's work that are written with greater subtlety, penetration, and dramatic power, and none in which the rôle of the unconscious in human behaviour is more clearly grasped. It is suggestive that he should have called the chapter that exhibits this understanding most fully, "Analysis."

Naturally, it is possible to see a reflection of certain of the author's personal experiences in the story. Toward the end of it the cuckold, who thinks of marrying again, takes Velchaninov to visit the family of the girl to whom he hopes to become engaged; he wants to show the man that he too can conquer a heart; he wants to parade his clever friend before the family; he must test the behaviour of this lady in the presence of a brilliant man of the world; and, perhaps, secretly from himself, he is strangely tempted to put himself again in the shameful position in which he had been placed years previously by the same Velchaninov. The family on whom the two men call is largely patterned on the Ivanov household, with its jolly crowd of young people who made the summer of 1866 so pleasant for Dostoevsky. The character of the cuckold's dead wife in some particulars remotely recalls that of Dostoevsky's first wife. Indeed, it has been suggested that the story is anchored in his relations with Marya Dmitrievna, that is in effect a cuckold's confession, and also a repudiation of the attitude he had adopted toward his rival at the time when he was courting her. Some colour is lent to these notions by the fact that he conceived the story shortly after his wife's death; yet they remain wholly conjectural. It is not necessary to assume such a basis for this anatomy of cuckoldry. His interest in every form of humiliation was sufficient to draw him to such a subject, and he needed but the shadow of an actual experience to release his imagination.

The year and a half that remained of this second exile saw no relief from the old miseries of want, worry, ill health, and isolation. As before, he took refuge from them in his work, upon which he spent all the intensity of which his nature was capable.

A new idea had begun to haunt him while he was still busy with the final chapters of *The Idiot*. As a matter of fact, he had been thinking about it for a year or so. It was a project for a colossal novel on atheism. The pivotal figure was to be a staid, comfortable member of the middle class who, at the age of forty-five, suddenly loses his faith. In his quest for God he was to mingle with all manner of people, to search the hearts and explore the minds of nihilists, monks, sectarians, Catholics, Orthodox priests. In the end he was to recover his faith and establish it on the Russian Christ. Here Dostoevsky felt he would say his final word. If only he could write this book, he would be content to die. If he did not write it, it would torture him to death. But he was not ready for it yet: he must first read a whole library of religious and anti-religious works. And in any case, it wasn't the sort of thing he could write abroad.

In the fallow months that followed the completion of *The Idiot* his mind kept returning to this mighty theme. Several characters took shape in his head, among them an ardent Catholic, modelled somewhat on Loyola's right-hand man, Saint Francis Xavier, the Apostle of the Indies. All that Dostoevsky had done until now he dismissed as "trash and introduction," compared to the titanic "parable of atheism" he was planning. He would give the rest of his life to it. As he brooded over the thing, it altered, so that by the time he had finished *The Eternal Husband* he saw the novel still as a work on a tremendous scale and concerned with the problem, which was his lifelong torment, of the existence of God, but he had conceived a new plot. It was to be the life of a great sinner, from his unhappy childhood through years of transgression and crime to his final regeneration. Dostoevsky first touched upon this theme of redemption in the last pages of *Crime and Punishment;* it coloured faintly his original drafts for *The Idiot*. Now that he was seeing it more clearly, he decided to make it the cornerstone of a vast work. He would break this up into three, or possibly five, novels which, though connected with one another, could be published separately.

The first one would deal with the hero's early years. The illegitimate son of a landowner of gentle birth, the motherless boy is entrusted to the care of strangers. They are a corrupt and dissolute couple, who disgust him. The child withdraws into himself. From the first he instinctively feels that he is destined for great things. Books help him to escape into a dream world. The sensitive, refractory boy has as companion a crippled little girl. He is in the habit of beating her, yet he confides to her his most private thoughts. Already the question of the existence of God frets him. "I am God," he tells her, and forces her to worship him. Later, together with the little cripple, he goes to live with his father and stepmother. Accused by her of a theft he had not committed, and whipped by his father, he repudiates him and takes refuge in the servant's quarters. The stepmother has a lover and the boy witnesses their love-making. The father knows that his bastard knows he is a cuckold. Then the boy watches his father being done to death by his own serfs ("Alas poor ghost!"). Boarding schools: Souchard's, Chermak's (Dostoevsky's old schools). Further humiliation and injustices. The boy despises adults and seeks deliberately to earn their disapproval. He tests himself, and tries to purge himself of fear and to develop will power. He resolves to become rich, so as to gain power and also the right to scorn people. But is power worth having? At moments "the pure ideal of the free man flashes before him." He runs away from school and becomes involved in a murder. Back in Moscow, he falls in with a schoolmate, a lad of French parentage and corrupt to the marrow. The two plunge into debauchery. With this companion he steal the jewels out of an icon frame. In court he declares himself an atheist, and is committed to a monastery for correction.

Part two: "The Monastery." Here the routine of monastic life is to be carefully set forth. What a chance to show the strength and beauty of the Russian spirit! All manner of men inhabit monasteries and visit them. There will be an opportunity to introduce monks of militant piety, sectarians, characters modelled on Belinsky, perhaps on Pushkin. But the centre of the stage is to be occupied by a saintly old churchman living in retirement, and the delinquent boy, "a wolf cub and a nihilist." An affection grows up between the two, though sometimes the lad torments his aged friend. The latter preaches meekness and extols "the living life," but with little effect. Indeed, the boy's unbelief becomes "organized" in the monastery. He leaves it unregenerate. Still clinging to his dream of wealth as a source of power, he believes that he is destined to become the greatest of men, and he treats everyone with disdain. What he has learned from his saintly mentor is that in order to conquer the world he must first conquer himself.

The titles of the three subsequent novels are: "Before Exile"; "Satan and the Female"; "High Deeds." The hero has a long, arduous road to travel before he achieves salvation. His difficult pilgrimage will offer an opportunity to present a panorama of Russian life, and be the more meaningful because he yields to the temptations of the intellect as well as those of the flesh.

So much can, with some difficulty, be gathered from the few rough jottings for *The Life of the Great Sinner* extant and from a letter to Maikov. It is also evident that Dostoevsky had a definite idea as to the style that he would use. He would give up his usual dramatic effects and write with the quiet simplicity that marks the nameless lives of saints which had cast their serene light over his own boyhood. In fact, it was to be just such an edifying story, every incident in it, however vile, carrying some hint of the grace to come, the final victory of the spirit.

Significantly enough, while the outline offers a vigorous sketch of the sinner, the saint is left blurred and unreal: no acceptable psychological clue to the hero's reformation is given. Whatever Dostoevsky said or felt to the contrary, he was not now, nor was he ever to be, sufficiently at peace to undertake this tranquil and pious tale. Certainly the epic tone was not in accord with the exigencies of his temperament either as a man or a writer. *The Life of a Great Sinner* went unwritten. It remained, however, a source that fed all his subsequent work. Traces of it are present even in the novel of a totally different tenor to which he now turned.

I V

While he was brooding over *The Life of a Great Sinner* he was at the same time planning another novel. He owed one to Katkov, who had been supporting him all this time, and the hour was not ripe nor his situation propitious for undertaking the more significant work. He felt that he had struck a rich vein, and he was working it with ease and pleasure. Surely the novel would be ready by the autumn of 1870. He would not try, he decided after some hesitation, to make it important as art; it was to be simply a pamphlet. Once and for all he would pour out his wrath upon the traitors to the Russian people and the Russian God, and let literature go hang.

The new year, 1870, found the couple without resources, and with many of their belongings in pawn. How would they manage until the autumn? They had had to keep postponing the baby's baptism because there was no money to pay for the ceremony. At least there was one great expectation: Pasha, yes, the impossible Pasha, armed with power of attorney, was trying to arrange for a separate edition of *The Idiot*. It would mean a thousand roubles! January passed, February . . . had he embezzled the money? Had he lent it to a boon companion? The boy was always full of wild schemes and crazy ambitions. In desperation Dostoevsky offered a novel to *Zarya*, asking for a sizeable advance. It would be the first part of *The Life of a Great Sinner*. He would do his best with it, even if he had to write it abroad.

By March it transpired that Pasha's negotiations had come to nothing. And Kashpirev, the publisher of *Zarya*, was silent. And the grocery was refusing credit. And the baby was teething. And Maikov was writing that *The Eternal Husband* struck him as somewhat forced. So it was plain, then, that he was losing his grip! Life was closing in around him. He must escape somehow. At the end of April, he was off to Homburg and the tables.

This time Anna's distress was increased by the fact that she had to conceal the nature of his trip both from her mother, who was still with them, and from her brother, who had recently arrived in Dresden. The money he gambled away must have been part of the advance which finally came from *Zarya*. The publisher had sent him five hundred roubles and promised to remit a hundred roubles monthly. The very first remittance having failed to arrive on time, the wolf was soon again at the door and, to make matters worse, the baby took sick. Dostoevsky managed, however, to work away at the novel for Katkov, but his heart was no longer in it. There was some fatal flaw in the thing. He was sorry he had begun it. He would much rather have busied himself with something else. And would *Russky vestnik* print his drivel? If only he could get back to Russia!

Summer brought with it a series of violent attacks, the like of which he had not had for a long time. For a month work was out of the question. When he was able to get back to his desk, he suddenly perceived what was wrong with the novel. And then in a flash he saw a new plot with a new hero. After a fortnight of agonizing indecision he made up his mind: he put aside the entire pile of sheets—over two thousand roubles' worth of copy—and began the whole thing afresh. It was a truly heroic decision. As August had already set in, it was obvious that he would not get through with the novel by Christmas, as he had hoped. In fact, there was no telling when he would finish it. And what of the novel he had promised to *Zarya*, and on which he had taken such a large advance? Well, those people would have to wait, or else have their money refunded, whenever he could scrape it together. What was much worse, he had managed to disappoint Katkov, and that after he had solemnly promised to hand in copy in time for publication during the year. Would not the long-suffering man at last tire of his procrastinations and throw him over? In any event, there was to be another winter of exile.

Another winter, besides, of pinching and worrying, and trembling over every thaler. Oh, if he could have an assured livelihood for two or three years, like Turgenev or Tolstoy, he could write a thing about which people would be talking a century hence. His new project was so fine, so rich in meaning, that he was awed by it himself. But he knew he was going to ruin it in his haste and turn out a half-baked product. He had the vision and the fire, but where was leisure and peace in which to shape his stupendous imaginings? Meanwhile, he worked away fiercely. He kept changing the plot and recasting what he had written. It was a task like Penelope's. He piled up such a mountain of notes that he could no longer find his way among them. It was only on October 19 that he was able to send off the first chapters. They appeared in the issue of *Russky vestnik* for January, 1871, as the first instalment of *The Possessed*. Two further instalments in February and April completed Part

One. He confided to Sonia that he had written this first part at least twenty times. None of his novels had cost him such excruciating labour.

Do what he might, the work would not satisfy him. How could he accomplish anything when the hunger for Russia was tearing at his vitals? It frightened him to see what homesickness was doing to Anna. She missed the good black bread, the deep drifts, the creak of the sledges gliding over the hard-packed snow, the booming of the bells, so different from the thin chimes of Western churches. What was worse, she was fretting over affairs at home—the family real estate, a share of which was to come to her, was, she knew, badly mismanaged in her mother's absence. Besides, in Petersburg she might add a bit to their income by doing a little stenography in her spare time. The baby, though amiable and possessed of a healthy appetite, was a drain on her energies, since she nursed it herself and wanted the domestic help that was so easy to secure at home. Dostoevsky was sure that if they were only in Russia, her apathy and exhaustion would vanish.

Communications from home reached him seldom and generally in a roundabout way. The most staggering piece of news was that Pasha was about to be married. It was hard to believe it. What changes these four years must have wrought in the boy he had left behind! Pasha, steadily employed, settling down, and with a nice girl, too! Dostoevsky was filled with pity and fear when he thought how young the two of them were, how unprepared for their venture, how little he could do in a material way to help them. In reply to what he called Pasha's "romance in several parts," announcing the news, he wrote his stepson a long, tender, if somewhat sententious letter. He warned the young man of the seriousness of the step he contemplated, of the necessity for mutual respect; spoke of the influence of a good woman as a man's "second and final education"; urged him to continue his studies, so as to be worthy of that gifted, cultivated, and lovable man, his father, whom physically he so much resembled.

The bleakness of the winter was increased by the war, which had been raging since July. If the siege of Paris added to the excitement of living, high prices and straitened credits made hardships for everybody, not least for a poverty-stricken foreigner. When the war was young, Dostoevsky, who was not a pacifist either by nature or conviction, was inclined to look at it with a hopeful eye. Perhaps it would prove a healthy stimulant and, among other things, rescue science from the morass of materialism. Disaster might rouse even the French to new life. Perhaps Russia would begin to see through the Germans and abandon its traditional Germanophile policy. His sympathies were vaguely with the French, not because he liked them more than he did the Germans, but because he hated them a little less. As the war dragged on, month after month, he was increasingly irritated by the jingoism of the people among whom he was living. He heard, so he wrote home, a white-haired savant shout: *"Paris muss bombardiert sein!"* So that wa the fine fruit of Western learning. The Prussians owed their victory to their schoolmasters. What an obscene thought! The schoolmasters had raised a generation worthy of Attila.

Sometimes the small shopkeepers with whom he dealt would show him letters their sons had written from the front. It wasn't those sick and hungry lads under fire who were shouting for blood. No, it was the professors, the banner-bearers of culture, who clamoured for the triumph of brute force! Who says "young Germany"? On the contrary, a dead people. And France, too, would go to the dogs, unless a strict ruler were somehow put into power there. At heart Dostoevsky cried: a plague on both their houses! The future lay with Russia. She must prepare for the inevitable conflict over the Balkan Slavs. She must build roads, fortresses, add at least a million rifles to her equipment, take thought for taxes and military service. (His military education had not been wholly lost on him). Russia's strength was her spiritual unity. But she must become fully conscious of her high mission, must bring back the true Orthodox faith to a blind world that has denied Christ. The whole of Russian history was an epic of Orthodoxy. True, the present age with the decay of the nobility and the general disintegration that followed the freeing of the serfs was a sad passage. But look ahead two hundred years: look at Russia in the glory of her full stature, of her spiritual maturity, beside a Europe brutalized and undone! Russia would yet spread the gospel of love, though she had to beat her ploughshares into swords to do it. He clung to his convictions with more passion than consistency. Did he once ask himself how far the Idiot, his

Christ—man, would have assented to this programme of prepared-ness?

He was far from writing anything like *The Idiot* at this date. He was struggling like a madman with that savage satire, *The Possessed*. He wasn't sure where it would take him, but it was a mighty, exhilarating effort in an otherwise dreary existence. Dres-den was as alien to him as when they had first come there. They had made some acquaintances among the many Russians settled in the city. The expatriates only made him feel how far he was from home. It was horrible to find that the children in some fam-ilies did not know their native tongue. Contacts with the Russian colony were only an annoyance to him. When one compatriot called twice to discuss the state of Russian literature with him he re-fused to see her. Confound Russian literature! He was killing him-self to get his copy out on time for *Russky vestnik*.

v

This exile must be brought to an end! He had been telling Maikov and others that he had fled abroad to save his health, to escape his creditors. The real reason why Anna had snatched him away from his Petersburg circle had somehow been obliterated from his mind. But now he was willing to face the worst at home rather than endure another year abroad. He had figured that they would need at least seven thousand roubles to return to Russia. Next he set the sum at three thousand, then at two thousand. Now he decided that one thousand must suffice. It might mean debtors' prison, but was that worse than Dresden? He would brave the consequences of the step. There was one circumstance which raised his hopes of securing this sum: it would come from a new edition of *Crime and Punishment*, issued by Stellovsky at the end of 1870. But it soon became clear that the money would not be forthcom-ing without a lawsuit.

A few weeks before Easter he dreamed that he was talking to Aunt Kumanina in her drawing-room, when he noticed that the pendulum of the clock had stopped swinging. He went over and pushed it, but after two or three strokes it stopped again. Dosto-evsky took his dreams seriously. Once when he had a mysterious dream about a full moon dividing into three parts and giving birth to a shield with a halo, he asked all his friends to interpret it for him. On the present occasion he recounted his dream to an acquaintance, who suggested that he inquire about the old lady, and indeed he soon learned that she had died. As he had long since received his share of the inheritance, this event was of no immediate consequence to him.

Again it was Katkov who saved them. He sent a remittance at Easter and promised the necessary thousand by June. But would the money come in time? Anna was expecting to be confined again in July or August, so that the slightest delay would force them to remain in Dresden and inflict another year of exile upon them. They rejoiced over the baby's coming. This time it must be a boy. They joked happily about the future of "Mr. N.N." But the fear of another year abroad left Dostoevsky too worried to work, and he was ill himself. Spring brought on a series of attacks, which were followed by long periods of intolerable spiritual anguish, as was always the case when the seizures came after a long interval. He took one hundred and twenty thalers and went to Wiesbaden.

All fell out as usual: he lost everything and had to beg Anna to send him the fare that would take him home. He swore to himself that he would not risk that money. The day it arrived there was fear in his heart. The previous night he had dreamed of his father, seeing him in the same terrifying guise in which he had appeared only on two previous occasions, each time boding calamity. Futhermore, shortly before that he had dreamed that Anna's hair had turned white.

With the fare in his pocket, he wandered into the casino just to watch the play. Ten times running he guessed the outcome correctly. After that, could he hold back? How fine it would be if he could bring home even a small sum! And for a whole year he had been wanting to redeem Anna's ear-rings. At nine-thirty he left the rooms half crazed: the last pfennig was gone.

He found himself running to the Russian priest: To clear his soul? To confess? He hardly knew. It was dark, the streets were strange, he lost his way. Was this the Russian church? No, it was a synagogue. He was brought up short, went home, and wrote to Anna. He must have another thirty thalers. By what shall he

swear that he will not take them to the tables? He has deceived
her once. She has the right to despise him. But she must believe
him now. He is not utterly mad. Now he will work, work for her,
for Lubochka, for "Mr. N.N." One thing is certain: a new life is
dawning for them all. A miracle has been vouchsafed him. The
abominable fantasy that has tormented him for ten years has been
swept away. It had fastened itself upon him, kept him from thinking of his work for nights on end—now he is blessedly free of
it, and forever. In the past, only half of him had belonged to
Anna. The other half had been given to that accursed passion.
Now he is wholly hers. Of course, things would not be easy at
once. There would again be trips to the pawnshop, but not many.
He would write to Katkov. Soon they would be back home and
make a fresh beginning.

His only worry was Anna. How would she raise the money
again for the fare back, and how would she explain matters to
her mother? He made up a story for her to tell the old lady: he
had had an attack, soiled the mattress, and in his embarrassment
paid for a new one. In his last letter he warned her that as he
could not afford meals on the way, he would come home hungry.
Would she not have at least a bite ready for him? And, out of
Christian charity, also a package of cigarettes?

Anna could not have taken very seriously his vows to renounce
the tables—she had heard such protestations too often. But this
time, as events were to prove, he spoke truly. The mad dream had
inexplicably lost its old power over him. He never gambled again.
Dostoevsky has furnished no clue as to how he found release from
his obsession. In *The Gambler,* which dates from the period before
the passion had taken complete hold of him, he imagined a man
unable to free himself from it. In *A Raw Youth,* which was written some three years after he played for the last time, he has his
young hero take a fling at roulette, but soon escape the spell of
the tables. The boy is aware that gambling gives him an acute joy
"filtered through torture," one of those ambivalent emotions which
Dostoevsky was the first to depict with such insight. The youth tells
himself, when his fever is at its height, that if he sticks to the game,
it is simply to test the strength of his will, for he believes that "if
one has perfect control of one's will, so that the subtlety of one's

intelligence and one's power of calculation are preserved, one cannot fail to overcome the brutality of blind chance and to win. . . ."
This idea of defeating chance by calculation is obviously the essence
of Dostoevsky's Wiesbaden "system." The idea is strangely out of
character and throws no light either on the origin or the passing
of his gambling mania.

When he returned to Dresden, it was hard to resume work. There
was the fearful uncertainty as to whether Katkov would send the
money in time for them to make the great removal. And along with
their private unrest there was the public excitement of those May
weeks. He had foreseen a conflict in France between town and country, and now civil war had indeed broken out, but it was between
the Paris Commune led by communists, socialists, and that lot, on
the one hand, and the rest of France, on the other.

Writing to Strakhov two days after the slaughter of the Communards was over and Marshal MacMahon had declared law and
order restored, Dostoevsky reflected on the lesson of the Commune.
Its failure, he felt, was rooted in the very nature of socialism. Those
men had to fail. Reason could never rebuild the world. It was a
treacherous guide through the tangle of desires and impulses that
make up man. Christ was literally the only Saviour. The downfall
of the West was the direct consequence of the fact that under the
tutelage of the Roman Catholic Church men had forsaken Him. If
Belinsky (how this ghost haunted him!) had lived to see the burning
of Paris by the Communards, he would have said: "That's a digres-
sion—wait, mankind will yet build its life on rational principles
and win happiness." He would have gone further: he would have
blamed the failure of the Commune not on socialism, but on nationalism, on its being a *French* Commune. Why, he wanted to see
Russia a "vacant nation, capable of putting itself at the head of a
common human enterprise"! What a madman! He had cursed
Christ in unprintable words. But whom would Belinsky set up in
His place? Oh, the little soul, the mean, obtuse, self-satisfied creature that he was, this typical liberal—full of hatred, impatience,
irritation, and petty self-love, self-love above all. Even as a critic
he lacked the true flair.

The venom sputtered from Dostoevsky's pen, as he poured himself out to Strakhov. He was like a man wrestling with a demon, like

Luther flinging his inkpot at the devil's head. But this devil was no black fiend with horns and a tail—it was a slender, pale, consumptive little man with big eyes, it was his old mentor, or was it another small, pallid, fervent person—the young Fyodor Dostoevsky? He wrote wildly, savagely, with hatred, impatience, irritation, perhaps with self-hate above all.

But now he could forget the Communards and the Catholics, the vapid French and the abominable Germans. They were going home! The money had arrived from Katkov in time. They paid their debts, redeemed their belongings, burnt as many papers as possible for fear of being held up at the frontier, and at long last shook the dust of Dresden from their feet.

On July 9, 1871, they arrived in Petersburg. It a was clear, warm day. As they drove past the Trinity Cathedral, where their marriage had been solemnized, they muttered a prayer, and the baby, imitating her parents, made the sign of the cross. In the four years that they had been away, the city had scarcely changed. And what had those years done to him? They had visited him with poverty, isolation, sickness, death, but he saw now that through it all he had lived deeply and intensely. His faith had been tried in those fires. He believed. Or at least he wanted desperately to believe, without apologies or qualifications, in the simple whole-hearted fashion of the peasant who worships the miracle-working icon. The future was full of uncertainties. He was practically beginning life again, and that at fifty. Between him and destitution stood sixty roubles and the contents of two trunks. But no matter. He had something to say. A word that clamoured for utterance. If only he had time, if only he had peace in which to shape it, so that it would come clear and resonant, for Russia, for the world to hear!

CHAPTER TWENTY-ONE

A BOOK OF WRATH

THE FIRST days at home were hectic. To the fatigues of the journey were added the troubles incidental to settling in a furnished flat. Anna was helpless. The baby needed constant attention. And, of course, there was a descent of friends and relatives. It was a comfort to find that Emilia Fyodorovna was now in reasonably comfortable circumstances, with both her boys earning money. The widow appeared to have come to realize that her brother-in-law had a family of his own to care for. Pasha, on the other hand, though now a married man, still seemed to expect help from his stepfather.

Just a week after their arrival, Anna presented her husband with a son, whom they named Fyodor after him. Chaos reigned in the two dingy rooms, which were crowded with the *accouchée*, the infant, the baby, an incompetent domestic, and the harassed father, when he wasn't out running errands. Under these conditions, how could he think of work? Especially since he was in momentary expectation of an attack, brought on by excitement and lack of sleep.

Gradually matters righted themselves. Katkov was as always a very present help in time of trouble. They were able to rent a small flat and to furnish it on the instalment plan. Anna had to buy practically everything: her pots and pans, which had been left with a friend, were gone; her china and glass, including some precious heirlooms, which had been deposited with her sister, had been broken by a careless maid; their winter things, left in pawn, had been forfeited by Mikhail's quondam mistress; Pasha had disposed of the library, and of the other objects entrusted to his care returned only two icons minus their silver mountings. He had, after all, not changed much. He was now proposing that he and his bride should live with them. He was told to shift for himself. The untried young girl, who had known when to snatch her husband away from his demanding relatives, had learned in the bitter years abroad how to hold her own against them. Her friends found her aged and reproached her for her dowdiness. She was indifferent. If she looked older than her years and was not attractive to other men, so much the better: it would save Fyodor a jealous pang. And saving him, guarding him, that was her one care.

What she had now chiefly to protect him against was the creditors. As soon as his return became known, they swooped down upon him. They cursed, they wept, they threatened to attach the furniture, they talked about debtors' prison. Dostoevsky would come back from an interview with them tearing his hair and on the verge of an attack. Then Anna took matters in hand and faced unaided the swarm of boorish retired officers, tearful widows, and insolent shyster lawyers who had bought up the promissory notes and were now coming to collect. She explained coolly that they could not attach the furniture because, being bought on the instalment plan, it still belonged to the shopkeeper, that all the family possessions were in her name, and that if they chose to send Dostoevsky to debtors' prison, he would go, and they would have the pleasure of paying his keep until his time was out, as was customary.

The creditors gave in and exchanged the promissory notes for agreements involving payment in instalments. Anna was counting on money from real estate which she had inherited earlier, but of which she was only now to come into possession. There was another cruel disappointment in store here. Through the carelessness and dishonesty of those who had been managing the property for her, it proved a dead loss. She succeeded in getting stenographic work, as she had hoped all along, but it was out of town, and she was forced to give it up for the sake of her husband's peace of mind: he was of too jealous a disposition to tolerate it. He was perhaps excusing himself when he wrote in *The Brothers Karamazov* that among the jealous "are men of noble hearts." As a result all that they had to depend on for their living and the payment of the debts were his literary labours and her managerial skill.

Dostoevsky took more than one flying trip to Moscow to see Katkov, and spent New Year's Eve at his sister Vera's as he had five years previously. How sad and shabby everything was there now! He tried not to dine there, so as to avoid adding to the household expenses of the orphaned family. There were his own worries, too, and plenty of indignities, but he was in his element again, at home, among his own, no longer living on print and memories, as he had been doing all these years. And at last there were like-minded people with whom he could discuss the ideas about which he felt so strongly. There were Maikov and Strakhov, and he made a few new contacts now. He fell in with Danilevsky, whom he had not seen since the days of the Petrashevsky circle. The man had written a remarkable book, *Russia and Europe*, which had stirred Dostoevsky deeply when he had read it in Florence. Here was someone who saw eye to eye with him in the matter of the superior genius and high destiny of the Russian people.

As the season wore on, Dostoevsky even ventured to give a dinner or two. He regularly attended Prince Meshchersky's Wednesdays where, among the most distinguished people he met was a lean, cool-eyed, scholarly-looking man, Senator Pobedonostzev. The eminent jurist, formerly tutor to the crown prince, was to acquire sinister fame as the power behind the throne when his quondam pupil became emperor. The fact that this learned dignitary had recently translated *The Imitation of Christ* must have made him all the more interesting to Dostoevsky, and, indeed, in spite of a fundamental difference in their natures—Pobedonostzev was stern, hard, and utterly consistent in his conservatism—the two had much in common and were soon on a friendly footing. The senator, like Dostoevsky, was hostile to the political institutions of the West and to the rationalist spirit informing them. Although the gentry had a place in his scheme of things, he too pinned his faith to the instinctive virtues of the peasantry, which he regarded as the bulwark of the Orthodox Church and the autocratic State. Back of it all was a distrust of human nature, which Dostoevsky shared to a greater extent than he realized.

That first winter brought an impressive proof of the novelist's growing fame. The Moscow Maecenas, Tretyakov, commissioned the already renowned Perov to paint Dostoevsky's portrait for his

private gallery. Before taking up his brushes, the painter visited
the flat on Serpukhovskaya Street every day for a week. Dostoevsky talked to him freely and by the time he sat down to pose he
was quite at his ease. When the painting was completed, Anna
who had been present during the sittings, saw on the canvas not
the jealous husband, or the anxious paterfamilias, or the plagued
debtor, or the mad gambler who had made her life more miserable than she was ever willing to admit. She saw the man whom
she would surprise in his study, so absorbed in his own thoughts
that ne would afterwards deny her having entered the room. Whatever the merits of Perov's portrait as a work of art, he produced
an authentic and satisfying image of the novelist: the broad shoulders are slightly bowed; there is coarse strength in the hands, in spite
of the narrow wrists and long fingers; the face, framed in thinning
hair and a soft straggling beard, is waxen, big-browed, sensitive;
the temples are hollowed, and there are lines of suffering under the
sombre, smouldering, inquisitorial eyes—the eyes of a man bent
inward upon himself.

If the winter had its satisfactions and interests, with the turn of
the season fortune turned, too. The family gave up their flat and
rented a little house for the summer at Staraya Russa, a town some
one hundred and fifty miles away, among the lakes of the Novgorod
province, which, what with the mineral waters and the bathing, was
something of a health resort, and cheap. They went all this distance
not so much for the sake of the unweaned infant, who might have
taken a prize at a baby show, but for Luba, who at two and a half
was frail and thin, and whom her father loved "more than anything
else in the world." The day after their arrival they discovered an
alarming bump on her wrist—she had sprained it before they came
away. The local doctor said it was no sprain but a fracture, and the
bones had not grown together properly. There was nothing for it
but to return at once to Petersburg for an operation, leaving the
infant behind to get along as best he could on cow's milk. The operation went off successfully, and Dostoevsky returned alone to his
two treasures at Staraya Russa: the baby and the manuscript of
The Possessed. During the fortnight that Anna had to stay in the
hospital, watching Luba every moment to see that she did not
break the cast, she learned that her only sister had died abroad

and had to witness the scene when the news was broken to her sick mother.

Fretting over how Anna and little Luba were faring, Dostoevsky was dreadfully unhappy. Staraya Russa was a dirty hole. The people, he wrote to his wife, were "terribly queer, stupid and coarse" (no better than the Germans or the Swiss?). The heavy rains had turned the town into a sea of mud. There was nothing to read. Work was impossible. Life was so boring that if it weren't for the baby he would go mad. He almost regretted the absence of attacks: they would be at least a distraction. The night after he wrote this to Anna he had a violent seizure. He kept on having bad dreams: surely they must be in for a run of ill luck.

Indeed, no sooner did Anna come back to Staraya Russa than she was taken sick, and was so sure that she was dying that she said her last farewells to her family. But she recovered, and during the rest of the summer the fates were kind, so that Dostoevsky could keep steadily at his work. Dissatisfied with what he had done on the third (and last) part of the novel, which had occupied him since the beginning of the year, he rewrote it completely. It was only finished in the autumn, and appeared in the issues of *Russky vestnik* for November and December, 1872, after an interval of nearly a year.

II

On November 26, 1869, the body of a young man, with stones tied to the head and feet was discovered in a pond on the grounds of the Moscow Agricultural Academy. Investigation disclosed that the youth, a student at the Academy, had been a member of a cell of a secret revolutionary society and that he had been killed four days previously by his comrades. The leading spirit of the organization, the initiator and the chief perpetrator of the crime was one Sergey Nechayev.

Dostoevsky first became acquainted with the case through the Russian newspapers in the Dresden library. Anna's brother, a student at the Agricultural Academy, who had come to Dresden several weeks before the murder, does not seem to have known the victim and could only tell his brother-in-law something about the temper of the students at the college. Murders always fascinated Dostoevsky, and this one had a special interest for him. It was just as he had predicted. This was what nihilism led to. It was bound to result in wanton killing. Here was the very stuff for a book against the revolutionists, a savage lampoon, a lash with which to flay the rebels against the human and divine order. Although the earliest reference to a story he was writing, in the nature of a political pamphlet, occurs in a letter dated April 5, 1870, he appears to have been planning a novel of the revolution before he ever heard of the Nechayev case. Without this event, however, *The Possessed* would either never have come into being or would have been a different book.

The trial of Nechayev's followers—he was himself in hiding abroad—was under way in Petersburg when Dostoevsky returned from Dresden. The proceedings were fully reported in the papers, for the first time in a case of this kind, and those columns were so much meat to the novelist. He was just then busy with the second part of his work, in which the conspirators figure prominently. The testimony showed Nechayev to be a man of a cold, forceful, daring, utterly unscrupulous nature, yet left him something of an enigma. He had planned to organize the society in small units, whose activities were hedged about with secrecy and whose members owed strict obedience to their superiors, and he had indeed made the initial step toward achieving his goal. The emblem of the organization was an axe, and its aim was a series of terroristic acts culminating in a popular rising, which was scheduled for February 19, 1870, the ninth anniversary of the emancipation of the serfs. The Tsar himself was to be temporarily spared, with a view to executing him publicly at a solemn festival of the liberated people.

The most startling item brought out in the course of the trial was a printed document in code, found in the possession of one of the conspirators: *The Revolutionist's Catechism*. It was apparently the work of Bakunin. With harsh precision it defines the duties of the revolutionist. It opens with the declaration that he is "a doomed man" and proceeds thus: "He has no interests, no affairs, no feelings, no attachments of his own, no property, not even a name. He is wholly absorbed by one exclusive interest, one thought, one passion: revolution." He has broken with the codes, the conven-

tions, the morality of the civilized world. "Whatever promotes the
the triumph of the revolution is moral, whatever hinders it is
immoral, is criminal." (Lenin will restate this idea with fresh conviction). Friendship, love, gratitude, honour itself must be sacrificed to "the cold passion for the revolutionary cause." The
revolutionist must insinuate himself everywhere, crippling those
enemies whom he does not destroy, turning everyone and everything to his purpose. In this war the foulest means are fair, and so
he will make common cause with the highwayman, "the true and
only revolutionist in Russia." The objective is "the complete emancipation and happiness of the people, that is of the unskilled
workers." Yet the task of ordering the new society the revolutionist leaves to the future: "Our business is passionate, complete,
ubiquitous, ruthless destruction."

The reader who turned from his newspaper to the instalments
of *The Possessed* as they appeared in *Russky vestnik* could not help
recognizing in the fictive conspirators a resemblance to the men
whom the sensational trial brought into the limelight. In drawing
the young Verkhovensky, the ringleader in the novel, Dostoevsky
may well have had an eye on *The Revolutionist's Catechism*. Certainly he used Nechayev himself as a model for his character. The
young man arrives in the provincial town where the action takes
place and proceeds to form a group of five, this being a unit of a
vast secret organization which he hopes to set up and which he
pretends is already in existence. In order to seal with blood the
pact that binds the five and above all, perhaps, to satisfy a private
animus, he plans to have them kill a former member of the group
who had lost his faith in the cause. Verkhovensky throws the town
into a turmoil, twists everyone round his finger, from the wooden-
headed governor on down, sets them all dancing to his fiendish
fiddling, instigates arson, carries out the murder (the details closely
approximate those in the Nechayev case), and vanishes, leaving
death and destruction in his wake.

Dostoevsky grants the young Verkhovensky, if grudgingly, flashes
of selfless enthusiasm, but spares no effort to render him odious; he
is disgustingly vain, greedy, deceitful, capable of every vileness, a
moral moron, and without originality, without genius to redeem
his vices. It is hinted that, to crown his infamy, this would-be

saviour of humanity is at one and the same time preparing the revolution and informing the Government against his comrades (as a
matter of fact, at one time Nechayev was suspected, though unjustly,
of being an agent-provocateur; Dostoevsky was anticipating the
career of the double-dealers who were to infiltrate the revolutionary movement and of whom the notorious Azef was the most startling example). As for Verkhovensky's satellites, they are a set of
"sullen dolts," conceited eccentrics and scoundrels, with only one
or two naïve dreamers in the whole mad, quarrelsome crew.

To destroy the Church, to undermine the foundations of society,
to poison the very springs of life—these are the aims of Verkhovensky and his comrades. True, Verkhovensky proposes that, when
the ramshackle structure has crashed to the ground, he and his
followers will build "a stone edifice." But it is obvious that he cares
nothing for building, and as for his followers, one of the characters
justly observes that they would be the first to be unhappy if the
millennium arrived. Nor is there any agreement as to what form this
rational, secular, artificial society will take. Will it be, as the Fourierist member of the Five would demand, a phalanstery? Or perhaps a world in which a fraction of mankind exerts a benevolent
despotism over all the rest who, by a system of spying, slander, and
murder, are eventually transformed into a slavish herd living in
animal innocence and contentment—the earthly paradise mapped
out by the mournful Shigalyov? In the interest of absolute equality
—which is incompatible with his scheme—he would cut out Cicero's
tongue, put out Copernicus' eyes and stone Shakespeare. He admits
with consternation that although the starting point of his plan is unlimited freedom, it ends in unlimited despotism. Yet his solution
of the social problem is, he believes, the only possible one. The
nihilists may profess devotion to freedom, but lacking religious
regard for the individual and for the spiritual bread he lives by, they
are bound to enslave him in the end. To this thesis Dostoevsky will
return again and again.

It may be that he modelled Shigalyov on Pyotr Tkachov, a former
contributor to *Vremya* and a defendant in the Nechayev trial. One
of the earliest Russian followers of Karl Marx, he held ideas to
which Marx would not have subscribed. The author of *The
Possessed* may have looked into the book that the young man pub-

lished in 1869. Therein Tkachov argued that for social harmony the abolition of classes was not enough—it was necessary to eradicate whatever made for rivalry between individuals and so whatever enabled a man to stand out among his fellows.

By the time the novel was published in book form, he believed that he had written "almost a historical study," as he said in a letter to the future emperor Alexander III, who had expressed the desire to know what the author thought of his own work. It was designed, the novelist wrote, to show how such a monstrous phenomenon as the Nechayev movement had arisen through the divorce of the intellectuals from the masses. The liberals of the forties, too deeply concerned for humanity to care either for their country or their God, had begotten the revolutionists of the sixties. Why, the spiritual father of Nechayev was none other than Belinsky!

Strange how, with the passage of years, that figure took on sinister proportions! Yet it was not Belinsky, but his disciple, Turgenev, whom Dostoevsky made the butt of his scorn. His hatred for this fellow writer had grown steadily since he left the scene of their quarrel. By now the man had become for him the embodiment of that indifference to the Russian God and the Russian folk that he so abominated. No wonder that in a novel which lumped the liberals with the extremists in a wholesale excommunication, he should hit out at one whom he considered both a personal and a public enemy. Indeed, the contemporary reader had no difficulty in recognizing the features of Turgenev, as man and writer, crudely and maliciously caricatured in those of Karmazinov, the celebrity who is visiting the town in which the action of the novel takes place. Few pages in this angry book are so spattered with spittle and gall as are those on which Karmazinov appears.

It is significant that a tender-minded liberal of the type that flourished when Dostoevsky and Turgenev were young is the father of the ruthless archconspirator in the novel, and the tutor of another youth marked for perdition. The novelist deals almost as mercilessly with Verkhovensky senior as with his fiendish offspring. The parent is a babe at fifty, a vain, self-indulgent babbler, spending his useless days as the pensioner of a rich woman who is bound to him by an affection strangely compounded of contempt, hatred, and jealousy. And yet there is a touch of the quixotic about the man, a faint con-

sciousness of his own degradation, a spark of aspiration not wholly
smothered in ashes. And so Dostoevsky concludes by taking the
sentimental old sinner to his heart, grants him a Christian end, and,
what is more, puts into his mouth the more obvious message of the
book.

Toward the close of the novel, offended by his patroness, the old
Verkhovensky takes to the road, alone and on foot, with no idea
whither he is bound, but with some crazy notion of upholding the
ideal of freedom. The wanderer falls mortally ill and on his death-
bed a chance companion reads him passages from the Gospels,
including the one on the devils who entered into the swine—the
epigraph of the novel. It flashes upon the dying man that this is
a parable of his country. Russia had been sick for generations, she
had been possessed of unclean spirits, but now these devils have
entered into the swine, that is, himself and his son and the rest of
that unhappy lot. "And we shall cast ourselves down," he cries,
"demented and raving, from the rocks into the sea, and we shall
all be drowned—and a good thing, too, for that is all we are fit
for. But the sick man will be healed and 'will sit at the feet of Jesus,'
and all will look upon him with astonishment. . . ."

The novelist may have flattered himself that he had produced
"a historical study," and indeed some of his material was drawn
from life, but the conspirators he painted were really devils in
whom he believed without having seen, and whom he was out to
exorcize. The nihilists of the early sixties had recognized themselves in Turgenev's Bazarov. The liberals of the seventies joined
with the extremists in dismissing Dostoevsky's picture of the revolutionists as malicious misrepresentation, portraits of psychopaths,
signifying nothing. It was infamous to identify the cause of Russian
freedom with Nechayev, a fanatic whom even like-minded men indignantly repudiated for his unscrupulousness! Anyone not completely swayed by prejudice could see that those who took up arms
against the older order were inspired by the highest motives. What
a hotchpotch of venom, bigotry, anachronism the book was! As
though in the days when the action takes place Russian radicals
were still reading Fourier or drawing blueprints for the millennium.
They were either engaged in the peaceful propaganda of socialist
ideas or, in yet smaller numbers, they were plotting mass insurrec-

tion. The fewest were advocating the seizure of power by a handful of conspirators. The man had obviously jumbled wry memories of the rebel circles of his youth with furiously distorted views of their more recent avatars. It was not only Dostoevsky's contemporaries who thus castigated *The Possessed*. It has remained on the blacklist of the radicals. In 1913, Gorky was protesting against the staging of a dramatized version of the novel by the Moscow Art Theatre, and the following year the Austrian Social-Democratic Party succeeded in suppressing its performance in Vienna. In our own day the novel has, of course, been condemned by Soviet opinion.

Dostoevsky could neither treat the revolution with Turgenev's genial, half-deprecatory interest, nor, like Tolstoy, leave it alone. He kept returning to the subject, with his usual vehemence, and in the compulsive fashion of a man who bites on a sore tooth. It is plain that the confused, blackened, and distorted picture of the revolutionary movement that he drew in *The Possessed* was the work of a man blinded by fear and fury. He failed utterly to do justice to the idealism that burned with so clear a flame in these early revolutionists, and with a fanaticism that savours of the renegade, he misrepresented both their programme and their tactics.

Yet read in the light of Russia's recent history some pages of *The Possessed* seem to foreshadow the character and course of the revolution that was to take place half a century later. For one thing, they suggest that the upheaval is likely to go beyond political and economic changes. "A new religion is coming instead of the old one," young Verkhovensky lets fall in discussing the prospects of the movement. Point is given to the remark by the fact that what is called "communism" to-day is a quasi-religion sharing the dogmatism, the dynamism, the intransigence of some of the older faiths. That the revolution would find a weapon against the Church in militant atheism is another of Dostoevsky's intuitions borne out by the event. He had Myshkin, in *The Idiot,* observe that Russians easily succumb to the temptation of atheism and that they hold to it with the conviction of the believer. In *The Possessed* a convert to the revolutionary cause chops up his icon with an axe and burns candles before the works of Vogt, Moleschott and Büchner, the exponents of the crude materialism of the day.

III

First conceived as a pamphlet against the radicals, *The Possessed* contains elements that are not an inevitable part of such a conception. The book has two main nodes of interest, at least two distinct, if related, plots. One is built around the conspiracy captained by the younger Verkhovensky, the other is centred about the career of Stavrogin, the quondam pupil of the elder Verkhovensky and the only son of the great lady who is his patroness. Indeed, it is the brilliant and enigmatic figure of Stavrogin that dominates the novel, although his connection with the theme of revolution, which is the prime mover of the book, is indirect.

While the novel was still in embryo Dostoevsky imagined him as a man with immense spiritual energy which, for lack of an objective, made his whole life one of "storm and disorder." Should he be drawn as a complete sensualist, playing with life and ending as a suicide? Or perhaps at the last he would find Christ, the Russian Christ, the Saviour of the Orthodox folk, possibly through contact with some pious recluse, and become "a new man." Obviously, these notions derived from the other projects that were at the same time occupying Dostoevsky: the novel on atheism and *The Life of a Great Sinner*. The Stavrogin of *The Possessed* is pictured as an irretrievably lost soul. At the height of his powers he is stricken with an impotence of the spirit, a lack of essential heat. A former disciple says of him: "If Stavrogin has faith, he does not believe that he has faith. If he hasn't, he doesn't believe that he hasn't." In his last estimate of himself he says that he can neither affirm nor deny, that he derives pleasure equally from good and evil, but that his pleasure is as feeble as his desires are petty.

Stavrogin, as he lives in the pages of the novel, does not sufficiently resemble this Laodicean. For all the novelist's insistence, one cannot quite credit Stavrogin's weakness or the completeness of his depravity. Dostoevsky's condemnation of his hero is akin to Milton's judgment on Lucifer, whom he could not help making attractive. He loves his unhappy villain: hadn't he told Katkov that he had taken him from his heart? It is not impossible that the image of Speshnev, that romantic companion of his youth, was present in his mind when he was drawing Stavrogin. There is a mighty force in this man, the secret of the fascination he exercises over all who encounter him, including Verkhovensky, who, believing in his extraordinary aptitude for crime, plans to make him the leader of the revolution. In fact, there is something idolatrous in the young nihilist's attitude toward Stavrogin—it is as though Dostoevsky could scarcely imagine a man, however irreligious, who did not eventually bow down to someone or something. But Stavrogin's force, being without direction, wastes itself in perversities, intellectual vagaries, and monstrous experiments. He toys with revolution, as he flings himself into debauchery, wallows in mud, essays crime, simply to escape from the aimlessness of his life. He marries a servant-girl, crippled and an idiot, who is secretly in love with him, partly to satisfy a perverse desire for self-injury, and also because it titillates him to outrage people's sense of the fitness of things. Stavrogin's tragedy was to his creator but another symptom of the disease with which a rootless, and hence godless, generation was afflicted. The descendant of a long line of gentlemen, he had lost the distinction between good and evil because, the novelist would have us believe, he was out of touch with the people.

Among the ideas he conjures with are the most precious articles in Dostoevsky's credo: the Russians are the one "God-bearing" people, possessing "the keys of life" and destined to "save the world in the name of a new God"; the Catholic Church has failed to preserve the purity of the Christian ideal, and in its greed for temporal power is indeed serving Antichrist, thus working the ruin of Western civilization; "socialism is from its very nature bound to be atheism, seeing that . . . it intends to establish itself exclusively on the elements of science and reason"; nations do not live by reason, which has no power to distinguish good from evil, but by faith, each in its own holy mission. The astonishing thing is that Dostoevsky offers these beliefs as the dubious treasure found by the spiritually bankrupt Stavrogin at the end of one of his blind alleys, just as in *The Idiot* he makes that devious rascal, Lebedev, the mouthpiece for some of his most cherished sentiments. Furthermore, it is in the limited, fanatical mind of Stavrogin's disciple, Shatov, that the idea of Russian Messianism finds permanent lodgment. It was a passing fancy with its brilliant originator; it is the rock of faith for his dull follower. This uncouth plebeian is possessed of complete integrity, ferocious earnestness, and a strong will-to-believe, but he is a man who, instead of mastering his convictions, is overpowered by them. What is more amazing than all this is to hear the atheist, Stavrogin, vainly striving with his unbelief, credited with the very words in which Dostoevsky, some sixteen years earlier, tried to express the perfection of his own faith to the devout woman who had befriended him as a convict: "If anyone could prove that Christ is outside the truth, and if the truth really did exclude Christ, I should prefer to stay with Christ, and not with the truth."

It was as if Dostoevsky had a need for deliberately casting a shadow of doubt upon his avowed convictions. Thus he impeached his own fanaticism. His private letters and his publicist essays show him cherishing a faith that his imaginative writings indirectly call in question. Was he so firm a believer that he could allow himself the luxury of blasphemy? Or was the placing of his credo in this ambiguous light a way of confessing his private doubts without offence to his conscience? In the course of one of those dialogues that are the peaks of Dostoevsky's art Stavrogin puts to Shatov the direct question: "Do you believe in God?" and receives the frantic answer: "I believe in Russia. . . . I believe in her Orthodoxy. . . . I believe in the body of Christ. . . . I believe that the new advent will take place in Russia. . . . I believe . . ." When Stavrogin insists: "And in God? In God?" Shatov can only stammer: "I . . . I will believe in God." One is inclined to read this as an indirect acknowledgment of the infirmity of his own faith on the part of Shatov's creator.

At the same time that he was indoctrinating Shatov with religious nationalism, Stavrogin planted in the receptive mind of Kirillov the seeds of a God-defying arrogance. By his own admission, he was not deceiving either disciple: in persuading them he was simply trying to find himself—a statement that appears to apply with equal force to the man who projected himself in these several characters. While Shatov piously accepts life, Kirillov is a Promethean rebel, refusing it on the terms on which it is offered. A man "swallowed by an idea," he is a fanatic and a visionary. He knows ecstatic moments of "eternal harmony," such as Myshkin knew just before an epileptic attack. This experience apparently leads him to the conviction that life need not be "the vaudeville of devils" that it is, that supreme happiness is possible on earth. But the prerequisite is to overcome the fear of death. Thereby the idea of God will be destroyed, for man has invented deity to protect himself from the horror of extinction. Kirillov, with naïve arrogance, believes that he is the first human being to refuse to devise God. Yet this atheist is a man of a profoundly religious temper. "God has tormented me," he says, "all my life." Existence without God is unthinkable and unbearable for him. The void must be filled: since God does not exist, he argues, I am God (the same thought had been attributed to the Great Sinner). If heaven is empty, it behoves man to use his "terrible freedom" and assert that attribute of his own godhead, his self-will. And what clearer proof can he give of it than by freely surrendering his life? Accordingly Kirillov resolves to kill himself. By another mammoth non-sequitur, he decides that through this act of self-crucifixion all humanity will be redeemed: man on earth will enter into glory and undergo a physical transformation. For man in his present state—here as elsewhere Dostoevsky was anticipating Nietzsche—is something to be surpassed.

Kirillov carries out his intention, but his suicide, far from being the apocalyptic event he had expected, is a gesture as futile as it is ghastly. His death does not even profit Verkhovensky, who made him take upon himself the blame for Shatov's murder. Kirillov's fate is, of course, intended as an object lesson in the deadly effect of atheism. The lesson is apt to be lost on the reader, in spite of the power with which Kirillov is presented, because of the quality of the reasoning that leads him to suicide. What this figure, like that of Shatov, does attest to is the tormenting insistence of the novelist's doubts and, no less, the strength of his religious need. "The chief question . . . by which consciously or unconsciously, I have been tormented all my life," he wrote to Maikov in 1870, "is that of the existence of God."

I V

One of the crucial points in the novel is a conversation in which Shatov, seeing Stavrogin's feet of clay, yet unable to cast down this idol, rises against him in a passion of love and hate, and calls him to account. At the close of this scene the rebellious disciple urges his false teacher, just as Sonia urged Raskolnikov, to kiss the earth that he has defiled, water it with his tears, and ask forgiveness. A clarifying commentary on this admonition may be gathered from the obscure words of that pitiful sibyl, Stavrogin's wife, to the effect that Mother Earth is really the same as the Mother of God, and that from the tears with which men water the earth springs joy. Shatov also bids Stavrogin give up his wealth and try to find God by toiling in the sweat of his face like a peasant (Tolstoy will exalt this notion into a system). He ends by telling Stavrogin to go and see Tikhon, a retired archpriest who is living in a local monastery. In the novel as it stands, nothing further is heard of the matter. But Dostoevsky did actually write the scene in which Stavrogin visits the saintly hermit—it will be recalled that the early plans for the novel provided for such an episode.

What brings the young man to Tikhon's cell is the need to confess an unspeakable crime, the memory of which is a continual torture to him. Dostoevsky's writings hold nothing more subtle and powerful than the account of the crime as it is unfolded in Stavrogin's confession, which he handed to Tikhon in the form of a printed statement. He had begun by injuring a little girl somewhat in the fashion in which Rousseau had wronged the servant girl Marion: he had suffered the twelve-year-old Matryosha to be flogged in his presence for the suspected theft of his knife, knowing that she was innocent. And then, as he savoured the pleasure of his own meanness, he was stung by a vile thought. He did not obey the impulse immediately. Indeed, for two days he did not come near the house where Matryosha lived, and where he kept a room for assignation purposes. By way of diversion, he committed a theft. He went back to the house, went away again, and finally returned, bent on carrying out his intention. All the while he was convinced that he could abandon it, were he so minded. Stavrogin insists on this point, in order to remove any suspicion that he was irresponsible. Any shameful act he might commit, any humiliating situation in which he might find himself, was a source of keen pleasure to him, yet he could control his emotions, no matter how violent. Though the child's sensuality, which he had himself aroused, moved him momentarily to revulsion and pity, he accomplished his purpose, after which he went off to spend the night elsewhere.

The following day he was drawn to the scene of his crime, torn between hatred of his victim and fear of discovery. But these emotions did not long distress him. The child, blaming herself, kept the secret. He decided to leave the city and, coming to the lodging to settle accounts, learned that Matryosha had been ill and delirious. Believing that he would find her alone in the evening, he returned then without knowing why, but with a vague feeling that his presence would bring matters to a head. In an obscure way he became the author of another crime: his apparently innocent visit was the goad that drove the little girl to hang herself, and he did not leave the place until he had satisfied himself that she had done so.

For a while, the confession goes on, he remembered the affair with irritation, and it was shortly afterwards, in a fit of desperate boredom, that he married the crippled idiot. His subsequent trip home and extended travels abroad wiped the evil memory out of his mind, until one day, waking from an afternoon nap in which he had had an exalting dream of a Golden Age, a trick of association recalled the whole hideous episode to him, and thereafter he knew no peace. Although feeling able to free himself from the obsession, he believed that he would cling to it until madness overtook him. In an effort to save himself from his torments, he planned to commit another crime, bigamy, but instead he had his confession printed with the idea of making it public at the proper moment.

The scene between Stavrogin and Tikhon, which was to form the ninth chapter of Part Two or the first of Part Three, does not figure in the novel, and indeed was not published in full until 1922. The magazine rejected it as too unsavoury for its pages. Early in 1872, while Dostoevsky's affairs were in disorder and he was spending his time driving from one creditor to another, he kept devising substitute versions of the chapter which would not offend "the chastity of the editorial office," as he put it to his niece Sonia. But none of them proved acceptable, and in the end the chapter was not published, nor did it appear in the separate edition of the novel. Dostoevsky must have had reasons other than the publisher's or the public's squeamishness for omitting it from the final version of his work. As has been seen, while the image of Stavrogin was still inchoate, the novelist had considered the possibility of redeeming him in the end. As the work progressed and Stavrogin claimed a more important place, he abandoned this idea. Possibly he felt that Stavrogin confessing his sin, even if he did so rather in a spirit of challenge than of Christian humility, was out of key with the picture of a soul utterly lost. In any event, it is regrettable that he discarded the chapter, since aside from its intrinsic value, it clarifies certain situations in the novel, which, as it stands, are rather puzzling.

Stavrogin's talk with Tikhon concludes on the archpriest's horrified prediction that the young man is on the brink of another atrocity, which he will commit in order to escape publicly acknowledging the one he has just confessed. And, indeed, Stavrogin does end his career with a double crime: for one thing, he renders himself morally guilty of the murder of his lawful wife and of her brother by taking no steps to prevent it, though aware that it is imminent. His failure to interfere is dictated by his vague thought of marrying a girl who is deeply in love with him, although her love, as is often the case with Dostoevsky's characters, sometimes assumes the guise of hatred. Furthermore, he takes this pure passionate creature when, in an impulsive moment, she offers herself to him. He hopes somehow that her love will redeem him, but knows at heart that he is incapable of loving her. The mob, smelling out his part in the murder, lynches her as "Stavrogin's woman," so that in a sense his hands are stained with her blood as well.

After the tragedy, Stavrogin's first thought is to expatriate himself and settle in Switzerland with a woman who loves him enough to be content with the rôle of a nurse to him. Suicide, he tells himself, would be the final lie in a life of deception, for it would argue a despair he cannot feel. He overcomes this scruple, however, and ends by hanging himself. He has placed himself beyond the pale of humanity by his inability to distinguish between good and evil, and this last act is merely a dramatization of that moral law. What with the edifying end of the elder Verkhovensky, the transcendental self-destruction of Kirillov, the assassination of Shatov, the death of his wife and her infant, the lynching of the girl, the killing of the thug who had murdered Stavrogin's wife and brother-in-law, the conclusion of this turbulent novel matches any Elizabethan drama for bloodiness. Dostoevsky's text in *The Possessed* might well have been that on the wages of sin: the sin of divorce from the people and the consequent loss of God.

v

In the spring of 1908 the Russian papers carried accounts of the sensational trial of a certain Duloup, an instructor of French in several of the more select Petersburg schools, who was charged with raping a ten-year-old girl. In connection with the case the name of the author of *The Possessed* was mentioned, with apologies, and some old gossip about him found its way into print. According to one story thus published, the novelist, following with morbid fascination the trial of a man accused of the same offence, came to identify himself with the criminal. "There were moments," he is reported to have said, "when it seemed to me that the accused got into the dock by mistake, and that it was not he but I who had outraged the little girl, although I had never before laid my eyes on the unhappy child." As the proceedings drew to an end, he found himself under compulsion to victimize the little girl in his turn, and indeed, when the trial was over he carried out his purpose. Overcome with remorse, he opened his heart to an old friend, who advised him to do penance by confessing the crime to the man whom he hated most, and so Dostoevsky made a clean breast of it to Turgenev. The tale is supposed to have been circulated by Dostoevsky's schoolmate, that scandalmonger, Grigorovich.

Another story, printed at the same time, had it that at a large gathering, the discussion turning on shameful acts committed by decent people, Dostoevsky told about a man who got into talk with a governess on the street and then seduced both her and her young charge. "That scoundrel," he is said to have blurted out, "was I." He is reported to have made the same confession to a lady of his acquaintance. The more recently published memoirs of a minor writer, a contemporary of the novelist, offers a variant combining the elements of the two previous versions. Dostoevsky comes to

Turgenev and tells him a detailed story about the governess and her charge, but ends by asserting that he invented the whole thing for his host's entertainment. Dostoevsky's reputed pedophilic offence is said to have been frequently mentioned in literary circles during the eighties. It was alleged to have occurred before his arrest.

These rumours would not merit serious attention, were it not that two years after the novelist's death the same damaging allegation was made by none other than Strakhov, Dostoevsky's intimate, the companion of his travels, the chief contributor to his reviews, the witness to his second wedding, the friend of the household, the man to whom Dostoevsky's widow entrusted the labour of preparing, in collaboration with Orest Miller, the official *Life and Letters* of her husband. Upon the publication of the book Strakhov sent a copy of it to an acquaintance with a note in which he remarked that the task, which had been more or less forced upon him, had been a good deal of a burden. He also sent a copy to his friend Leo Tolstoy, and followed it up with a letter, dated November 28, 1883. Herein he confessed that while working on the book he had had to combat a feeling of disgust for his subject, and closed with a resigned admission that the performance was simply another piece of eulogistic cant. After portraying his late friend as a selfish, dissolute, vicious creature, he wrote: "He was drawn to abominations, and he boasted of them. Viskovatov began telling me how he boasted that in a bathhouse he . . . a little girl brought to him by her governess."

This astounding document was not published until 1913, when both correspondents were in their graves, and was first brought to the attention of Dostoevsky's widow a year later. The devotion she had borne her husband when he was alive had long since turned into idolatrous worship of the memory of the departed. She had once described him to Tolstoy as "the kindest, the tenderest, the most intelligent and generous man" she had ever known. Naturally Strakhov's portrait appeared to her a monstrous calumny, the work of malice and envy, perhaps the belated revenge for a slight put upon him by the dead. She says as much in her posthumously published reminiscences, where she deals with Strakhov's letter, while ignoring the other versions of the rumour. Of course she indignantly denies his charge of perversion. To satisfy such a craving, she argues, one must be a rich man, and that her Fyodor had never been. And how absurd to drag in Professor Viskovatov, a casual acquaintance who had never even been in the house! The story goes back to a variant of "Stavrogin's Confession," she suggests, pointing out that when Katkov rejected the chapter in its original form, Dostoevsky rewrote it, introducing a governess and a bathhouse, and then read it to some friends, Strakhov among them. They advised him against this version too, on the grounds that to implicate a governess in so hideous an affair would be to lay himself open to the charge of attacking the movement for the emancipation of women. And it was thanks to this piece of fiction, she concludes, that Strakhov ascribed Stavrogin's crime to Dostoevsky!

The widow is candid enough in her memoirs, but inclined to emphasize the brighter parts of the picture. Thus, she passes over in silence the murder of her father-in-law, of which she could scarcely have been ignorant. In any event, no trace of the variant of "Stavrogin's Confession" that she mentions has been discovered so far. As for the cost of gratifying the perverse desire, it could not have been great: a contemporary points out that the shameful traffic went on openly in the Petersburg "Passage," the arcade where, any night, Dostoevsky might have seen little girls as wretched as those who had wrung his heart in the Haymarket on his London visit. Further, even if Strakhov was, as Dostoevsky felt in his latter years, a fair-weather friend, capable of treachery, it is difficult to believe that he wilfully twisted the facts with a view to defaming the dead man in the eyes of posterity. There are no plausible motives for his bringing falsely so grave a charge against his late companion, in a letter addressed to the master whom he deeply reverenced.

At the same time Strakhov's letter, though apparently sincere, is of doubtful value as evidence. The allegation it contains is plainly a piece of hearsay, omitting all reference to place and time, and not even completed: "Viskovatov *began* telling me. . . ." Viskovatov was a professor at the University of Dorpat, who seldom came to Petersburg and whom Dostoevsky seems to have disliked. It is not even certain that he had the story at first-hand. But assuming that Dostoevsky did thus unbosom himself to the man, it is still open to question whether he was confessing an act he had committed or indulging his morbid fantasy.

Strakhov's letter in itself is a psychological puzzle. Three days after Dostoevsky's funeral he had been writing to Tolstoy in quite a different tone: "In his [Dostoevsky's] presence I longed to be both wise and good, and the deep respect we felt for one another, in spite of foolish misunderstandings, was, as I see, extremely dear to me." Were these sentiments merely in the nature of a conventional wreath laid on the grave, and withering as soon? Certainly it is hard to reconcile them with the ugly effigy of the man he presented two years later. Perhaps this was as much the product of blind emotion as the widow's glorification of her late espousèd saint. In spite, then, of the weight Strakhov's name lends to the charge, it must be considered not proved.

It may well be that, as the widow suggested, the ugly rumour arose simply in connection with the suppressed chapters of *The Possessed,* either as they now stand or in some other form that has not come down to us, and has no foundation in fact. But here, too, proof is lacking. "The truth must be sought somewhere between," as the chronicler in the novel observes in commenting upon the veracity of Stavrogin's confession. Surely there is some significance in the fact that Dostoevsky here presents so nakedly intimate a picture of this perversion, and further, that the same motif crops up in his writings with a curious persistence.

The theme is first adumbrated in a story written when he was only twenty-seven, "A Christmas Tree and a Wedding," where a middle-aged man casts guilty glances at a little girl still playing with dolls. There is an ever so faint hint of it in the treatment of an adolescent boy's first awakening in "The Little Hero," the story he wrote in prison. When he was courting Anna Korvin-Krukovskaya in the winter of 1865 he entertained the ladies of the family one day by relating a scene from a tale he had sketched out in his youth. He imagined, he said, a comfortably situated middle-aged man waking up one morning and plunging into pleasant reveries; suddenly in the midst of this agreeable occupation the man becomes vaguely troubled; his apparently baseless uneasiness grows; something hovers tantalizingly on the edge of his consciousness and vanishes before he can seize it; abruptly the recollection flashes upon him: years earlier, after a night of debauch, spurred on by drunken companions, he had violated a child. In *The Insulted and Injured,* little Nellie is in the clutches of a procuress and barely escapes being victimized by a middle-aged pervert. The depraved Svidrigailov in *Crime and Punishment* is said to have outraged a girl of fourteen who ended by killing herself. (In this respect, as in others, Svidrigailov is the sketch, where Stavrogin is the finished portrait). The night before he shoots himself, in a state between sleeping and waking, he sees the familiar face of a fourteen-year-old girl who lies in her coffin: ". . . she had destroyed herself, crushed by an insult that had appalled and amazed that childish soul, had smirched that angel purity with unmerited disgrace. . . ." The meaning of this fantasy is underscored by his subsequent nightmare. Before he decides to commit suicide he engages himself to a girl under sixteen. In *The Eternal Husband* the middle-aged cuckold also comtemplates marriage to a schoolgirl, and, like Svidrigailov is represented as a man whose sensuality is aroused by innocence and immaturity. Again, in *A Raw Youth,* the same inclination is vaguely ascribed to Versilov. According to a preliminary note for the novel, he seduces his thirteen-year-old step-daughter, who eventually hangs herself. To judge by the notes for *The Brothers Karamazov,* Dostoevsky had at one time intended to make Dmitry Karamazov guilty of Stavrogin's crime.

Why did Dostoevsky choose this particular offence as a symbol of evil? Why was he haunted by it? The morbid sexual act may have been a phantasy of Dostoevsky's, with the incidental effect of intensifying his sense of guilt. In *The Brothers Karamazov* the prosecutor observes that epileptics are "tormented by pangs of conscience, often without cause; they exaggerate and often invent all sorts of faults and crimes." Holding that "epilepsy is apt to be associated with moral perversity," Havelock Ellis writes that Dostoevsky had "manifold perverse impulses." It is not necessary to conclude, however, he adds, that the novelist "carried morbid impulse to completed action." Wilhelm Stekel states that the epileptic fit is a substitute for a crime, "or, it may be, for a sexual act that is a crime," and suggests that in Dostoevsky's case the crime may have been child rape. The assumption that he was obsessed by a pedophilic craving, even though he did not satisfy it, would explain his preoccupation with the theme. He harped upon it for the same reason that the victim of a phobia constantly seeks to project the eventuality he fears; he kept returning to it, one surmises, for the sake of the vicarious experience and in obedience to the urge to confess.

CHAPTER TWENTY-TWO

"THE ACCURSED YEAR"

So HE had freed himself from the burden of another novel. There it was—a great, sprawling, awkward thing. It had less structural unity than its predecessors. When would he learn to master his material? When would he restrain himself from crowding the stuff of several novels into one, "without measure and harmony?" Perhaps never. Form, finish, craftsmanship were important, yes, but they were beyond him. He must always overreach himself, must always be stammering and stuttering with the urgency of what he had to say. At any rate, there was heat in *The Possessed*, and some plain speaking. He had poured out his wrath upon the unbelievers and the rebels and taken the opportunity to settle a personal score. He had fought furiously in defence of God and country. He knew that not all his blows had struck home, but he probably did not realize that he had inadvertently shown the chinks in the armour of his own faith.

And now he must be at it again. The end of one book was but the beginning of another. His novels had something unfinished, something tentative about them. Repeatedly he was forced to return to the problems that he raised in them. The struggle to speak out all that was in him would never end. Long before he had written finis to *The Possessed* new projects began to ferment in his mind. In January, 1872, when only the first two parts of that work were completed, he had paid a visit to Katkov in Moscow and outlined for him the subject of his next novel. About the same time he had confided to a friend that he was reading up in preparation for a journey to the East: Constantinople, Greece, and the Holy Land. While he was still in Dresden he had been dreaming of going there and bringing back a book which would cover the expenses of the trip. He had told Anna prior to their engagement that he had before him three choices: to go to Jerusalem and perhaps settle there, to live a gambler's life in Europe, to get married. Well, he had married; he had followed his gambling urge; and the East still beckoned him. There could be no thought of settling there now; he had a wife and two children on his hands. He would stay there less than a year and come back with a book. The journey could only have meant a pilgrimage to the sources of the Orthodox faith. The book could only have been a story of Christ. Some years later he was to list such a work among the things he promised himself to write before he died. He never made the pilgrimage. He never wrote the book. Nor, when *The Possessed* was finished, did he turn at once to another novel. He needed a rest from the strain of fiction-writing. In the meanwhile, how would they all live?

He had little to hope for from the litigation over Aunt Kumanina's estate in which he was now engaged. It will be remembered that during his sojourn in Dresden, Dostoevsky, misled by false news of the old lady's death and an equally false report as to the provisions of her will, had made inquiries preliminary to claiming a share for himself and for Mikhail's family. His brother Andrey, one of the executors, informing him reproachfully of the true state of affairs, he had replied in a tone of injured innocence that he had never had any expectation of benefiting by the will, considering that he had received all that was due to him. He had repeated this to his niece Sonia, adding that in all conscience he believed that he owed Aunt's estate interest on the ten thousand roubles he had had from her. But Aunt Kumanina having actually departed this life and her will coming up for probate, he felt differently about the matter. In addition to the Dostoevskys, the will mentioned descendants of a half sister of the deceased. If the Dostoevskys could successfully contest the will as having been drawn up when the testator was not of sound mind, the entire estate would go to them. His former protestations notwithstanding, Dostoevsky, together with his brothers and sisters, instituted proceedings to annul the will. They dealt with two lawyers, both of whom he thought incompetent and one of whom he suspected of being in collusion with the enemy, the other branch of the family. There was thus precipitated a bitter feud, in which he found himself ranged against not only his distant relatives, but his own brothers and sisters, who denounced him as a robber, because, if they won the suit, he would be legally entitled to a share in the estate from which the will excluded him. This, although he assured the family that he was fighting for their interests and would not claim anything beyond the expenses incurred by him in connection with the case. It was settled in favour of the Dostoevskys, but then the situation was further complicated by the fact that the youngest sister, dissatisfied with the arrangements, brought suit against the rest of the family. In February, 1874, Dostoevsky received a little over four hundred roubles, which barely covered his share of the costs. The court also granted him a portion of the tract of land which was all that was left of Aunt Kumanina's substantial estate, and, contrary to his promise, he eventually took possession of it.

Even while this unfortunate lawsuit was in progress, he was engaged with other affairs of a practical nature. He had been nursing the idea of going into the publishing business since his early youth. Now his ambitions had narrowed down to bringing out his own works. He had not been able to find a publisher either for *The Idiot* or *The Possessed* after they had been serialized. With the book trade what it was in Russia, the only way to make his novels pay as they should was to issue them at his own expense. In spite of the grave warnings of friends, Anna enthusiastically embraced the idea, entered into the scheme with her characteristic energy and good sense, and rapidly became the sole factotum in the enterprise. It was decided to issue *The Possessed* first. Its publication was announced in one of the newspapers on January 22, 1873. That morning Dostoevsky rose late, sulky as usual, but after two cups of piping hot coffee he was able to ask Anna cheerfully how the book business was going. When she replied that it was going well, he remarked that she must have sold one copy, whereupon she produced three hundred roubles and a slip of paper showing that she had disposed of one hundred and fifteen copies, for cash, since nine o'clock that morning. The venture was a huge success. Within a twelvemonth they sold three thousand copies. For the next thirty-eight years Anna was to keep up the business of publishing her husband's works.

He had further money-making schemes in his head. While still abroad, he had played with the idea of compiling, on his return home, a reference work of some sort, perhaps in the form of a

POLINA SUSLOVA

year book—Liza, in *The Possessed,* cherishes a similar notion. He had had, too, a plan for starting a newspaper. Now more than ever he needed to make some direct response to the questions that were flung at him by life in Russia. Yet these notions came to nothing for want of funds with which to start the ventures. He was therefore glad to accept the editorship of a weekly owned by his new acquaintance, Prince Meshchersky, at a salary of three thousand a year, with additional payments for whatever contributions he might make.

Grazhdanin (The Citizen), as the paper was inappropriately called, had been founded the previous year by that young aristocrat as an organ of reactionary opinion. In one of its first issues it called for an end to the liberal reforms with which the reign had opened. The prince had the highest connections—he was on friendly terms with the heir apparent—and an inordinate ambition for journalistic laurels, but limited funds and a more limited mentality. He was, besides, championing a most unpopular cause. As a result, the paper, which counted among its few subscribers chiefly ecclesiastics and members of the court circle, was dragging on an inglorious existence, the butt of the press generally. It was this leaky ship, flying the colours of the aristocratic clique, that the former political prisoner, the author of humanitarian stories, the intellectual proletarian, the Christian democrat, engaged to captain.

I I

Dostoevsky entered upon his duties at the end of 1872. His decision to edit *Grazhdanin* was another instance of his capacity for getting himself into wrong situations. He had been at it only a few weeks when he cursed himself for having shouldered this responsibility. He was totally unfit for a task that required steady application and businesslike regularity. Moreover, the circumstances under which he worked were extremely trying. Although he was nominally the sole responsible head of the publication, in practice the owner, who was also a prolific contributor, insisted on exercising his prerogatives and interfered at every turn. The crotchety prince, whose wretched writings Dostoevsky had to spend hours licking into shape, neither respected his editor's opinions nor spared

his feelings. There would be wrangling and procrastination through
the week, and then all-night sessions in order to bring the issue out
on time. And there were a thousand minor vexations. The owner
allowed only scanty funds for running the paper, and as a result the
people with whom the editor had to deal were frequently careless
and disagreeable. And even a patriotic publication, exempt from
preliminary censorship, could not avoid trouble with the authorities.
Dostoevsky had not been at his duties a month when he failed to
comply with some minor censorship regulation, and accordingly
was sentenced to forty-eight hours in jail. He served his term over
a year later, relieving the tedium by reading *Les Misérables* and
listening to the keeper's admiring comment on *Crime and Punishment.* In the autumn the sale of the weekly was suspended because
of an article criticizing the Government's handling of the famine
situation in a certain province. There were things that Dostoevsky,
for all his loyalty to his sovereign, could not stomach. Later on,
an article against a *bête noire* of his, the Russians of German ex-
traction, who were favoured in high places, again brought down the
wrath of the authorities.

The summer was the most trying time. The family was at
Staraya Russa, but he, chained to the editorial desk, had to stay
in the capital. The city was hot, dusty, deserted. He was alone. He
missed Anna terribly, and the sight of the empty beds in the nursery
hurt him. When there was a cool spell, he worried lest the
children catch cold. He kept wondering if they were forgetting
him. He dreamed of them: frightful nightmares in which little
Fedya fell out of a fourth-storey window, or in which Luba, orphaned and in the clutches of a wicked woman, was being flogged
to death with heavy rods such as were used in punishing soldiers,
and, at her last gasp, was crying: "Mamochka! Mamochka!" The
nightmares drove him half mad, for he believed firmly in premonition. For years his nights had been wrecked by terrifying dreams
of fires, assassinations, and bloody battles. He did pay flying visits
to the family, but good as it was to be with them, the trip tired him
and the pressure of extra work on his return exhausted him. He
did not get enough sleep and was often feverish. Sometimes he
had to work in the twilight state that followed an attack, and nearly
fainted at the end of a long session. He did not know how he held

out. Moreover, his salary and income from the sale of *The Possessed* notwithstanding, he was still making trips to the pawnbroker, and the debts were mounting.

One of the few satisfying contacts that he had during those dreary weeks was with Pobedonostzev. The senator, who had recently been honoured by an appointment to the Imperial Council, went out of his way to show his interest in the editor and to give him the benefit of his advice, to the end of helping a publication which sought to stem the tide of reforms. He even contributed anonymously to its pages. Dostoevsky could not but have been flattered by these attentions from a man of such eminence.

There was yet another person who relieved his loneliness. Often that summer he worked not in his study or at the editorial offices, but in the printing house, where he would read proof, edit manuscripts and even do some of his own writing. He was drawn there by the presence of a young woman, the proof-reader. She strikingly resembled his first wife and, like more than one of the women to whom he was attracted, was touched by the liberal notions of the time. For her part, the girl did not find this haggard, tense, distrustful, peevish man easy to work with. Her early experiences with him were distinctly disagreeable. He took an unmannerly pleasure in vexing her. And though he seemed locked within himself and perfectly controlled, he could rage like a boy in a tantrum.

As the weeks went by, a kind of intimacy sprang up between them. There were still days when he would come in, with the slow, dragging gait of one who had worn irons, in a mood so black that she dared not approach him. Sometimes he would plague her with questions about herself and freeze if she attempted to retort in kind. Here was an overbearing, intolerant man, who demanded nothing less than one's complete adherence to his way of thinking. But there was at least one moment when his pettiness and crustiness fell away, and he surprised her with the face of the genius she reverenced, young, radiant with animation, noble with spiritual power. There were times when he was genial and open with her, and they would talk freely, though there was always the risk of his snarling if the sceptic in her peeped out. If she caught him muttering to himself and gesticulating, she would know that he was dramatizing a scene preparatory to writing down a bit of dialogue.

Occasionally they would sit over the ill-smelling galleys deep into the small hours, the room in darkness except where a single kerosene lamp shone on their work, on the pale, heated faces, and on his lean, knotty-fingered hand crushing another cigarette butt in the sardine-tin overflowing with ashes. At the end of one such late session, as the exhausted proof-reader was preparing to go home, he noted her bedraggled look and was put in mind of a story he had heard (or more probably invented), which he proceeded to relate. Some young men, walking through the streets late at night in an exalted mood and reciting Schiller, came upon a prostitute and were so outraged by her appearance that they spat at her. Dostoevsky observed that, at this hour and in this state, his companion, the honest working-girl, might be mistaken for such a woman—truly, he wished that she were and that he might go to court along with her and make, oh, such a speech, against her virtuous defamers!

One night in June, having pressed her to admit that this world was but the threshold to other worlds, he repeated after her in an unforgettable voice: "To other worlds!" and lifted his arms in an ecstatic gesture toward the transparent summer sky, crying out what a glorious, what a tormenting thing it was to speak to people of those worlds beyond this. Again, he broke off his work to say to her, in the tone of one revealing a great and terrible secret: "And these liberals don't even suspect that soon there will be an end to everything . . . to all their progresses and chatter! They don't know that the Antichrist is already born . . . and his coming is near!" When his companion failed to show complete acquiescence in his belief, he struck the table with his fist and shouted with prophetic fervour: "The Antichrist is coming! Coming! And the end of the world is near at hand, nearer than people think!" It was to be half a century before Dostoevsky's world came to an end.

With the return of the family from Staraya Russa in the autumn, home became a cheerful place again. There was, moreover, something of a social life for Dostoevsky. He joined the Association of Lovers of Religious Education and the Slavic Charitable Society, went now and then to their meetings, and enlarged the circle of his acquaintances. It now included a learned, pious, and charming youth who was the son of the greatest Russian historian then living, and the brother of one of Dostoevsky's most passionate admirers. The flowing locks, pale face, and deep eyes of this Vladimir Solovyov made him look like Annibale Caracci's Christ, Dostoevsky believed, and reminded him, too, of the companion of his youth, Shidlovsky. Indeed, his intense spirituality, his amorousness, his fits of childlike laughter, his verse-making, his devotion to philosophy, combined to make him seem to the older man the very reincarnation of that lost friend.

As for his work, it was scarcely less of a burden than it had been during the summer. Instead of proving the relatively easy and agreeable affair he had expected, it sapped his energies and gave him nothing in return. There were not infrequent clashes with the owner of the paper. One day Prince Meshchersky sent in an article in which he recommended the establishment of cheap, attractive dormitories for students, to the end of preventing the spread of revolutionary propaganda among them. The dormitories, the author pointed out, would be advantageous to the students, and would enable the Government to keep them under surveillance. Using his editorial authority, Dostoevsky deleted the lines about the opportunity that this arrangement would give the Government to spy upon the youth. "I have the reputation of a man of letters," he wrote to the prince, "and besides, I have children. I don't intend to ruin myself. Moreover," he concluded, in a line that he struck out, "your idea is wholly contrary to my convictions, and cuts me to the heart." One suspects that this was not the only occasion when Dostoevsky's views were at variance with those that prevailed in the *Grazhdanin* circle.

As "the accursed year," so he described it in a letter to Anna, drew to an end, life became a nightmare. There was nothing for him but to resign the editorship, which he did with a sigh of relief.

III

In spite of all the attendant difficulties, Dostoevsky's journalistic activities afforded him a distinct satisfaction. The pages of *Grahz-*

danin gave him an opportunity to present some of his convictions —hitherto confined to private communications—directly and unequivocally, as he could not in his fictions. At last he had a chance to speak his mind plainly on matters that interested him. Every week or so he contributed a piece under the general title, *A Writer's Diary*, in which he offered chatty comment on any subject that struck his fancy. These fugitive pieces, like his later work as a publicist, are of small interest in themselves, but they should be accorded a measure of attention for the light they throw upon his personality and upon his fictional writings. The diary is a prolix and rather dull medley of reminiscence and anecdote, opinion and invective, observation and prophecy. The tone is always personal, informal, at once dogmatic and uncertain. The diarist asserts, anticipates objections, modifies his assertion, shifts his ground, returns to the original assertion.

Only occasionally do the dusty pages glow with life when, abandoning opinion and reportage, he notes the fancies that pass through his mind as he walks the Petersburg streets on a summer Sunday, trying to pierce the masks of the passers-by. Again, he gives free rein to his imagination and draws little sketches that might be cartoons for his canvases: a man of the people who drives his wife to suicide; a widowed workman and his little boy on a Sunday visit to a relative; a young peasant who, accepting a blasphemous challenge, is about to shoot at the Host, but has a vision of the Crucifixion, collapses in a dead faint, and spends the rest of his life in penance. Once, for want of more suitable copy, Dostoevsky offered his readers a macabre skit, in which the narrator overhears the conversation of the denizens of a cemetery. Assuming that some sort of life goes on in the grave for a short while, the dead are shown planning to spend the period of respite in unbridled debauchery, such as the restraints of life on earth had denied them. A humble tradesman is the only decent soul among these lecherous corpses.

Repeatedly the discussion revolves around the peculiar genius of the Russian people. The features of the nation's psychology, as marked by the diarist, show a suspiciously striking resemblance to the lineaments of his own nature. The Russians, one learns, know no measure, whether sinning or repenting; they are apt to trample upon the very things they hold sacred; they are the chastest and most foul-mouthed people; the abyss summons them, and embracing self-destruction they leap into it; their deepest need is suffering—without it even their happiness is incomplete. In their anguish they are sustained by the love of Christ, whom they adore. Dostoevsky was speaking, of course, of the unspoiled masses. "Thirst for *pravda* (righteous truth)" is also theirs. "The delicate reciprocity of lying," another Russian characteristic, presumably applies to the educated classes only. Dostoevsky notes ominous signs of demoralization among the common people, but is not disturbed: secure in their Orthodox faith, they will be saved: "Light and salvation will shine forth from below." In denouncing the laxity of the new courts, he points out that the Russian masses entertain a truly Christian view of crime: it is not his environment, but his own evil will that makes the criminal, yet the community shares the moral responsibility for the crime—the guilt lies equally upon all. This may or may not have been the belief of the people, but it was that of Dostoevsky, whose self-identification with all criminals may well have been one way of acknowledging his own unappeasable sense of guilt.

He loses no opportunity to lash out at "the leaders of European progressive thought," at all these Mills, Darwins, Strausses. In the heads of their Russian followers, he laments, their materialistic theories turn into "adamantine axioms." He is willing to concede that, while these men spurn religion, their intentions are "humanitarian and majestic." But, he insists, give them a chance to build a new society, and the result would be "such darkness, such chaos, something so crude, blind and inhuman," that the edifice would be cursed out of existence before it was finished. The mind, having rejected the guidance of Christ, it bound to go astray—"that is an axiom."

The essayist tries his hand at literary and even at art criticism, and he comments at length on a temperance play. When he looks backward, his attention is centred on outstanding men he had known. There is a warped passage about Herzen, "the born expatriate," alienated from his land and its ideals. The decidedly good-natured account of the author's few meetings with Chernyshevsky contrasts with the biased pages about his contacts with Belinsky. An enthusiastic believer in ethical socialism, a worshipper of reason, an atheist rejecting Christianity as "a false and ignorant humanitarianism condemned by modern science and economic principles"—such is Dostoevsky's picture of his former master. He offers a retrospective estimate of the Petrashevists, too. Like the rest of them, he states, he had been infected with "theoretical social- ism" that saw things "in a pink and paradisally-moral light," and dominated minds and hearts "in the name of some generosity." And yet, under proper conditions, he asserts, he and the others could have become the followers of that monster, Nechayev. In any event, as they stood on the scaffold listening to their death sentence, they felt anything but repentance.

Besides the Diary, in the latter part of his incumbency Dosto- evsky contributed reviews of foreign affairs, partly a matter of shears and paste. He gave most of his attention to France, where the issue between the legitimists and the republicans was then hang- ing in the balance. He is not content with the rôle of a mere chronic- ler. He seeks to go beneath the surface, reading a religious meaning into the political drama. His reflections, however, are sometimes as unrealistic as they are unenlightened. The journalist is apt to retire abruptly, to reappear wearing the mantle of the prophet and uttering warnings, predictions, dark oracles. He sees in the conflict between Church and State in Germany the preliminary skirmish in the coming struggle between God and the new society that seeks to usurp His place. The Franco-Prussian war is to him a clash between the Catholic and Protestant civilizations, a clash bound to recur again and again. He intimates that the royalist movement in France may be really a gigantic international scheme to restore the tem- poral power of the Pope. Should he fail here, he will join forces with the proletarians and embrace communism, for the Catholic Church would rather see Christianity perish than surrender its secular dominion. But that "lofty soul," Henri V, the claimant to the French throne, should know that his mission is not to save the worldly power of the Church, but to give battle to Antichrist, who is even now at the gates. Only by restoring her to Christ could France be saved from the evil effects of her revolution. But can she be saved at all? Has the source of her life dried up? Perhaps, Dostoevsky hints broadly, another great nation is destined to lead Western humanity.

CHAPTER TWENTY-THREE

THE TONGUE OF ADOLESCENCE

I T TOOK Dostoevsky several months to wind up the red tape connected with his resignation from *Grazhdanin,* so that it was only in April, 1874, that he was again a free man. While he had been slaving away at his editorial duties, he had told himself that he would need a long rest before he could take up his own work in earnest. But he was to know no respite. He was still in harness when he set to thinking seriously about, and jotting down notes for, another novel. Momentarily the new work presented itself to him as a "fantastic poem-novel" which he sketched out thus: "Future society, commune, uprising in Paris, victory, 200 million heads, terrible plagues, depravity, destruction of art, of libraries, a tortured child. Wrangling, lawlessness. Death." But his mind quickly turned away from such remote scenes to others nearer home, characters resembling Myshkin or Stavrogin, to figures out of *The Life of a Great Sinner,* all enveloped in an atmosphere reeking with the odour of a "chemically disintegrating" society. These images were as yet fluid and an acceptable plot was still to take shape.

But suppose Katkov had already stocked up on fiction for the coming year. Where could he go with his novel? Before he had a chance to communicate with the editor of *Russky vestnik,* however, he received a visit from Nekrasov, of all people—Nekrasov with whom he had fallen out so many years ago, and whose path since then had diverged completely from his own. For some time now the man had been editing *Fatherland Notes,* the review in which Dostoevsky's early work had appeared, and had succeeded in turning it into the successor to *Sovremennik,* which had been suppressed by the authorities. Anna, overcome with curiosity as to what had brought the distinguished visitor to their humble dwelling, did not hesitate to eavesdrop and was astonished to hear the editor of the

315

great liberal review ask her husband to give him his next novel, naming a much higher rate than the one paid by Katkov. Nekrasov was not the man to let his political opinions stand in the way of capturing an important author.

Dostoevsky replied that he was under moral obligation to offer his work to Katkov first, but should there be no place for it in *Russky vestnik*, he was ready to give it to Nekrasov's review. The higher rate was a great temptation. He then went to see Katkov in Moscow and found him willing to go as high as Nekrasov, but unable to offer an advance, inasmuch as he had just bought *Anna Karenina* for publication the following year. Regretfully Dostoevsky parted from the man who had so long been his publisher and agreed to turn over his novel, *A Raw Youth*, to the liberal review.

Spring was now well under way, and with the help of the sizeable sum he had received from Nekrasov he was able to take the family to Staraya Russa. They were back in the same house in which they had summered the previous year. Situated on the outskirts of the town, it was more like a cottage in the country, with its flowers, its fruit trees, its vegetable garden, the detached bathhouse in which Dostoevsky could steam himself. When his little daughter grew up to be a woman she still remembered the tiny rooms furnished in Empire mahogany, the mysterious mirrors, green with age, the trapdoors and winding stairs, and recognized some features of the place in the house where old Karamazov was murdered. The family liked this retreat so well that they kept returning to it season after season and, in the end, bought it from the owner's heirs.

From Staraya Russa Dostoevsky went to Ems in June for the cure. For some time he had been suffering from an affection of the lungs, which may have been aggravated by his spending long hours in the overheated plant where *Grazhdanin* was printed and thence going into the cold and damp of the Petersburg winter.

Ems was romantically situated in a pleasant valley, but the prices, the prices! To be in time at the spring, he had to rise with the whole town at six o'clock, which meant that he must retire at ten, and how then could he write? Surely not when the sun was blazing in the streets and his fellow lodgers were noisily going about their business. But it was not really a question of writing yet; he was only drawing up the preliminary plan, and he could make very little headway. Possibly he was no longer capable of writing. Perhaps his attacks had robbed him not only of his memory, but of his imagination as well. But no, it was still active enough; when he looked over his notes, he realized that his scheme was suffering not from poverty, but from superabundance: he was trying to squeeze the stuff of four novels into one. But there was still time. If only he could shape a workable plot, the rest would follow easily.

But after all, he had come here not to write, but to take the waters. He did so, conscientiously and resentfully, hating everything —the crowd, offensive Germans and no less disgusting Russians, that pushed and shoved around the *Kurhaus*; the band music that always began with a dull Lutheran hymn; the climate; the food. Before he left he had come to abominate every house, every bush, and looked on everyone he met in the street as a personal enemy. When he compared this fashionable resort, frequented alike by the German emperor and his own tsar, with the Omsk prison, he decided that as a convict he had been better off.

There was one thing to be said for Ems—his health did benefit by the cure. What interfered with the treatment was two severe epileptic attacks, which were all the more discouraging since the seizures now occurred less frequently: on the average, once every six weeks. Nothing else was to be expected of such a vile hole as this.

He was horribly homesick. He worried about the children. He longed for Anna, though for one brief period, perhaps the first in his life, as he put it, he felt like a mummy. He thought about her continually—she had every virtue, he wrote to her, except that she was a little absent-minded, and slovenly. He assured her that she need not fear that he would be unfaithful: he wanted her and no one else; he simply could not think of another woman; yes, there was an end to all that; habit had become too strong for him; he was a family man once and for all. She must have feared that he would succumb to temptation of another sort: What was to prevent him from rushing off to the tables? But he didn't. He stuck it out at Ems and left with his chest condition improved and with two alternate outlines for his novel. Before returning home he went to visit the little grave in the Geneva cemetery and took some cypress twigs from there to Anna. He also brought her some black silk for a gown.

He was back with the family at Staraya Russa in August. He was facing a period of strenuous work. Would his health hold out? And would they scrape along? The advance on the forthcoming novel would soon have been spent, and he could get no more out of the tight-fisted Nekrasov until he had a substantial amount of copy to show. The money that had been trickling in from the sales of *The Possessed* and *The Idiot,* published early in the year, was a drop in the bucket. What worried him most of all was that Nekrasov would insist on deleting from his unwritten manuscript certain passages inconsistent with the liberal tendency of the review. In such an event, there would be nothing for him to do but withdraw his work and refund the advance, God knows how. And where would he take his book? They must economize, and speedily. At Anna's suggestion, they decided to winter at Staraya Russa, thus saving on rent and living expenses and providing Dostoevsky with quiet in which to work. She also looked forward to having more of him than winters at the capital gave her.

During the months that followed, the lower story of the spacious old house on Ilyinskaya Street, where they established themselves, was the scene of domestic joys and earnest work. Of course, he was never free from the threat of an epileptic attack. He had a violent seizure on December 28, at eight o'clock in the morning, in bed. He described his state of mind on regaining consciousness in these broken words: "Felt troubled, sad; remorse and fantastic mood. Was very irritable." He recorded in detail another fit which struck him down April 6 of the following year. It occurred half an hour after midnight and was preceded by a strong premonition. He had just rolled some cigarettes and was pacing the floor, when he dropped in the middle of the room, remaining unconscious about forty minutes. When he came to, he found himself sitting at his desk, pen in hand, and noted that he had rolled four cigarettes in an unconscious state—an instance of the automatism that usually follows the seizure. He had a headache and pain in his sides and legs, and the fear of death was so strong in him that he dared not lie down. An hour later he tried to write an account of the attack, but could scarcely marshal the words.

The seizures came at irregular intervals. When the attack was delayed, he and Anna would await it anxiously. Concealing her fears, she would try to watch her husband without his noticing it. He might drop anywhere. Once he was almost drowned in the bathtub. They would place a mattress next to the couch on which he slept, in case he should have a seizure in his sleep and roll off. When she heard the eerie cry that preceded the fit—it rang in her ears after thirty-five years—she would rush over to him and draw his head down to her breast, lest he hurt it in falling, and stuff a handkerchief into his mouth so as to prevent him from biting his tongue.

That winter at Staraya Russa, however, was a singularly peaceful one. Anna and the children kept well, and his cough was better. Never had life been so quiet, so orderly, so like the monotonous existence of a respectable burgher; never had he been so much the good family man. He would give the children sweets, romp with them, and, to distract the little girl, who was given to weeping, would get up a mazurka of an evening, in which the whole family participated. As darkness settled over the sleepy town, he would tell them fairy tales or read them fables. They had, he thought, sensitive, poetic natures, and he was pleased by it, as long as they didn't take to this accursed business of writing. At bedtime he always came in to give them his blessing and say their prayers with them, preferring the little prayer of his own childhood: "All my hopes I place in thee, Mother of God; shelter me under thy mantle." It was only late at night, after the children had long been asleep, and Anna, having played her customary games of patience, had been sent to bed, that the good burgher was changed into the rapt writer. He worked into the small hours, the only interruption being the sound of the fire alarm—conflagrations were frequent and apt to wipe out whole blocks. He would rouse Anna when he heard the signal, and while he reconnoitred, she would dress the children and pack the manuscripts. But the scourge spared them.

In the afternoon Anna would make a fair copy of what he had written the previous night for his revision. He knew, as she had once said, that she did not understand his business, and she sometimes admitted that what he dictated was incomprehensible to her, yet he valued her criticism as that of a candid common reader. By October he was able to inform Nekrasov that he could definitely count on having the novel the following year. Indeed, the first instalment was being set up in the latter part of December. Just then it became a matter of public knowledge that *Anna Karenina* was to run the next year in *Russky vestnik*, and Dostoevsky was overcome by the fear that Nekrasov, knowing that his author's market was closed, would make him dance to his piping. He insisted to Anna that, even if he had to beg in the streets, he would not sacrifice a single line where his convictions were concerned. His fears of editorial interference proved groundless, however, and the first instalment of *A Raw Youth* appeared in the issue of the review for January, 1875.

Once during the winter and once again in the spring Dostoevsky went to Petersburg to see the editor, chiefly with a view to securing further advances. Nekrasov, who liked the novel, was friendly and even generous. His old cronies, Maikov and Strakhov, however, struck him as rather chilly. Were they vexed with him for having sold himself to the enemy? Well, Maikov would come round in the end, but Strakhov, he wrote home, was "a dirty seminarist and nothing more." He'd played the deserter once before, after the failure of *Epokha*, and then come running back upon the success of *Crime and Punishment*. There was another fly in the ointment during Dostoevsky's winter trip to the capital: he had to listen to praise of *Anna Karenina* on all sides. He read the current instalment under the bell—he was taking compressed air treatments— and found the novel nothing extraordinary,—indeed, "rather dull." And to think that the count was getting just double his own rates for this stuff!

Soon after his second visit to Petersburg Dostoevsky went to Ems again for a repetition of the cure. Once more there was a succession of dreary weeks filled with boredom, homesickness, anguished fears. He had left Anna in a delicate condition, and for some reason she thought she was going to present him with twins. He was worried about himself, he was worried about the family. He tried to find comfort by reading the book of Job and was filled with an ecstasy that brought him close to tears. He had to work—there wasn't a line written for the August instalment of the novel—he couldn't work, and besides he ought not to work: it might interfere with the cure. Still, he made an effort, producing nothing. The subscribers would simply have to wait till the following month. Once he was back home, he would get on with the book. Perhaps the novel was a failure, but no matter; his powers were still with him, he would do something yet.

Indeed, when he was back at Staraya Russa he was able to make progress with the novel in spite of the interruption caused by the birth of the baby. It was a boy, and they called him Alexey, for Saint Alexey, Man of God, whom Dostoevsky particularly revered. They stayed in the country till autumn, and on a fine Indian-summer day returned to Petersburg. The trip, for a family including two small children and an infant, as well as a wagonload of household goods, was no simple matter. They had to travel part of the way by steamer, and as the harbour was too shallow for the boat, the passengers went out to board it. Stout peasant women offered their broad backs, for a consideration, to those ladies and gentlemen who were too squeamish to wade to the rowboats that took them to the steamer. Having been the first to be thus transported, Dostoevsky stood in the boat and received, one after another, the children, who were screaming with fear. In the confusion the travellers almost lost the precious chest containing the manuscript of the next instalment of the novel. But they managed to reach the capital safely. There, in spite of the disturbance of settling in a new apartment, Dostoevsky succeeded in finishing the final section of the novel, which appeared in the November and December issues of the review.

II

Dostoevsky's first tale, written in his early manhood, dealt with the tragedy of a broken-down middle-aged clerk; now, himself a middle-aged man, he was attempting, in *A Raw Youth*, to speak with the tongue of adolescence. Miraculously, he succeeded. What freshness there was in the writing, and that coming from a man past fifty, Nekrasov said to the author, on reading the first part of the novel in proof. Indeed, what one might expect Dostoevsky to have learned—sobriety in the invention and handling of his plot and his characters, economy of means, and clarity of thought—is missing;

but what the years might well have erased—understanding of a boy's heart, a sense of the urgent heat, of the anguish of youth—is triumphantly there.

The story is in effect a partial autobiography of the "raw youth," an account of a crucial year, the twentieth, in Arkady's life. It is set down with a mixture of brusqueness, tenderness, and spluttering bravado that admirably conveys a turbulent emotionalism struggling with a shamed consciousness of *naïveté* and inexperience. Although bearing the name of his mother's legal husband, a former serf, the boy is really the son of a gentleman, and he is painfully aware of his false position. He had a neglected childhood, and at boarding school (a thinly disguised and blackened picture of Souchard's or Ghermak's) suffered untold humiliations to which he responded by further abasing himself before his tormentors. All the while he was remaking the world in his imagination and withdrawing into himself, consumed by a longing for his true father, an idealized image of whom he had built up in his heart.

He was still at school when he conceived his "Idea": he would deliberately cut himself off from all human associations and dedicate himself to the systematic accumulation of the wealth of a Rothschild, not for the sake of the power that it would bring, but for the mere consciousness of such power. This "Idea" was an old conception of Dostoevsky's—a variant of it may be traced back through *The Life of a Great Sinner* and *The Idiot* to the early story, "Mr. Prokharchin." On the one hand, Arkady's project is a compensation for his humiliating circumstances; on the other, it offers the attractions of an ascetic discipline. On graduation he proceeds to carry out his plan, when he receives a summons from his real father, Versilov, to come to Petersburg. Without abandoning his "Idea," he sets off for the capital, drawn there by the dream of finding and at last possessing his father, and with vague notions of punishing him for his sins and avenging him on his enemies. Yet another motive impels him: into the lining of his coat is sewn a document which delivers into his power a young widow of high rank and great beauty between whom and Versilov there is an obscure and potent bond. In Petersburg young Arkady is certain to meet this Katerina Nikolayevna Akhmakova and to triumph over her.

Upon his arrival there develops a complicated series of events which, though presented with a concern for realistic precision, are in the main crude and tangled melodrama. The document in Arkady's possession is desperately sought by Katerina Nikolayevna because, were it shown to the wealthy old prince, her father, she would be disinherited; by Versilov's legitimate daughter (Arkady's half sister) who wishes to marry the doddering old man for his money; by Versilov himself as a weapon in his weird combat of love-hate with the beautiful widow. The plot entails seductions, suicides, threatened duels, gambling, a legal contest over a will, with blackmailers, counterfeiters, and political conspirators enlivening the scene. Directly or indirectly, the raw youth is involved in the interplay of these greeds and lusts.

When he catches his first glimpse of the enchanting lady, she snubs him cruelly, but he feels himself protected from her insults by his possession of the letter which puts her in his power; moreover, the hatred he thought he bore her dissolves into a tenderness for her as his potential victim. This emotion develops into a passion which has all the feverish excitement and rarefied exaltation of adolescent love.

Not for a moment does the boy cease to hunger secretly for his father. When he first came to Petersburg, he did not know whether he hated or loved him, but his whole being was bound up with him, and he was continually trying to puzzle out the mystery of his character. The boy's pent-up resentment finally finds vent in an indignant outburst against Versilov, in which he bids his mother choose between this man and himself. Yet when Versilov glances at him with hatred, he rejoices, knowing that at last his father has taken serious notice of him. One generous gesture on the man's part is enough to make his son's repressed love for him find release, and, the father taking the first step towards him, the boy flings himself into his arms. He throws himself upon his new-found parent "like a starving man upon bread," idolizes him, tyrannizes over him, and yet still withholds some part of his confidence. As for Versilov, he is tender towards his son and treats him with a kind of patient wisdom, but also has his reserves.

Arkady comes in contact with all manner of people, including a set of young radicals, with whom he is out of sympathy, and an original of Kirillov's stripe whom he—and, one feels, his creator, too—deeply admires. This young man, having convinced himself that the Russians are a second-rate people, with no rôle to play in history, commits suicide. What with one interest and another absorbing him, Arkady allows his Rothschild "Idea" to fall into abeyance. He is so sure of his devotion to it that he can permit himself to drop it temporarily without compunction. His plan, he believes, is not so much an idea, as what he calls an "idea-feeling": a theory so transfused by emotion as to be impermeable to reason and only to be dislodged by a stronger feeling. Far from following the ascetic discipline upon which he had resolved, he plunges into a life of easy excitements, playing the dandy and gambling, all on borrowed money. He is weak in the knowledge of good and evil, and instinct is a doubtful guide. What now makes him walk on air is the sudden graciousness towards him of the beautiful Katerina Nikolayevna. He cannot keep his transport to himself and makes a clean breast of it to his father, only to discover with horror that in this enigmatic man he has a rival! One blow follows another, until the curtain of illness mercifully falls between him and the consciousness of his degradation.

During his convalescence Arkady suddenly encounters his nominal father, the pious vagabond, Makar Ivanovich, who is on one of his rare visits to his "family." Dostoevsky had proclaimed often enough that the Russian masses were alone the vessel of the true religion. In Makar he attempted to present a concrete embodiment of the faith by which the people lived. Like the hero of *The Idiot*, he exemplifies the Christian virtues of humility, non-resistance, and selfless love, a saintliness which he has not attained through sin, but which is native to him. But while Myshkin has an aristocratic background, Makar is a former house serf, a servant and the son of a servant, with the superstitions and prejudices of his class. His place in the pattern is that of a foil for the divided souls that people the novel. But he has the artificiality of a figure contrived to illustrate a theory. His serenity, in contrast to the mad passions of the others, fails to be impressive, because he is outside of life, not coping with its problems.

Arkady is at once drawn to the old pilgrim, who has now come to the end of his journeys. "He has something firm in life, and all

the rest of us here haven't anything firm in life to stand on," cries
the boy in defence of the old man, when someone, with invidious
intention, calls him a tramp. The firm thing in Makar's life is an
orderly, a religious view of the universe, a humble happy sense of
his own place in it, and therewith a serene acceptance of life and
death. It is just this dignity, a decorum religious in its basis and
producing a kind of aesthetic satisfaction, what Arkady calls "seemliness," that he admires in the old man. Usually the adolescent
strives to cut loose from the familiar, familial, "seemly" background; the raw youth, on the contrary, mortified since childhood
by the irregularity of his position, yearns to achieve a father, a
family background, a comforting sense of "seemliness."

His enthusiasm for his nominal father moves the boy to another
indignant outburst against his real father, and not having fully recovered from his illness, he suffers a relapse. In his delirium he has
a dream; his beautiful lady enters, abject fear in her face, and fawns
upon him, in the hope of gaining the document which is in his hand;
he flings it to her contemptuously, and is about to leave her when
Lambert, a former schoolmate turned professional blackmailer,
eggs him on with a leer to demand "the ransom"; on seeing them
together, the woman who had given him such exalted moments is
suddenly transformed into a lewd creature; his first horror, his
disgust and pity at once give away to a new feeling "strong as the
whole world"; he savours the shamelessness of it as he answers the
invitation of her insolent lips.

The youth perceives clearly the significance of this dream and
interprets it in a fashion that anticipates psychoanalytic theory. It
reveals to him that for all the urgency and sincerity of his moral
yearning, there is in him a secret lust for what he feels to be depraved—that he has "the soul of a spider." The latent desires that
his conscious mind dared not confront were revealed to him in
his dream: ". . . in sleep the soul presented and laid bare all that
was hidden in the heart. . . ." In a story written shortly after this
novel was completed Dostoevsky had the narrator observe: "Dreams
seem to be moved not by reason, but by desire, not by the head, but
by the heart, and yet what complicated tricks my reason has played
sometimes in dreams . . .," and again: ". . . it happened as it always
does in dreams when you skip over space and time, and the laws of

existence and reason, and only pause upon the points for which the heart yearns." Throughout Dostoevsky's work there is scattered evidence that he had an uncanny insight into the nature of dream life.

In his previous dealings with both his father and the lady, Arkady had been strangely disingenious—in the midst of the transports of discovering his father, at the height of the pure ecstasy aroused in him by Katerina Nikolayevna, with "music in his soul," he lies almost casually to them both about the document. It is the dream that discloses to him the dual nature of his impulses. "It has always been a mystery," he reflects, "and I have marvelled a thousand times at that faculty in man (and in the Russian, I believe, more especially) of cherishing in his soul the loftiest ideal side by side with utter baseness, and all quite sincerely."

Arkady's dream is not merely revealing, it is also prophetic. He does not obey his first impulse and destroy the incriminating document; instead he listens with a thirst for shamefulness to Lambert's proposal that they use it to blackmail Katerina Nikolayevna, but with a sudden revulsion of feeling, abandons the plan. It is only when, by eavesdropping, he learns of his father's mad passion for the lady and her ambiguous attitude towards him that he makes common cause with the blackmailer, and decides to demand of her both money and her virtue in exchange for the document. He tells himself that he will show his father the sort she is, and thus save him from his infatuation; actually, he is moved by jealousy of Versilov. Again his better self prevails, and he resolves to surrender the document freely and to effect a general reconciliation, when he discovers that Lambert has stolen the letter. The final scene is as implausible as it is sensational and involves Versilov's frustrated attempt to murder the lady and kill himself. Yet Dostoevsky manages to ring down the curtain on a happy ending.

III

The novel is not confined to the adolescent's oscillations between good and evil. With his usual lack of measure, Dostoevsky brings in another motif, which runs parallel to the first and to some extent overshadows it. It is the story of the raw youth's father,

Versilov. There is an air of enigma, of mystery about him, which is never completely dispelled. His son succeeds only partially in puzzling out the riddle, nor does the reader fare much better. A gentleman of intelligence and cultivation, a man of the world who has managed to run through three fortunes, he is capable of extreme quixoticism as well as of the lowest intrigues, neither consorting with his social position. He is the sort of man to whom queer gossip clings. It is rumoured that at one time he had run after little girls, and again that he had had a phase of religious fervour so intense that he practiced asceticism. Is his the strong, proud nature of one unwilling to bow to man and therefore seeking a God to bow down to? He is evasive about his faith, but on one occasion describes himself as a philosophical deist. At any rate, he is far from being a Christian: he advises his son to shut his eyes and hold his nose in order to love his neighbour, since love him one must, adding: "I believe that man has been created physically incapable of loving his neighbour." (Among the notes Dostoevsky made for the novel there is this jotting, clearly belonging to the same complex of ideas: "Undoubtedly Christ could not love us such as we are. He tolerated us. He forgave us, but, of course. He despised us"). He has none of his creator's violent animus against atheists, but one hears Dostoevsky's voice when Versilov grieves over the way they hiss God and pelt Him with mud, as also when he speaks of the forlorn lot of man, stripped of immorality and orphaned of God, and of the eventual return of Christ, ending with the rapturous hymn that greets "the last resurrection."

While leading a parasitic, meaningless existence, Versilov prates of the spiritual leadership of the class to which he belongs and of his own championship of the Russian idea. The rôle of the nobility is connected in his mind, as it was in Prince Myshkin's, with the mission of his country. This mission is the harmonizing and the reconciling of the separate principles for which each European nation stands. The true Russian gentleman, promenading his melancholy through the declining West, he sees himself as the only good European, worshipping every stone that tradition has hallowed, dreaming of Europe's lost Golden Age (this passage is lifted bodily from the unpublished chapters of *The Possessed*, where the dream is Stavrogin's), and seeing before him its fading sunset. For some unexplained reason Versilov at one time almost committed the cardinal sin of expatriation; it would have been the act of a "crippled" soul, a "book man," a wanderer, with no roots in his native soil (the act of a Raskolnikov or a Stavrogin).

Oddly enough, this homeless aristocrat is made to share Dostoevsky's disgust with the materialistic's solution of the social problem, "turning stones into bread," and rejects what he calls the "Geneva idea," which he aptly sums up as "virtue without Christ." Dostoevsky must have been thinking of the conference of the League for Peace and Freedom that had so outraged him when he attended its sessions in Geneva. It was a characteristic thrust at the socialists, and he allowed himself one more where Arkady, at a gathering of young hotheads in the house of one, Dergachov, repudiates their rational millennium as a thing of "barracks, common lodgings . . . atheism, and common wives without children," and refuses to give up his "entire personality" in exchange for the "mediocre advantage" of their system. The group is rather closely patterned on the Dolgushin circle which, in July, 1874, while Dostoevsky was taking the cure at Ems, was being tried in Petersburg on the charge of having secretly printed and disseminated appeals inciting the masses to rebellion. Whether because Dostoevsky was writing for a liberal periodical, or because he was now able to recall his own youthful errors with some equanimity, the pages about the Dergachov set do not carry the venom that exudes from *The Possessed*.

One of the less successful of Dostoevsky's inventions, Versilov is a wavering, insubstantial, incoherent image that one never quite seizes upon. He lacks the opacity and solidity of a character existing in his own right; he suggests something transparent and fluid in which one sees plainly floating fragments of Dostoevsky's thinking. The one unmistakable feature of his make-up is his duality. He is afflicted with what Myshkin calls "double thoughts," the simultaneous presence of contradictory impulses. "I can with perfect convenience," he observes on one occasion, "experience two opposite feelings at one and the same time, and not, of course, through my own will." On another occasion he describes his state of mind thus: ". . . It is as though my mind split in two. . . . It's just as though your double were standing beside you; you are sensible and rational yourself, but the other self, close beside you, wishes at any cost to do something perfectly senseless, and sometimes something very funny; and suddenly you notice that it is you yourself who wants to do that amusing thing, and goodness knows why; that is, you want to, as it were, against your will; though you fight against it with all your might, you want to." He analyses his condition thus just before he breaks in two pieces the revered icon that Makar, the pilgrim, had bequeathed to him, an act which at once dramatizes his emotional division and represents his rebellion against his moral obligations. Versilov's son, who resembles him in this respect, goes so far as to erect his simultaneous allegiance to good and evil into a "faculty" of the human race, and particularly of his compatriots. There is also another character, the worthless young prince, who is an example of the "roomy" heart. In fact, none of Dostoevsky's other novels offers so thorough a study of emotional ambivalence.

The theory crops up repeatedly in Dostoevsky's writings, that the Russian nature is peculiarly "broad," being able to harbour at the same time contradictory impulses. But when he put forward this notion, was it because he had closely examined his countrymen, or was it because he imagined them to be much like himself? A lady of his acquaintance complained to him that she was plagued by a duality of impulses that compelled her constantly to do things she knew she should not do and left her in a maze from which only an expert psychologist could extricate her. In his reply to her letter, Dostoevsky wrote that this was a trait common to humanity, though perhaps exaggerated in her, adding: "That is why you are akin to me, because this duality of yours is like my own to the dot, and I've had it all my life. It is a great torment, but at the same time a great delight. . . ." He knew of only one remedy: "If you believe (or strongly wish to believe), give yourself wholly to Christ. The torments of this duality will be greatly reduced, and your soul will find release. . . ." Nowhere does he indicate so unambiguously as in these lines, written the last year of his life, the therapeutic function of his own faith or of his will to believe.

Versilov's lack of emotional integration shows itself most clearly in the history of his relations with Katerina Nikolayevna. It is not quite plain how the affair began, and from the first it seems to have been an ambiguous one, in which love and hatred, high-mindedness and baseness, were curiously commingled. When the novel opens the two are far apart, but one gathers that under his professed scorn for her the old passion still glows, while her attitude toward him is one of apparent fear. His son's raptures over her rouse the smouldering fires, and thenceforward his every move testifies to the strife within him of conflicting emotions. Goaded by jealousy, he betrays his son's confidence and writes her an insulting letter, bidding her refrain from seducing the boy. He tries to interfere with her prospective marriage. She writes him a calm and friendly letter asking that their relations be brought to a peaceful end, and he feels miraculously released from his obsession. Almost simultaneously old Makar dies. At last Versilov can marry that gentle creature, the raw youth's mother, who for so long had been his wife in fact but not in name. A new life is about to begin. He has no sooner joyfully announced his intention to his son than he turns around and offers marriage to Katerina Nikolayevna. He sends her the proposal through his legitimate daughter—he is a widower—who is herself plotting to become the lady's stepmother. Katerina Nikolayevna refuses him, but consents to see him. At the meeting he shows himself possessed by passion, while she seems to want nothing but friendship. In his despair and rage he lends his support to the blackmailer, expecting to see her humiliated, and it is when she is confronted by Lambert that Versilov completely loses his self-control and attempts to kill both her and himself, but only inflicts a slight wound on himself.

The object of Versilov's passion is not much more clearly drawn and not much more comprehensible than he. She is guided by sordid considerations and yet is described as a woman of irreproachable purity. She speaks of herself as a peaceful person, liking cheerful companions, and yet as being "a little after Versilov's kind," and, indeed, he tells her that they are "possessed by the same madness." It is the raw youth who discovers in her "the ideal woman," effortlessly perfect, the embodiment of what Versilov called "the living life," something which is the very opposite of the cerebral and theoretical, something so simple, natural, and direct that one fails to notice it and so goes seeking it in impossible places all one's days. The "earthly queen," Katerina Nikolayevna, sometimes seems to be antipodal to that utterly selfless woman, Arkady's mother, who embodies the spiritual principle, so that Versilov, with his emotions divided between the two, is a man torn, as it were, between heaven and earth. He loves the mother of his illegitimate children with a "humane and general love," whereas what he gives Katerina Nikolayevna is "the simple love that one feels for woman." One cannot escape the feeling that Dostoevsky was groping here for a symbolic expression of his more recondite thoughts about man's destiny, but the characters did not compose into a significant pattern—the symbol eluded him.

It has been suggested that Versilov's passion for Katerina Nikolayevna was Dostoevsky's way of symbolizing the striving of this vagrant man to re-establish his bond with his native soil. Such an interpretation is as ingenious as it is dubious. What is less debatable is the primary intention behind the book, the urge that animates it. The novel was still in embryo when Dostoevsky told a friend that he had come out from the shadows of the underground and was now capable of producing a work of a serene and healing character. Certainly, *A Raw Youth,* unlike *The Idiot* and *The Possessed,* offers an attempt at a happy ending. The event toward which this creation appears to move is the healing of a sick spirit, the exorcism of a demon, the regeneration of a man. When the story opens the raw youth is "a bundle of all kinds of *amour propre,*" as he describes himself, dedicated to his inhuman "Idea." The experiences of the year with which the book deals results in drawing him away from his madness; the very recording of them helps to effect the re-education of the young man. A new life is beginning for him, but, as in the case of Raskolnikov, this is merely indicated, and no attempt is made to depict it.

As for Versilov, at first he had been conceived as another Stavrogin, and he was to have had the same fate. In the end, however, the novelist had decided to make him not a "cold" atheist, like that lost soul, but a "hot" one, an anguished unbeliever. Therein lies the secret of his salvation. His bullet wound healed, he begins to lead a new life—the catastrophe has been for him a spiritual catharsis. His marriage to Arkady's mother is in abeyance, but one is given to understand that he will never leave her side and that he is free of his passion for Katerina Nikolayevna. He has become wonderfully softened and sweet-natured and has received what the old pilgrim, speaking of a sinner's conversion, had once called "the gift of tears." One leaves him as he sits beside his lifelong companion, stroking her hair, kissing her hands, and "with the light of perfect happiness in his face." Alas, nothing could prove more clearly than this treacly ending that Dostoevsky was incapable of portraying the shriving of a sinner.

CHAPTER TWENTY-FOUR

A WRITER'S DIARY

NOT ALL of *A Raw Youth* had been published, indeed, not all of it had been written, when Dostoevsky came to the desperate conclusion that the novel was "lost," and that it would be "buried with all honours under universal contempt." He was thinking chiefly of the critics, whom he had definitely alienated by *The Possessed*. As a matter of fact, their hostility was somewhat mitigated because *A Raw Youth* appeared in a progressive review. But the author himself must have been even less pleased with his work than usual. This effort, more than previous ones, gave him reason to feel that his performance lagged painfully behind his intention, and that, as Versilov puts it, the thoughts did not always ripen into words. He was never to know the sense of accomplishment, his reach always exceeding his grasp, but he was sustained by a feeling of the great potentialities within him. A few months before his death, when he was deep in *The Brothers Karamazov*, he wrote to an acquaintance: "Just imagine, at moments of inner accounting I am often painfully aware that I have expressed literally not one twentieth part of what I want, and perhaps am able, to say. What saves me is the constant hope that at some future time God will send me so much inspiration and power that I shall express myself more fully, in a word, that I shall utter everything that is locked up in my heart and my imagination."

In some ways, however, *A Raw Youth* could not but be a satisfaction to him. In no other work had he so fully objectified that sense of duality which dogged him all his life, and his straining toward a faith which would integrate his divided self and would give him spiritual health. Besides, the story of *A Raw Youth* was a partial realization of a project he had long had at heart. In Arkady's unprotected childhood, in his dream of isolation and power, in his association with a corrupt schoolmate, in his moments of tenderness and aspiration, in the influence upon him of a saintly old man (his legal father), one recognizes elements that were to have formed part of *The Life of a Great Sinner*. Yet nothing could be further from the serene piety that narrative was to breathe than the violence and sordidness which crowd with melodramatic incident the pages of this novel. Would he ever achieve sufficient inner quietude to write that edifying tale?

Meanwhile, he was not really dispirited. He was fifty-five, and not in the least weary. The years had "flashed by like a dream." He knew that he had only a short time ahead of him, yet he felt, so he wrote to Andrey, as though his life "were only beginning." And here was Andrey's daughter getting married! How well he remembered the night when his father had come to wake him and Mikhail to tell them that their little brother had come into the world. His own children were growing up, and he was practically a grandfather, what with Pasha raising a large family. Dostoevsky learned to his horror that one of the babies had been relegated to a foundling asylum. Marya Dmitrievna's offspring, now a man in his thirties, had not improved with the years. Unable to hold on to a job, he remained a drain on his stepfather's purse and, thanks to his lies, his pretences, his general irresponsibility, an unmitigated nuisance to the end. In spite of everything, Dostoevsky continued to feel a duty toward the black sheep, and indeed, an obstinate affection for him. There was nothing to lessen Anna's dislike of her husband's stepson, and although little Lubov and Fyodor adored the clownish fellow, she did all she could to keep the two households apart.

Whether or not Dostoevsky agreed with his wife in this matter, he certainly wanted only the best influences in his children's lives. He felt that he must exert himself to nourish their minds in these impressionable years, to give them memories that would always sustain them. Naturally, their upbringing was a religious one. He made a point of taking Lubov, while she was a very little girl, to the midnight Easter mass. Her reminiscences present the man who introduced child psychology into literature as a fond, but unimaginative and pedantic parent, bearing some resemblance to his own father. He took the children to the opera and, finding that a comic operetta had been substituted for the serious work on the programme, was about to take them away at once. Only their tearful protests restrained him, and he was annoyed to see that they enjoyed the entertainment. When they were about seven and five years old, he read them Schiller's *Robbers*, a performance that had the natural, if unintended, effect of putting them to sleep. Later on Scott and Dickens were their fare. The first book he gave his little daughter was Karamzin's *History of the Russian State*, the ponderous work that had been read aloud in the family circle in his own childhood.

The fruit of his and Anna's tender nurture was to prove disappointing. Lubov grew into a vain, hysterical, greedy spinster, whose egotism and spitefulness knew no bounds. As her father had suspected, she eventually turned to literature, but produced only a few feeble tales. She spent most of her adult life in health resorts and died, an expatriate, in 1926, a few years after having written a biography of her father that does her no credit. As for Fyodor, a sufferer from depression, allergy and nervous disturbances, he was not without amiable traits. He appears to have been a believer but not to have shared his father's views about Orthodoxy or the Russian people, of whom he had a low opinion. A well-to-do dealer in cotton before the Revolution, he achieved something of a reputation among turfmen with his stables. He died at the age of fifty, leaving one son.

Fortunately, Dostoevsky had no second sight with regard to the future of his children. Their immediate needs were a sufficient cause for anxiety. There were still debts. What should he turn to next? Anna's publishing venture—she had by this time issued several of his novels—was bringing in money, but not enough. He decided that the best step to take would be to resume the *Writer's Diary* he had run as a department in *Grazhdanin*. But now it was to be a wholly independent enterprise, a one-man review, financed and written by himself alone. He looked upon it as a preparation for the big novel that he was projecting. When a friend wrote him deploring the fact that he had engaged on a task unworthy of his powers, he answered that a writer must not only understand his craft, but must also know, "to the last detail and with the utmost precision," the reality that he depicts, and that his work on the *Diary* was a means of keeping abreast of current problems and, particularly, of studying the younger generation. He added that at his age "one can easily lose touch with the times if one relaxes the least bit." This was, however, not his sole motive in undertaking the venture. He also had a vague notion of disseminating his views and rallying a like-minded group around himself.

The unique journal made its début in January, 1876, and thereafter appeared none too regularly every month for two years. Anna, aided by an office boy, acted as business manager and factotum, and occasionally the nursemaid or a stray relative would be pressed into service to help with the work of wrapping, addressing, and mailing.

The period that he devoted to the *Diary*, as far as Dostoevsky's private life was concerned, was unwontedly even and devoid of incident. The summers were spent in the country, the first one, as usual, at Staraya Russa. Again he went to take the cure at Ems. whence he wrote one desperate letter after another to his Anya, his angel, his all, his alpha and omega. He is racked by loneliness, by boredom, by "literary anguish," this time not over the next instalment of a novel but the next issue of the *Diary*. And the waters do not seem to help him. Next summer he must go to Munich; there is a *Wunderfrau* there who cures the incurable; if she fails him, he can always return to Ems. He is tormented by nightmares, by fears of an attack, by anxiety over the children, and by a passionate need of his wife. Separation is becoming increasingly difficult for him. He is in love with Anna all over again and more than ever. It is a new love. He is a new man. Of course, he still has his whims and his hypochondria. How different the two of them are! He, with his simple nature—she so complex, so wide-hearted. The more he thinks about her, the more he marvels at her. She has, he writes her, a "vast intelligence," she could rule a kingdom. For himself he asks nothing better than to be ruled, indeed, enslaved, by her. If she went out more, she would have a whole string of admirers. Jealous as he was, he was prepared to suffer, if only she could have more diversion. Next winter she must certainly get herself fashionable clothes and lead something of a social life.

Next winter she stayed home, attending to her domestic duties and, in addition, acting as business manager for the *Diary*. By the end of the day she was too tired to accompany her celebrated husband to the evening parties that he now began to frequent. Society was in a mood to welcome a literary lion who, for all his queerness, spoke for God and Country, and Dostoevsky, on his part, was not averse to accepting the invitations of aristocratic hostesses. When he returned home, in the small hours, Anna would be up to serve him tea and listen to his account of what had been said and what the ladies wore—he was a poor hand at this, having no eye for colour and being ignorant of the vocabulary of fashion. She had her small pangs of jealousy, but feeling herself to be a mediocre, homely woman, no longer young—she was thirty—was content simply to serve and adore him. She had answered one of his passionate letters from Ems by saying that she was proud to be loved by "the most magnanimous, most noble-hearted, purest, most honest, saintliest of men." She knew she didn't deserve such love. "You are my sun," she had written, "you are up on the mountain, and I am lying below and only worship."

The summer of 1877 he did not take the family to Staraya Russa, but to his brother-in-law's estate in the South, and omitted his usual trip to Ems. He had to leave them in July, however, and go to Petersburg to see an issue of the *Diary* through the press. It was a horrible experience. Upon his arrival he had a seizure in his sleep, so that for several days he worked in a befogged state, and at night the fear of death was heavy upon him—if only he could see them once before the end! And Anya, Anya, after ten years of married life he was still madly in love with her. He missed her furiously, he prayed to her as to an icon. The days were distressing: he had to visit relatives, to settle accounts with booksellers, to run to the printer, to attend to all the worrisome details of mailing the issue, and in the intervals try to clear the house of the cockroaches that infested it. To make a bad matter worse, he did not hear from Anna. At the end of a night of insomnia he found himself pacing the floor in tears, trying to stifle his sobs so as not to be heard by the old servant, who kept screaming in her sleep.

On his way back to the country he made a long detour to visit briefly the village of Darovoye where his childhood summers had been spent. He cursed this trip which was delaying his getting back to the family, but what could he do? He would soon be in no shape to stand the hardships of such a journey, and for the sake of his work he must refresh his remembrance of things past. "If one refused oneself these impressions, how, then, and about what would an author write?" he asked Anna in one of his unhappy letters. It was more than forty years since he had seen the place. He chatted with the peasants, went to see all the spots that stood out in his memory, and walked the road between Darovoye and Chermashnya on which his father had been murdered. The impressions of this visit did assist a work of the imagination which was vaguely shaping itself in his mind and which was soon to occupy him completely. For the present, however, he went on with the *Diary*.

I I

Dostoevsky had started this enterprise with the notion of offering his readers the entries from an actual diary such as might be kept by an author keenly responsive to the passing scene. But he soon realized that this was impossible, and so had to abandon his naïve idea and content himself with something more like conventional journalism. In tone and substance the *Writer's Diary* differs little from his contributions to *Grazhdanin*. Having, however, more space at his disposal here, he could widen the scope of his discussion and elaborate his views more fully, with the result that he involved himself more frequently in contradictions. He skips from one topic to another as fancy leads him, his subject matter ranging from spirit rapping to the science of fortification. As before, he indulges in polemics, and in autobiographical digressions. It is curious that in this *Writer's Diary* he deliberately refrains from commenting on current literature, making an exception of *Anna Karenina*, which he holds up as proof of Russia's national genius. He also touches briefly on *Virgin Soil*, but does not take advantage of this opportunity to remark upon the Populist movement with which Turgenev's novel deals. Indeed, it is noteworthy that in spite of Dostoevsky's avowed eagerness to keep abreast of the times and in spite of his preoccupation with nihilism, the *Diary* scarcely mentions the revolutionary movement which had been growing since the early seventies.

The one occasion that called forth a comment from him was the unprecedented event of December 6, 1876, when a group of students and working men assembled in the capital, before the Kazan

DOSTOEVSKY'S SECOND WIFE

DOSTOEVSKY IN 1880

Last portrait. Photograph taken in Moscow in June, 1880

Cathedral, and raised a red flag bearing the inscription, "Land and Liberty," the slogan of an underground revolutionary organization. Dostoevsky granted that the youth who took part in the demonstration may have been moved by a generous impulse, but he described them scornfully as "a whipped-up herd in the hands of a set of shrewd scoundrels." A year later a group of radical students in Moscow were beaten up by rowdies, and some young men from the university wrote to Dostoevsky asking his opinion of the incident. In his reply he conceded that the youth were animated by a noble spirit. He pointed out, however, that the propagandists who had "gone to the people" had failed because they despised the very masses they were trying to save and, above all, scorned the faith by which these lived. He therefore advised his correspondents, if they really wished to accomplish their ends, to respect the common people as the only healthy part of a rotten social organism, and to believe in God.

The views he had set forth in his earlier attempt at journalism and which are also present, sometimes quite explicitly, in his imaginative writings, are reiterated, in greater detail, in the *Writer's Diary*. It is natural that the problem of crime, which had always absorbed him, should hold a prominent place in these pages. There is lengthy comment on some of the sensational trials of the day, as well as an obvious interest in the more gruesome details of the crimes. The juries and the prestidigitating lawyers, the mechanical justice meted out by the state come in for obloquy. But what Dostoevsky finds particularly revolting is the notion that the criminal is not responsible for his crime, that this is an effect of, and a protest against, the environment, that it can be rooted out simply by abolishing poverty, that it is, in fact, a social disease. No! he cries: "Crime is hidden more deeply in human nature than socialist physicians think." Evil is metaphysical, not a question of nerves or stomach. And then, in at least one noteworthy instance he acted on the very theory that he abominated. He read the account of the trial of a young peasant woman who had attempted to kill her little stepdaughter, and was struck by the fact that she was pregnant at the time. It occurred to him that it was the woman's condition that had led to her act. He said as much in the *Diary;* he went to visit her in prison; his suspicion was confirmed; he made an issue of it.

The fact that she was given a retrial and eventually acquitted on the grounds of temporary insanity was in no small part due to his efforts.

One looks in vain for intellectual consistency here. He will assert that the character of a nation depends on its form of land owner- ship, and interpret the history of France after the revolution and the career of the middleclass in terms acceptable to a Marxist. At the same time he takes the position that religion is the determining factor in the course of human affairs and that history is a battle of "ideas," that is, of the faiths by which the nations live. In the Western world the struggle is between Catholicism, Protestantism, and Eastern Orthodoxy. Since Protestantism is negative in essence and therefore negligible, the conflict resolves itself into that between the worldly dream of Rome and the ideal of the Orthodox Church. Both envisage the ultimate union of mankind, but by what different means! Catholicism, more Roman than Christian, would unite men by force, relying on temporal power. This, Dosto- evsky repeats endlessly, is a betrayal of Christ, a denial of His religion. From the failure of this Judas Church sprang socialism, or communism—the terms are used interchangeably (it will be re- called that the novelist foisted this notion on Prince Myshkin). Dostoevsky had never missed an opportunity to pour out his venom on the socialists; he did not now. They, too, would enslave man- kind, but without pretending to do it in the name of Christ. Their aim is to set up, in a God-bereft world, a human ant-hill, a mechan- ical congeries ruled by science. Their doctrine is the blackest calumny on human nature; it would mean utter economic con- fusion; it would destroy liberty; it would drown the world in blood. The *Diary* is haunted by the sinister plotting of Catholics and Com- munists.

On the other hand, Eastern Orthodoxy, obedient to the Saviour's precepts, repudiates coercion. The guardian of that faith, Russia alone holds by the true Christ, clinging to His garment with the rough hand of the peasant. In the West there is nothing to hold the greedy, lonely individuals together. Only in Russia is the sense of human brotherhood alive, only there can a real society arise. In the fulness of time she will unite men, not by appealing to self- interest or force, but through active love in the spirit of Christ, and mankind will become "like a great and magnificent tree shadowing the happy earth." Russia is well equipped for this task, for her people possess—and here the diarist was harping on an old idea of his—"the instinct of pan-humanity." This enables them to sympathize with alien ways of living and will eventually make it possible for them to achieve a synthesis of the European national cultures—which the diarist has so often and somewhat gleefully pronounced dying or dead.

At least once Dostoevsky declares that the one world he envisions will include not only the Japhetic peoples, but "even the seed of Shem and Ham." On other occasions he seems to restrict it to "the great Aryan race." Throughout, the *Diary* exhibits an animus against the Jews. Disliking these aliens with their peculiar ways and their traditional Messianism, which is an affront to his own belief in Russia's Messianic rôle, he practically indentified the Jewish "idea" with the predatory materialistic individualism of the bourgeois West, and repeats glibly all the charges of the Jew-baiters. In an expansive moment he disclaims, however, any personal feeling against the Jews, allows that the Russian masses neither hate nor despise them and will eventually accept them as brothers. He goes as far as to advocate extension of full civil rights to his compatriots of the Jewish faith, only to add in the same breath that they already have more rights than the natives and that at the first opportunity they will invade the countryside and make the life of the peasantry worse than under the Tartar yoke. In *The Brothers Karamazov* Alyosha, an exemplar of Christian love and charity, is asked: "Is it true that at Passover the Jews steal children and cut their throats?" His answer is: "I do not know." At the time when the novel began to appear a group of Jews in the Caucasus was tried on a charge of ritual murder, and the long-lived lie was being revived in the reactionary press, including *Grazhdanin*, of which Dostoevsky had been the editor.

Much space is given to the Near Eastern question. In the summer of 1876 a ripple of sympathy and admiration for the Balkan Slavs, who had risen against their Turkish oppressors, ran over the country. Collections were taken up for the victims, war orphans were given refuge, Russian volunteers joined the Serbian forces. To the diarist this is "an epoch-making period." A great unifying and purifying emotion, he writes, is sweeping over Russia. The gap between the masses and the intellectuals is closing. Clearly deep within the folk there is a thirst for suffering in a good cause. The people know that Russia exists solely for the purpose of championing Orthodoxy. Surely a nation capable of such a crusade is "spiritually intact."

Dostoevsky greeted the formal opening of hostilities against Turkey on April 24, 1877, with religious enthusiasm. That day he noticed a crowd around a newsboy as he was on his way to the bank in a droshky with Anna. They stopped to buy a paper. It contained the war manifesto. He directed the coachman to drive them to the Kazan Cathedral. Ceaseless masses were being served before the icon of Our Lady of Kazan. He disappeared in the throng within the cathedral, and half an hour later Anna found him, so absorbed in prayer that he scarcely recognized her. There could be no thought then of going to the bank. He put away the text of the manifesto among his most precious papers.

The apostle of Christian love is by no means a pacifist. The diarist sees a powerful moral stimulus in wars and he believes this one to be a step toward the fulfilment of the high destiny of Russia, which, he never tires of repeating, is to unite mankind in Christ. The conflict will bring all the Slavs together—the Orthodox Slavs, of course —under Russia's motherly wing, and the world will witness an example of a true confraternity of peoples, not of a political federation based on self-interest.

Other more momentous results will issue from the struggle, Dostoevsky vaticinates. The Russo-Turkish conflict will turn into a European war. Taking advantage of the fact that Russia, Germany's "eternal ally," has her hands full in the Near East, the Jesuit conspirators will manoeuvre France into attacking Germany. France may suffer a fresh defeat and be reduced to the status of Poland. In that case the Catholic Church, which "used to whore it with the mighty of the earth," will turn to the common people. The Pope will appear before them "barefoot, poor, and naked." He will proclaim that Christ taught communism, he will sanction the use of force, and offer to head the revolution of "the fourth estate."

At this point the crystal ball becomes clouded. Demos will accept the Pope's leadership at once. Demos will accept it only when wearied by endless carnage. Russia will join Germany in slaying the double-headed monster of Catholicism and communism, and then the two countries will divide the world between them. But no, Russia will hold aloof, and ride out the storm. Oh, Europe will be drowned in blood! The nations of the West are ranged against one another, each a house divided against itself, each threatened by a "Red" revolt—not that Dostoevsky regards the latter eventuality as an unmixed evil, since it holds the promise of the destruction of the bourgeois civilization he abominates. Russia, on the other hand "a mighty world apart," stands united, free from discord, monolithic (in an unguarded moment the diarist blurts out, however, that the large non-Russian contingent of the population necessitates a strong army). No matter what happens, "the future of Europe belongs to Russia."

Before undertaking her great historical mission, Russia has to perform a smaller task without delay. As soon as the war has been won, she must take possession of Constantinople, and of its hinterland and the Straits. Surely, as the head of Eastern Orthodoxy, she has a moral right to the ancient capital of Byzantium. This will prevent the little Balkan states from quarrelling over that prize. It would be wrong to suspect any less unselfish reasons for such an annexation: throughout her history, writes Dostoevsky, Russia has been an example of "political disinterestedness." Be that as it may, the *Diary* resounds with the cry: "Constantinople must be ours, conquered by us Russians from the Turks, and remain ours forever." The Moslem population need not be deported or exterminated; it can take to peddling soap and dressing-gowns like the Volga Tartars. If Orthodoxy is to fulfil its historic destiny with the aid of the sword, is it less a denial of Christ than Catholicism? The question apparently never occurred to Dostoevsky.

As a political writer and commentator on current events he cuts a sorry figure. But when he abandons all pretence of dealing with objective facts and turns a feuilleton into an apocalypse, his utterances take on a fragile kind of validity. The peculiar tension that belongs to his fictions dominates his view of history as well. A sense of drama, of catastrophe, of the imminence of great and terrible events, haunts these pages. "The present century, it seems to me," he writes, "will end in Old Europe with something colossal, that is, with something not exactly like the upheaval with which the eighteenth century concluded, but with something equally colossal, elemental, and terrible, and also resulting in a change of the face of the world, at least in the western part of old Europe." But, as in the novels, he holds out the promise of redemption. Russia will be the Messiah of the nations.

end

III

Now and then the novelist peers out of the pages of this *Diary*. He builds up a situation, he sketches in a group of characters, with no more to go by than a reported casual encounter on the street. At least two complete stories detach themselves from the matrix of his general discourse. The first of these allows the reader to catch the novelist in the very act of taking hold of his subject. One sees here how an external impulse sets his imagination moving along a familiar path. In the issue for October, 1876, he quotes a newspaper notice about a poor seamstress who committed suicide by throwing herself from a window, an icon clasped in her arms; and he remarks that the thought of this gentle soul "involuntarily torments the mind." The following issue is devoted to a story, "A Gentle Soul," which ends with a woman leaping to her death, an icon clasped in her arms.

In form the story resembles "Notes from the Underground." Indeed, the middle-aged pawnbroker who is the monologist here is another denizen of the underground who has harboured a sense of humiliation and injury ever since a single cowardly act had resulted in his discharge from his regiment and subsequent ostracism. Attracted by a destitute sixteen-year-old girl who brings her poor trinkets to his shop, he saves her from the unwanted attentions of a fat grocer by marrying her. He does not quite conceal from her his conviction that he has thus put her in his debt. He loves her, but when she offers him affection, he does not respond. Secretly he cherishes the thought, if half disbelieving it, that, though outwardly a heartless money-grubber, he is actually a proud, noble soul, wronged and misjudged. He plans to have his young wife discover the truth by herself in the hope that she will then admire and adore him. Meanwhile, he perversely continues to put barriers between them by studied coldness and niggardliness. She rebels against him, indeed comes to loathe him and is even ready to attempt his life. But his unexpected courage, when he faces her revolver, paralyses her hand and ends her revolt. His affection for her is now complicated by pity for her in her defeat and pleasure in her humiliation. Believing himself rehabilitated in her eyes and basking self-complacently in his triumph, he is content to delay reconciliation until she returns to him of her own accord. Yet a trifling incident throws him at her feet in a gust of rapturous tenderness. He opens his heart to her, and she promises to be a faithful wife to him. But while he is out getting passports for their projected trip abroad, she destroys herself. "Why did she die?" the bereaved man keeps asking. There is a large element of uncertainty in the situation, as in many situations of Dostoevsky's fashioning. What is least in doubt is the undergroundling's tragic fault in committing a crime against love: possessed by a perverse pride and a thirst for domination, he had played havoc with his bride's affection and delayed too long the gift of his own.

"The Dream of a Ridiculous Man" is the title of the other story inserted in the *Diary*. The "Ridiculous Man" is a solitary who might have stepped out of Dostoevsky's early writings. The misery of knowing that he cuts an absurd figure is overlaid by a conviction that nothing matters, has ever mattered, will ever matter, since the world has no objective existence outside of his consciousness. He decides to kill himself.

On the night that he has chosen for the act he is accosted in the street by a panic-stricken little girl begging for help. He repulses her brutally: pity has no meaning in a world which is only illusory and which will vanish anyhow in two hours when he has shot himself. But he finds that he does pity the child and is ashamed of the way he has treated her. Something does matter. His solipsistic obsession is dispelled: his is not the only self that exists. Somehow the incident with the little girl has restored him to a sense of the reality of the world. Instead of blowing out his brains, he falls asleep in his room and has a dream.

He dreams that he dies, and thereafter is carried through space to a replica of our earth. As he approaches it, he is pierced by a longing for that other earth he had left behind and a jealous fear that he may forget it. "Is there torment upon this new earth?" he asks himself. "On our earth we can only truly love with torment and through torment. . . . I want torment in order to love. I long, I thirst, this very instant, to kiss with tears alone the earth that I have left, and I don't want, I won't accept life on any other." Landing, he finds himself in the midst of an Eden, on an island of the blessed, where the lapping of the emerald waves, the rustle of the young leaves, the flutter of birds' wings, all seem syllables of love. The men and women who people this paradise are like our first parents before the Fall. They are radiant with beauty and serenity, innocent of pain and evil alike, and free of desires. They are without knowledge, but they possess wisdom, and there is a living bond between them and the universe. They love, but know neither lust nor jealousy, nothing of the cruel sensuality that is common to all men on earth. They bear children, who are the children of all, since they are one family. They are spared heavy toil and illness, and death is euthanasia. Here is an elaboration of the dream of the Golden Age that Dostoevsky had given to Stavrogin and later bestowed upon Versilov—a rather jejune Eden, almost recalling the sunny Chautauqua scene from which William James longed to flee to an Armenian massacre for "an agreeable change."

The stranger tells the denizens of this blissful planet that he has had a presentiment of their beatitude, and wonders how it is that on earth he could not hate men without loving them, or love them without hating them. And then, carrying about with him as he does the earthly contagion, he corrupts this innocent world. These radiant beings come to know shame and sorrow and exalt them both. They break up into separate groups, each waving its own flag. Men come forward with a scheme—the hint at socialism is too broad to be missed—for bringing people together again, "so that each, without ceasing to love himself best, at the same time might not interfere with others, and all might live together in something like a harmonious society." Wars are fought in the name of this idea. Crime and suicide flourish. The man from earth walks among these people then, wringing his hands and weeping, but loving them more than in the old days when they were still blameless and beautiful and ignorant of pain—yes, and loving the land they have polluted more that he had loved it in its purity. In his remorse, he seeks crucifixion at their hands, but they laugh at him for a madman, as he had been laughed at on earth. Intolerable grief seizes him, and he awakes.

Few of Dostoevsky's writings reveal so unambiguously the anatomy of his feeling about life. The very fact that the moral he tacks on to it should be such a complete *non sequitur* is a further revelation. The dream, he tells us in conclusion, has saved the would-be suicide from carrying out his intention. It has given life significance by showing him that evil is not the normal condition of mankind, and that happiness is possible on earth. The only requisite is that men should love one another as themselves. Dostoevsky had asserted that he would stand with Christ against truth. Here he stands with Christ against the true meaning of his story. It bespeaks an attachment to the earthly, with all its shame and pain, beyond any devotion to the crystalline beatitudes of heaven.

The two stories have the theme of suicide in common. Repeatedly in the *Diary* he returns to this subject, which is a constant element in the pattern of his novels. He accounts for the suicide epidemic that he believed he saw around him, as he accounts for the spiritual breakdown of so many of his characters, by the want of a belief in the immortality of the soul. His argument for it is bare-faced pragmatism. The absence of this belief robs life of its meaning, makes it indeed "unnatural, unthinkable, and intolerable." In *The Possessed* the young Verkhovensky tells of how "a grizzled old stager of a captain," after hearing some young men make short shrift of religion, stood up and said: "If there's no God, how can I be a captain then?" He might as well have said: "If my soul is not immortal, how can I be a captain then?" To Dostoevsky these two elements of the religious consciousness are inseparable, indeed, identical, and are, moreover, the basis upon which alone the life of mankind can be maintained. Except in the service of some higher principle, every effort loses its meaning. The idea of immortality, he asserts in the *Diary*, is the highest on earth, and the source of every good, even of the love of humanity. One can offer small comfort to a man if his life is a brief and miserable interval between two oblivions. Unable to help one's neighbour, one hates him. Was the need satisfied by the belief in the immortality of the soul

related to that morbid fear for the integrity of the self that manifested itself so clearly in his youth and that he seems never to have
quite lost? In any event, one can understand why he discredited
and indeed abominated the agnostic with a conscience and a purposeful life: the very existence of such people was a denial of the
faith he professed.

It was no vague disembodied survival that he laid claim to.
He made his position clear in a letter written shortly after he suspended the *Diary*. At the end of 1877 he found in his mail an
anonymous manuscript, accompanied by a note from a friend of
the author's. He had previously received a communication from
the same pen, setting forth, in a fashion after his own heart, the
need for brotherly union, if a true human society was to be realized. But now he had before him a much more remarkable, indeed
a startling piece of writing. It has since disappeared, but there is
evidence that herein the author summoned all to labour for the
achievement of immortality, not merely the immortality of the
living but the resurrection of the ancestors who lay in their graves—
this, rather than procreation, being, in his opinion, humanity's
supreme task.

Dostoevsky pondered this manuscript and showed it to Vladimir
Solovyov. Since his young friend's return from a long stay abroad,
where he had been studying the mystics and having visions, an
intimacy had sprung up between him and Dostoevsky. Neither
of them smiled at the mad project; on the contrary, they received
it with enthusiasm. And when, in March, 1878, Dostoevsky acknowledged the receipt of the manuscript, he wrote: "At bottom,
I am completely in accord with these thoughts. I read them as
though they were my own." He went on to say that the essential
point in the essay was "the duty of resurrecting the ancestors who
lived before us, a duty which, if fulfilled, would put a stop to
childbirth." But, he asked his correspondent, was this raising of
the dead to be taken in an allegorical and ideal sense, or literally
—was it to be, as religion asserts, resurrection of the body? Pursu-
ing the subject with a kind of theological earnestness, he suggested
that it would of course have to be a different kind of body, perhaps
resembling the body of Christ in the state in which it was between

the resurrection and the ascension. He concluded: "I tell you now forthwith that we, at least Solovyov and I, believe in real, literal, individual resurrection, and that it will take place on earth."

The question Dostoevsky put to his correspondent did not go unanswered. Some time later the author of the curious manuscript sent him a fuller statement of his position. He made clear that what he believed in was "a material, visible, palpable" resurrection, to be achieved by the common effort of mankind, without any miraculous intervention, through control of the forces of nature. Much in this essay was congenial to Dostoevsky's way of thinking. It was the expression of a selfless soul, who felt acutely that each was responsible for all, who desired men to live neither for themselves nor for others, but *with* all.

It is not known whether Dostoevsky ever received this third communication and, indeed, whether he ever learned the identity of the man who had conceived this plan—which might have originated with a character in *The Possessed*—of reversing the life process and, through united filial effort, bringing all the departed into the world of the living again. Believing that any thought or feeling which contained an element of truth was not an individual possession, the author of these manuscripts left them anonymous and had others to sign his letters. His name was Nikolay Fyodorov, and he was an obscure library assistant in Moscow, known to a limited circle for his prodigious learning, his complete self-effacement, and the originality of his thinking. It was only after his death, in 1903, that his followers published his writings. These unique documents reveal a mind that was a grotesque cross between that of an early Christian heresiarch and that of a thoroughgoing materialist. Whatever Dostoevsky saw of them was calculated to attract him. Yet if at one time he subscribed to Fyodorov's fundamental thesis, he did not take seriously the duty of resurrection. Apparently he was content with the Orthodox view which holds that it is not to be won by human effort, but lies in the gift of God. Like every imaginative writer, Dostoevsky had his own way of conferring immortality on men and women, but certainly he did not raise them in incorruption. It may be recalled that in the one story in which he dealt with life after death, he depicted with macabre humour a posthumous salacity.

IV

D. H. Lawrence said of Dostoevsky that while "professing love, all love," his nose was "sharp with hate" and his running "shadowy and ratlike." This is an apt description of the man revealed at his worst in the *Diary*. The very writing is so often evasive, slippery, unctuous, snarling. On the one hand he exhibits a violent animosity against the peoples of the West, the Catholics, the Poles, the Jews, the Socialists; on the other, he preaches reconciliation, brotherly love, universal union, in the name of Christ. It is plain that these views, as indeed all his opinions, were not a matter of intellection but of feeling—they were rooted in his personality. His nature was too complex to fall wholly within a simple formula, yet the analysis of the epileptic make-up in medical literature throws some light upon the paradox of his thinking.

The "epileptic character" is marked by irritability, fits of anger, a large capacity for hatred—all the earmarks of an aggressive, destructive disposition. If the epileptic's criminal impulses are inhibited, he overcompensates for them by an attitude of "clammy, saccharine kindliness and solicitude," as one psychiatrist puts it. His oppressive sense of guilt and the consequent desire for atonement express themselves in an emphatic religiosity. This is a well-recognized feature of the epileptic temperament and, as the same author suggests, gives a new meaning to the ancients' term for the falling sickness: "the sacred disease." The zealot is bent upon spreading the faith. He considers it his mission to bring peace and harmony and to root out evil. He is unaware that the source of the evil is within himself. It is probable that a psychological mechanism such as this was partly responsible for Dostoevsky's violent prejudices, for the sadistic strain in his novels which won him the reputation of a "cruel genius," for his religious bias, and for the Messianic zeal which was his and which he attributed to his race.

In Strakhov's letter to Tolstoy, which has already been quoted, he drew a portrait of Dostoevsky that is of particular interest in this connection. "I cannot," he wrote, "consider Dostoevsky either a good or a happy man (which is in substance the same thing). He was malicious, envious, dissolute, and he spent his whole life in a state of agitation which was pitiable and which would have made him ridiculous, if he had not at the same time been so malicious and so intelligent. For his own part, he considered himself, as Rousseau did, the best of men, and the happiest. . . . In Switzerland in my presence he ordered a waiter about in such a way that the man took offence and spoke up: 'But surely I am a human being, too!' " Strakhov went on to say that such scenes occurred continually because Dostoevsky could not restrain his malice, and that his spiteful outbursts were marked by a womanish suddenness and obliquity; further, that he himself readily took offence, indeed rather enjoyed insults, and never fully repented his own nastiness. After remarking that Dostoevsky, "possessed of a bestial sensuality, had no taste whatever, no feeling for womanly beauty and charm," Strakhov observed: "The characters most resembling him are the hero of *Notes from the Underground*, Svidrigailov in *Crime and Punishment*, and Stavrogin in *The Possessed*."

"With such a make-up," Strakhov wrote, "he was at the same time very much inclined to a sweet sentimentality, to lofty and humane reveries, and these reveries are his particular tendency, his literary muse, his road." He could not recall, he said, "a single impulse of true kindness, a spark of genuine, cordial warmth, even a single moment of real repentance" on the part of Dostoevsky. Had he been able to do so, he could have forgiven him all his faults. "But merely putting oneself on a pedestal as a fine man, mere cerebral and literary humanitarianism—God, how disgusting it is! He was a truly unhappy and wicked man who imagined himself happy, a hero, and loved tenderly himself alone."

It is plain that in some respects this damning portrait is not true to life. Certainly Dostoevsky did not consider himself either the happiest or the noblest of men. He knew himself too well for that. Nor was he the monster of selfishness and perversion Strakhov paints him. The pages of this biography bear sufficient witness to the fact that, on the contrary, he was capable of true kindness, of disinterested generosity, of a humility that was not merely inverted self-vaunting. Marfa Brown, that piece of human flotsam, felt ennobled by her contact with him. Strakhov distorted the likeness by over-simplifying it and exaggerating its uglier aspects. Roughly speaking, however, his interpretation of his friend's nature is in agreement with the pattern of the epileptic character. But whether or not those "lofty and humane reveries" were, in the language of the school, a reaction-formation, their suspect origin cannot invalidate their worth, since they were, as Strakhov rightly said, his "muse," and dictated some of the finest passages in his novels. It is noteworthy that it was not only the vicious Smerdyakov whom Dostoevsky made an epileptic, but also the Christlike Prince Myshkin, suggesting in a shadowy way that the epileptic in him had a share in both.

Tolstoy, saying in his reply to Strakhov that Dostoevsky was "all conflict," that he was caught in "a struggle between good and evil," came nearer than the philosopher to an understanding of the law of Dostoevsky's being and, also, of his art. He was a hater; he felt himself to be a sinner, a guilty man. And so he strained after love, atonement, communion. In his effort at self-integration, he sought to impress himself upon the world, to fulfil his religious mission, to purify, to unite the hearts of men.

CHAPTER TWENTY-FIVE

THE PROPHET

FROM the first the *Writer's Diary* found a sizeable audience and was something of a financial success. Some months the edition would run to as many as six thousand copies. Not a few people relished the personal note and the informal manner of the journal, and the author's obvious sincerity, even if they were irritated by his intellectual confusion. In spite of his retrograde opinions, there was an eager restlessness about him that was apt to disarm his antagonists. He had vaguely hoped to secure a following which might make itself felt in public affairs, and indeed the expressions of sympathy he received from his readers made him feel that numbers of his compatriots shared his point of view. But he succeeded chiefly in attracting feeble souls, many of them women, who confided in him, who looked up to him as their oracle or their mentor, and who heaped his desk with pleas for suggestions as to their reading, for advice on the choice of a career, and requests for spiritual aid and comfort.

He replied whole-heartedly, if at all. Sometimes he forgot whether he had answered or not—his memory was so wretched that he could not remember the faces of people whom he had met, or recall the plots of his own novels. Besides, he had a great distaste for letter writing. "If I ever go to hell," he told one correspondent, "the punishment imposed on me for my sins will be to write ten letters a day." Yet, as far as time and memory allowed, he did his duty and, indeed, showed a warm interest in the problems presented to him. He explained, he counselled, he soothed, he warned. He advised at least two young women in affairs of the heart, saying: "If you don't love him, don't marry him." He reassured and encouraged a despairing schoolgirl who had failed to pass her examinations. To a young man with literary ambitions he wrote that there was no reason why he should not, at least temporarily, take up some practical occupation. In his own youth, he said, although he knew that he was destined to be a man of letters, not an engineer, he had been among the first at the engineering school, and for a time had practised the profession for which he had been trained He bade the fond mother of an eight-year-old boy teach him the Gospels, because "you can't find anything better than Christ," and surprisingly enjoined her to retain a sense of measure in her love for the child, lest she spoil their relations. The rôle of father confessor could not have been wholly disagreeable to him, yet there were times when he realized the absurdity of his position. In such a moment he wrote to a stranger who had invited his assistance: "You believe that I am the kind of person who sustains hearts, releases souls, banishes sorrow. Many write me in this strain, but I know for a certainty that I am rather apt to instill disillusion and disgust. I am not skilful at lulling to sleep, although sometimes I have tried to do it. And, of course, what many people want is to be lulled to sleep."

In the summer of 1877 Dostoevsky was under the impression that the *Diary* was going downhill. In any case, he decided to suspend it the following year. He might later on issue a larger publication, of which it would form only a department. But now he must give it up. He was tired, he was ill, he wanted to start work on his novel.

Part of the December issue, which was the last one, he devoted to a friendly estimate of Nekrasov, who, after horrible sufferings, had recently died. The event had touched Dostoevsky more than he would have believed. The two had long been in opposite camps, but since the publication of *A Raw Youth* in Nekrasov's review their relations had been friendly, and the man's cruel illness had drawn Dostoevsky closer to him. Upon learning of his death, he spent the night pouring over his poems. He was confirmed in his feeling that they were the work of a man who had sustained a deep wound in his early life, who had sinned privately against the ideals that he upheld publicly, but who had redeemed himself through suffering, a man who exemplified the moral duality and turbulence of the Russian nature—in fine, a man like a character in a Dostoevsky novel. And as he read, not only what Nekrasov had told him of his personal history, but the points at which he had touched his own life, came vividly before him, chiefly, of course, that dawn hour, now thirty-two years behind him, when Nekrasov had burst in upon him, proclaiming him a genius.

He went with Anna to the funeral—Nekrasov was buried in the section of the Volkov Cemetery reserved for men of letters, and as they stood there he begged Anna not to have him laid to rest here, among his enemies. To give the talk a lighter tone, she described in detail the magnificent funeral she would give him provided he promised to delay the occasion as long as possible. Years later she was to adduce as an instance of her gift of second sight the fact that the ceremony, as she had then pictured it, closely resembled her husband's actual funeral.

He might occasionally think and speak of death, but he intended to hold on a good while yet. On Christmas Eve he made the following entry in his notebook:

"Memento. For Whole Life.

"1. To write a Russian *Candide*.
  2. To write a book about Jesus Christ.
  3. To write my reminiscences.
  4. To write *Commemoration of the Dead*, an epic.

"(All this, in addition to the last novel, and the proposed edition of the *Diary*—that is, minimum ten years' work, and I am now fifty-six)."

There is every reason to believe that by the "last novel" Dostoevsky meant the work for the sake of which he was suspending the *Diary—The Brothers Karamazov*.

II

The plot of Dostoevsky's last novel, at least in its essentials, seems to have presented itself to his mind complete from the start, and he was spared the distress of having to revise and recast it. He made occasional jottings for the novel in his notebook while he was still issuing the *Diary,* and when, at the beginning of 1878, he suspended it, he set to work in earnest on *The Brothers Karamazov*.

In the spring his labours were interrupted by a tragic event. Little

Alyosha died suddenly of a seizure, and Dostoevsky believed that the fatal malady was epilepsy, which he had passed on to the poor baby. Heaven could not have punished him more terribly. This was evidently the great sorrow prophesied to him by the fortune-teller he had consulted the previous winter. It was not like the death of their first-born, when they had been alone in a strange land, without other children to comfort them. But nothing could make the loss easier. He spent the night praying beside the crib where the little body lay, and a friend coming in the morning found the parents so helpless with grief that she had to attend to the details of the funeral for them.

To divert her husband, Anna persuaded him to go on the trip he had so long wished to make to Optina Pustyn, a venerated monastery, famous for the wisdom and loving-kindness of its elders, particularly Father Amvrosy. Dostoevsky went first to Moscow, in some trepidation, to see if Katkov would buy his yet unwritten novel. If the publisher refused, he was determined to go on with it anyway, but what would they live on meanwhile? Katkov, however, was agreeable and promised a sizeable advance.

From Moscow he went on to the monastery, in the company of Solovyov. It was Anna who had arranged this, believing that for all his otherworldliness, the eccentric young philosopher would be able to take care of her husband in the event of an epileptic attack. In spite of the difference in their ages and temperaments, Dostoevsky found Solovyov's company extremely congenial. This young man of twenty-five, the author of several philosophical treatises, had already reached conclusions similar to his own on such matters as the state of the West, the mission of Russia, the moral maximalism of Christianity, the nature of socialism. This last Solovyov condemned as the ultimate expression of the bourgeois spirit, his own view being that the Church was the society toward which all others should move, since men will not be satisfied with less than perfection. This carefree mystic had, moreover, a gift for formulating and organizing ideas with an easy grace that the novelist may well have envied him. Expansive in the company of those he loved, Dostoevsky must have talked freely on his favourite themes to the young man. Solovyov recalled that on one occasion he spoke of "the woman arrayed with the sun" who is mentioned in Revelation, and of her crying out "in pain to be delivered" of a man-child, declaring that the woman was Russia, and the child, the message she carried for the world. It was also to Solovyov that he confided the main theme and the plan of *The Brothers Karamazov*.

Theirs was not the traditional leisurely pilgrimage on foot, with halts by the wayside and nights under the stars. They made the long journey by train and carriage, cruelly jolted about and sleeping in wretched peasant huts. It was only on the third day that Dostoevsky saw the white walls and blue cupolas of the monastery against the background of pine forest. He did not spend more than two days there. He had gone, as any simple person might go, in bereavement, to seek religious solace. But he went more particularly as a novelist in search of local colour, his memories of pilgrimages made in childhood with his mother being insufficient for his purpose. What he saw at Optina Pustyn he used in the monastery scenes of his novel. Indeed, the consolation that was offered him by Father Amvrosy he put into the mouth of *staretz* ("elder") Zosima, in the touching passage of *The Brothers Karamazov* in which he comforts the peasant woman for the loss of her child. The pitiful words of the woman herself echoed Anna's when her baby died. Dostoevsky's art had for him a kind of religious significance, so that he could turn every part of his experience, no matter how private, how sacred, to its uses, without any sense of immodesty or profanation. When Tolstoy underwent conversion, he rejected his art as belonging to that sinful life from which he had turned away. For Dostoevsky there was no division between his fiction and what he had of faith.

When, his pilgrimage over, he came back to Staraya Russa, where the family was summering as usual, he could concentrate on his book, The apartment in town holding too many painful memories of little Alyosha, in the early autumn there were the distractions incident to moving into a new flat—this was to be Dostoevsky's last home. Nevertheless, by November he had completed the opening chapters of the novel. Indeed, the first instalment of *The Brothers Karamazov* was published in the January issue of *Russky vestnik* for 1879, and further instalments continued to appear during the subsequent months.

In order that the novelist might suffer fewer distractions, the family went to Staraya Russa that year earlier than was customary with them. When they got there the town was buzzing with whispered comment on the hanging of an officer of the local regiment who had been discovered to be a member of a militant revolutionary organization. Executions of terrorists were then rather common, occurring on the average about once a month. The previous year Dostoevsky had been present at the public trial of Vera Zasulich, who had fired upon the brutal Governor General of Petersburg, and though he felt that her acquittal was justified, he was afraid she would be made a heroine. If only there were some legal formula equivalent to the Scriptural admonition: "Go and sin no more!" This kind of Christian anarchism could hardly have been to the taste of Pobedonostzev who, upon the assassination of Alexander II, wrote to his pupil, the emperor's successor, urging him to show no clemency toward the regicides. Dostoevsky's attitude this time, to judge by a letter he wrote to his eminent friend, was not so much one of horrified indignation as of wonder over the terrorist's state of mind. To the run of loyal citizens, he commented, people of this type appear insane, but it must be acknowledged that these lunatics have their logic, their moral code, their God; yes, and they believe that the whole world will yet come round to their way of thinking. Did it occur to Dostoevsky that these "lunatics" might have their will with his country? "Sometimes," he wrote to Pobedonostzev a few months later, "a silly and sinful thought occurs to me: what will become of Russia when we, the last of the Mohicans, die?"

As was his habit, he worked at night, stimulated by cup after cup of strong tea, bitter as beer. What with the back-breaking strain under which the novel put him, the trying weather—he wrote to the sound of trees crashing in the storm—the serious illness of both children, not to mention the distress of watching, even from a distance, what he called "the insane antics of the press and the intellectuals," by midsummer he felt badly in need of the cure. It was to be his last trip to Ems. He found the place more execrable than ever. The landscape was ravishing; how he hated every stone in it! At the concerts they played nothing but Wagner, "a most tedious German blackguard." His loneliness was abysmal; he wrote to Anna that for four weeks he hadn't heard his own voice. Prison had been better. He didn't know how he stood it without her. After

twelve years of married life she attracted him more than she had
as a girl of nineteen. She filled him with an inexhaustible rapture
which was increasing with the years. The only thing that she lacked,
for wifely perfection, was frankness. His own outspokenness was
so complete that she reminded him jestingly that his letters might be
read by the censor, and in later years, before allowing them to be
published, with anxious modesty she expurgated the most intimate
passages. "You will say," he wrote to her, in one of these, which
stressed the importance of the physical basis of marriage, "that this
is only one side, and that the grossest. No, it is not gross, and besides, at bottom, everything else depends on it."

The anxious father was not lost in the passionate husband. He
was a prey to nightmares and gloomy thoughts. He kept thinking
of his death. Men were selfish. The world was a cold place. The
children! What would become of them when he was gone? Something must be laid aside for them, he insisted, as his father had
before him. He must finish the *Karamazovs,* establish his reputation
with it, then resume the *Diary,* and with money from the subscriptions buy a place in the country. By the time the children are
grown, it will have trebled in value, and with a stake in the land
they will be substantial citizens. Either because it was remotely
located, or because he had a guilty feeling about retaining it, Dostoevsky took no account of the land that represented his share in
the Kumanina estate.

Meanwhile, he was not saving; on the contrary, he was spending money. His letters bristle with the figures of his outlays. He
drops the glass he used at the spring; it costs him five marks, and
he buys another one for four; he sighs over the loss, which he
sets at nine marks, and besides, it is a bad omen. In spite of the
demands of the cure, his boredom, and his anxieties, he manages
to do a little work, about two hours a day, and sends off the section
devoted to Father Zosima. Good riddance! The old man had been
sitting on his neck long enough.

Letters from home are infrequent and are not always reassuring.
Anna has gone off on a long journey to inspect, at long last, the
land left by Aunt Kumanina. She has hopes of coming to an agreement regarding the division of the property with the coheirs, those
"pickpockets, cheats, and sharpers," as Dostoevsky calls these

kinsmen. He is worried about the indignities to which Anna will be exposed, and the hardships the children, whom she has taken with her, will suffer. They will have to stop in a dirty peasant hut where they will be starved, and their belongings will be stolen (alas, the virtues of the Russian masses on which he harped so much were, after all, only potential). He is better pleased with the news that the family is planning a visit to a monastery. They must pray for him— he is a great sinner. One letter brings word of the death of Emilia Fyodorovna. Curious, that on the eve of her passing he had had a dream—he had set it down the next day as was his habit—of Mikhail bleeding to death.

I I I

Dostoevsky had obligated himself to complete the novel within the year 1879. A little more than half the year had gone by when he discovered that, as usual, he could not keep his promise. He had overestimated his strength, he was writing more slowly than he used to, and he was more self-critical. But surely the following March would see the publication of the last instalment. When he came to write Book Eight, which contains the great scene of revelry in the tavern, it grew beyond the bounds he had originally set for it and so the delivery of it was delayed. He had intended this book to conclude Part Three, but suddenly decided that the novel would gain if he added another book to this section. He refused to be hurried. Haste would ruin his reputation now and for all time. The thing was being read everywhere, by the younger generation, by high society. He must do his best. When he finally dispatched the additional chapters, he was dizzy with the strain. The winter months sped by, and the end was still far off.

The season held fewer anxieties than usual. Anna and the children were well, and his own health had benefited by the cure at Ems. His epileptic attacks were now less frequent, occurring on the average about once every three or four months. He believed, however, that owing to his enfeebled condition, his resistance to them was lessened and the after-effects lasted longer. As he was in the habit of taking notes on his more striking dreams, so too he would occasionally make jottings on his seizures. Of the next to the last one he noted that it occurred with a sharp change in the weather

and was followed by a state of mind that he described thus:
"Ragged thoughts, migration into the past, dreaminess, melancholy, feeling of guilt. . . ."

The family's material circumstances too were less of a worry.
They had at last paid off the creditors, the novels—they had already
brought out five of them—were selling steadily, it was no longer
necessary to beg Katkov for advances. Besides, since the beginning
of 1880 there had been an additional source of income, however
modest: the practical-minded Anna had set up as a book-seller on
a mail-order basis. What with Dostoevsky's increasing age, his failing health, and his careless generosity to whoever held out a hand,
be it a professional panhandler or the equally importunate Pasha,
Anna felt that she must think of the future. The eight hundred and
eleven roubles that the business netted her the first year promised
well. When her husband died, however, she discontinued the enterprise, nor would she sell the good-will of the firm—to attract
customers, it had been established in Dostoevsky's name—lest the
new owner bring that name into disrepute.

Meanwhile, the successive instalments of *The Brothers Karamazov,* as they appeared in *Russky vestnik,* were finding an increasingly enthusiastic audience and rolling up the novelist's fame. He was
more and more in demand when a literary evening was to be held
for the benefit of the Fund for Needy Authors, on which he had
drawn more than once, or for some similar cause. He read not only
from his own works but from his favourites among the Russian
masters—Pushkin, Gogol, Nekrasov. If as a reader he lacked
Dickens' dramatic quality, he had the power of hypnotizing his
listeners with his low, cracked voice and passionate delivery, so
that those who heard him once never forgot the experience. On
these occasions he was accompanied by Anna, his "faithful squire,"
as he called her. She would bring up the rear, carrying the book,
the cough lozenges, the extra pocket handkerchief, the plaid in
which he was to wrap his throat when the reading was over. Her
presence was a comfort, and he made a practice of starting to read
only after he had assured himself that she was in the audience. But
on the other hand, what with so many cavaliers about, kissing his
wife's hand and paying her polite attentions, his jealousy would
often get the better of him.

More than ever was he being lionized by the *haut monde*. Pobedonostzev, now Procurator of the Most Holy Synod, was as gracious
as ever. For some time Dostoevsky had had the privilege of a visit
with him regularly on Saturday evenings after mass, when they
would have heart-to-heart talks which lasted beyond midnight. He
gave private readings from his works to aristocratic audiences, and
was a frequent guest of Countess Tolstoy, the poet's widow, a highly
cultivated lady. He presented his novels to the Heir Apparent
with expressions of ardent devotion to his person, and on December 16, 1880, was received by the future Alexander III and the
Grand Duchess, who a week later attended one of his readings. He
also became acquainted with the Tsar's nephew Constantine, the
only Romanov to attain some prominence as a man of letters. The
Grand Duke was most gracious to Dostoevsky and introduced him
to other members of the imperial family.

It is said that in the drawing-room of Countess Mengden he was
presented to the Emperor himself, an honour rarely conferred upon
a writer. Dostoevsky was somewhat taken aback to discover that the
handsome man dyed his side whiskers (he was about to contract
a morganatic marriage with the beautiful Princess Yuryevsky, nearly
half his age, who had been his mistress for years and had borne
him three children). It was a further disappointment to the author
to learn that the Tsar had read few of his works and to find that
when the conversation touched on freedom of conscience it was
gently but firmly directed into other channels. Apparently at Pobedonostzev's suggestion, the Tsar instructed the tutor of his two
younger sons to arrange for his charges several meetings with the
novelist. It was hoped that contact with this passionate defender
of Church and throne would exert a beneficent effect upon them.
One of the Grand Dukes was to die by the hand of a revolutionary
in the stormy days of 1905.

One may find an explanation of Dostoevsky's popularity with the
aristocracy in the state of public affairs at this time. The war from
which he had hoped so much had ended in a diplomatic defeat, and
therewith seriously shaken the prestige of the government at home.
The political climate favoured the growth of the revolutionary
movement. This had now taken a new turn. The attempt, made in
the middle seventies, to propagandize the peasants peacefully had

failed, and so too had the effort to rouse the masses to armed insurrection. Accordingly, terrorist tactics were adopted, first in retaliation for police brutality, then as a means of frightening the government into concessions and so demoralizing it as to enable the revolutionists to seize control.

The two years of shootings and dynamitings were beginning to have their effect. In high places there was the feeling that the government was being besieged. At the reception held in the Winter Palace on February 19, 1880, to celebrate the twenty-fifth anniversary of Alexander II's reign, the Tsar looked to a French diplomat like "a ghost," while the old chancellor, Prince Gorchakov, gave the impression of a mummy taken out for an airing. "I'm done for, I'm done for," he kept muttering, as he leaned against a column so as not to fall. "We are disturbed by the spectacle of these ruins . . in this palace that trembles," the diplomat wrote in his diary. Society in the capital was panic-stricken. To the numbers of gentlemen and ladies who were frightened by the threat of violent revolution Dostoevsky's doctrine of mystic nationalism was a grateful one, and his enthusiastic monarchism a moral support. It was only natural that Pobedonostzev should hold the novelist to be a man who, as he wrote to a friend, "fitted the times" and was indeed "irreplaceable."

Did the distinctions and glories heaped upon Dostoevsky remind him of those early social triumphs that he had retailed in his letters to Mikhail with such breathless zest? He was not as thrilled by it all now, and more self-assured, but even his less highly stationed hostesses recognized that he was not quite at ease in the drawing-room, that he belonged unmistakably to the lower middleclass and though not vulgar was quite without taste. While his official rank was that of a *dvoryanin* (noble), he had the manners, the habits, the standard of living of an intellectual proletarian lacking elementary financial security and used to indignities and humiliations.

One could not be sure of his mood. Sometimes he was reserved and conventional, and only the perspicacious discerned that this was a mask. Again, he might march in sullen and unapproachable, looking as if he expected momentarily to be insulted. He would retire to a corner, eyeing every newcomer suspiciously and simmering with malice—the crotchety, subtle old man. Only the place and the company would restrain him from making himself unpleasant, and so he would sit, his head drooping, his look withdrawn, his lower lip in a pout, and not brighten up until he had managed to instill a drop of poison into a remark. One young woman, meeting him for the first time, at an evening party, saw "a greyish face, a thin, greyish beard, a distrustful, frightened look, and shoulders hunched as though with chill. . . . He looked shrunken together, meek and guilty." She saw him for the last time in the Marquesa Paulucci's ballroom, seeming somewhat out of place at the brilliant gathering in his ill-fitting frock coat and looking as though his thoughts were elsewhere.

Occasionally, if his hostess coaxed him sufficiently, he would consent to give a reading, and then the sickly-looking, sunken-chested man with the whispering voice would seem to take on stature and presence and would throw the guests into "a kind of moral rapture." Sometimes he would unbend to speak freely on his favourite topics. Thus to the Vicomte de Vogüé, a member of the French diplomatic corps, who was married to a Russian lady, he expatiated on the superiority of the Russian race, giving his listener the impression of a cross between a bear and a porcupine. Again, the viscount heard him vaticinate about the end of European civilization in the accents of a Daniel. The writing, Dostoevsky proclaimed would appear on the wall of the Café Anglais, Paris would go down in all her pride, and the old world would meet its doom.

The viscount pictures the novelist as a small, dry man, bent and worn by sixty bad years, "faded rather than old, having the ageless look of the sick, with his long beard and blond hair, and in spite of everything, possessing that catlike vitality of which he spoke one day." To the Frenchman, Dostoevsky's features had the stamp of the Russian peasant: the broad nose, the small eyes blinking under the arches of his brows, the forehead with its bulges and furrows. He noted also the temples, hollowed as though beaten in by a hammer, the mouth of a sufferer, and the convulsive twitches of the whole face. "Everything in this man was of the common people, and there was in him an inexpressible mingling of grossness, subtlety, and gentleness . . . and something disturbing, perhaps the concentration of thought on this proletarian mask."

IV

In order to escape from dinners, soirées, and concerts, from society women looking for spiritual solace and young people in search of advice, Dostoevsky again left for Staraya Russa early in the season, but he was not to get as clear a space for work on the novel as he had hoped. Late in May he found himself in Moscow, having been delegated by the Slavic Charitable Society, a highly respectable body, to attend the ceremonies connected with the un-veiling of a statue of Pushkin on Strastnaya (now Pushkin) Square. Forthwith a dinner was given in his honour, on a scale in accordance with the city's traditions of hospitality. What impressed him most about the affair was that "its refinement reached a point where, after the coffee and liqueurs, two hundred magnificent and expensive cigars were passed around."

As the proceedings were delayed by the death of the empress, Dostoevsky spoke of returning home: he was worried about Anna and the children; he had to complete the next instalment of his novel. His Moscow friends would not hear of it: they would send a delegation to his wife to beg her to allow him to remain; they would send a delegation to Katkov to request an extension of time. He stayed on, but he was in distress: he was homesick, and fretted by a dozen petty matters. There were his expenses. True, they were not likely to be heavy, since the municipality paid for his room and board, but that was embarrassing: he felt constrained to eat outside of the hotel so as to reduce the bill that would be presented to the *Duma*—they mustn't think he was a hog. It was bad enough that before he learned of the arrangement he had ordered stamps freely and had sent back the coffee, complaining that it was too weak. There was one outlay that especially weighed upon him—the wreath he would have to place on the statue: it would come to fifty roubles (in the end it was only fourteen). And then suppose it should rain on the day of the unveiling, and he were to catch cold and cough in the middle of his speech. That speech! He had already half prom-ised it to two different publications. He slept badly and had con-tinual nightmares about Anna being unfaithful to him. And all the time he was thinking: my book, my book! He took comfort in a visit to some high Church dignitaries who told him that they counted themselves among his readers and were honoured by his visit. "So they value a man," he wrote to Anna, "who stands up for God." What was keeping him in Moscow above all was the feeling that he must fight for his cause. The issue between the Slavophils and the Westerners would be drawn at the celebration; he couldn't run away from the battlefield.

At last the great day was upon him. He was afraid of it. He would have to be on his feet from early morning until late at night, and only then, worn out by the exercises, heavy with the food and drink of the banquet at the *Duma*, he would have to give a reading from Pushkin that demanded particular poise and mastery. Meanwhile the split in the ranks of the delegates had grown more apparent, Turgenev heading the liberals. Tolstoy, who was then immersed in religious problems, was not even present, having dismissed the whole affair as a farce; it was rumoured, as a result, that his mind was unbalanced. So Dostoevsky lost his last opportunity of meeting the man. Only once were they in the same room, the occasion being a lecture by Solovyov. But Tolstoy had stipulated on setting out that there should be no introductions, and his wish was respected. Thus it was that Dostoevsky never satisfied his desire to come face to face with his great contemporary.

The unveiling went off smoothly, and Dostoevsky's reading in the evening was brilliant, but Turgenev got the greater ovation. Of course, the man had a *claque:* students and Westerners. Dostoevsky noted that the people from whom he won his own applause were mostly those in the more expensive seats, though there were plenty of other people who came up afterwards to shake his hand and tell him: "You are our prophet, we are better men since we have read the *Karamazovs*." The next day, at a literary dinner following the public session of the Society of Lovers of Russian Literature, he was confirmed in his opinion that his own followers had true enthusiasm, while Turgenev's were mere *claqueurs*. But he was deeply troubled. He was to make his speech the next morning, and he was afraid that he would lose even more sleep than usual and that he would have an attack.

He delivered his address on June 8, at the second session of the Society, which was held in the high-ceiled eighteenth-century hall with its double colonnade, where the nobility gave balls and received the imperial family and where, forty-four years later—it was by then transformed into the House of the Trade Unions—the body of Lenin was to lie in state.

Dostoevsky spoke in moved tones, his voice soft, tense, urgent. The appearance of Pushkin, he declared, was a prophetic sign, an earnest of the fulfilment of his country's high destiny. Pushkin was the first to portray the Russian intellectual, dreaming of universal happiness, but helpless because he had no roots in his own soil; and Pushkin was also the first to exalt the purity and moral integrity of the Russian woman. He had, above all, the peculiarly Russian gift of identifying himself utterly with men of alien races and cultures; where Shakespeare's Italians were Elizabethan Englishmen, Pushkin could miraculously sink himself into the being of a Spaniard, a Serb, a Moslem. His country's genius, to which the poet's was so deeply akin, was to understand all, to reconcile all, to unite all. To be truly a Russian was to be *vsechelovek* "a panhuman," a brother to all men. Russia might be backward, poverty-stricken, ignorant, yet precisely because she was not distracted by material wealth, she was gloriously destined to achieve the union of mankind in obedience to the law of Christ.

Dostoevsky's speech came toward the end of three days of oratory which, rather than tiring the public, had keyed its nerves to an extraordinary pitch. It was delivered in a charged atmosphere. It was spoken by a man who, for at least some of the audience, wore the halo of martyrdom, to whom others looked for moral guidance, and in whom all recognized the author of masterly works, especially that extraordinary novel, then in course of publication, *The Brothers Karamazov.* There was something in the worn face, in the low, broken voice, in the smoldering passion of the utterance, that cast a spell upon his listeners. The message, while in essence it offered nothing new to those familiar with Dostoevsky's publicist writings, was a thrilling one: it stirred generous emotions; it opened glowing vistas into the future; it flattered democratic sentiment; it satisfied the craving that men have always felt to be assured that they belong to the chosen people.

Small wonder, then, that his speech formed the climax of the occasion. "No, Anya, no," he wrote, "you can never picture to yourself, never imagine, the effect it produced." His words were interrupted repeatedly by salvos of applause. When, toward the close, he proclaimed the universal union of men, the hall rocked with emotion, and when he ceased "there was a shout, a roar of ecstasy"; strangers embraced, men wept, and swore to lead better lives. Great ladies, state dignitaries, students, swarmed to the platform to embrace him. Turgenev, too, kissed him, with tears, and said: "You're a genius, more than a genius!" Aksakov, who was to have been the next speaker, ascended the platform and declared that Dostoevsky's speech was a historic event. Like the sun, it had scattered clouds, and henceforth there would be brotherhood and good will. The public shouted assent, and men again embraced one another, weeping. The sitting was adjourned, and Dostoevsky tried to escape into the wings, but he was followed by the throng, above all, by the women: "They kissed my hands, they tormented me." One student collapsed at his feet. He was himself ready to faint, exhausted by emotion. Two old men told him that they had been enemies for twenty years, but on this day they had composed their differences: "You are our saint, our prophet," they said. " 'Prophet! Prophet!' people cried in the crowd." Was he at last being accorded the rôle he had essayed time and again? This was a moment such as redeems the miseries of a lifetime.

At last the programme of the morning was resumed. At the end of the session over a hundred ladies stormed the platform and crowned him with an enormous laurel wreath. Truly, an acrid observer remarked, Dostoevsky, in company with Turgenev, had succeeded in usurping the honours intended for Pushkin. In the evening the festivities were concluded with more readings from Pushkin, and Dostoevsky's part was to recite the lyric, *The Prophet*, a fact which, in view of the acclaim he had received, seemed suddenly providential. Late that evening—it is Anna who tells the story—after all the visitors had left, he hired a droshky, drove to the site of the monument and, not without some difficulty, lifted the enormous wreath he had received, laid it at the feet of the statue, and made a low obeisance to the poet.

The enthusiasm that had greeted his address of the morning,

though violent, had, not however, been unanimous. There was a minority of radically-minded young people whom Dostoevsky had antagonized the moment he opened his mouth. They perceived an ugly irony in his reference to the Russian "wanderer"—everybody knew he meant the socialists—who would not be content with less than universal happiness. They were disgusted by his praise of Pushkin's Tatyana, who stupidly remained faithful to her aged husband instead of following the dictates of her heart. They were outraged by his enjoining the intellectual to humble himself, and his rhetoric regarding Russia's mission seemed to them not only wrong-headed, but dangerous. Turgenev afterwards confessed that Dostoevsky's sentiments were extremely distasteful to him, though at the time he too had succumbed to the hypnotic effect of the address, and come up to press the speaker's hand, as did several other liberals and Westerners. Indeed, what Aksakov had meant when he described the speech as "an event" was that it healed the breach between the two factions, the Westerners and the Slavophils. Had not Dostoevsky made it plain that the true Russian was inevitably a good European? The peace proved, however, but a short-lived truce. As soon as his burning words appeared in cold print—the oration was published in the daily owned by Katkov who, as a notorious reactionary, had been denied admittance to the exercise by the organizing committee—the two camps were at loggerheads again.

The liberal press, while sympathizing with Dostoevsky's veneration for the masses, pointed out the inconsistencies of his position, intimated that the same things had been heard before from the same source—as a matter of fact, he had expressed them in the pages of *Vremya* twenty years earlier—that in any case there was nothing original in national self-vaunting, that Russia's "pan-humanism," far from being a mystic virtue, was merely a sign of her backwardness and of her natural tendency to appropriate the achievements of the other nations, and finally, that the Russian people, instead of being capable of leading mankind, stood in urgent need of the civilizing influences of Western enlightenment. He was deeply wounded by this criticism: why, his opponents were treating him as though he were a thief or an embezzler! When, in August, he printed his speech in the form of an issue of the *Writer's Diary*, the only one for the year 1880, he supplemented the text with introductory remarks and a prolix reply to his critics.

Herein he reiterated his belief that social betterment depended not on reformed institutions, but on the spiritual regeneration of the individual; that each nation existed merely to safeguard and promote the religion that alone bound its members together; that European civilization, based on greed as it was, had nothing to offer Russia, which possessed the true Christian enlightenment won by centuries of suffering. Why speak of Europe? She was doomed. "The final accounting, the payment of the bill," was to come sooner than people imagined. A fraction of humanity could not exploit the rest with impunity much longer. And was not such exploitation the very cornerstone of Europe's social system? A final catastrophic "political war" was impending. It might break within the next decade. The factories and the banks would close and starving millions be thrown upon the pavement. "Do you think that proletarians will wait patiently, dying of hunger, as they did before?" No, the propaganda of socialism, the International, the Paris Commune, have changed all that. "They will hurl themselves upon Europe, and the entire old order will come to a final crash." Russia would be the rock against which those stormy waves would be shattered.

By the time this issue of the *Diary* appeared, he believed that as far as his progress on the novel was concerned, he was on the last lap. There were a thousand interruptions: letters of all descriptions, manuscripts that eager unknowns sent to him to place for them, student deputations, visits from strangers who threatened to kill themselves on the spot if he did not solve their insoluble problems. There was no time left to read, to see the children, to live. The night hours were the only ones he had for work. Until the day, early in November, when he dispatched the final pages, he toiled furiously. What he was writing was so original that he expected no praise from the critics, but he put his trust in the public. Except for those few passages that wrote themselves, it was frightfully hard work, so hard that it made him physically ill. Sometimes, after having written a chapter on which he had been taking notes for three years, he had to discard it and rewrite it altogether. For ten, for twelve hours he would sit hunched over his desk, and at six o'clock in the morning, when the city was beginning to wake, he had not yet gone to bed. And this when the doctors had warned him that he must have his night's rest. It was worse than hard labour in Siberia! But the whole of literate Russia was waiting for him to put a close to the novel; that he should end it fittingly was a debt that he owed to himself, to literature, to God.

CHAPTER TWENTY-SIX

"HURRAH FOR KARAMAZOV!"

ONE OF the most widely known of Dostoevsky's books, *The Brothers Karamazov* is the greatest of them and that which most richly repays exploration. Like other major works of his, it is a crime novel and has the obvious appeal of a superbly managed detective story. But this tale of murder and mystery contains elements undreamt of in the philosophy of purveyors of thrillers. There is in it not only the conflict that results from the pressure of one character upon another; there is also the drama of the mind that belongs to the novel of ideas. Without offering that definite message that he was always striving to utter, this, among all his works, holds the sum of his experience, the substance of his vision.

Though the design of the novel has the involutions usual with Dostoevsky, the main outline of the plot, which revolves around the crime of parricide, is fairly simple, and the fact that in the main it has to do with one family helps to sustain its unity. Similarly, the protagonists, while creatures of flesh and blood, possessing the complexity common to his characters, yield their symbolical meaning more readily than is generally the case. It is the eldest son, Dmitry, who holds the centre of the stage most of the time, yet each of the Karamazovs is drawn with a firmness, an insight, an imaginative power, that sets them among the most authentic characters in fiction.

The old Karamazov is a small landowner who has risen from the position of a clownish hanger-on to that of a shady, and successful, entrepreneur. A creature scarcely capable of a moral scruple or an impulse of natural affection, he is little more than a bundle of coarse appetites, a kind of vicious Falstaff, built upon lust as upon a rock, yet with something of a Rabelaisian geniality about him. True, the spiteful, shrewd old sot has moments of "spiritual terror," and in his cups is not beyond discussing the existence of God and the chances of immortality, but this flicker of religious feeling serves only to show up more sharply his greedy sensuality.

The father's carnality has been transmitted to the sons, but in a sublimated form. He was married twice, the first time to a spirited, pretty, and dowered girl who ran away from him, the second time to a poor, meek, long-suffering orphan whom he drove to her grave. It is as though the finer substance of these women had purified and humanized, in the sons, the man's gross animalism, so that the children born of these unions grew souls. At the same time they all shared, to a greater or lesser degree, the dark, earthly power which was the heritage of the Karamazovs. Dmitry, the first-born, has much of his father in him. He too is a sensualist, a man driven by his lusts, knowing no measure, no discipline, no restraint. Yet this passionate soul possesses an unreflective moral sense of an adolescent acuteness, so that he comes to feel a community of suffering and guilt with all mankind. He may do low things, but he pays for it by the injury to his sense of honour. He may do cruel things, but none has a greater gift of pity than this rough, uneducated, impulsive fellow. Though he sinks to the depths of degradation, he knows his own baseness; from the filthy pit he reaches out to clutch the hem of divinity, and he is capable of rising to the peaks of generosity and religious exaltation. He quotes Schiller's *Hymn to Joy,* and it is as though Dostoevsky were introducing him with a musical motif, fitting enough because there is a kind of music in his heart, a gaiety singing in him, for all his savagery. Grushenka, the kept woman who is the object of his fierce desire—the very woman after whom his father lusts—is made of simpler stuff than Dmitry, but is at bottom his feminine counterpart: a somewhat coarse, hot-blooded creature, capable of cruelties and indeed of a craftiness altogether foreign to Dmitry, but having also his humanity and his largeness of spirit.

In Ivan, the younger brother, the Karamazov vigour runs along another channel. He is not wanting in the zest for living that is his inheritance, and he has a more exacting conscience than he knows, but he is, above all, intended to be the pattern of the intellectual, the doubter, the trafficker in the subtleties of the mind. Not that he is a cold rationalist, dealing in airy abstractions. He is a man who is anguished by the problems that he fastens upon. It is his tragedy to be caught in the trap of sterile dialectics. Like all those characters of Dostoevsky's who succumb to the temptations of the intellect, he stumbles, he goes astray, he is lost. The handsome, theatrical Katerina Ivanovna, with whom he is involved and to whom Dmitry is for a time betrothed, is a woman who, as Dostoevsky phrased it, "constantly invents herself." She is another twisted, lacerated soul, one who suffers by forcing herself to live beyond her spiritual means and, without realizing it, is in love only with what she believes to be her own moral excellence.

If Dmitry comprehends the life of the senses, and Ivan that of intellect, Alyosha, the youngest, embodies the life of the spirit. Although he is a novice at the local monastery, he is no wan mystic, but a smiling youth whose red cheeks and sturdy frame consort ill with his cassock, one who has in him, too, the dark Karamazov strain and knows his moment of racking doubt. It is not without significance that the girl, Lise, whom he eventually intends to marry (he has been bidden by his religious superior to leave the monastery for the world) is a hysterical, sensual child, with perverse caprices and an equally perverse charm. During a conversation in which she parades her abnormal impulses before him, he drops the remark that there are moments when everyone loves crime; and when she observes that everyone secretly relishes Dmitry's having killed his father, Alyosha acknowledges that there is truth in what she says. But if the boy inherits something from his father in the flesh, he shares with his spiritual father, the "elder" Zosima, the gift of mystic ecstasy, of unstinted love. He represents another attempt on Dostoevsky's part to portray the Christian; another character who approaches Prince Myshkin in simplicity of heart, intuitive wisdom, radiant serenity, selfless compassion. Indeed, in the notes for the novel, Alyosha is referred to as "the idiot."

While he was writing the book, Dostoevsky observed in a letter that, taken together, "these four characters" epitomized the cultivated Russian of his day. He might have said that they compromised the complex of appetites, questionings, and aspirations that belong to human nature generally.

There is yet a fourth son—the bastard, Smerdyakov. The drun-

ken Karamazov begot him upon a half-witted vagrant, not in the
heat of lust, but cold-bloodedly, deliberately, in the spirit of a
buffoon playing an obscene practical joke. The offspring of this unnatural union is a moral idiot, like his father in his want of conscience, of common pieties and human attachments, but, unlike him,
having no gusto for life; indeed, he is sexless, the only emotion of
which he is capable being hatred. A flunkey from the crest of his
pomaded hair to the tip of his polished calf boots, he is loathsome
as a reptile or a slimy cellar-growth. Significantly, Dostoevsky,
always ready to besmirch the faculty of reason, gives this dandified
monster a logical mind and an extraordinary shrewdness. Smerdyakov is a masterly parody of the intellectual, a distorted image,
as it were, of Ivan, in which his finer features are thrown out of
focus, his baser ones magnified.

The background of the novel is crowded with people: peasants,
schoolboys, merchants, and, in the ample chapters devoted to the
preliminary investigation and to Dmitry's trial, magistrates and
lawyers. Through Alyosha, the revered "elder" Zosima is brought
into the picture, and the life of the monastery becomes part of the
pattern. That scatter-brained lady, Mme. Khokhlakova, furnishes
the comic relief, and the divinity student, Rakitin, is another nasty-
minded, scoundrelly embodiment of Dostoevsky's pet abomination,
the nihilist. Then, too, there are the miserable Snegirevs, a family of
poor folk who suffer from Dmitry's violence and are comforted by
Alyosha's compassion.

As regards the dramatis personae alone, this is the most comprehensive of Dostoevsky's novels. Some fifty men, women, and
children move through its pages. There is more of the furniture of
ordinary life here than in most of his works, some slight awareness
of the rhythms of nature, and, at one high moment, the mystic sense
of man's communion with the universe. As the reader surrenders
himself to this book, he is caught up into a closed world, which has
amplitude, solidity, variety. It is a world in which human beings
live furiously the life of the senses and with equal intensity the life
of the mind, engaged as they are with issues of the moral and religious order—and passionately so engaged.

II

Dostoevsky lays the responsibility for the murder of the old Karamazov, around which the plot revolves, chiefly upon Ivan and Smerdyakov. It is Smerdyakov who actually kills the old man and robs him of the three thousand roubles he had put aside to buy Grushenka's favours. But it is upon Ivan that the burden of guilt lies most heavily. In his moral confusion, he arrogated to himself the right to decide who was worthy and who unworthy of life, and gave himself license to desire the death of his horrible old father. Yet, since he held his wish to be inoperative, it was possible for him to believe himself beyond reproach. He desired his father's death without willing it, but Smerdyakov, being of coarser perceptions, interpreted crudely what he knew to be Ivan's feeling. Having overheard him put forward the theory that to a man without faith in God and immortality "everything is permitted," and attributing to him his own mercenary motives—every member of the family stood to gain by the old man's death—Smerdyakov decided that he had Ivan's tacit consent to the murder. Ivan's irresponsiveness to his innuendoes he took to be the caution of a shrewd man who wished to furnish no evidence of his connivance, and when Ivan left town after Smerdyakov's hints of what might occur in his absence, the bastard believed he had the other's mandate to go ahead. He was not wholly mistaken: even before his departure Ivan felt the claw of conscience.

In the course of his conversations with Smerdyakov after the crime has been committed, the horrifying truth dawns upon him: it was his own criminal desire, which he believed safely locked within his breast, that had guided the hand of the murderer. The scenes in which these two are confronted contain the subtlest drama that can be found in Dostoevsky's pages. In *Crime and Punishment* he showed the thinker compelled to action. Here he cries out that the wish is father to the deed, that the will to crime is equivalent to, or perhaps more evil than, the act. This is the doctrine of Christian maximalism: "Whosoever hateth his brother is a murderer."

If Ivan bears the brunt of the responsibility, his two brothers

are not unimplicated in the crime. Dmitry wished to kill his father
and was capable, in a fit of passion, of carrying out the murder.
Indeed, suspicion falls upon him, and as circumstantial evidence
is overwhelmingly against him, he becomes the victim of a judicial
error and is sentenced to hard labour in Siberia. In deciding to bear
the cross of his undeserved punishment, he is prompted not merely
by a desire to atone for his disorderly life, but by the feeling that
he is responsible for the sins of all mankind. As for Alyosha, he
certainly did not wish his father's death. His sin was wholly one
of omission: he failed to love enough, above all, he failed to draw
into his spiritual orbit his wretched half brother, Smerdyakov.

Early in the book one finds the Karamazovs gathered in the cell
of Father Zosima, to whom they have come for arbitration of a
quarrel between the old man and Dmitry. While they await the
"elder," the conversation turns upon an article published by Ivan on
the unlikely subject of the ecclesiastical courts. Therein he maintained that the State should be absorbed by the Church, if the social
ideal of Christianity was to be realized. After this idea has received
the monks' hearty approval, a member of the company reports
another theory of Ivan's. According to this, the moral law is the
fruit of the belief in God and immortality; destroy that belief and
"everything would be permitted"; crime would be sanctioned; a
limitless, savage egoism, to the point of cannibalism, would become
the rule of conduct. Father Zosima at once recognizes that Ivan is
a man struggling with unbelief, and that in his despair he formulates
these diverse ideas at which he mocks inwardly, but that if he cannot
give an affirmative answer to the question of the existence of God,
he will never decide it in the negative: hence his agony. The gathering in the cell concludes with a scandalous scene to which the
"elder" puts an end by bowing before Dmitry, in reverence, as he
explains later, to the suffering in store for him. One wonders with
Merezhkovsky why the saintly *staretz* singles out Dmitry rather
than Ivan, who is potentially the greater criminal, and hence the
greater sufferer: Dmitry would kill his earthly father, Ivan is capable
of attempting upon his Heavenly Father.

Ivan opens his heart to his brother Alyosha in a section of the
novel that Dostoevsky himself considered its culmination. The
famous scene is laid in a screened-off corner of a shabby tavern,

and the two talk of first and last things to the popping of corks,
the clicking of billiard balls, the shouts of waiters and the drone
of a mechanical organ. It is a marvel, Ivan tells the young novice,
that the idea of God should have entered the head of "the savage
and vicious animal" that man is. For his own part, he is ready to
grant the existence of God, and even to admit that all creation
moves toward an ultimate harmony, but he cannot justify the ways
of a Deity who includes in His scheme the suffering of the innocent.
He fails to recognize suffering as part of the divine pattern. And he
proceeds to exhibit specimens from a collection of cruelties with
which he would confront this unfathomable God. "The tears of
humanity with which the earth is soaked from its crust to its core"
fill him with a bitterness that has no issue but rebellion, a rebellion
anticipated by Ippolit (in *The Idiot*) and Kirillov (in *The Possessed*).
He rejects God's world, he returns his entrance ticket to millennium, preferring to stay outside, intransigent, unreconciled, unfor-
giving. Is there a being in the whole world, he asks, who has the
right to grant absolution to torturers of the innocent? Alyosha points
to Christ. Thereupon Ivan retells a "poem in prose" he has composed, though not written down—"The Grand Inquisitor."

Christ returns to earth, appearing in Seville at the time of the
Inquisition. He is recognised and adored by the people, but is
thrown into prison by order of the Grand Inquisitor. The venerable
churchman visits the divine captive in His cell and tells Him that
on the morrow he will have Him condemned as the worst of heretics,
and that at a sign from him, those who had just kissed His feet
will heap the embers when He is burned at the stake. A long
harangue follows. The gist of it is that the Grand Inquisitor accuses
Christ of the unpardonable error of having brought men the promise
of freedom. Satan had warned Him in the Wilderness that men were
bound to abuse that gift or reject it altogether as an intolerable
burden. That "wise and mighty spirit" bade Christ give men contentment and bind them to Him forever with the aid of miracle,
mystery, and authority. But He had rejected these as diabolical
temptations and chose to leave men free to come to Him, as souls
capable of attaining their full stature. This has proved too exalted
a view of mankind. Human beings are ignoble and vicious and,
solicitous of the happiness of these poor creatures, says the Grand

Inquisitor, the Church of Rome, while speaking in the name of Christ, has, in fact, allied itself with Satan. Before it will have achieved its purpose, however, it will undergo severe trials. Men are slaves, but rebellious ones. Now they are in revolt against the Church, and they will go further in wickedness. The time will come when they will follow leaders who will absolve them from all moral responsibility, declaring that there are no criminals, no sinners, but only the hungry, who should be fed before virtue is asked of them (here the Grand Inquisitor's prophecy is in substance an argument Belinsky had once advanced in Dostoevsky's hearing). With no faith save in the promise of material well-being held out by science, they will destroy the temples and attempt to build another Tower of Babel, but only end with "cannibalism" (one recalls the remark of a character in *The Idiot* that people who begin by denying God end by devouring each other). After centuries of bloody confusion some will destroy themselves and there will be those who will destroy one another. The rest, in their disillusionment and despair, will crawl back into the fold of the Church, with no thought but to lay down their freedom at its feet, and be saved from themselves. Then the Church will emerge in triumph from the catacombs into which it will have been driven. Using the means Christ had spurned, including the sword of Caesar, it will proceed to secure peace and happiness for all under the aegis of the universal state. It will give men bread, comforting lies, rules of conduct, a unifying faith—in exchange for their liberty. And they will find joy in unquestioning obedience, hug their chains, and know the contentment of a well-fed herd. Alone the priestly *élite* will be martyred, shouldering the weight of secret unbelief and of free choice between good and evil.

Having finished, the Grand Inquisitor waits for his prisoner to speak. For all reply Christ gently kisses the old man. The Grand Inquisitor then sets Him free, but, nowise shaken in his convictions, bids Him never, never return to interfere with the work of the Church.

"The Grand Inquisitor" is, of course, another thrust at Catholicism. Obliquely, "socialism" (or "anarchism"—Dostoevsky confused the two) is condemned as well. The builders of the Tower of Babel do not invoke the name of Christ as do the priestly rulers envisaged by the Grand Inquisitor, but they too despise man while loving him, they too seek to force happiness upon him, and relieve him of the onus of freedom, which is the heart of his humanity. The "poem" echoes Myshkin's tirade against the Church of Rome and elaborates Shigalyov's sketchy blueprint for Utopia (in *The Possessed*). Obviously it has a compelling actuality in our age as at once a dramatized epitome and an impeachment of the totalitarian position. It is a tract for the times.

"My socialist," wrote Dostoevsky to his publisher, referring to Ivan Karamazov, "differs from the general run of socialists in one respect: while they are 'conscious Jesuits and liars,' who do not concede that their purpose is to reduce mankind to the state of cattle, he frankly admits that he shares the Grand Inquisitor's views." Ivan's stand, as presented in the novel, is by no means so unequivocal. One gets the impression that while he may be inclined to share the Inquisitor's conception of human nature, and to accept his way out of the human predicament, he nevertheless regards that way with aversion. The reader is apt to see, as the novelist allows Father Zosima to see, that here is no cold sceptic, no callow blasphemer, but a puzzled, tormented man, at war with himself.

In the latter part of the novel Ivan is brought face to face with a devil quite different from the one mentioned in the "Grand Inquisitor." This private demon of his is represented as a shabby gentleman of middle age, sporting an eye-glass and fond of puns and broad stories. The ambiguous creature is drawn so as to suggest that he has an objective existence, yet to all intents and purposes he is Ivan's hallucination, the embodiment of his baser self, his mimic, as Satan, in Tertullian's phrase, is "the ape of God." One of the notions on which he harps, in self-justification, is that he also serves in the scheme of things: evil is the necessary foil for good, the logical complement of it, as darkness is of light. Dostoevsky apparently put this in the devil's mouth as an ugly platitude, an example of that vulgar common sense which he epitomizes. Yet when the devil says that without him life could not go on, that suffering makes it real, he is using an argument employed by Dostoevsky himself in seeking to justify the ways of God. Two years before he began the novel he had written to a friend that if Christ rejected the first temptation of the devil, choosing to feed man's spirit only, it was because He wanted humanity to learn what life meant, through struggle, through self-sacrifice, through suffering. So readily did he welcome pain—a characteristic of those who carry about with them a potent sense of guilt—that the ancient idea of the religious value of suffering had for him an intimate significance.

In the course of his conversation with Ivan, the devil reminds him of another composition of his, "The Geological Upheaval." Herein Ivan imagined humanity, the idea of God and immortality discarded, the hope of heaven abandoned for the joys of earth, infinitely extending its conquest over nature by the exercise of the will and the development of the sciences. Death is serenely accepted, and love, being transitory, is all the more intense. But, the poem runs, such a state of affairs is, after all, remote and uncertain. For the present, any individual who is so bold as to reject God and immortality may jump over the "former slave barriers of the former slave-man," and assume that "everything is permitted." If the opening of "The Geological Upheaval" reminds one of the dream of "the ridiculous man," the end takes one back to Raskolnikov. Ivan's argument with the devil is strongly reminiscent of Raskolnikov's debates with himself. The devil would have it that conscience is merely a matter of habit, and he who gives it up will be as a god, a man-god. He taunts Ivan by telling him that in confessing his part in the crime he will "perform a deed of heroic virtue" without believing in virtue. Ivan, like Raskolnikov, is driven to confess somewhat against his will. He despises the "rabble" to whom his confession will be addressed. He is simply not strong enough to be the man-god.

The scene between Ivan and his devil presents a divided soul confronting with horror its own division. Alyosha, who is plainly the novelist's spokesman at this point, feels that the forces of hell and heaven are battling for his brother, and prays that he may be compelled to confess and so find salvation. The prayer is granted: before the court Ivan declares that Smerdyakov committed the murder, and that he had incited the valet to do it, adding, "Who doesn't desire his father's death?" Ivan's mind gives way, as so often the body of a Dostoevsky hero breaks down in a spiritual crisis. It is suggested that he will recover, drawing on the inexhaustible Karamazov vitality. But, like the regeneration of Raskolnikov, that is another story. In *A Raw Youth* Dostoevsky did attack the problem of a sinner's regeneration, but without success. Shatov, in *The Possessed*, abandons the hopes and hatreds of a revolutionist to embrace Dostoevsky's own brand of religious nationalism, but this regeneration is merely reported, and that unconvincingly, not depicted. Dostoevsky believed that he had himself known such a change of heart when, in Siberia, he repented the errors of his youth, but whether or not the experience was an actual event in his life, he was unable to realize it in his art.

III

"The blasphemy of my hero will be solemnly countered in the next book, and I am working on it full of fear, trepidation, and awe, for I consider my task—the defeat of anarchism—a deed of civic heroism." Thus Dostoevsky wrote to the managing editor of *Russky vestnik*, having mailed the first half of Book Five, in which Ivan sets forth his subversive views. In the letter accompanying this next book, devoted to Father Zosima, he said that although he had not succeeded in expressing a tenth of what he wanted to, he considered this the climax of the novel. Pobedonostzev, having read the instalment in which Ivan speaks out, wrote flatteringly to Dostoevsky, but noted with regret that he had not, so far, refuted the young atheist's ideas. To his illustrious correspondent, Dostoevsky repeated that the answer to Ivan, though not indeed a logical rebuttal, point by point, was contained in the section dealing with Zosima, a figure in the creation of which Pobedonostzev was to claim that he had had a part. But would his readers understand? Had he made himself clear? He was worried. He had to meet the requirements of the art of fiction while driving his point home. To some people certain passages would seem either over-spiritualized or absurd, and in the light of common day they were absurd, but from a more inward point of view, they were deeply true. He had written those pages with great love. He would force men to admit, he had previously told his editor, that a perfect Christian was no abstraction, but a palpable reality, and that Christianity alone would medicine all of Russia's ills. Here—he spoke as though he had not written *The Idiot*—was a subject of absolute originality. He approached it with a proud humility. "For the sake of it," he concluded, "I am writing the whole novel."

Father Zosima, who as a *staretz*, possessed the gifts of a spiritual counsellor and healer, had been introduced early in the narrative, Dostoevsky seeking, in more than one scene, to illustrate his wisdom and compassion. But it is only in Book Six, "The Russian Monk," that he attempted a rounded picture of the man, and set forth, in a more or less systematic way, the substance of his faith. Most of his beliefs are familiar enough to the reader of Dostoevsky, and only the more important of them need be restated. There is a bond of union among all living creatures. Hence, when one man sins, all share the guilt. The terrible isolation in which men live must come to an end. The true society can never be achieved by means of science or enlightened self-interest, but only if men desire it enough, only if men love one another. If love cannot justify suffering (nothing can, in the light of mere reason), it robs it of its sting. Hell is simply the inability to love. (Ivan, a denizen of that hell, is bound to find the problem of evil a stumbling-block). The gates to a heaven on earth cannot be forced. Men will turn freely to God. In the West, the proletarians resort to violence. In Russia Christian brotherhood will be won through meek faith. The Christian world is at present no better than heathendom and rests only on some seven righteous men, but society will yet be transfigured and, at some remote time, take on the character of "a single, universal, and all-powerful Church," the State having dropped away and withered like a sloughed skin.

The Church as the ideal toward which society should move was indeed, Dostoevsky had told Solovyov, the central idea of his novel. It must have been reassuring for his ultraconservative friends, such as Pobedonostzev, to realize that this was a millennial hope rather than a practical programme. If "elder" Zosima's teachings, so dear to Dostoevsky, were to be carried out literally, what would become of the established order? The novelist was an untrustworthy ally. He knew no measure, no restraint. His Christianity was dangerously tinged with anarchism. No enemy of statehood has so clearly exposed, in the chapters on Dmitry's trial, the cruel clumsiness of Leviathan in meting out justice, as this avowed monarchist. An instinctive animus against the State, a conception of it as a soulless monster, a cold machine, was characteristic of pre-revolutionary Russian thought, and Dostoevsky was here at one with many of his compatriots with whom he was otherwise in disagreement.

On one point his theology was quite heretical. That the naïve faith of the peasant, which he was always crying up, fed on the miraculous he was undoubtedly aware. Indeed, his own being thirsted after it. In "The Grand Inquisitor" Christ, on coming to Seville, makes a blind man see and raises a child from the dead. Nevertheless, in the same "poem," it will be recalled, miracle is spurned by Him as a diabolical temptation and espoused by the Church of Rome as a means of enslaving men's minds. In a note for the novel Father Zosima admonishes his flock thus: "Children, do not seek miracles, for miracles kill faith." Dostoevsky, exalting freedom of conscience, of necessity took this stand. He was, however, uneasy about his deviation from orthodoxy in rejecting miracles. He explained apologetically to his editor that he had not invented the episode of the rapid corruption of Father Zosima's dead body: a similar occurrence had taken place in a monastery on Mount Athos. The incident was needed for the story: the scandal was a convenient way of testing the strength of Alyosha's faith. The novelist declared that he would be last to cast doubt on the miraculous power of holy relics. If he did not have the courage of his convictions, he had no small-minded fear of contradicting himself.

For years, indeed, ever since he had conceived the grandiose project of the *Life of a Great Sinner,* Dostoevsky had wanted to enshrine in a novel, against the monastic background, the image of some saintly man, some rock of the Church. The unpublished chapters of *The Possessed* contain a faint outline of such a character in such a setting. And now at last his dream was a reality. A reality? Scarcely. He believed that he had a firm grasp on the figure of his Pater Seraphicus, as he called Zosima, and that the "elder's" faith was his own. "I cherish," he wrote, "the very same thoughts that Zosima expresses," although, of course, he would have worded them differently, had he spoken in his own character. He had managed to set forth Zosima's credo and had been successful in sketching in the man's background. But the *staretz* himself, whose life, whose works, whose personality, above all, was to be a refutation of Ivan's "blasphemy," somehow remains a pale abstraction, a mere ghost compared to the solidity of a Karamazov.

Mawkishness and unctuousness mark the whole section in which the career and doctrine of Zosima are retailed in a style borrowed from religious writings. It is totally wanting in the impact, the tension that one associates with Dostoevsky. The story of Zosima's life opens with the account of the last days of his brother, a young man dying of consumption, who accepts his end with angelic joy. The situation parallels that of Ippolit in *The Idiot*, but there, it will be remembered, the boy rebels against his fate. That passage has a savage thrust, carries a tearing grief, while the history of the monk's brother is intolerably insipid and unreal. There are flaws in Father Zosima that must disconcert even those who have no quarrel with his point of view. When the old Karamazov half worthy rather of the Grand Inquisitor. The figure of the "elder," advises him, among other things, to close up his drinking-houses: "If not all, close at least two or three"—a counsel of imperfection worthy rather of the Grand Inquisitor. The figure of the "elder," though wrought with patient care and pious intention, is one of the least convincing of the novelist's creations.

Whether or not he remained satisfied with the chapters on him, Dostoevsky came to feel that something more was needed by way of rebuttal than the argument to be drawn from the account of the life of the *staretz*. Indeed, he jotted down in his notebook, the whole novel was an answer to Ivan. Of course, it is no more a logical answer than is the section on Zosima—dialectic was not Dostoevsky's strong point. Yet it remains true that, for all their kinship with their harrassed brother, Dmitry and Alyosha represent an attitude of yea-saying to life which triumphs over, though it does not cancel, Ivan's doubt and negation.

In the superb figure of Dmitry the passionate affirmation is most effectively symbolized. The high words of Schiller's "Hymn to Joy" are on the lips and more truly in the heart of this rough army officer, who does not stop short of peculation and who lives so carelessly and loosely. He will carry this song with him as a convict into the mines, underground. Like Ivan, Dmitry has his vision of evil, but whereas the younger brother scorns so botched a world, the elder, confronted in a dream with the misery of mankind, feels that it is all the result of a cruel misunderstanding. The suffering can be wiped out. He will erase it himself by some heroic act. The sobs will be turned into a song of joy. He wakes from the dream, prepared thereby ultimately to accept his own suffering—his punishment for a crime that he did not commit. Dmitry's self-abnegation, which is a token of his spiritual rebirth, points the moral that was in Dostoevsky's mind when he set as an epigraph to the novel the text: "Except a corn of wheat fall into the ground and die, it abideth alone: but if it die, it bringeth forth much fruit."

If Dmitry's heroism is passive—as that of a Dostoevsky character must be—both in his hugging of his cross and in his periods of rebellion against it, he is still embracing life, as only a Karamazov can. In a different way, Alyosha makes the same response. His ecstasy is not less intense, but purer. He obeys literally Father Zosima's behest to kiss the earth and water it with his tears, and gives to the precept a human meaning. After his brief moment of temptation caused by the scandal attending the death of the *staretz*, Alyosha returns to the cell where the Gospel is being read over the corpse. As he listens, kneeling, to the recital of the passage on the marriage of Cana, he falls into a gentle doze and dreams that both he and his beloved "elder" are at the wedding feast, drinking the new wine, "the wine of new joy." In the state of ecstasy to which the dream brings him, he wakes, leaves his dead, and goes out into the soft glory, the starred mystery of the night. His heart swollen with rapture, he throws himself on the ground, kisses it, and, sobbing, vows to love the earth "for ever and ever."

This scene is of profound significance. It is the consummation toward which Dostoevsky had been moving all along. Alyosha's gesture is the symbol of a spiritualized sensuality such as man knows only in the rarest instances. It is as though in giving Alyosha this dream and the exaltation that followed upon it, Dostoevsky had been able to overcome his own division, to unite the physical and spiritual man as he bridged the gulf between carnal and spiritual love. Herewith he utters a syllable of the Word he had for so long been striving to say.

IV

The father-son relation is a major theme in *A Raw Youth*. There Dostoevsky is concerned with a youth's search for and discovery of his father. In *The Brothers Karamazov* he shows the sons possessed by a murderous hatred for their unnatural parent, and builds the novel upon the murder of the old man by his bastard, with the tacit connivance of at least one of his legitimate sons. Here he was driving home the same moral lesson that he had sought to point in *Crime and Punishment:* that the mind, having abandoned the religious attitude toward life, may not be able to return to that haven save by the road of crime. It is mere conjecture that in fashioning the plot he was influenced by Fyodorov's philosophy, in which filial devotion was the sum and substance of piety and, by the same token, parricide the archcrime. The psychoanalytic view has it—and this suggestion seems to thrust deeper—that what Dostoevsky in essence did in this novel was unconsciously to re-enact the murder of his father by the outraged serfs, and his own reaction to it. This was allegedly, as has been indicated in an earlier chapter, an overpowering sense of guilt, due to the fact that the assassination fulfilled the boy's unconscious death wish. The tragedy, with its emotional repercussions, had, it is held, brought on his epilepsy, had informed his thinking, and had strongly affected the play of his imagination. It is his last novel which is his fullest confession, it is here that the whole complex, which had shadowed his life for forty years, is seen less darkly than in any other of his works. Those who read this meaning into *The Brothers Karamazov* are bound to put special emphasis on whatever points to an identification of the author with the two men most deeply involved in the murder: Smerdyakov and Ivan. Much has been made of the fact that the novelist afflicted the actual assassin with his own disease. Freud goes so far as to say that he did so "as if he were trying to confess that the epileptic, the neurotic, in him were a parricide."

There can be small doubt as to the identification of the novelist with Ivan Karamazov. This character, in some respects a portrait of the author as a young man, is, to a large degree, a self-revelation. Ivan has Dostoevsky's lust for life, his acute sense of evil, his capacity for cruelty toward others—particularly those he loved —and toward himself, and that duality Dostoevsky recognized to be his own, a source of perpetual anguish and perverse pleasure. Was it true that when he had Ivan said that he could not understand how it was possible for a man to love his neighbour, he was describing precisely his own sentiments? So Strakhov contended in a letter to Rozanov, who was a close student of Dostoevsky's work and, it will be recalled, for a time the husband of Polina Suslova. In reply Rozanov made the comment that Dostoevsky's harping on love was very suspicious: "It is as though he were blowing on his frozen fist and stamping his feet in the cold." A more plausible picture of both Ivan's attitude and his creator's is given in *The Dream of a Ridiculous Man*, where the narrator soliloquizes thus: ". . . in my hatred for the men of our earth there was always a yearning anguish: Why could I not hate them without loving them? Why could I not help forgiving them? And in my love for them there was a yearning grief: Why could I not love them without hating them?"

Strakhov spoke of Dostoevsky's hatred of his neighbour in connection with his unfaith, saying that this was the secret of his torment. But it is more probable that Dostoevsky, rather than being without real faith, was torn by doubt, and that what he projected most effectively in Ivan was the quarrel within himself between a strong religious disposition and the obstinate, sceptical voice of reason. He had always insisted that his was not a naïve childlike faith, but that his "hosannah" had "passed through a crucible of doubts." His pillorying of Ivan was indirectly a self-flagellation.

There is in the eldest brother, Dmitry, a healthfulness, a physical exuberance, that makes it difficult to see in him the lineaments of his creator. Yet they are certainly there: the strong sensuality, the unrestraint, the extremism, the longing, most intense at the moment of utter debasement, for spiritual grace. This rough, vigorous, passionate man shares Dostoevsky's roomy-heartedness and lack of integration. "Yes, man is broad, too broad, indeed. I'd have him narrower," he observes in a reflective moment. He is perplexed by the contradictions within himself. "What to the mind is shameful is beauty and nothing else to the heart." Beauty is terrible to him because "here the boundaries meet and all contradictions exist side by side." He is horrified by the thought that there is "beauty" in physical lust as well as in spiritual exaltation: in "the ideal of Sodom," so he phrases it, as well as in "the ideal of the Madonna," and the fact that a man may cherish both at once confuses him painfully. Here one finds an echo of the Idiot's "double thoughts," a repetition of the Raw Youth's wonder at "that faculty in man (and in the Russian . . . more especially) of cherishing in his soul the loftiest ideal side by side with the most abject baseness, and all quite sincerely." Indeed, one may go back as far as *The Gambler* to find a similar observation, made this time by an Englishman: "Russians alone can combine in themselves so many opposites at the same time." The problem of dual impulses, of psychic hermaphroditism never lost its reality for Dostoevsky.

In Ivan, in Dmitry, in the old Karamazov, the novelist embodied his own mental conflict, his emotional disorder, his carnality. Through these characters, and that of Smerdyakov, he could give his own dark impulses their freedom, because they were disguised, like the elements that rise to consciousness in the dream. Alyosha, on the other hand, represented the man he would so gladly have been: armoured in faith, strong to overcome temptation, rich in love, wise in compassion. The same need was satisfied by fashioning the image of Alyosha and that of Father Zosima. Dostoevsky failed to realize the "elder" because, one suspects, this character was derived from the surface of his mind. The presentation of a perfect Christian, with no trace of the human weakness to be found in Alyosha Karamazov and in Prince Myshkin, with no grain of that evil will which was to Dostoevsky fundamental in human nature, was a task beyond his powers and, indeed, foreign to his genius, however deeply devoted to such an enterprise he felt himself to be.

In Dostoevsky the instinct and vision of the novelist were at one with the commitments and fervour of the believer, or rather the would-be believer. To labour, once again, to the greater glory of God was his manifest intention in writing *The Brothers Karamazov*. Small wonder then that in the novel faith is allowed the final word, the faith of the simple folk. On the very last page Alyosha affirms his belief in the literal resurrection of the dead. In answer to the boys' question as they stand at the grave of little Ilyusha, he says: "Certainly we shall rise again, certainly we shall see each other and relate to each other with joy and gladness all that has happened."

Carried away by love for their mentor and comrade, the children shout: "Hurrah for Karamazov!" The cry is not merely an amen to Alyosha's pious affirmation. Like the "Hymn to Joy" that celebrates the lust of insects as well as the vision of angels and that Dmitry rapturously quotes, it may be taken as a hosanna to all of life, in its earthliness and in its moments of transcendence.

CHAPTER TWENTY-SEVEN

"DO NOT DETAIN ME"

IT APPEARS from the brief and lame foreword to *The Brothers Karamazov* that Dostoevsky intended to follow it up with a sequel. In the novel as it stands Alyosha takes a subordinate part, but in the author's mind he was the hero of the tale, the drama related there was a mere incident of his youth, and his story proper was to be the substance of a second volume in which the same characters were to figure. Very little is known of Dostoevsky's plans for this book, and that little is doubtful. It is said that Alyosha was to become involved in the revolutionary movement, commit a political crime, and be executed. According to a more plausible version, and one nearer to his unfulfilled project for *The Life of a Great Sinner*, he was to marry Lise, abandon her, fall into temptation, go astray, and at last find his way back to the monastry, where he was to end his days, a beloved teacher, surrounded by a flock of children.

For the present, however, this sequel was not to be thought of. The enterprise to which he turned forthwith was the *Writer's Diary*. The thought of it had been with him while he was writing the novel. There were things he felt impelled to say to his compatriots without the indirections of fiction. As early as August, 1879, he was writing to Pobedonostzev: "I have, I really have something to say, and just in the way in which you would have me say it." He expected, on resuming the *Diary*, to appeal to this eminent friend for advice, as he had previously done. How gravely he regarded his task may be judged from the words he wrote to an acquaintance just before embarking upon it: "Having decided to issue the *Diary* again next year, I have often prayed to God on my knees to grant me a pure heart, a pure, sinless word, spoken without irritation, without envy."

The Brothers Karamazov was still on the stocks when he began making jottings for the forthcoming *Diary*. Some of them were incorporated into the sole number that appeared. It is of a piece with its predecessors. There is the same rambling, muddle-headed, opinionated comment on the topics of the day, with some excursions into political philosophy and occasional flare-ups of prophetic fire. The issue opens with an attempt, only half serious, to touch upon the financial questions which then occupied everyone's attention, but soon Dostoevsky leaves this difficult ground and turns to such familiar matter as the antinomy of Russia and Europe, the alienation of the intellectuals from the masses, the mission of the Russian people.

Here is once more the same medley of populist sentiment and monarchist faith, of Christian professions and jingoistic bluster. "Above all," he writes, "I stand for the masses, I believe religiously in their soul, in their great strength, which no one among us knows in its full scope and grandeur." Among his notes for the issue is the round statement: "The ideal of beauty is the Russian people." However lacking the masses may be in other ways, at least they have something to live by: their God and their tsar. The Orthodox faith is their one spiritual treasure. As for the bond between the people and the Tsar, it is like that between a father and his children, a bond that is the adamant foundation of all Russian history, past, present, and to come. In fact the father of his people was just then hiding in his palace as in a prison, the object of a manhunt on the part of some of his children. One of the very men who were plotting against the tsar's life lodged just above the Dostoevsky flat, and was arrested the very night the novelist was taken mortally ill. In Dostoevsky's eyes the terrorists were the ultimate dreadful symbol of the division between the intellectuals and the people. That he was not a simple-hearted believer in his monarch's paternal good will, however, may be seen from a jotting in his notebook to the effect that he would serve the tsar even more faithfully if the latter would really come to believe that the people were his children. "Only," he adds wistfully, "he is taking a little too long to believe it."

The way for the tsar to show his fatherly confidence in the people is by inviting them to speak freely before him. First of all, the peasants should be asked to tell their needs, in a straightforward fashion, without resorting to any semblance of a Western parliament. The details of this happy scheme Dostoevsky is content to leave to the authorities. He says merely that "the inquiry may be conducted locally, by districts and cottages." At last the man of the soil will become vocal, and this will have momentous effects. For one thing, perhaps the old wall that has been standing between the classes and the masses will crumble. The honest utterance of the plain man—that will be Russia's salvation, that, rather than the "crowning of the edifice" of which so much talk is heard. The cryptic phrase referred to a constitution establishing parliamentary government. Any direct mention in the press of this consummation, which liberals had devoutly wished for generations, was taboo, and even the euphemism for it was used with circumspection.

Not everyone in higher government circles saw the salvation of the old order in bloody reprisals against the terrorists. There were those who favoured liberal reforms along with a firm attitude toward subversion. They gained ascendancy when Count Loris-Melikov was appointed Minister of the Interior after heading a Supreme Commission for the Maintenance of State Order and Public Peace. He went so far as to propose the establishment of a consultative legislative Commission, which was to include elected delegates from zemstvo boards and municipal councils, in addition to functionaries and appointed experts. The plan, which was taken to be the first step toward representative government, was dubbed by a humorist "the bob-tailed constitution."

Dostoevsky has nothing but scorn for the idea of a parliamentary régime. To the people this could only mean a change of masters, a change for the worse. He heaps contumely on "the white vests" (the prospective Russian M.P.s) and their "talkery." Their efforts, he writes in the *Diary,* are bound to be a failure. "They will only knock their heads against each other in the dark." In his notebook he abuses the constitution, the "European wench," in unprintable terms. What angers him above all is the notion of interposing anything between the people and their tsar. In essence what Dostoevsky wants is a dictatorship of the peasantry—a crowned dictatorship. And in the fullness of time this peasant empire will become an all embracing Church, a spiritual union in Christ. This is what he calls "Russian socialism," contrasting it with the soulless materialistic socialism of the West. This transformation of State into Church, one reads in his notebook, will be the true "crowning of the edifice," but a couple of pages further on he observes realistically that the Church as a living institution has been in a state of paralysis since the time of Peter.

Christianity versus socialism, the solution of the social problem by love or by reason—this dilemma vexed Dostoevsky to the last. He has no doubts as to which will prevail: "A new sudden spirit will blow." Certainly Russia has nothing to fear, although the future is fraught with danger. The end of the world is coming, he prophesies, falling into his old apocalyptic strain. The close of the century will be marked by such a cataclysm as has never been seen before. But Russia must stand like a rock, and the waves will break on her shore. "No, we have no socialism, not at all," is his last word.

As though he needed to reassure himself on this point, he kept returning to his other favourite idea, namely that morality is rooted in faith. "Moral ideas," he jotted in his notebook, "spring from religious feeling. Logic can never justify them." And again: "Conscience without God is a horror; it may go astray to the point of immorality." The sole touchstone of morality is Christ. "But this," he goes on, "is no longer philosophy; this is faith; and faith is [as unmistakable as] the colour red." As though not yet satisfied with his formulation of the idea, he stages a brief debate with a utilitarian, which concludes thus: "To turn the other cheek, to love another more than yourself, not because it is advantageous, but because you like it to the point of its becoming a burning feeling, a passion. 'Christ was mistaken'—admitted. This burning feeling says: I would rather stay with the mistake, with Christ, than with you." It is the conviction that he believed he had acquired in prison a quarter of a century previously and that he had then expressed in practically identical terms.

In the same breath he preaches turning the other cheek and advocates, in his *Diary*, a public policy of shrewdness and violence. In Europe, he writes, Russia should lie low, all the while working hard at home, in secret preparation for the coming conflict. But in the East aggressiveness must be the order of the day. "In Europe

we were hangers-on and slaves, Asia we shall enter as masters."
Besides, the Russians, though Europeans, are also, and perhaps
more truly, Asiatics. Skobelev's victory over the Turkomans on
January 12, 1881, which completed the conquest of Turkestan,
seems to him of immense historic significance, since Asia might
play a decisive part in the future of the country. With its vast ex-
panses, the continent is perhaps destined to save Russia from communism. Alexander I had made a capital mistake, he argues, in
failing to come to terms with Napoleon after driving him out of the
country: had he done so, the two might have divided the world,
France securing the West and Russia the East. Napoleon would
have failed in the end, but Russia would have retained the East
and, as a sea power, could easily have defeated England. That old
error must be rectified: Russia must face East. "To Asia! To Asia!"
Dostoevsky cries, and the last public utterance of this apostle of
Christian love was a cheer for Skobelev's conquering battalions.

II

The year 1881 opened auspiciously. The novel was a huge sec-
cess in every respect—a staggering number of copies, fifteen hundred
in all, were sold within a few days after its publication in book
form. Furthermore, subscriptions to the *Diary* were pouring in.
Dostoevsky's health seemed better than usual, although it was clear
that only his nervous energy sustained him. He went out a good
deal and even consented to take part in private theatricals arranged
by Countess Tolstoy. As the month wore on, however, and the
publication date for the first issue of the *Diary* approached, he was
again in his customary hectic state. Would the censor pass the
remarks on summoning the spokesmen of the peasantry? It was a
matter of great importance to him, since he intended to return to
the subject repeatedly in the course of the year. By Sunday, January
25, the entire copy for the issue was in the hands of the printer and
Dostoevsky had received a reassuring word from the censor, who
was a personal friend of the countess, that the text would not be
tampered with. The day found him, relieved at having the issue
safely off his hands, in a good mood, and the house was full of
guests. Before the afternoon was over, however, his irritability got

the better of him, and he had a little tiff with one of them over a trivial matter.

That evening his sister Vera, who had come from Moscow on a visit, was dining with the family. The meal began pleasantly enough, with jokes and reminiscences, but soon the guest steered the conversation toward that sore subject, the Kumanina inheritance. Indeed, she had come as an envoy of the other sisters, all of them incensed by Dostoevsky's having secured through litigation a share in the estate to which the will did not entitle him. Vera's mission was to persuade her brother to give it up, and she did not mince words in denouncing his greed and cruelty. She ended by bursting into tears, and he, mortified beyond words, left the table before dinner was over and fled to his study. The ugly scene was destined to be the last in a long feud. As he sat at his desk, his head in his hands, he suddenly realized that they were wet with blood that was trickling from his mouth: he was having a haemorrhage.

Such is his daughter's account of what occurred. Strakhov's reminiscences lend some slight support to this story. On the other hand, Dostoevsky's wife says nothing in her memoirs of any family quarrel. According to her, the haemorrhage of the lungs came late at night and was caused by the strain of moving a heavy piece of furniture.

There was a second and more serious haemorrhage on Monday afternoon, but he made light of it and tried to soothe his frightened children by showing them a humorous weekly that had just come. He was sufficiently himself to write with his own hand a letter—his last—to *Russky vestnik*, pleading for the immediate payment of a sum owing to him, on the grounds that he was "in extreme need of money." The doctor arrived, and in the course of the examination there was another flow of blood, which so weakened him that he fainted. On recovering consciousness, he called for a priest, confessed, and received extreme unction. As soon as the priest left, Anna came in with the children to congratulate him upon having taken the sacrament. He gave the children his blessing and bade them love each other and take care of their mother. He asked her to read them the parable of the prodigal son. Then he bade them never forget what they had just heard, trust in God, and, should they fall into evil ways, remember that God's forgiveness was infinite and that He would rejoice in their repentance as the father had rejoiced in the return of his prodigal son. When the children left the room, he turned to Anna, thanked her for the happiness she had brought him, and begged her forgiveness for any unkindness he may have shown her.

On Tuesday he seemed better. He was cheerful, called in the children, and even spoke to them, in a whisper. As the day wore on he began to fret about the *Diary*. Then the make-up man came with news that the issue had been passed by the censor, but that the copy was seven lines too long and would have to be cut. With Anna's help the difficulty was ironed out, and Dostoevsky was able to rest. Meanwhile news of his illness had got abroad, and expressions of sympathy began to pour in.

A quiet night followed. Waking while it was still dark, Anna, who had slept on a mattress beside the divan where he lay, found his eyes were fixed upon her. She bent over him. He had been awake for hours, he whispered, and added that he knew he would die that day. He asked her to light a candle and give him his Bible. She handed him the copy of the New Testament which had been presented to him in Siberia on his way to prison, and which he always kept by him. He was in the habit of opening it at random and telling his fortune by the passage upon which his eye lighted. He opened it thus now and bade her read. The words she read at the top of the page were these: "But John detained him, saying: I have need to be baptized of thee, and comest thou to me? But Jesus answering said unto him: Do thou not detain me, for thus it becometh us to fulfil all righteousness." " 'Do thou not detain me,' " Dostoevsky repeated; "that means I shall die." And he closed the book.*

He was calm, and tried to comfort Anna, speaking of the chil-

* This account figures in the reminiscences of Dostoevsky's widow. She told an early biographer of her husband that the reading of the Bible took place in the afternoon of the day he died. The page in question bears the following inscription in her hand: "Opened by me and read at Fyodor Mikhailovich's request on the day of his death at 3 o'clock." The passage on which he lighted was Matthew III, 14-15. In the King James Version it reads: "But John forbade him, saying, I have need to be baptized of thee, and comest thou to me? And Jesus answering said unto him, Suffer it to be so now: for thus it becometh us to fulfil all righteousness." This is some-

dren, reminding her of their happiness together, assuring her that in the fourteen years of their married life he had not been unfaithful to her even in thought (had he utterly forgotten Polina?). She tried to turn his mind to other things and begged him to rest. He obeyed her and was silent, but she knew by his expression that he was still brooding on death, though it held no terrors for him. Did she read his face aright? In her account of those last hours, she is plainly intent upon painting a picture of a truly Christian passing. He was dying at the height of his powers, with his work unfinished and just when, for the first time, there was some hope of going on with it unhampered. Was he confronting his end with the submissiveness with which he had accepted his prison sentence, or was he relinquishing his hold with the reluctance of one who shared the Karamazov lust for life? Did he feel no shudder of dread, had he at last recovered that faith in which he could confidently murmur his childhood prayer: "All my hope I place in thee, Mother of God; shelter me under thy mantle"?

Late in the morning all hope was abandoned. The one thought that seemed to oppress the dying man was that he was leaving Anna and the children without means. Certainly they could not depend on the income from his published works. Where would they turn? He kept whispering broken words of pity to Anna, as she sat beside him holding his hand. Several times the children came in for a brief moment, and he gave little Fedya his chief treasure: his New Testament.

As the day wore on the apartment filled up with friends and relatives. Pasha rushed in, demanding to be admitted to the sick room, but was prevented. He was excited. He kept insisting that, as his father had as yet made no disposition of his property, a notary should be summoned at once to draw up a will.

Toward seven in the evening Dostoevsky had a haemorrhage so severe that he lost consciousness. The doors of the sick room were opened, and people filed into the shabby, gloomy chamber. It was an added agony for Anna to share his last moments with these outsiders, some of whom were not even friends, but she was helpless.

what different from what Dostoevsky's wife read. The book before her was a copy of the 1820 edition of the Russian New Testament. In later editions the text of verse 15 was corrected to bring it closer to the original and so to the English translation.

The motionless figure lay on the divan, and there was no sound but the whistle of weak, difficult breathing. His head was thrown back upon the pillow, and a light nearby fell squarely upon the white forehead and cheek and a smudge of blood on the chin. The two children knelt at the head of the couch, making the sign of the cross over and over in a frightened, hurried way. Anna clung to his hand. At last the priest came to murmur the prayer for the dying. It was eight thirty-six when the doctor, bending over the body of Fyodor Dostoevsky, caught the last beat of that divided heart.

CHAPTER TWENTY-EIGHT

"LIFE BEYOND LIFE"

During his last years Dostoevsky's publicist writings had considerably coloured his reputation. Death, retiring the journalist, advanced the novelist, but at the moment of his passing the tributes were paid to both. And the loudest acclaim came from the conservatives. Pobedonostzev, writing to the heir apparent, lamented the loss of an ardent Christian and patriot, and was told in reply that the man was truly irreplaceable. Church and State united to turn the stupendous funeral into quasi-official ceremony. There were some to whom the spectacle of the bishops eulogizing the Russian Marquis de Sade, as Turgenev put it, was food for irony. There was a handful of radicals who looked upon the dead man as one who had, after all, once fought in the cause of freedom. Indeed, it was rumoured that some students were restrained from marching behind the coffin carrying fetters in memory of Dostoevsky's political martyrdom. But on the whole it was as the apostle of pity and love, the spiritual guide, the humanitarian that he was remembered in the public orisons.

A month later the capital was agitated by another funeral, that of Alexander II, who had been killed by a terrorist bomb. His successor, piloted by Pobedonostzev, pursued a policy or repression which postponed until the reign of Nicholas II the hour of reckoning, and made it the more terrible when it came. During the grey eighties people adopted a "brighten-the-corner-where-you-are" attitude and engaged in self-cultivation. In such an atmosphere Dostoevsky's work was apt to be prized mainly for the problems of the individual conscience that it poses.

As the century drew to a close these novels found an increasingly receptive audience. The literary world, having entered upon its *fin de siècle* phase, exhibited a romantic, anti-rationalist bias. The tide of individualism ran so high that Nietzsche rivalled Marx in popu-

larity. A large group was submitting itself to the discipline of philosophy. The more tender-minded intellectuals finding the materialist
doctrines chill and cramping, looked for some comforting faith.
Soon God-seeking and God-building became the fashion. Some
preached a new synthesis of flesh and spirit, others, a communal religious consciousness; all inclined to share a belief in the Messianic
rôle of the Russian people and a mystic sense of imminent doom.
Both the neo-romantics and the neo-Christians adopted Dostoevsky
as their spiritual father. At the same time the industrial development
of the country, and the consequent growth of the city population,
with "its sick hurry, its divided aims," made the fictions of this
intellectual proletarian more actual. There were those on the Left
who cried down his work as socially dangerous. But even in revolutionary circles there were some who valued him not only as a
novelist, but as a man whose work carried a rebellious strain and
a profoundly democratic sentiment. This in spite of the fact that his
opinions continued to give aid and comfort to the monarchists and,
during the first World War, the expansionists.

At the fall of the empire the influence of Dostoevsky was part
of the very air that literate Russia breathed. There was hardly an
imaginative writer who did not owe him something, by way of
manner, if not of matter, so that even those who did not read him
could not escape him. By this time his writings belonged to the
body of European culture. Abroad, as at home, his prestige was
at once an effect and a contributing cause of the reaction against
the positivism of the previous era. The Western world showed
toward his performance an intellectual hospitality that, along with
other virtues, he had summarily denied it. Translations of his novels
had begun to appear while he was still living. A decade after his
death the bulk of his work was accessible in German. Then France
welcomed it, and shortly before the first World War his collected
fiction began to appear in English. If he came to his new public with
the credentials of a naturalist and a critic of the social order, he
appealed to it largely as an interpreter of that strange and wonderful
thing, the Russian soul. As time went on, however, and new de-
velopments in psychology became familiar to the general, his novels
ceased to seem so exotic.

It was during the war and the calamitous decade following it that his vogue in the West, especially in Germany, reached its peak. The few deprecatory voices were lost in a chorus of acclaim. The reason why people turned to Dostoevsky in those troubled times is not far to seek. The sadism fostered by the war lent this "cruel talent" a new resonance. Further, the world of his fictions was congenial to men who had a sense of being caught in the grip of catastrophe. Some saw him as a prophet of Europe's doom. To others he appealed as the apostle of a revivified Christianity, or as the keeper of the keys to the unconscious, in which the West must immerse itself before it could take up the task of building anew.

A reaction against what amounted to a cult of Dostoevsky was inevitable. It occurred in Great Britain and America in the years immediately preceding the second World War. Simultaneously his influence waned in Germany under the impact of Nazism, which because of its xenophobia seems to have made but a feeble effort to claim him as a proto-fascist.

Since the end of the war there has been a revival of Dostoevsky's vogue. Witness the flood of new translations, biographies, critical works. It is noteworthy that the emphasis of the commentators has been less on the novelist's art, than on his thinking, on the ideas to which his fictions give body and pressure. Re-examination of the values of liberal democracy has brought some of his writings into focus, and much of his work has acquired new relevance by virtue of the intensified concern with religion. More than one author has been at pains to harmonize Dostoevsky's views with the teachings of Catholicism—not an easy task, considering his hostility toward the Church of Rome and his infirmities as a theologian. On the other hand, his vehement anti-intellectualism, which leads him to cast reason in the rôle of the villain of the human drama, his reliance on faith as a means of apprehending reality, his tendency to place his characters in extreme situations, his emphasis on the individual's self-determination through free choice, his sense of tragedy—all this has enabled the existentialists to recruit him for their camp, at least for its Christian sector.

Whatever the vicissitudes of Dostoevsky's reputation, his popularity has apparently been confined to the intellectual class. One gets the impression that even at the height of his vogue his work was largely caviare to the general, at least in the English-speaking countries. An author anxious to reach the common reader, he has been, instead, to a large extent a writer's writer, finding particularly responsive members of his public among his fellow literati. Has he not left his mark on the fiction of the Western world? Indeed, attempts have been made, if not always successfully, to specify the debt owed him by certain novelists. It is difficult to escape the feeling that Dostoevsky's art has helped to free imaginative literature from what Arthur Symons called "the bondage of exteriority."

At home, with the destruction of the old order, his popularity has naturally suffered a setback. In the beginning his prestige commanded the respect of the new régime. He was second only to Tolstoy in a list of authors to whom monuments were to be erected according to a decree signed by Lenin on July 30, 1918. In a speech made at the unveiling of Dostoevsky's statue in Moscow that same year he was declared to have been a harbinger of the revolution. Three years later the Commissar of Education gave him a place of honour among Russia's "great prophets."

Before long, however, the encomia grew less frequent and a decidedly chilly tone crept into them. The fewest critics denied that he was a writer of major stature, but many of them found both his dogmas and his doubts counter-revolutionary, when they did not seem unreal. Soviet writers were warned against the influence of a novelist whose work exuded the poison of petty-bourgeois individualism and who, furthermore, failed to see that evil in human beings was the consequence of a social system based on the exploitation of man by man. Maxim Gorky had long been inveighing against Dostoevsky as a decadent and a defamer of human nature. Speaking in 1934 at the First Congress of Soviet Writers, he laid at the novelist's door the fact that after the abortive revolution of 1905 the intelligentsia had turned away from the radical movement.

At the same time there was no lack of critics who attempted to find a place for Dostoevsky in the cultural heritage of communism. The enterprise was not entirely hopeless. He had been, after all, a disciple of Belinsky and a "Petrashevist." His apologists could point to the tonic strain of rebellion in his works, to the insight into the pathology of the soul of man under capitalism that they offer, to the fact that he abominated the bourgeoisie, to his high conception of Russia's world mission. It was possible to emphasize the part that socialism and revolution play in his work, and at worst pay him the tribute due a mighty adversary, whom all enemies of communism must plagiarize. Altogether, while the zigzags of the literary party line naturally affected comment on the novelist, a certain amount of freedom in interpreting his writings was tolerated. The 125th anniversary of his birth did not go unnoticed. A dramatization of one of his tales was performed at the Moscow Art Theatre. Shortly afterwards several books appeared which tended to rehabilitate him in the eyes of the Soviet public.

Then came a sudden reversal. These books were scathingly denounced in the press. One critic, quoting Gorky to the effect that Dostoevsky was "the evil genius" of the Russian people, declared that there was nothing more harmful than to try to impart "a pink glow" to this novelist's "reactionary countenance," the more so since he was widely read in the Soviet Union.

As a matter of fact, long before this outburst, hostility toward Dostoevsky must have prevailed in influential quarters. This, no doubt, accounts for the neglect into which Dostoevsky studies fell after the middle thirties. But the preceding dozen years had been a period of fruitful research: it had witnessed the appearance of a new edition of his works, with all the apparatus of scholarship, as well as the publication of the bulk of his literary remains and of much factual material relating to his life and writings.

Thus, a clearer view has been gained of this flagrantly inconsistent man, this stubbornly ambiguous genius. Yet, as the present study should have indicated, ignorance of some intimate facts concerning him has not, and probably never will, be dispelled. He remains a Rembrandtesque figure, moulded by light struggling against an enveloping darkness. Before leaving him, it seems fitting to recall briefly those elements of his performance that touch us most dearly.

I I

Dostoevsky's work, like Shakespeare's, addresses itself to more than one level of intelligence. It engages the mature mind by its psychological wizardry and its wrestling with fundamental moral and religious problems, but it also makes, by reason of its emotionalism and melodrama, a more elementary appeal.

He had a sense of dedication and he regarded his novels as his testament, but this did not blind him to the fact that he dared not be a bore. Though he took on the rôles of both journalist and prophet, his chosen craft, his livelihood was the writing of fiction, and he used all the means he knew of holding the attention of his public. In his most serious works, perhaps partly because he published these long narratives in instalments, he employed without compunction, and without skill, all the stock in trade of the mystery tale, the *roman-feuilleton*, the detective story. Perhaps, too, he felt that the heavy dialectical passages called for compensating thrills.

Prodigality, excess, diffuseness, prolixity are the hall-mark of his writing, and he can be very clumsy; his work lacks finish, a sense of measure, the restraint in which Goethe saw the sign of the master. Packed with incidentals, complicated by sub-plots, thick with philosophical argument, burdened with rather footless pronouncements, his novels are nevertheless dynamic. Instead of the contemplative quietude, the provincial indolence in which so much nineteenth-century Russian fiction is bathed, theirs is a breathless sense of crisis, of upheaval, of drama. What assists this effect is that the main action occupies only a few days, with gaps equivalent to intermissions between acts. Dostoevsky's mastery of dialogue contributes further to the dramatic quality of his novels. The air of the theatre he thus brought into his work was thoroughly congenial to him. In the scenes of pathos, of rapture, of nightmare, especially where the characters speak almost as naked souls, this indifferent and awkward stylist finds phrases that, in his own words, veritably "scratch the heart."

Now and then one surprises him behaving as though he had the conscience of a realist. He tried to seize upon and cope with the passing moment, and liked to allude to matters of current interest, especially a sensational murder. *The House of the Dead* is to a large extent a piece of reportage. In the preface to *The Brothers Karamazov* he was careful to indicate that the action took place "thirteen years ago," that is in the middle sixties, shortly after the introduction of the jury system: the details of Dmitry's trial by jury occupy a generous section of the book. To avoid errors in the pages dealing with the trial, he made it his business to consult a lawyer. He begged the editor, who was reading his proof, to find out exactly what uniform school boys were wearing at the time and, if necessary, to make changes in the text. He had written earlier to an acquaintance who had much to do with children, asking for some examples of schoolboys' talk, habits, beliefs, misdemeanours. For the sake of the section on Father Zosima he read the lives of saints and other devotional literature and, as will be remembered, visited Optina Pustyn, modelling the monastery in the novel largely on that retreat. He told his editor that in describing Ivan's hallucination he was not overstepping the bounds of possibility: physicians with whom he had discussed the matter had reassured him on this point. He said further that every item in Ivan's collection of atrocities committed against children was based on reports of actual occurrences. All these things, he wrote, "happened, *were*, they are printed in newspapers, and I can show where—I have invented nothing."

The realist reveals himself in other ways than in concern for faithfulness of representation. More than once the tale is related not by the omniscient author, but by a participant in the action or an innocent bystander who is an eyewitness of some of the events and has hearsay knowledge of others. Dostoevsky was skilful in telling the story in the first person, but rather awkward in his use of what Henry James called "the impersonal author's concrete deputy." In employing both devices, however, it is clear that his intention was to enhance the verisimilitude of the account. The very texture of his writing, coarse and loose as it is, suits a workaday naturalism. The total absence of metaphor is noteworthy. Here is none of the perfection of phrasing that attracts attention to itself and reminds the reader that he has to do with a literary work. It is chiefly because of extreme slovenliness, concealed to some extent in translation, that his style is obtrusive. In a literature the tone of which had from the first been set by the gentry, he established the language of the democratic middle class.

It would be erroneous, however, to place Dostoevsky within the realistic tradition. Not infrequently he failed to live up to his own precept that a writer must know "down to the last detail" the milieu he is depicting. He was not the shrewd observer, the historian dealing with things as they are, that he sometimes fancied himself to be. His task was not to set down his impressions of the shifting world as it flowed past him. The run of average experience seen with the

eye of common sense—the sort of thing that the British novelist
is adept at—is incommensurate with the substance of his novels.
"What to most people verges on the fantastic and exceptional," he
wrote to Strakhov, "is for me sometimes the very essence of the
real." It will be remembered that he dated his birth as a writer from
a moment of "vision." He had a predilection for prosy, shabby
backgrounds, but he treated them with a kind of romantic gusto,
reminiscent of Versilov's liking for the tavern where "it's all so
vulgar and prosaic that it borders on the fantastic." He spoke of
himself, and truly, as a realist in a higher sense. His business, he
said, was to explore "all the depths of the human soul."

To this task he brought rare insight and intuition. His characters
—excluding, of course, the conventional caricatures and lay figures
—are for the most part people in whom the ordinary impulses are
exaggerated, sometimes perverted, and who are subjected to some
overwhelming strain. They are given to ecstasies and agonies, they
go to extremes intellectually, they are apt to want integration and
stability. These men and women are drawn with an extraordinary
understanding of the ambivalence which latterly has been recognized as fundamental to human nature, with an appreciation of the
rôle that the subconscious plays in shaping attitudes and behaviour,
of the function of the dream in disclosing hidden wishes and dreads.
The world he imagined would have been a different place, if so many
people in it did not behave compulsively, love where they hate and
hate where they love, suck pleasure out of pain, show themselves
at once noble and base. It suggests a conception of the psyche as a
complex of responses subtler and more ambiguous, less subject to
the control of reason than had been generally believed. Dostoevsky
thus anticipated findings of later students of the mind. The novelist,
who came after him could scarcely have taken their readers on such
revealing journeys if they had not travelled along the passages that
he had tunnelled out.

Behind the conflicting impulses and unstable emotions, far below
the play of the intelligence, at the very core of the personality, perhaps synonymous with it, there is the will. It manifests itself in
freedom of choice, man's dearest possession, without which life is
unendurable. This view, which is set forth in "The Notes from the
Underground" and implicitly denied by the Grand Inquisitor.

Dostoevsky accepted, but with an important proviso. Granted that it is an evil thing, even for ends ostensibly just, reasonable, advantageous to the individual, to coerce or bribe the will, but woe to it when it is an instrument of unbridled self-indulgence and intransigent self-regard! The supreme act of the will is free surrender in love. Only by losing itself in God can it find itself. With Dostoevsky, psychology abutted on religion.

He was anything but a systematic thinker, and he thought with his viscera. Yet beating like a pulse in each of his books is some dominant *idea*, some problem of the moral or religious order. This is not a matter of dispassionate intellection, but rather in the nature of what is called in *A Raw Youth* "idea-feelings." Arising from and finding issue in emotion, they owe some of their power to the warmth and urgency of the human voice that gives them utterance.

His preoccupation with ideas lends some of his characters a symbolic quality, which is accentuated by their relation to one another. Nevertheless for the most part they possess a compelling reality, having the solidity and opacity of men and women who cast a shadow. The authority with which they are portrayed may be due to the fact that in exploring "all the depths of the human soul" Dostoevsky proceeded both by observation of his fellows and by pitiless introspection. His performance was not a flight from himself, as is the case with some artists, but a kind of *amor fati*, a hugging of his destiny. In his novels one finds, however veiled, distorted or transfigured, the projection of the forces and potentialities within himself, the embodiment of his own fears and desires, his loves and his hates, his rebellion and his submission. Vital to an understanding of his work is the fact that it was the theatre of his own inner conflict.

The struggle, one ventures, was between his sceptical intellect and his urgent will-to-believe, between his ugly impulses and his desire to cling to the image of moral perfection. He was a man who felt intensely and, though capable of compromise in practical affairs, exalted the extremist, the intransigent, the one who knows no limits in his pursuit of good or evil. Unable to face stoically a purposeless, godless world, he trampled upon whatever threatened his faith. If, as has been truly said of D. H. Lawrence, he "turned his intellect into a giant slave of his intuitions," the slave was in perpetual rebellion. He might revile, he might degrade his rational member, but he could not subdue it.

III

In the climatic scene which ends with Ivan Karamazov reciting his fantasy, "The Grand Inquisitor," he asks Alyosha what it is that "during a momentary halt in a tavern" Russian boys talk about. And he answers himself: "Of the universal questions, nothing else: is there a God? Is there immortality? And those who do not believe in God talk of socialism or anarchism, of the transformation of all mankind according to a new pattern, so that, what the devil, it all comes to the same, they're the same questions tackled from the other end."

There is a large group of people in this age who are apt to tackle these problems "from the other end" and to reject some of Dostoevsky's solutions. Particularly for the secular-minded, much in his thinking impairs a full response to his work. His fictions move within the sphere of religion, a religion strongly tinged with nationalism and bound up with the idea of Russia's Messianic mission. They are, too, a vehicle for his aberrations and obsessive prejudices, bizarre or worse. It was not partiality for free enterprise that made him inveigh endlessly against what he called socialism. He abhorred it because he saw its adherents as atheists, dedicated to a mechanistic philosophy and so determined to devise a rational, planned, and inevitably dehumanizing society. What will span the "echoing straits" between men, between nations? The question was one of his chief preoccupations. By way of an answer, intended as an alternative to the "socialist" solution, he could offer only a beatific vision: a polity transfigured into a universal Church, innocent of all coercion and authority, in effect the City of God.

One can share Dostoevsky's distrust of scientific control as a means of achieving the good society. One can readily sympathize, too, with his anguish at the thought of life being a ceaseless flux, devoid of meaning and purpose, yet fail to see eye to eye with him in regard to the consequences of disbelief. "How is man going to be good without God?" cries Dmitry Karamazov. The thesis that morality hangs upon belief in God and immortality is indeed the burden of Dostoevsky's mature work. At the mid-century Dmitry's cry is not echoed from the pulpit alone. Yet there are those who retort, and with reason: has man been better with God than without Him? One recalls a passage from Tolstoy's *Confession*, a work composed at the very time when *The Brothers Karamazov* was being written: "Then and now the public profession and confession of Orthodoxy was chiefly met with among people who were dull and cruel and who considered themselves very important. Ability, honesty, reliability, good nature and moral conduct were more often met with among unbelievers."

By his exaltation of suffering Dostoevsky places another stumbling-block in the reader's path. The difficulty is that he failed to recognize the distinction that Kierkegaard drew between "tribulations" and "temptations": on the one hand, suffering which is due to external causes and which can and should be eliminated, and on the other, unavoidable suffering which results from a situation involving a moral choice.

Above all, one remembers against him his alliance with the forces of bigotry and oppression. Nevertheless, it must be acknowledged that his novels affirm, if not without ambiguity, the basic humane values which men can only neglect to their grave hurt. The world of his imagination centres upon the integrity and inviolability of the individual self, and the longing for human fellowship is of the tissue of his work. These stories, these novels were composed by a man who denied the competence of science to legislate for a being only partly within the natural order, and who celebrated "living life" as against everything that smacked of the mechanical and the cerebral. He was aware of, indeed, he exaggerated, the burdens and dangers of freedom. Hence his dire predictions of what would happen if the religious sanction of morality collapsed. Yet with his "principal" mind—it will be recalled that Aglaia in *The Idiot* attributes to everyone a "principal" mind and a subordinate one—he knew that freedom is the essential of man's humanity. The idea dominates and shapes some of his most pregnant writing.

Rebellion both frightens and fascinates him. In his attitude toward the revolutionary complex he is like Raskolnikov, dreaming that he was repeatedly murdering the old harpy, who kept laughing at him, refusing to be killed. His orthodoxy, both political and

religious, is highly suspect. While fighting on the side of the angels
he is too persuasively the devil's advocate. The novelist's moral
maximalism, with its raptures and its agonies, is inimical to all
reformist and middle-of-the-road thinking. Gorky rejoiced in
Dostoevsky's vogue abroad, believing that this "poisonous talent"
would weaken the complacency of the Western middle class.
No radical has poured out more venom upon the solid bourgeois
than this reactionary. No one has shown more effectively the miseries
of indigence and the way in which a man's soul may be mutilated
under oppression. He was himself, after all, a penniless intellectual,
alienated from the people whom he idealized, having no real bond
with the upholders of the ancestral order. His professions of loyalty
to the *status quo* notwithstanding, his novels point to disorder and
corruption behind the social façade, suggesting impermanence and
upheaval. Few novelists have so relentlessly explored man's capacity for cruelty and depravity, and while his contemporaries,
impressed with the advance of science and technology, spoke confidently of progress, he was haunted by visions of wars and revolu-
tions, disintegration and collapse. His work speaks with special
authority to an age that has supped on horrors and that has been
well named one of anxiety.

Whatever course history may take, a large part of Dostoevsky's
work, so warm with compassion, so crowded with people inwardly
seen, powerfully projected, so big with questionings, will trouble
the blood, kindle the imagination, move the mind toward a concern
with ultimate things. His major novels should continue to provide
the reader with the sense of having glimpsed the human drama at
its most intense, of having shared in the enterprise to which Dostoevsky at an early age promised to devote his life: the unravelling
of the mystery of man.

BIBLIOGRAPHY

I. GENERAL REMARKS

The most complete and textually reliable edition of Dostoevsky's writings is that issued in Moscow in 1926-30. Its scholarly apparatus comprises variant readings, lists of the editions which appeared during the novelist's lifetime, and information on the manuscripts extant, including preliminary drafts and notes. The amply annotated Soviet edition begun in 1956 contains his fiction only. The quotations from the novels and stories are taken from Constance Garnett's translation, first published in London, 1912-20, in twelve volumes, each separately titled. In every instance the quoted passages have been collated with the original and in some cases altered. The Modern Library edition of *The Possessed* New York, 1936, includes the suppressed chapter of the novel, translated by the present writer. He has revised the Garnett translation of *The Brothers Karamazov* and *The Idiot*, which the Limited Editions Club, New York, brought out in 1933 and 1956 respectively; the novel mentioned first was reprinted in 1949 by The Heritage Press, New York. A rendering of *Crime and Punishment*, by Jessie Coulson, appeared in 1951. David Magarshack's retranslation of that novel and of *The Possessed* (under the title *The Devils*) came out in 1953, and of *The Idiot* in 1956. With the publication of *The Diary of a Writer*, New York 1949, 2 v., and of *Winter Notes on Summer Impressions*, New York 1955, the bulk of Dostoevsky's non-fictional work has become available in English.

Only the first three of the projected four volumes of a complete Soviet edition of Dostoevsky's letters have been published so far. With its abundant notes, it is an indispensable repository of data on our author. The first volume of a French translation of this work appeared in Paris in 1949. Dostoevsky's letters to his wife were published separately in 1926; an English translation of them was brought out in 1930. There are two selections from the novelist's correspondence: *Letters of F. M. Dostoevsky to His Family and Friends*, New York 1914; Dostoevsky: *Letters and Reminiscences*, New York 1923.

Aside from *The House of the Dead*, which is thinly disguised autobiography, and certain passages in *The Diary of a Writer*, Dostoevsky left no account of his works and days. Much of the testimony of his contemporaries went into the making of his first biography, published in 1883. Thereafter some additional matter of no little weight found its way into print, but it was only in the first two decades of the Soviet period that numerous publications released a flood of light on the subject. In 1956 a collection of hitherto unknown Dostoevsky texts was announced for publication in the near future as a volume in the series entitled *Literaturnoe nasledstvo*. A list of reminiscences about Dostoevsky is contained in *Seminari po Dosto-*

evskomu, edited by Grossman, Moscow 1922. The latter's *Zhizn i trudy Dostoevskovo*, Moscow 1935, is a useful compilation in the nature of a strictly factual chronological outline of the novelist's life.

To the devotion and industry of his widow we owe a comprehensive catalogue of Dostoevskiana: *Bibliograficheski ukazatel sochineni i proizvedeni iskusstva, otnosyashchikhsya k zhizni i deyatelnosti F. M. Dostoyevskovo: 1846-1903*, St. Petersburg 1906. A sequel to this Bibliography, covering the years 1903-23, is to be found in v. 2 of *Dostoevsky; statyi i materialy*, edited by Dolinin, and another list, bringing the record to 1930, is contained in v. 13 of the first of the Soviet editions of Dostoevsky's works mentioned above. Komarovich surveyed the literature on Dostoevsky in *Dostoevsky: sovremennye problemy istoriko-literaturnovo izucheniya*, Leningrad 1925, and summed up later research in *Neue Probleme der Dostojewskij-Forschung: 1925-30 (Zeitschrift für clavische Philologie*, Leipzig 1933-34 v. X-XI). Much non-Russian Dostoevsky literature is noted in Romein, *Dostjewskij in de Westersche kritiek*, Haarlem 1924; Minssen, *Die französische Kritik und Dostojewskij*, Hamburg 1933; Helen Muchnic, *Dostoevsky's English Reputation*, Northampton, Mass. 1939.

Mme. Dostoevsky was instrumental in founding the department of the Moscow Historical Museum devoted to the manuscripts and relics of her husband. This material has been transferred to the Dostoevsky Museum, located in the novelist's childhood home, the apartment in the wing of the Mariinsky Hospital for the Poor, now the Hospital for Social Diseases. There are, too, Dostoevsky museums at Staraya Russa and at Darovoye, where the novelist spent his summers as a boy. Dostoevsky mss. are also kept in the Central Archives, Moscow, the Institute of Russian Literature attached to the Academy of Sciences, Leningrad, and the Leningrad Public Library.

II. REFERENCES

Abbreviations and symbols for titles frequently cited:

A   Dostoevsky, *Polnoe sobranie khudozhestvennykh proizvedeni*, Moscow-Leningrad 1926-30, 13 v.

AD   *The Diary of Dostoevsky's wife*, New York, 1928: tr. of *Dnevnik A. G. Dostoevskoi*, 1867 g., Moscow 1923.

AN   A. G. Dostoevskaya, *Vospominaniya*, Moscow 1925.
       Die Lebenserrinnerungen der Gattin Dostojewskis, München 1925, is a complete German translation of this volume. *Vospominaniya A. G. Dostoevskoi: F. M. Dostoevsky v 1871-2 gg., in* Dolinin, ed., *Dostoevsky: statyi i materialy*, v. 1, contains some matter not included in Mme. Dostoevsky's reminiscences as issued in book form.

AV   A. M. Dostoevsky, *Vospominaniya*, Leningrad 1930.

B   O. Miller and N. Strakhov, eds., *Biografiya, pisma i zametki iz zapisnoi knizhki Dostoevskovo*, St. Petersburg 1883; this volume, which is the first attempt at a biography of the novelist, consists of three separately paged sections; the last two are indicated by Roman numerals following the page reference.

BK   Dostoevsky, *The Brothers Karamazov,* tr. by Constance Garnett, New York 1929.

BY   *Byloe,* Petrograd.

CP   Dostoevsky, *Crime and Punishment,* tr. by Constance Garnett, New York 1916.

D   Dostoevsky—all spellings and grammatical cases.

DO   Dolinin, ed., *Dostoevsky: statyi i materialy,* Petrograd 1922-24, 2 v.

DP   Dostoevsky, *Pisma,* Moscow-Leningrad 1928-34, v. 1-3.

DT   Dostoevsky and Turgenev, *Perepiska,* Leningrad 1928.

GD   Grossman, ed., *Dostoevsky na zhiznennom puti,* Moscow 1928, v. 1.

GL   Grigorovich, *Literaturnye vospominaniya,* Leningrad 1928.

GM   *Golos minuvshevo,* Moscow.

GS   Grossman, *Seminari po Dostoevskomu,* Moscow 1922; some of the contents are reprinted from a work edited by the same author: *Tvorchestvo Dostoevskovo,* 1821-1881-1921, Odessa 1921.

HD   Dostoevsky, *The House of the Dead,* tr. by Constance Garnett, New York 1923.

HT   —— *An honest thief and other stories,* tr. by Constance Garnett, New York 1919.

ID   —— *The Idiot,* tr. by Constance Garnett, New York 1917.

IS   *Istoricheski vestnik,* St. Petersburg.

K   S. S. Koteliansky, ed., *Dostoevsky portrayed by his wife:* the diary and reminiscences of Mme. Dostoevsky, New York 1926.

KA   *Krasnyi arkhiv,* Moscow.

KN   *Krasnaya nov,* Moscow.

L.   Leningrad (in imprint).

LD   Aimée (Lubov) Dostoevskaya, *Fyodor Dostoeyevsky, a study,* London 1921; first published in German: *Dostojewski geschildert von seiner Tochter, A. Dostojewski,* Erlenbach-Zürich 1920.

lit.   literaturnyi (various forms of the adjective).

LM   *Literaturnaya mysl,* Petrograd.

M.   Moscow (in imprint).

NV   *Novoye vremya,* St. Petersburg.

P.   St. Petersburg or Petrograd (in imprint).

Pa.   Paris (in imprint).

PO   F. M. Dostoevsky, *The Possessed,* tr. by Constance Garnett, New York 1916.

PR   *Pechat i revolutziya,* Moscow.

RS   *Russkaya starina,* St. Petersburg.

RV   *Russky vestnik,* Moscow.

RY   Dostoevsky, *A Raw Youth,* tr. by Constance Garnett, New York 1916.

416 BIBLIOGRAPHY

SL *Slavia*, Prague.

SO *Sibirskie ogni, Novonikolaevsk.*

sobr. sobranie.

soch. sochinenie.

SP Shchegolev, ed., *Petrashevtzy, sbornik materialov*, Moscow 1926-28, 3 v.

U Dostoevsky, *Die Urgestalt der Brüder Karamasoff:* Dostojewskis Quellen, Entwürfe und Fragmente, mit einer einleitenden Studie von Sigm. Freud, Munich 1928.

VE *Vestnik Yevropy*, St. Petersburg.

VF *Voprosy filosofii i psihologii*, Moscow.

vosp. vospominaniya.

WN Dostoevsky, *White Nights and Other Stories*, tr. by Constance Garnnett, New York 1918.

WR Wrangel, *Vospominaniya o Dostoevskom v Sibiri*, St. Petersburg 1912.

YA Yanovsky, *Vospominaniya o Dostoevskom*, in *Russky vestnik*, Moscow 1885, v. 176.

Z Zamotin, *F. M. Dostoevsky v russkoi kritike*, Warsaw 1913, v. 1 (no more published).

ZS *Zeitschrift für slavische Philologie*, Leipzig.

Note: A number standing alone refers to a letter in Dostoevsky, *Pisma*, Moscow 1928-34, v. 1-3; in these volumes, which cover the years 1832 to 1877, the letters are numbered continuously.

CHAPTER ONE

i: GS 66 (tr.: K 268); RY 107; B 5-6; BK 43; HD 214; BK 14, 307; 523.

ii: AV ch. 1, *passim;* GD 36; 3; Grossman, *Put D.*, L. 1924, 27. Lyubimov, *K voprosu o genealogii D.*, in DO v. 2; AV 409-10; Volotzkoi, *Khronika roda D., M. 1933;* Arsenyev, *K proiskhozh deniyu D., in Novik,* Athens 1934, 2.

iii: AV ch. 1; A v. 4, 51; 383; AV 364; A v. 12, 224; B 119 111; GD 26; AV 403; A v. 11, 139; AV 91; Grossman, *Put D.*, 19, DO v. 2, 393,

iv: GD 25, 31-42; A v. 1, 517-18; *Dnevnik pisatelya*, Feb. 1876, ch. 1 (tr. *The peasant Marey* in HT); PO 29; Nechayeva, *V semye i usadbe D.*, M. 1939.

CHAPTER TWO

GD ch. 4-9.

i: W 145; AV 63-77; RY 112-15, 459; A v. 4, 56.

ii: AV 77-80; A v. 11, 168-70.

iii: AV 365-77.

iv: B 35-45; Maksimovsky, *Istor. ocherk razvitiya Glavnovo inzhenernovo uchilishcha,* P. 1869; RS 1900, v. 103, 327; GL 43-4, 58; Trutovsky, *Vosp. o D.,* in *Shchukinsky sbornik,* M. 1902, v. 1, and in *Russkoye obozrenie,* P. 1893, 1.

CHAPTER THREE

i: 10, 12; Alekseyev, *Ranni drug F.M.D.,* Odessa, 1921; Prokhorov, *Die Brüder D. und Sidlovskij,* in ZS 1930, 3/4; 16; *Russki arkiv,* 1907, 1, 381; ZS 1930, 3/4, 319; 10. 16, 14.

ii: 11 AV 378-81; 13; DP v. 1, 470; AV 87-8, 109; Stonov, *Seltzo Darovoye,* in *Krasnaya niva,* M. 1926, No. 16; Nechayeva, *Poyezdka v Darovoye,* in *Novyi mir,* M. 1926, 3; AV 413-14; 14; AV 375; 12; WR 171; 14.

iii: AV 381; Prokhorov, *Pochemu D. vyshel v otstavku?* in *Lit.-khud. sborn. Krasnoi panoramy,* L. 1929, 12; 14, 17, 596, 18; B 35, 41; AV 125-43; 19; GD 72-3; B 50-1.

CHAPTER FOUR

i: B 49-53; 21-27; AV 384-96; 26; v. 1, 477.

ii: 27-8; A v. 12, 30-3; GL ch. 7; Panayev, *Lit. vosp.,* L. 1928, 502-03; Annenkov, *Vosp.,* L. 1928, 447-50; Turgenev, *Soch.,* P. 1898, v. 12, 48-9.

iii: 29-31: Sollogub, *Vosp.* in IS 1886, v. 24, 561-62; 32.

iv: 33, 36-40; Rammelmeyer, *D. Begegnis mit Belinskij,* in ZS v. 21.

v. 41, Panayeva, *Vosp.,* L. 1927, 196-99; Nekrasov, *Kamennoye serdtze,* in his *Tonki chelovek,* M. 1928; Panayev, *Sobr, soch.,* M. 1912, v. 5, 7; Yezhemes. lit. pri. k *Nive,* P. 1901, 11, 392-93; Chukovsky, *D. i pleyada Belinskovo,* in his *Nekrasov,* L. 1926; Ashevsky, *D. i Belinsky,* in *Mir Bozhi* P. 1904, 1.

CHAPTER FIVE

i: 41; GL 147-50; YA 801; A v. 11, 135; 42, 44-7.

ii: 34; YA 32, 78; RY 28-9.

iii: GL 139-40; Yazykov, *Pismo v redaktziyu,* in NV Mar. 2, 1881, no. 1799, 2; Yanovsky, *Bolezn F. M. D.,* in NV Feb. 24, 1881, no. 1793; Trutovsky, *Vosp. o D.,* in *Shchuk. sbornik,* M. 1902, v. 1; Vs. Solovyov, *Vosp. OD.,* in IS 1881, 3-4; *The Insulted and Injured,* tr. by C. Garnett, London 1915, 49; 78, 398; Neznakometz (pseud. of A. S. Suvorin), *Nedelnye ocherki i kartinki: O pokoinom,* in NV Feb. 1, 1881, no.

1771, 2-3; DO v. 2, 393; B 141, ftn.; Neufeld, *D.: Skizze zu einer Psychoanalyse*, Leipzig 1923; Burchell, *D. and the Sense of Guilt*, in *Psychoanalytic Review*, Albany 1930, v. 17; Amenitzky and Segalov, *Bolezn D.* in *Nauchnoye slovo*, M. 1929, 4; Freud, D. und die Vatertötung, in U, (tr. in *The Realist*, London July 1929, and in *Partisan Review*, New York Fall 1945); Carr, *Was D. an epileptic?* in *Slavonic Review*, London 1930, v. 9; Squires, *F. D.*, in *Psychoanalytic Review*, 1937, 10.

CHAPTER SIX

i: GD 154; Semevsky, *Butashevich-Petrashevsky*, M. 1922; GM 1915, 11, 37; SP v. 3, 200; Leikina, *Petrashevtzy*, M. 1924, 25; SP v. 1, 169; RS 1872, v. 6, 84; Rourke, *The Trumpets of Jubilee*, New York 1927; SP v. 2, 153; GM 1913, 4, 114; GM 1916, 4, 189-90; Considérant, *Le socialisme devant le vieux monde, suivi de Jesus-Christ devant les conseils de guerre*, par Victor Meunier, Pa. 1848; SP v. 1, 115-17; GM 1915, 11, 42-3; 316; DO v. 2, 380-87. Also GD ch. 13; Komarovich, *Yunost D.* in BY 1924, 23; Chulkov, *D. i utopicheski sotzialism*, in *Katorga i ssylka*, M. 1929, no. 51/52.

ii: GM 1915, 12, 44; KA 1931, 46, 165-67; *D. i petrashevtzy* in DO v. 1; Leikina, *Petrashevetz Speshnev*, in BY 1924, v. 25; *Delo petrashevtzev*, M. 1937-51, 3 v. (see Index in v. 3, s.v.D.); Dolinin, *D. sredi petrashevtzev*, in *Zvenya*, 6; Belchikov, *D. v protzesse petrashevtzev*, M. 1936.

iii: YA 815-17; 51-54.

iv: YA 809; AV 188.

CHAPTER SEVEN

i: Semevsky, *Sledstviye i sud po delu petrashevtzev*, in *Russkie zapiski*, P. 1916, 9-11; SP v. 1, 165-67; Shchegolev, *Alekseyevsky Ravelin*, M. 1929; GM 1915, 11, 24-9, and 12, 42-3; 52-5; SP v. 3, 200-07; 55-56.

ii: SP v. 1, 201; *Russkie zapiski*, P. 1916, 11, 33-4; 57; SP v. 3, 207-08, 328, 335.

iii: SP v. 1, sec. 3; 58; B, 117-22; *Russkie zapiski*, P. 1916, 11, 44-5, A v. 11, 138; CP 146; ID 57; GD 192-93.

iv: 58, 60; GD p. 197, 199.

CHAPTER EIGHT

i: *Poor Folk*, tr. by L. Milman, Boston 1894, XIV; Z 8; Boehm, *Pervyye shagi D.*, in SL 1933, 1/2; Čizevskyi, *K probleme dvoinika*, in Boehm, ed., *OD., sbornik statei*, Prague 1929, v. 1; Vinogradov, *Stil peterburskoi poemy Dvoinik*, in DO v. 1; Avanesov, *D. v rabote nad Dvoin-*

ikom, in Piksanov, ed., *Tvorcheskaya istoriya,* M. 1927; Otto Rank, *Der Doppelgänger,* Leipzig *1925;* Boehm, *Skupoi rytzar Pushkina v tvorchestve D.,* in Russki Inst. v. Prage, *Pushkinski sbornik,* Prague 1929; Trubeckoj, *The Style of "Poor Folk" and "The Double,"* in *Amer. Slavic and East Europ. Review,* 1948, 4.

ii: *Petersburgskaya Letopis,* in A v. 13; (tr. *Petersburger Träume,* in *Die Weisse Blätter,* Zürich 1918); Komarovich, *Peterburgskie felyetony D.,* in Oksman, ed., *Felyetony sorokovykh godov,* L. 1930; *Boehm, Dramatizatziya sna,* in Boehm, ed., *O. D., sbornik statei,* Prague 1929, v. 1.

iii: A v. 2, 473-78; Belchikov, *Kak pisal romany D.,* in PR 1928, 2; A v. 2, 480-83.

iv: Boehm, *Gogol i Pushkin v tvorchestve D.,* in SL 1928, 7; *Grossmann, Hoffmann, Balzac, D.,* in *Sofiya,* M. 1914, 5; YA 806-07; 44; *Peterburgskaya letopis,* in A v. 13, esp. 30-32; A v. 13, 156; WN 198; See also Antziferov, *Peterburg D.,* P. 1923; Passage, D. *the Adapter* Chapel Hill, N.C. 1954.

CHAPTER NINE

i: 60; B 125-27; A v. 11, 10; Frantzeva, Vosp., in IS 1888, v. 32, 358-60; Grossman, *Grazdanskaya smert D.,* in *Liter. nasledstvo,* 22/24.

ii: Torkarzewski, *Siedem lat katorgi,* Warsaw 1918; Khranevich, *D. po vosp. ssylnovo polyaka,* in RS 1910, v. 141; Brailovsky, *D. v Omskoi katorge i polyaki,* in IS 1908, v. 112; GS 55; 60.

iii: Nikolayevsky, *Tovarishchi D. po katorge,* in IS 1898, v. 71; Vyatkin, *D. v. Omskoi katorge,* in SO 1925, 1; DP v. 1, 166; 60; 61; Cherevin, *Polk. de Grave i D.,* in RS 1889, 2; 60; BK 638; 61; BK 824; GS 55.

iv: IS 1895, 450; 60, 62-6; Skandin, *D. v Semipalatinske,* in IS 1903, 9; Gerasimov, *D. v. Semipalatinske,* in SO 1924, 4, 1926, 3; Gerasimov, *Gde zhe otbyval D. katorgu?* SO 1927, 4; Sytina, *Vosp. o D.,* in IS 1885, v. 19; WR 17-8; Stackenschneider, *Dnevnik i zapiski,* M. 1934, 445.

v: RS 1910, v. 141, 610; B 17-20, 11; D., *Das politische Gedicht auf die europäische Ereignisse von 1854,* München 1920; 75; A v. 11, 138; WR. 18-38; Smith and Isotoff, *The Abnormal from within,* in *Psychoanal. Review,* v. 22.

CHAPTER TEN

i: WR 38-9, 50-3, 63-7; B 271; Feoktistov, *Propavshie pisma D.,* in SO 1928, 3-4; 68-9, 71, 74, 76, 79.

ii: 78, 80; DP v. 1, 527-30.

iii: 81-2; *Polnoye sobr. zakonov,* P. 1856, v. 31, no. 30877; 84, 83, 86-8, 91-6

CHAPTER ELEVEN

i: 93-6, 98 101, 75, 102-08.
ii: WR 83-4; 105-11; 451, 114, 112, 115-19; Lit. nash., 22/24, 729.
iii: 120, 133.
iv: 121-28, 130-32, 134-43; GL 422; Olisov, *K prebyvaniyu D. v g. Tveri*, in KA 1923, 4.

CHAPTER TWELVE

i: 61; Kozmin, *Bratya D., i prokl. Molodaya Rossiya*, in PR 1929, 2-3; 140; Dolinin, *K tzenzurnoi istorii pervykh dvukh zhurnalov D.*, in DO v. 2; *D.-redaktor; Vremya i Epokha*, in A v. 13, 559-80; B 179-240; A v. 13, 526, 212-13; Knyazhnin, *Mater. dlya biografi Grigoryeva*, P. 1917, 285; Steklov, *Chernyshevsky*, M. 1928, v. 2, 319-24; Leikina, *Reaktzionnaya demokratiya 60-ykh gg: Pochvenniki*, in *Zvezda*, L. 1929, 6; Komarovich, *D. i shestidesyatniki*, in *Sovr. mir*, P. 1917, 1; Dolinin, *D. i Strakhov, and Pisma Strakhova k D.*, in Piksanov, *Shestidesyatye gody*, M. 1940; Shestov, *O pererozhdenii ubezhdeni u D.*, in *Russkie zapiski*, Pa. 1937, 2.
ii: B 213; *Trudy Publ. Biblioteki SSSR*, M. 1934, v. 3, 106; B 175, 213-14; ID 224-25.
iii: B 171; IS 1901, v. 86, 1032; DP v. 2, 412; B 173-74; 122; Schubert, *Moya zhizn*, in *Yezhegodnik imperat. teatrov*, P. 1911-12, 145-47.
iv: A v. 13, 350-51; DO v. 1, 359-68; GS 71; 75, 127-28; HD, 187, 76-7, 282; Z ch. 2; *D., Pervaya zapisnaya knizhka*, in *Zvenya*, 6.

CHAPTER THIRTEEN

i: RY 464; 152; Herzen, *Polnoe sobr. soch.*, P. 1920, v. 15, 354; 157; B 240-45.
ii: Dolinin, *K tzenzurnoi istorii zhurnalov D.*, in DO v. 2; AV 294-95; B 264; DT 58-60; 168, 171-74; Guralnik, *Sovr. v borbe s zhurnalami D.*, in Akad. nauk, *1 v. otd. lit. i yazyka*, M. 1950, v. 9.
iii: Dolinin, *D. i Suslova*, in DO v. 2; A. Suslova. *Gody blizosti SD.*, M. 1928 (tr.: Suslova, *D. ewige Freundin*, München 1931).
iv: 175-79: Herzen, *Polnoe sobr. soch.*, P. 1920, v. 16, 526; 180; Grossmann, *Put D.*, L. 1924, ch. 6; LD ch. 10.

CHAPTER FOURTEEN

i: 181; B 265-69; DT 87; 182-83; GS 57; 294, 185-95, 197-98, 200-01; Vysheslavtzev, *D. o lubvi i bessmertii* in *Sovr. zapiski*, Pa. 1932, v. 50 (tr.: *Über Christus*, in *Der unbekannte D.*, München 1926); AD 376; 221; S 51-2 LD ch. 9; 221; IS 1904, v. 95, 510.

ii: 297, 214-15, 203, 221; AV 299; 189, 196, 207-13, 217-21; B 269-76; *Otryvki iz zapisnoi knizhki D.: 1861-63*, in *Lit. gazeta*, M. 1931, 8.

iii: Skaftymov, *Zapiski iz podpolya sredi publitzistiki, D.*, in SL 1929, 8; Belchikov, *Chernyshevsky i D.*, in PR 1928, 5; Charles S. Peirce, *Chance, Love and Logic*, New York 1923, 275: Chernyshevsky, *Polnoe sobr. soch.*, P. 1906, v. II, 259; 193; Komarovich, *Mirovaya garmoniya D.*, in *Atenei*, L. 1924, 1-2; Dolinin, *V tvorcheskoi laboratorii D.*, L. 1947, 148; Zakrzewski, *Polpolye*, Kiev 1911; Beardsley, *D.'s Metaphor of the "Underground,"* in *The Journal of the History of Ideas*, 1942, 3.

CHAPTER FIFTEEN

i: AV 301; 221-22; DP v. 1, 402; Prokhorov, *Nerazvernuvshisya roman D.*, in *Zvenya*, 6.

ii: Kovalevskaya, *Vosp. i pisma*, M. 1951; 212; Streich, *D. i syostry Korvin-Krukovskie*, M. 1931; 240; 245; K 24; Slonim, *Tri lyubvi D.*, New York 1953, 309.

iii: 235, 226-27; DP v. 2, 225-26; 245, 386, 361, 228, 221-22; S 117; 228-31; A v. 12, 208; DT 193; AN 218; 232-33, 235-37, 318, 222; Suslova, *Gody blizosti s D.*, 129.

CHAPTER SIXTEEN

i: 241; *Iz arkhiva D. Prestupleniye i nakazaniye, neizd. mater.*, M. 1931; *Raskolnikoffs Tagebuch, mit unbekannten Entwurfen und Briefen* München 1928; Danilov, *Kompozitzionnye priyomy v Prestuplenii i nakazanii D.*, in *Izvestiya Akademii nauk*, ser. V 11, Otd. obshch. nauk, L. 1933, 3; 243; B 285; N. von Vogt *K biografi D.*, in IS 1901, v. 86; 244, 250, 294, 153, 257.

ii: 227, 234, 304; *Iz arkhiva D. Prestuplenie i nakazanie*, 66; A v. 5, 61; Alexander and Staub, *The criminal, the Judge and the Public*, New York 1931, The Neurotic Criminal; Florance, *The Neurosis of Raskolnikov*, in *Archives of Criminal Psychodynamics*, v. 1, no. 2, 1955.

iii: 234; B 290; Weinberg, *Iz vosp.*, in BY 1906, 4; RV 1889, 3, 159; Glivenko, *Raskolnikov i D.*, in PR 1926, 4; Grossmann, *Ispoved odnovo yevreya*, M. 1924, 79 (tr.: *Die Beichte eines Juden in Briefen an D.*, München 1927); 586; CP 364; *Partisan Review*, Fall 1945, 541; Kardiner, *The Bio-analysis of the Epileptic Reaction*, in *Psychoanalytic Quarterly*, Oct. 1932, 477; BK 765.

CHAPTER SEVENTEEN

i: 250, 178; Boehm, *Igrok D.*, in *Sovr. zapiski*, Pa. 1925, 24; Savage, *D.*, *The Idea of The Gambler*, in *The Sewanee Review*, Spring 1950.
ii: AN 25-49 (tr. in K 3-50); 265.
iii: 256-57; CP 433; 258-63; AN 49-71.
iv: AN 72-91; DP v. 2, 174; 265; AD 23.

CHAPTER EIGHTEEN

i: DP v. 2, 26; AD; 265; Herzen, *Polnoe sobr. soch.*, P. 1922, v. 18, 40; Streich, *Vechnaya lubov D.*, in *Ogoniok*, M. 1933, 18; LD 187-88.
ii: 266-77; DP v. 2, 250.
iii: 278-79.
iv: AD 237-38; 279; *Russki arkhiv*, M. 1902, 9, 148-49; *Russkoe obozrenie*, M. 1894, 1, 28; DT 179; Turgenev, *Pervoe sobr. pisem*, P. 1884, p. 194; Yarmolinsky, *Turgenev*, New York 1926, ch. 30.
v: AD 404; AN 112; ID 410; 279-80, 284; James Guillaume, *L'Internationale*, Pa. 1905, v. 1, ch. 5; Steklov, *Bakunin*, M. 1926, v. 2, 376.

CHAPTER NINETEEN

i: 285-87; *Iz arkhiva D. Idiot, neizdannye materialy*, M. 1931; 288-95.
ii: AN 117-18; 296-302; DO v. 2, 374-48; 303-07; AN 121-24; 308-09, 292, 296, 302, 310-12; AN 124-28; 314-19.
iii: 292, 294; ID 430; 309; ID 375, 587; 323; Dorovatovskaya-Lyubimova, *Idiot D. i ugolovnaya khronika yevo vremeni*, in PR 1928, 3.

CHAPTER TWENTY

i: 323-24; Z 123; AN 126; 322, 321-28, 331; AN 125-28; Schurig, *D. in Dresden*, in *Das Inselschiff*, Leipzig 1921, 85; 329-31.
ii: LD 161, 332; DP v. 2, 458; 330; AV 335-37; 331, 339; AV 338-43; 332-36; AN 129; DP v. 2, 183; Boehm, *Razviortyvenie sna*, in *Uchenye zapiski uchebnoi kollegii v Prage*, Prague 1924, v. 1, fasc. 2; Petrovsky, *Kompozitziya Vechnovo muzha*, in *Trudy Gos. Akademii khud nauk*, M. v. 3.
iii: 318, 321, 328; *Plan "Zhitiya velikovo greshnika,"* in *Dokumenty po istorii literatury i obshchestvennosti*, M. 1922, v. 1; Plan of the novel *"The life of a great sinner,"* in *Criterion*, London 1922, v. 1, 10; 336, 345-46.

iv: DP v. 2, 213; 343, 345-46, 340; DP v. 2, 283; 354-62; Komarovich, *Nenapisannaya poema D.*, in DO v. 1; 363, 353, 357, 362, 369, 328; A v. 11, p. 18; 365.

v: 348, 321, 353, 376, 361-62, 364-65, 369, 372, 374-75, 383-84, 386, 144, 373; AN 135; 380-82; RY 278; 371, 387-93; AN 135-39.

CHAPTER TWENTY-ONE

i: AN 144-46; DO v. 1, 483; AN 146-54, 170-72; BK 407; 394; AN 154-55; 325; AN 155; 389; AN 155-68; 406.

ii: Kozmin, ed., *Nechayev i nechayevtzy*, M. 1931; AN 130; 345; *Borba klassov*, M. 1924, 1-2, 262-73; Lenin, *Soch.*, M. 1925, v. 17, 323; PO 396; B. Kozmin, *Tkachev i revol. dvizh. 60-ykh gg.*, M. 1922, 116-20: PO 616; Z ch. 4; Krasnovskaya, *Gorki i D.*, in KN 1931, 56; PO 381; *Spor o Bakunine i D.*, L. 1926.

iii: *Der unbekannte D.*, München 1926; *Zapisnye tetradi F.M.D.*, M. 1935; A v. 7, 591-92; Boehm, *Evolutziya obraza Stavrogina*, in *Trudy V Syezda Akad. Organ. zagranitzei*, v. 1; Grossman, *Speshnev i Stavrogin*, in *Katorga i ssylka*, M. 1924, 4; Hessen, *Stavrogin als philosophische Gestalt*, in Cyzevski, ed. *D. Studien*, Reichenberg 1931; PO 579; 356; PO 234; Werner, *Tip Kirillova u D.*, in *Novyi put*, M. 1903, 10-12; Camus, *Kirillov*, in his *The Myth of Sisyphus*, New York 1955; Bulgakov, *Russkaya tragediya (Besy)* in *Russkaya mysl*, M. 1914, 4; 346; PO 106; 346; Rahv, *D.* in *The Possessed*, in his *Image and Idea*, 1945; Howe, *D.; The Politics of Salvation* in *The Kenyon Review*, Winter 1955.

iv: PO 238; A v. 7, 553-86, 592; *Sovr. mir*, P. 1913, 10, 307-10; K 231-34; Dolinin, *Ispoved Stavrogina*, in LM 1923, v. 1; 397.

v: Botzyanovsky, *Spletnya o D.*, in *Rus*, P. 1908, 159; Yasinsky, *Roman moyey zhizni*, M. 1926, 168-69; Nikolski, *Turgenev i D.*, Sofia 1921, 30; RV 1901, 125; *Sovr. mir*, P. 1913, 10. 307-10; AN 15, 285-92; Slonim, *Tri lyubvi D.*, 199-200; Levitzky, *Biograf. slovar prof. i prepod. Yuryevskovo univ.*, Dorpat 1903, v. 2, 359-62; 505; *Sovr. mir*, P. 1913, 9, 266; S. Kovalevskaya, *Vosp. detstva*, in VE 1890, 4, 626; CP 457, 459; RY 33; U 246; Stekel, *Conditions of Nervous Anxiety and Their Treatment*, London 1923, 357; Havelock Ellis, *Impressions and Comments*, 3d series, Boston 1924, 195; BK 765.

CHAPTER TWENTY-TWO

i: 385, 394, 351; AN 227; AV 348; 339, 428-31; AN 174-79; A v. 13, 580-93; Oksman, *D. v redaktzii Grazhadanina*, in Grossman, ed., *Tvorchestvo D.*, Odessa 1921.

ii: 433, 435-37, 439-47, 422, 453; Aleksandrov, *D. v vosp. tipografskovo naborshchika*, in RS 1892, v. 74; Pochinkovskaya, *God raboty s znamenitym pisatelem*, in IS 1904, v. 95; 437, 418; AN 181-82; 455.
iii: *Bobok*, in HT; A v. 11, 108-16, v. 13, 388.

CHAPTER TWENTY-THREE

i: Dolinin, *V tvorcheskoi laboratorii D.*, L. 1947, 11; AN 185-87; 469-70; LD 175-76; AN 224-25; 423, 474-86; DP v. 3, 328-29; Speransky, *D v semye* in *Illustr. Rossiya*, Pa. Feb. 21, 1931; AN 190-200; 490, 495, 505, 499, 518-32; AN 204-08.
ii: Komarovich, *Genezis romana Podrostok* in LM 1925, v. 3; 501; RY 375; HT 312, 315; RY 271, 375; Lapshin, *Obrazovanie tipa Krafta v Podrostke*, in Boehm, *OD.*, v. 1.
iii: *Nachalo*, P. 1922, 2, 229; RY 208, 54; 487; DP v. 3, 333-35; Setschkareff, *D. und das goldene zeitalter*, in *Festschrift für D. Cyzevskyi*, Berlin 1954; Kunkl, *Dolgushintzy*, M. 1932; ID 310; RY 206, 503; Junge, *Vosp.*, M. 1913, ix-xv; IS 1904, v. 95 533; Komarovich, *Roman D. Podrostok kak khudozhestvennoe yedinstvo*, in DO v. 2; *Handschrifte, Aufzeichnungen, Varianten und Briefe zu dem Roman Der Jüngling*, in *Der unbekannte D.*, München 1926.

CHAPTER TWENTY-FOUR

i: 524; Junge, *Vosp.*, M. 1913, xiii; 571, 488, 490, 510, 537, 610; LD 196-97, ch. 23; 544, 555-66; AN 214-17; DP v. 3, 368; 600-06; AN 224-26.
ii: 544; A v. 11, 491; Raskolnikov, *Zabytoe pismo D. k moskovskim studentam*, in KN 1932, 4; A v. 12, 210, 123-24, 60-62, 102, 76-90, 389; Steinberg, *D. und das Judentum*, in *Der Jude*, Berlin 1926, 4; Schwarz, *D. and Judaism*, in *Jewish Review*, London 1933, 4; Grossman, *Ispoved odnovo yevreya*, M. 1924, pp. 165-81; A v. 11, 324, 380-84, 430; AN 227-28; A v. 12, 324, v. 11, 267, 327, 398, 443, v. 12, 317; Kozlovsky, *Mechty o Tzargrade*, in GM 1915, 2; D. H. Lawrence, *Letters*, New York 1932, 238; A v. 12, 153.
iii: A v. 11, 425; Dolinin, ed., *Novyi variant Krotkoi*, in DO, v. 2; William James, *Letters*, Boston 1930, v. 2, 43-4; HT 322; A v. 11, 485; PO 210; B 117-18, 111; 551; U Einleitung, ch. 1 and p. 27; N. F. Fyodorov, *Filosofiya obshchevo dela*, Vernyi 1906. v. 1, pt. 3; Berdyayev, *Religiya voskresheniya*, in *Russkaya mysl*, M. 1915, 7; Gornostayev, *Rai na zemle; D. i Fyodorov*, Harbin 1929.
iv: L. Pierce Clark, *Clinical studies in epilepsy*, Utica 1917; *Perepiska Tolstovo so Strakhovym*, P. 1914, 307-10; ID 225; Sergeyenko, comp., *Pisma L. N. Tolstovo*, 1848-1910. M. 1910, 146 (tr.: K 234).

CHAPTER TWENTY-FIVE

i: 612, 545, 611; B 329-31, 11; 587-88, 594, 596; *Vestnik vospitaniya*, M. 1894, 1, 1-5; B 329, 11; 603-12; AN 227-30.
ii: U; AN 231-32; W 123-25; Vl. Solovyov, *Tri rechi o D.*, in his *Sobr. soch.*, P. 1901, v. 3, particularly p. 183; Levitzky, *Solovyoi D.*, in *Novyi zhurnal*, v. 41, New York 1955. Hessen, *La lutte entre l'utopie et l'autonomie du bien dans la philosphie de D. et de Solov'ev*, in *Le monde slave*, Pa. 1930, 2, 4; KA 1922, 2, 242-43; Pokrovski, *Brief History of Russia*, New York 1933, v. 1, 197; Gradovski, *Itogi*, Kiev 1908, 18; *Pobedonostzev*, *Pisma k Aleksandru III*, M. 1925, v. 1, 316; KA 1922, v. 2, 244-47; *Pisma D. k zhene*, M. 1926, letters nos. 132-47.
iii: U 551-613; Modzalevsky, *D. o "Br. Karamazovykh," neizdannye pisma, 1879-81*, in BY 1920, v. 15; *Pisma D. k zhene*, 365; AN 250-52, 247-49; LD ch. 27; Speransky, *D. v semye*, in *Illustr. Rossiya*, Pa., 1931, 9; AN 234-38; Vogüé, *Journal*, Pa. 1932, 180-81; NV (illustr. prilozh.) P. 1909, no. 12118, 7; *Sbornik pamyati A. P. Filosofovoi*, P. 1915, v. 1, 259; Stackenschneider, *Dnevnik i zapiski, 1854-1886*, M. 1934; Letkova, OD., in *Zvenya*, M. 1932, v. 1; Mikulich, *Vstrechi s pisatelyami*, L. 1929; Vogüé, *Journal*, 164; Vogüé, *Les ecrivains russes contemporains: F.M.D.*, in *Revue des deux mondes*, Pa., Jan. 15, 1885; Grossmann, *D. i pravitelstvennye krugi 1870 gg.* in *Lit. nasl.*, 15.
iv: W 148-60; Koni, *Na zhiznennom puti*, P. 1912, v. 2, 88-95; AN 230-31; GS 31; IS 1904, v. 95, 531; VE 1908, v. 1, 215-18; AN 264; *Neizdannye pisma iz arkhiva Ostrovskovo*, M. 1932, 523; *Zapis o poseshchenii D. Polivanovoi*, in GM 1923, 3; *Zvenya*, M. 1932, v. 1, 466-71; Z ch. 7; AN 265; A v. 12, 369-417, 411; U 604-09; *Pismo D.* in *Ogoniok* 1956, 6.

CHAPTER TWENTY-SIX

i: B 359, 111; BK 628; U 244, 320; *F.M.D., materialy i izsledovaniya, pod red.* Dolinina, L. 1935; Reizov, *K istorii zamysla Br. Kar.*, in *Zvenya*, 6; Čyzevskyi, *Schiller und Die Br. Kar.*, in ZS 1929, 1/2; Volynsky, *Tzarstvo Karamazovykh*, P. 1901 (tr.: *Das Reich der Karamasoff*, München 1920).
ii: Hessen, *Tragediya dobra v Br. Karamazovykh D.*, in *Sovr. zapiski*, Pa. 1928, no. 35; John 1 3, 15; Putzykovich in NV 1902, no. 9292; Grossmann, *Russki Candide*, in VE 1914, 5; Bulgakov, *Ivan Karamazov*, in VF 1902, 3; BK 68; Rozanov, *Legenda o velikom inkvizitore D.*, P. 1906 (tr.: *D. und seine Legende vom* Grossinquisitor, Berlin 1924); Berdyayev, *Veliki inkvizitor*, in VF 1907, 1; Rahv, *The Legend of the Grand Inquisitor*, in *Partisan Review*, 1954, 3; *D. i Pobedonostzev*, in KA 1922, 2, *passim*; B 368 11; U 532-50; 550; *D. o Br. Kar.*, neizd. pisma, 1879-81, in BY 1922, 15, 104.
iii: *D. o Br. Kar.*, in BY 1922, 15, *passim; Iz perepiski I. S. Aksakova*, in NV (illustr. prilozh.), P. 1909, no. 12118; BK 64; Vl. Solovyov, *Sobr. soch*, P. v. 3, 181; U 299; BK 40; B 368-9 11.

426   BIBLIOGRAPHY

iv: U 6, 7, xxix, xxx; Rozanov, *Lit. izgananniki*, P. 1913, v. 1, 251; HT 320;
B 375 111; BK 110; RY 376; *The Gambler and Other Stories*, tr.
by Constance Garnett, 126.; Vivas, *The Two Dimensions of Reality
in The Brothers Karamazov*, in *Sewanee Review*, Winter 1951.

CHAPTER TWENTY-SEVEN

i: A v. 9, 7, 8 (tr.: The Brothers Karamazov, Lim. Edit. Club, New York
1933, xxviii, xxix); Suvorin, *Dnevnik*, M. 1923, 16; KA 1922, 2, 245-7;
B 345-7, 355-75 11; *D., IZ zapisnoi knizhki*, in *Novyi put*, P.
1904, 1-2; A v. 12, 442; Frolenko, *Sobr. soch.*, M. 1930, v. 1, 149.
ii: AN 266-81; B 315-24; LD ch. 30; AN 268; BY 1920, 15, 133; U, plate
opposite p. 384; Hoffmann, *D., eine Biographische Studie*. Berlin 1899,
441; *Pamyati F.M.D.*, in RV 1881, 2.

CHAPTER TWENTY-EIGHT

i: *Pobedonostzev i yevo korrespondenty*, M. 1923, v. 1, 43; B 324-32, 111;
AN 273-81; Nikolsky, *Turgeney I D.*, Sofia 1921, 97; *Revue des deux
mondes*, Pa. Jan. 15, 1885, 355; Gorki, *Statyi*, 1905-16, P. 1918, 150-62;
Boehm, *Die Geschichtsphilospphie D. und der gegenwärtige Krieg*, in
Preuss. Jahrb., Berlin 1915, v. 159; Hesse, *The Br. Karam. and the
Downfall of Europe*, in *The Dial*, New York 1922, 6; Berezhkov, *D.,
na Zapade*, in *Trudy Gos. Akad. Khud. nauk*, Lit. sek., v. 3, M. 1928;
Schiller, *Legenda o D. v zapadnoyevr, lit. krit.*, in *Lit. i marksizm*,
M. 1928, 5; Mirsky, *D. im Westen*, in *Slav. Rundschau*, Berlin 1931;
Neuschäffer, *D. Einfluss auf den englischen Roman*, Heidelberg 1935;
Adamovich, *Sumerki, D.*, in *Posl. novosti*, Pa. Sept. 17, 1936; Arthur
Symons, *The symbolist movement in literature*, 1919, 8; Shestov, *Kierkegaard i ekzistentzialnaya filosofiya*, Pa. 1939; Yermilov, *Protiv
reaktz. idei v tvorchestve D.*, M. 1948; Fiske, *D. and the Soviet
Critics*, in *The Amer. and East Europ.* 1950, 2; Friedlender, *Obrazy
i temy D.*, in *Zvezda* 1956, 2.
ii: Grossmann, *Poetika D.*, M. 1925; V. Ivanov, *D. i roman-tragediya*, in
Russkaya mysl, 1911, 5-6 (tr.: *Freedom and the Tragic Life*, New York
1952); Poggioli, *D. and Western Realism*, in *Kenyon Review*, Winter
1952; Voloshin, *Prostranstvo i vremya u D.*, in SL 1933, 1/2; Lukacs,
D., in his *Der russische Realismus in der Weltliteratur*, Berlin 1949;
Yevnin, *O khudozhestv. metode D. v 1860-70 gg. (Izvestiya Akad.
nauk SSSR*, Otd. lit. i yazyka, 1955, v. 14, 6); 323; B 373 11.
iii: 346; BK 246, 639; Tolstoy, *Works*, London 1933, v. 11, 4; W. H. Auden,
The Double Man, New York 1941, 130; ID, 430; Gorky, *O literature*,
M. 1933, 52.

III. SUPPLEMENTARY LIST

Berdyayev, N. *D., An Interpretation,* New York 1934.

Capetanakis, D., *D.,* in his *The Shores of Darkness,* New York 1949.

Carr, E. H., *D.,* Boston, 1931.

Čyzevskyi, D., *D. und Nietzsche,* Köln 1947.

Gide, A., *D.,* New York 1926.

Goldenweiser, A., *D. i problema nakazaniya,* in his *V zaschitu prava,* New York 1952.

Guardini, R., *Religiöse Gestalten in D. Werk,* München 1947.

Kirpotin, V., *Molodoy D.,* Moscow 1947.

Lavrin, J., *D., a study,* New York 1947.

Lednicky, W., *Russia, Poland and the West,* New York 1954.

Levinson, A., *La vie pathétique de D.,* Pa. 1931.

Lossky, N., *D. i yevo khristianskoe miroponimanie,* New York 1953.

Lubac, H., *Le drame de l'humanisme athée,* Pa. 1945.

Meier-Graefe, J., *D., The Man and His Work,* New York 1928.

Mochulsky, K., *D., zhizn i tvorchestvo,* Pa. 1947.

Murry, J. M., *Fyodor D.,* London 1916.

Nigg, W., *D.; die religiose Überwindung des Nihilismus,* Hamburg 1951.

Noetzel, K., *Das Leben D.,* Leipzig 1925.

Shestov, L., *D. und Nietzsche,* Berlin 1931.

Simmons, E., *D.: The Making of a Novelist,* New York 1940.

Stepun, F., *D. Weltschau und Weltanschauung,* Heidelberg 1950.

Zweig, S., *Three Masters: Balzac, Dickens, D.,* New York 1930.

INDEX